This valuable study illuminates the idea of nobility as display, as public performance, in Renaissance and seventeenth-century literature and society. Ranging widely from Castiglione and French courtesy manuals, through Montaigne and Bacon, to the literature of the Grand Siècle, David M. Posner examines the structures of public identity in the period. He focuses on the developing tensions between, on the one hand, literary or imaginative representations of "nobility", and on the other, the increasingly problematic historical position of the nobility themselves. These tensions produce a transformation in the notion of the noble self as a performance, and eventually doom court society and its theatrical mode of self-presentation. Situated at the intersection of rhetorical and historical theories of interpretation, this book contributes significantly to our understanding of the role of literature both in analyzing and in shaping social identity.

David M. Posner is Associate Professor of French and Comparative Literature at Loyola University Chicago. He studied in France, Germany and Italy as well as his native United States, and has received fellowships and grants from the National Endowment for the Humanities, Villa I Tatti, the Newberry Library, the Lila Acheson Wallace Fund and the Almanor Scholarship Fund. Amongst his published work are essays on Montaigne, Rabelais and Corneille.

Cambridge Studies in Renaissance Literature and Culture 33

The performance of nobility in early modern European literature

Cambridge Studies in Renaissance Literature and Culture

General editor
STEPHEN ORGEL
Jackson Eli Reynolds Professor of Humanities, Stanford University

Editorial board
Anne Barton, *University of Cambridge*
Jonathan Dollimore, *University of York*
Marjorie Garber, *Harvard University*
Jonathan Goldberg, *Johns Hopkins University*
Nancy Vickers, *Bryn Mawr College*

Since the 1970s there has been a broad and vital reinterpretation of the nature of literary texts, a move away from formalism to a sense of literature as an aspect of social, economic, political and cultural history. While the earliest New Historicist work was criticized for a narrow and anecdotal view of history, it also served as an important stimulus for post-structuralist, feminist, Marxist and psychoanalytical work, which in turn has increasingly informed and redirected it. Recent writing on the nature of representation, the historical construction of gender and of the concept of identity itself, on theatre as a political and economic phenomenon and on the ideologies of art generally, reveals the breadth of the field. Cambridge Studies in Renaissance Literature and Culture is designed to offer historically oriented studies of Renaissance literature and theatre which make use of the insights afforded by theoretical perspectives. The view of history envisioned is above all a view of our own history, a reading of the Renaissance for and from our own time.

Recent titles include

28. Eve Rachele Sanders, *Gender and literacy on stage in early modern England*

29. Dorothy Stephens, *The limits of eroticism in post-Petrarchan narrative: conditional pleasure from Spenser to Marvell*

30. Celia R. Daileader, *Eroticism on the Renaissance stage: transcendence, desire, and the limits of the visible*

31. Theodore B. Leinwand, *Theatre, finance and society in early modern England*

32. Heather Dubrow, *Shakespeare and domestic loss: forms of deprivation, mourning, and recuperation*

A complete list of books in the series is given at the end of the volume

The performance of nobility in early modern European literature

David M. Posner

CAMBRIDGE
UNIVERSITY PRESS

PUBLISHED BY THE PRESS SYNDICATE OF
THE UNIVERSITY OF CAMBRIDGE
The Pitt Building, Trumpington Street, Cambridge, United Kingdom

CAMBRIDGE UNIVERSITY PRESS
The Edinburgh Building, Cambridge CB2 2RU, UK http://www.cup.cam.ac.uk
40 West 20th Street, New York NY 10011–4211, USA http://www.cup.org
10 Stamford Road, Oakleigh, Melbourne 3166, Australia

First published 1999

Printed in the United Kingdom at the University Press, Cambridge

Typeset in Times 10/12pt [VN]

A catalogue record for this book is available from the British Library

Library of Congress cataloguing in publication data

Posner, David Matthew.
    The performance of nobility in early modern European literature /
David M. Posner.
        p.   cm. – (Cambridge studies in Renaissance literature and culture: 33)
    Includes bibliographical references and index.
    ISBN 0 521 66181 1 (hardback)
        1. European literature – Renaissance, 1450–1600 – History and criticism.   2.
Nobility in literature.   3. Nobility of character in literature.   I. Title.   II.
Series.
PN721.P67   1999
809′.93353 – dc21
                                                                        98–53637
                                                                          CIP

ISBN 0 521 66181 1 hardback

Contents

Acknowledgments

This project has taught me that writing, while a relentlessly solitary activity, is also a collaborative effort, and I am happy to be able at last to acknowledge, however inadequately, some of the many debts I have incurred in the course of my work. The first and greatest of these is to Catherine Bangert Posner, my wife, who, in addition to being my most incisive reader, has constantly maintained her sense of humor and perspective throughout the entire process, thereby enabling me to maintain mine. The extraordinary *générosité*, *magnanimité*, and *franchise* of David Quint, under whose direction this book originated, have made my work far better than it would otherwise be. Likewise, François Rigolot, Alban K. Forcione, and Lionel Gossman have been invariably generous and conscientious in their reading and oversight of my work. Natalie Z. Davis and Thomas Pavel have also been kind enough to read and comment upon portions of the text.

Eric MacPhail has shown me that Bacon was wrong, and Montaigne right, about friendship. Pierre and Thelonious did all the work. To Giuseppe Mazzotta, whose generous encouragement and sage counsel came at a crucial time, I owe a special debt of thanks. I am likewise grateful for the kindness and support of my colleagues at Loyola University Chicago. Herbert Lindenberger and René Girard, my undergraduate advisors, opened intellectual doors for me in ways that I am only beginning to appreciate. Among the many other friends and colleagues who have contributed in various ways, I would like to mention Albert Russell Ascoli, Lorenz Böninger, Meredith Gill, Ullrich Langer, Norma MacManaway, Louisa Matthew, Glenn W. Most, Robert Norton, and Rachel Weil. I am grateful to the editor of the Cambridge Studies in Renaissance Literature and Culture, Stephen Orgel, for welcoming my work into the fold, and for his remarkable patience. In my revisions, I have been guided above all by the generous and thoughtful comments of Timothy Reiss, whose careful reading of the entire manuscript helped me to rethink and clarify a number of important issues. Josie Dixon, Maureen Leach, and Susannah Commings of Cambridge University Press were exemplary in their expertise and patience. My thanks to Loyola's Office of Research Services, and especially to David Crumrine, for timely financial assistance towards publication. I am grateful to the Barbara Piasecka Johnson Collection for permission to reproduce the cover image. Portions of the second chapter appeared in different form in *Montaigne Studies* and in *Romance Languages Annual*, while an earlier version of a part of the chapter on Corneille appeared in *Renaissance Drama*. My thanks go to these journals for allowing them to reappear here. All translations, unless otherwise indicated, are my own.

The libraries of Princeton and Yale and of the Ecole Normale Supérieure, and the Bibliothèque Nationale, made it possible for me to read what needed to be read, or at least to find what I ought to have read. Princeton University and the Almanor Scholarship Fund provided essential financial support. Finally, my parents, Robert and Sally Posner, have from the outset been unfailingly supportive, even if they had no idea what they were getting into when they taught me to read. This book is dedicated to them.

Edmund Spenser summed up the aspirations of a class and an age when he described, in the *Faerie Queene* (I, v, 1, 1–4), the state of mind of the Redcrosse Knight on the eve of a great tournament:

> The noble hart, that harbours vertuous thought,
> And is with child of glorious great intent,
> Can never rest, untill it forth have brought
> Th' eternal brood of glorie excellent...

This image of nobility – as something pure, unmediated, even innocent – is one which late Renaissance nobility liked to hold of itself, at a time when the possibility of artless, unconstrained public self-presentation seemed as if it were rapidly being foreclosed. The historical position and identity of the nobility were being threatened by the rise of the modern nation-state and the new power and importance of the princely court. A nostalgic yearning for a Golden Age of artless self-presentation thus formed an important part of the ideology of nobility in this period. Spenser's text itself executes a double movement of optimism and despair; even as these lines enunciate the idealized image of the "noble hart," they simultaneously suggest the impossibility of its realization. This comes about both through the self-conscious archaism of the *Faerie Queene* as a whole, situating itself in a nostalgically viewed and no longer accessible past, and through this passage's insistence on the inability of that "noble hart" to rest, to be content, until it has attained the "eternal ... glorie" – that is, the public fame, the perfect reputation always still to be achieved – that will render it immortal. In Spenser, internal virtue is not enough for the noble soul; that soul cannot rest, indeed noble identity cannot be said to exist, until it is confirmed in front of an audience.[1] It is this imperative of display, of the public performance of nobility, that is the subject of the present work.

The link between theatricality and ideas of nobility and courtly behavior in the late Renaissance, hinted at here in Spenser, is made far more explicit by other Renaissance writers, who regularly use the metaphor of the theatre to describe both the court and noble identity. To be sure, this usage is in part just another version of the ancient commonplace of the *theatrum mundi*;[2] but for authors and readers of the period, who are often themselves players on the stage of the court, it seems to acquire a particular urgency.[3] The present inquiry will investigate the reasons for this urgency and its futility. Starting with the concept – new in Spenser's time – of nobility as a quasi-theatrical performance before a courtly audience, and taking into account Renaissance sociopolitical and ideological contexts, I will investigate why nobility seems to become more difficult both to act out and to define as the Renaissance draws to a close. Building on the work of Norbert Elias, Stephen Greenblatt, and others, this study seeks ultimately to work towards an understanding of the role of literature both in analyzing and in shaping social identity. Elias's theatrical model of the absolutist court of Louis XIV, in which role-playing acts to suppress individual affect in the interests of the king and the State,[4] is counterbalanced by Greenblatt's model of Elizabethan and Jacobean court society, in which the courtly performer constantly adapts to the shifting matrix of power relations in the court, fashioning identities appropriate to whatever circumstances arise.[5] Where, for Elias, repression gives rise to civilization and the State, in Greenblatt's model repression acts merely to perpetuate itself, or to reproduce itself in new forms, a paradigm owing something not only to Elias but also to Michel Foucault. The present study, while indebted to these writers, will emphasize not so much the totalizing energies of the theatre of the court as the tensions and contradictions within it. These tensions – centering around the radical dissimilarity between, on the one hand, the nobility's literary or imaginative images of itself, and on the other hand its increasingly problematic position in historical reality – eventually doom the court society and its theatrical mode of self-presentation.[6]

Strongly "literary" texts – a loaded term which will be discussed below – best foreground these tensions, which is why I have chosen to focus on them. This is not to say that I have considered them in isolation. While I do not claim to have produced either a political or a social history, projects for which I would in any case be insufficiently qualified, the readings of literary texts here offered are necessarily conditioned by attention to the matrix of historical experience in which the texts themselves are embedded, without, however, thereby reducing the texts to mere appendages of history. While history generates the conditions of possibility for literature, modulating what a given text can articulate or reflect, a text also creates its own re-vision of history, laying claim to a certain (perhaps illusory) autonomy. Whatever its legitimacy, that claim generates a space, a zone of tension, between text and history, and it is this space that the present study seeks to explore.

Forming the backdrop for our discussion is the large-scale historical debate over the idea that there was a generalized crisis of European society in the late Renaissance and seventeenth century,[7] and that the nobility were particularly at risk.[8] This notion of crisis – by now a (much-contested) commonplace – conditions, if sometimes only negatively, most recent work on the problem of noble identity. While aspects of the problem vary with time and locale, its general features are fairly clear, whether in France or in England: a class of persons accustomed to considerable political and economic power and independence, and to a certain monopoly on violence, finds these privileges being challenged by a royal power, or state, interested in appropriating them for itself.[9] At the same time, this class finds itself facing competition in the form of parallel claims to "nobility" from other groups of persons whose skills are more useful to the new state, and who – owing more to that state's authority – tend to be more tractable. Each of these two competing groups therefore attempts to define itself against the other, even as they lay claim to the same vocabulary of identity, and compete for the same rewards from an increasingly powerful Crown.[10] Nor is this picture exclusively one of division and conflict; nobles, whether *épée* or *robe*, whether old nobility or "New Men," operate along with the Crown within a complex web of mutual interdependencies, in which no one element can do entirely without any other.[11] This web, however, is anything but stable, and its shifting strands produce a corresponding instability in concepts of nobility and noble identity. Nobility and noble comportment in this period are not a predetermined set of axioms, but rather a series of questions posed and re-posed, whose constantly shifting terms are variously imagined, projected, and described by their supposed or would-be possessors. Efforts by Renaissance nobles themselves, by the Crown or the State, and by contemporary writers on the subject, to define what nobility is, what it does, and who may have access to it, are therefore marked by a contentiousness and desperation mirrored in the descriptive and interpretative work of modern historians. It is perhaps not inaccurate to speak of a "crisis of the historians" surrounding the idea of late Renaissance nobility, so striking are the disagreements among students of the subject. However, the concern of the present study is not to decide whose view of the economic or social status of the various nobilities of the sixteenth and seventeenth centuries in Western Europe is, historically speaking, "correct"; instead, we will examine a point on which most students of the period actually do agree: that the nobility found itself, or – more importantly – perceived itself, to be in a period of difficulty, tension, and transition, in which certain previously secure ideas of what it meant to be "noble" were being challenged, modified, or replaced. (Whether these pre-existing models of nobility were in fact as stable as their adherents wished them retroactively to have been is less important than the desire that they be so, since it is this desire that – as will be seen – both produces and destroys claims to nobility.) In any event, disagreements between Renaissance or modern writers on nobility may reflect, more than anything else, the essential slipperiness of the subject; nobility, far from being what it invariably claims to be – something timeless, immutable, and consistent – is always being called into question by its actual or would-be possessors, as well as interested observers, whether critical or not. Terms and definitions, and the authority to control and manipulate them, are at all times being fought over, both because control over vocabulary is in this case not unconnected with actual political power, and because the terms are terms of self-definition, terms from which individuals construct their own identities.

Recent students of the period have therefore tended to link their examinations of noble identity to larger questions of identity and the structure of the self in the Renaissance and afterwards. Not only literary critics like Greenblatt, Jonathan Goldberg, or Timothy Reiss, but also historians like Kristen Neuschel or Jonathan Dewald, have engaged in a series of efforts to rewrite Burckhardt, searching for the genesis of modern concepts of selfhood.[12] Most of these revisions of Burckhardt's *Entwicklung des Individuums* reject his nineteenth-century optimism – an extension of the optimism of the Florentine *quattrocento* – in favor of a more pessimistic, not to say paranoid, vision of the individual's relationship to Renaissance society. These readings, conditioned to a greater or lesser degree by the Foucault of *Histoire de la folie* and *Surveiller et punir*, tend to see the fabrication of the self as a response to the repressive forces of Crown and State.[13] From Greenblatt's Thomas More to Dewald's memoir-writers, each critic's subject seems to become, in that critic's hands, the inventor of modern interiorizing subjectivity; this peculiar concidence perhaps means nothing more than that, like Burckhardt himself, modern readers are persuaded by the dazzling rhetoric of Renaissance performances of selfhood.[14] It might perhaps be more judicious to suggest that, while the self is always and everywhere being (in the etymological sense of *invenio*) "invented," the form taken by the self as *literary* subject, as constituted in writing and print, undergoes a transformation during this period, a transformation conditioned both by the actual political and historical circumstances of the writers and their subjects, and by what they thought those circumstances – and themselves – to be. Our study is therefore concerned with literature's intersection with the *myths* of nobility – imagined versions of what it was or should have been – as well as with its reality.

In what follows, we will begin by seeing briefly how one text in particular, Castiglione's *Cortegiano*, brings to the fore the overarching *topos* of the theatre that will govern the literary discourse of nobility in the late Renaissance. This discourse ranges from a literature of overt definitions of nobility, through a series of self-help books addressing the practical needs of actual or would-be courtiers, to more overtly "literary" texts, all of which conceive of the self and its relationship to society in explicitly theatrical terms. The next chapter explores Montaigne's versions of this theatrical model of the self in the dual contexts of his readings of classical texts and his own public career. Montaigne's assimilation and critique of the Italians, and his simultaneous readings of Seneca, Plutarch, and Tacitus, among others, are informed by the practical realities of his situation as a *noble de robe* in late sixteenth-century France. Early on, he posits a neo-Stoic model of nobility in which a radical scission exists between the social self and the "true," extra-social, moral self. He associates this version of the self with a putative transparency of language, and presents it in anti-courtly, anti-performative terms specific to the contemporary discourse of *épée* nobility. However, Montaigne's deployment of this model of identity exposes the instability of any discourse depending upon such terms as *franchise*, *générosité*, and so on, and shows neo-Stoic noble identity to be a mystification-dependent performance like any other. Indeed, Montaigne's conception of nobility depends precisely upon being able to demonstrate that there is an irreducible distance not just between social ("false") and private ("true") identity, but between the subject and *any* identity recognizable as such. The pose of the nobleman as a non-performer, one whose *parole* is a transparent (re)presentation of identity, is simply one performance among many, and the successful nobleman is one who can control and deploy an array of performative selves according to situational demands, while maintaining an essential separation between performer (however defined) and performance. Montaigne's performance of nobility also has ideological dimensions; it is designed, of course, to establish his own noble credentials in conventional *épée*-defined terms, but in so doing it rewrites those very terms in ways that paradoxically make the claims to noble identity of *nobles de robe* like himself more powerful than those of the "true" *noblesse d'épée*. Montaigne brings this about in two complementary ways: through ironizing traditional definitions of nobility, and through a surreptitious replacement of those definitions with others better suited to the growing court society of the late sixteenth century. Central to success on this new stage is the capacity for performance, and Montaigne goes to great lengths to demonstrate his own theatrical facility. Throughout the *Essais*, but particularly in the essays of the third book, Montaigne is able to present to the reader a multifarious array of selves, selves which both reveal and conceal themselves to and from the reader in ways which inevitably implicate that reader. The audience is inexorably drawn into playing an active role in Montaigne's *jeu de miroirs*.

Nascent in Montaigne's text is an opposition, or at least a dichotomy, between "public" and "private" (terms which he negates or ironizes even as his text generates them); but the presence of this quasi-doubling of the self foreshadows a sharper opposition in the next author to be studied, Francis Bacon. His *Essayes* bear little real resemblance to those of Montaigne; but, like the *Essais*, Bacon's text bears an isometric relationship, structurally and dynamically, to the model of noble identity it describes. The *Essayes* are a kind of manual, although perhaps not in the sense in which they have been conventionally understood as such; rather, they are a text whose rhetorical strategies mirror the performative and interpretive behaviors expected of its reader, the ambitious "New Man" eager to succeed at court. In its quasi-didactic intent, and in the particular form taken by that ædificatory impulse, it is consistent with Bacon's larger interest in how best to convey and understand information, as expressed in such works as the *Advancement of Learning* and the *Novum Organum*, where he says, "[w]e must lead men to the particulars themselves."[15] While the exact content of these "particulars" will vary according to the field of knowledge to which they belong, their structure and presentation will always be similar. Specific quanta of information are presented in an aphoristic discourse that compels assent by seeming clear and self-evident, while imperceptibly leading the reader to look beyond that appearance to the truth of the matter at hand. Bacon acknowledges the initial assent (the "contract of error"[16]) produced by the (potentially) specious truths of rhetoric as a tool, to be used to move the mind of the reader/beholder towards true understanding; however, he also acknowledges – and capitalizes on – the potential for deception, particularly in the arena of what he calls "civill Businesse."[17] He insists in this context on the utility, even the necessity, of the Lie, the performance that deceives the better to persuade; and what began as a quest for truth quickly becomes a drive to deceive without being deceived, to further one's own interests without regard for, and if necessary at the expense of, others seeking to do precisely the same thing. The dangers confronting Bacon's "New Man" produce an imperative of masking and dissimulation; whatever "real," "true" identity the performer in this treacherous court-world might possess is entirely irrelevant, since – if it exists at all – it is essential that it be concealed behind an array of masks. The *Essayes* therefore call into question the existence of *any* "private self," or at least any observable one; all that can be seen is the performance. This is true even between friends; in the first version of the essay "Of Frendship," Bacon posits the possibility of a relationship unmediated by masking or performance, but in the final version he rejects even this tentative gesture, and insists that the "frend" functions only as an auxiliary to one's own public performance, extending its range and effectiveness beyond what it could accomplish alone. In Bacon, what will become the "private sphere" may be imagined, but its realization, in the absolutist realm of Elizabeth and James, remains impossible. Bacon's consequent avoidance of the subjectivity of Montaigne calls into question the existence of any self other than that self's various roles on the public stage; when the house lights go up, the actor vanishes.

The next chapter turns to theatre *per se*, specifically that of Pierre Corneille, to explore responses on the stage to theatrical models of the noble self. Much of Corneille's work may be read as a set of carefully orchestrated variations on a single theme, one which dominates his dramatic *oeuvre*: the articulation of the conditions of possibility for the noble self. Defining that self as a quasi-theatrical role to be performed within a courtly context, he focuses on one particular moment in this theatre of state, namely the conflict, whether potential or real, between an independent-minded nobility on the one hand and centralizing royal authority on the other, with parallels both obvious and subtle with the real political situation of seventeenth-century France. In the theatrical court-world of Corneille, everyone must know their lines; deviating from the script, i.e. the modes of behavior proper to one's role, whether that role be King, Defender of the Realm, Sage Counsellor, or Virtuous Princess, is the worst possible error, and inevitably entrains the direst consequences.

This is, for example, what separates Don Gomès from Rodrigue in the first of Corneille's variations on this theme, *Le Cid*; both can legitimately (although not simultaneously) claim to be the Bravest Man in Castille, but Don Gomès's crucial error is to insist that he personally is essential to the well-being of the State. "Sans moi, vous passeriez bientôt sous d'autres lois, / Et si vous ne m'aviez, vous n'auriez plus de Rois."[18] ["Without me, you would soon be subject to other laws, / And if you did not have me, you would have no more Kings."] He fails to realize that the "moi" he considers so indispensable is not he himself, but rather the role he plays in the theatre of the state. His too-close identification with his role makes him a dangerously destabilizing force; he must therefore be eliminated. Rodrigue, on the other hand, while he fulfills exactly the same state-sustaining function, avoids confusing him*self* (a term which, as I shall attempt to show, is of questionable value in describing the Corneillean model of identity) with the role he plays. He also is willing to play that role in concert with his nominal liege lord, in an elaborate public ritual of mutual admiration, where they simultaneously acknowledge their reciprocal dependence on one another and assert their individual worth as uniquely necessary elements of the State. This kind of performance is possible only if all the actors on the stage speak the same language, the language of honor and nobility, sharing a common understanding of such key terms of the Corneillean vocabulary as *gloire, magnanimité, générosité, franchise, vertu,* and so on, terms which define the relations that exist between the various *personnages.*

Hence, the real conflict in *Cinna,* the next play to be discussed, is a lexical one, in which Emilie and Auguste struggle over who will control the discourse of true nobility. Emilie loses because she tries to retain sole ownership of certain key words, words which must on the contrary remain common property in the interest of the *res publica.* Auguste, on the other hand, triumphs because he is able, at the last, both to recognize that this discourse is public property and to demonstrate, through an act of supreme *magnanimité* – the entire renunciation of any private "self" – his complete domination of that discourse, the very discourse on which his antagonists base their opposition. That dominance can be sustained only because, just as in *Le Cid,* all the characters are ultimately willing to abide by the same set of discursive rules. This willingness evaporates in the plays that follow *Cinna,* and therefore the play's optimistic and transcendent resolution of the conflict between noble and king in the unique *personnage* of Auguste is without sequel. An elegiac note (admittedly present even in *Le Cid*) therefore comes to dominate the later works. The play of *noblesse* becomes a tragedy of nostalgia, in which the noble hero casts a longing glance back toward a time when men were noble and kings knew their place – a *bon vieux temps* which, like all such entities, seems always to have been written into the past, and to have been replaced by an inferior and corrupt imitation. The tension, in Corneille, between this elegiac vision of an idealized past and the grim reality of the historical present is finally unresolvable, leading inevitably, in such plays as *Suréna, général des Parthes,* to the forced exit of the noble subject from the stage.

By the end of the seventeenth century, the performance of nobility has become a dead-end spectacle in which the courtier no longer participates; he merely reads and watches, as if from afar, the odd antics of the "characters" presented on the metaphorical stage of La Bruyère's text – "characters" which are, of course, distorted versions of the courtiers themselves. The theatre of nobility becomes a tiny theatre of marionettes, in which aesthetic satisfaction comes not from being fooled into forgetting that the puppets are merely puppets, but on the contrary from being constantly aware of all the *ressorts,* from knowing at every instant that one is merely watching lumps of wood being jerked about by strings. For La Bruyère, this is both an aesthetic and a moral imperative; he insists that the reader look beyond and behind the glittering surfaces of courtly performance, in order to perceive the unflattering truths those surfaces strive to conceal. He is nevertheless compelled to acknowledge the persuasive power of those surfaces, and to recognize the difficulty of seeing through them. To avoid being drawn into this play of appearances, La Bruyère's text endeavors to situate itself – and its audience – "outside" of the world it both inhabits and observes. The noble protagonist moves away from being a *personnage*, performing a role in front of an audience, and towards becoming a *caractère*, under examination by a detached observer; but this movement always remains incomplete. The spectator, in La Bruyère's text, is inevitably and perpetually implicated in the spectacle, and indeed the spectacle itself seems to depend for its very existence on the presence and participation of the observer. Moreover, the mystification upon which that spectacle depends turns out to be irresistible, since the distinction that La Bruyère attempts to establish between *masque* and *visage* depends on the possibility that there are at least some cases where there is no distinction – where the performance is merely a setting forth of unmediated truth, rather than an attempt at persuasive deception or concealment. The problem thus becomes one of distinguishing between "true" and "false" performances, and – despite La Bruyère's strenuous efforts to demonstrate otherwise – it quickly becomes apparent that, for the observer at least, there is no reliable way of telling the difference. The pose of the detached observer, watching with amused indifference the impostures of those performing onstage, is itself a mystification, a rhetorical gesture no different than any other performed within the theatre of the court.

The work of La Bruyère seems to represent the ultimate development, or perhaps the last gasp, of what one might call the literature of the theatre of *noblesse*. It is itself a theatrical discourse, with a succession of *personnages* strutting across its stage, but it is also a meta-theatrical discourse which works extremely hard to unmask the mode of theatricality it describes. As such, it seems to want to leave behind a theatrical mode of presentation and to move towards a novelistic or narrative one, in that it speaks often in the voice of a remotely situated narrator, observing and describing in the third person the phenomena of the court. La Bruyère's text does not complete this movement; but, precisely because of its failure to resolve (or at least conceal effectively) the fundamental contradictions it so strongly foregrounds, it paves the way for the movement towards a narrative mode to be completed in the literature of the eighteenth century.

The theatrical discourse of which the *Caractères* are a kind of culmination is set in motion, in the early sixteenth century, by Castiglione's *Cortegiano*. Its dazzlingly aestheticized vision of courtly behavior, dominated by metaphors of performance and theatricality, engenders a seemingly endless proliferation of texts on questions of nobility, courtliness, and identity, all governed to a greater or lesser extent by the same *topos* of the theatre.[19] The *Cortegiano* can in some sense be held responsible for the entire range of such texts, from the sophisticated critiques of Montaigne or La Rochefoucauld to the compound platitudes of Cammillo Baldi or Eustache de Refuge. While these texts vary widely in complexity and sophistication, they all work within a discourse of public identity whose terms and conditions are largely established by Castiglione. This is not to suggest that Castiglione invents the problem, nor that he is the first to apply systematically the metaphor of the theatre to the question of public identity. On the contrary, the notions of public life as a kind of theatre, and of the individual-as-actor therein, are already commonplaces for Cicero, from whom Castiglione borrows not only the quasi-theatrical form of his work but also a number of key metaphors. But Castiglione's artful reformulations of classical *topoi* of theatricality have resonances for his Renaissance readers that even Cicero cannot always match.[20] It would nevertheless be misleading to claim that Castiglione effects a radical reversal of the Ciceronian ideal, or that Cicero himself proposes as his ideal orator a naïvely straightforward Mr. Smith *à la* Frank Capra. To be sure, Cicero insists, in a famous pun, that the orator should present himself to the public as *actor veritatis*, the advocate – and performer – of truth. However, even as he presents this ideal he complains that orators have abandoned the essential art of *actio* – delivery or performance – to mere *imitatores veritatis*, that is, *histriones* (theatre actors): "Haec ideo dico pluribus quod genus hoc totum oratores, qui sunt veritatis ipsius actores, reliquerunt, imitatores autem veritatis, histriones, occupaverunt."[21] ["I dwell on this because the whole area has been abandoned by the orators, who are the performers of truth, and taken over by the actors, who are merely imitators of truth."] Cicero immediately goes on to insist that the cultivation of this art is essential, since the orator cannot rely solely upon the naked truth to persuade his audience. On the contrary, since the minds of the audience are so often clouded by emotion, the orator must attempt to control those emotions through *ars* and *actio*, in addition to persuading through a rational presentation of truth.[22] Indeed, the concluding portion of Book III of *De Oratore*, which follows this passage, is concerned primarily with the application of *actio* to this form of non-rational persuasion, with extensive examples drawn from the theatre.

Castiglione's emphasis on the persuasive effectiveness of performance is therefore a development of something already present in Cicero, rather than a radical turning away from the Ciceronian ideal. The direction of this development is nevertheless significant and revealing. Castiglione recognizes the danger of persuading an audience of something they do not want to hear (a danger equally real for Cicero, although he was perhaps less willing to recognize it), and therefore moves away from the idea that the purpose of persuasion, and of its attendant *delectatio*, is to present potentially uncomfortable truths with overwhelming rhetorical force. The aesthetic pleasure brought to the audience becomes, for Castiglione, more of an end in itself; rather than being in the service of forensic persuasion, it is part of a larger context of princely *otium*, and functions for the performer primarily as a means of attracting favor and *onore* to oneself, and as a means of self-protection.[23] Even and especially when the noble courtier is performing that function most proper to his class, namely making war,[24] that activity becomes above all a performance designed not so much to serve the interests of the State as to impress one's employer.[25] One should be sure, when in battle, to perform one's heroic deeds as visibly as possible, and if it can be managed, right in front of one's boss.[26] The practical results – if any – of this martial performance, and of other, less overtly dangerous forms of showing off, are vastly less important than the perception thereof by the princely onlooker. In the discussion in book II, section 11, of masquerade ("lo esser travestito"), and of its great utility for showing off one's true (noble) identity through disguising it, Castiglione emphasizes that the success of the courtier's performance is determined by the audience reaction, and in particular by whether or not the audience "si diletta e piglia piacere" ["is delighted and pleased"]. Control of that reaction, through controlling the pleasure experienced by the beholder, thus becomes paramount.[27] This pleasure arises not from the audience's experience of the showing forth of some Truth, *à la* Cicero, but rather from its being deceived. Castiglione shows that the essence of the courtier's performance is a kind of multi-layered deception, in the form of a performed concealment – a concealment that pretends to be the opposite, to be an intentionally incomplete concealment that instead reveals, with a wink and a nudge, the "truth" behind its supposedly consensual pretense. Through performing "con abito disciolto," in a disguise meant to be seen into, the performer invites the audience to feel as though it is in on the joke. The audience's pleasure arises from its accepting that invitation, from being fooled into believing that, rather than being fooled, it is seeing beyond the mask (representing e.g. a *pastor selvatico*, a peasant) to the "real" (i.e. noble) visage underneath. The precise *locus* of this pleasure, as Castiglione makes clear, is the tension between what is actually seen and what is artfully hinted at, without however being revealed in what Bacon will call the "Naked, and Open day light"[28] of Truth. Nor could that shadowy something-hinted-at ever be thus revealed, as it is neither presence nor substance, neither essence nor Truth, but rather the reflection of the desire of the beholder, the very movement of "l'animo ... [chi] ... corre ad imaginar ..." ["the mind which rushes to imagine"]. In this specular performance, there is always something more – Castiglione's "molto maggior cosa" – than can be seen, or indeed be present; the desire for that shadowy *cosa* is the *delectatio* proper to this masquerade, and it is the eliciting of that desire that is the object of the courtier's performance.

The success of that performance, of its come-hither pseudo-revelation, is in turn dependent on a sort of meta-deception, another layer of pretense that likewise attempts to disguise itself as its opposite. The courtier's performance must persuade, but that effort at persuasion must itself be covered over by another persuasive effort, one that "demonstrates" to the audience that no effort at persuasion is being made. One cannot be seen to be doing what one is in fact doing, namely working very hard to persuade one's audience of a noble identity which – if it actually were what it claims to be – would need no rhetorical helps to impose its intrinsic veracity, its mathematical Identity with itself, on the minds and emotions of the audience. That such an effort of rhetoric is in fact needed suggests that the Identity being performed is not what it professes to be, or at least that the person laying claim to it has no intrinsic, "natural" right to do so. Effort must therefore be disguised as its opposite; one must persuade the witnesses to that effort of its absence.[29] This is *sprezzatura*.

Although Castiglione, when he introduces the concept (I, 26), coyly lays claim to at least lexical originality ("... per dir forse una nova parola [...] una certa sprezzatura... " ["to say, perhaps, a new word ... a certain *sprezzatura*"]), he knows perfectly well that he is once again recycling a Ciceronian commonplace. He even throws out a hint as to his source: "E ricordomi io già aver letto esser stati alcuni antichi oratori eccellentissimi, i quali ... sforzavansi di far credere ad ognuno sé non aver notizia alcuna di lettere..." ["And I remember having read about certain most excellent orators of antiquity, who ... tried to make everyone believe that they knew nothing at all about letters..."] The reading here recalled by the Count Ludovico da Canossa is book I of *De Oratore*; and the Count goes on to explain how such pretense made the orators' powers of persuasion all the more effective in the minds of their audiences, commending their example to the would-be courtier. However, Cicero's most explicit theoretical statement about this particular form of deception is found not in *De Oratore*, but in another dialogue, the *Orator*; and, in the tensions between the latter text's *diligens negligentia* and the *sprezzatura* of the *Cortegiano*, we find precisely those features of Castiglione's version of courtly identity that will be most productive – and problematic – for subsequent discussions of nobility and courtly behavior. When Cicero recommends to the orator a kind of studied nonchalance, he does not mean it as a general rule, to be applied to all types of rhetorical performance; the term appears in the context of a discussion of a specific variety of rhetoric, namely the plain style. After pointing out that a certain *non ingrata negligentia*, in addition to simply pleasing one's audience, can lead them to believe that the person speaking is concerned "de re ... magis quam de verbis" ["more about things than about words"], he continues,

...quaedam etiam negligentia est diligens. Nam ut mulieres pulchriores esse dicuntur nonnullae inornatae quas id ipsum deceat, sic haec subtilis oratio etiam incompta delectat; fit enim quidam in utroque, quo sit venustius sed non ut appareat.[30]

[...there is such a thing as careful negligence. Just as some women are said to be more beautiful when unadorned – it becomes them – so this plain style, even though unornamented, pleases; in both cases there is in fact something that is more attractive, but does not show itself.]

Castiglione appropriates from Cicero the notion of artful artlessness, as well as its seductive effect: that the audience, finding what it beholds "sit venustius sed non ut appareat," is incited to suspect, and desire, the presence of something more than what is actually seen. (While Castiglione's rewriting of *diligens negligentia* jettisons the explicit comparison with the woman made more beautiful and attractive by her non-use of external adornments, the model of a seductive *delectatio* is everywhere implicit in Castiglione's idea of the courtier's relationship with his or her audience.) But the *Cortegiano* expands the field of application of *diligens negligentia* well beyond the narrow limits of a single style of oratory; *sprezzatura* governs *all* courtly behavior, and indeed is its essential defining characteristic. Upon it depends *grazia*, grace, which must be seen to accompany the courtier's every action; upon it depends above all the crucial ability to persuade one's public of the presence of the "molto maggior cosa," that Something Else, always just beyond the reach of clear perception, which is the key to noble identity.[31]

For Cicero, as we have seen, the necessity of art, of studied performance, to the rhetorical process is the fault of the audience. The existence of Truth, and of its power to convince, are not called into question; were the audience only able to rise to a sufficiently high level of rationality, Truth would need no help from the orator in order to persuade. Castiglione is less optimistic. The "truth" of public identity is indeed called into question, as it not only should be but must be, since the entire idea of noble identity rests on an impossibly unstable foundation: that peculiar Something Else, always just beyond the bounds of what can be perceived clearly, always suggested but never made wholly manifest. It is that Something Else to which the elaborate, multi-layered deception of the courtier's performance is always trying to direct the audience's attention, without being perceived to do so; and if any of the levels of deception should fail, if the audience should be somehow undeceived, the whole performance collapses, and with it the performer's identity. This is not to say that the performer is necessarily practicing a consciously calculated deception upon the audience, nor that he is necessarily exempt from that deception. On the contrary, one might say that there is yet another meta-deception, another layer of pretense, one that includes the performer as well; performer and audience are engaged in a contract of mutual or collective deception, since both share the desire that the "molto maggior cosa" be genuinely present, that the performer be what both he and the audience would have him be.

This mutuality is governed by another of Castiglione's key words, *prudenzia*. Once again, Castiglione borrows a term central to Cicero's model of the ideal orator, but shifts its meaning to adapt it to a world in which consensual deception, rather than *veritas*, is the substrate upon which relations of mutual confidence are built. For Cicero, *prudentia*, while a useful tool for the orator,[32] cannot be divorced from *iustitia*, precisely because such a separation would entail losing the confidence of one's audience:

Harum igitur duarum ad fidem faciendam iustitia plus pollet, quippe cum ea sine prudentia satis habeat auctoritatis, prudentia sine iustitia nihil valet ad faciendam fidem.[33]

[Of these two qualities, then, justice has more power to inspire confidence, since, even without prudence, it has enough authority; but prudence without justice is worthless in inspiring confidence.]

This is not the place to enter into the question of how seriously Cicero intends his own audience to take such a sanctimonious maxim. What is important for us to notice is that Castiglione does not make even this ritual gesture towards anchoring prudence in some sort of moral virtue; his *prudenzia* is rather a question of selecting one's circumstances, and above all one's audience, so as to maximize the effectiveness of one's persuasive performance. The courtier should use (II, 6) "una certa prudenzia e giudicio di elezione" ["a certain prudence and judicious choice"] when for example committing acts of mayhem on the battlefield (II, 7), "per acquistar laude meritamente e bona estimazione appresso ognuno, e grazia da quei signori ai quali serve..." ["...to gain praise deservingly, and everyone's good opinion, and favor from the princes he serves..."] The exercise of this prudence may lead one to *seem* virtuous in the eyes of one's audience, to be sure, but virtue is not a necessary precondition. What is important is that one uses one's *prudenzia* to (IV, 18) "elegger bene" ["choose well"] one's audience, so that they will be the sort of persons most likely to be persuaded by one's performance. In other words, they must resemble the performer, at least insofar as they share the performer's desire for that "molto maggior cosa."[34]

For this mutual desire to be realized, for the performance to succeed, the audience must be persuaded; hence, for Castiglione's actor, opinion is the only thing that counts. This is made clear in the odd conclusion of the debate, early in the *Cortegiano*, on the precise nature of nobility, a debate which also owes much to Cicero. In *De Oratore*, the question of the relative value to the orator of birth as opposed to training is expressed in terms of *ingenium* [talent] versus *diligentia* [hard work]. Good genes, Crassus insists, are the first prerequisite to oratorical success (I. xxv. 113). However, Antonius will show that, talent notwithstanding, *diligentia* is indispensable, and indeed can work wonders, even (perhaps) compensating for shortcomings in *ingenium* (II. xxxv. 147–48). Antonius's remark that one of the functions of *diligentia* is to awaken an under-active *ingenium* is echoed in Castiglione's discussion (I, 14) of the *occulto seme* ["hidden seed"], a mysterious entity which appears, as the argument proceeds, to be by turns essential and irrelevant to the actual formation of noble identity. It may be a prerequisite to true nobility, but evidently hard work can compensate almost entirely for its absence; it may "porge una certa forza e proprietà del suo principio" ["grant a certain strength and property of its own essence"] to its possessors, but – as it is, after all, *occulto* – persons possessing it seem nevertheless to need to be "cultivati" through training and hard effort in order to manifest its fruits. It may confer genetic advantages upon its possessors, but there is no guarantee that those genetic advantages will be passed on; and in fact *nobiltà di sangue* seems to act primarily to shame its possessors into living up to the alleged virtues of their ancestors. One may indeed be "nato nobile e di generosa famiglia" ["born noble and of generous family"], but this does not relieve one of the responsibility of acting like it. The noble is, by definition, always attempting to bridge a gap between the unrealized potential of the flawed present and a supposedly actualized ancestral ideal.

The necessity of that attempt is what drives the performance of nobility in Castiglione. The inevitable inadequacy of that performance – one is always trying, or pretending, to be Something Else – and its consequent hollowness are what gives that performance its peculiarly paranoid character. This paranoia in fact pervades the entire text of the *Cortegiano*, but especially here, where it is perhaps closest to the surface, Castiglione is extremely careful to avoid direct confrontation with the inherent contradictions of his subject. The debate on the *occulto seme* is brought to a close, almost apologetically, by Canossa, who says that – like it or not – opinion determines reality, insofar as one's public identity is concerned. He insists on that opinion's inevitable fragility, and fallibility, precisely in order to show that it is essential that one must do everything in one's power to deliver a convincing performance, so as to manipulate the arbitrary – but crucial – first impression to one's advantage. The "truth" of the matter, whatever that may be, is entirely irrelevant; what counts is (I, 16) "la opinion universale, la qual sùbito accompagna la nobiltà" ["universal opinion, which immediately accompanies nobility"]. The real issue, that the calling into question of any "natural" correspondence between essence and appearance undermines the entire notion of noble identity, is here sidestepped by Canossa and Castiglione, a maneuver that later writers on the subject will be unable to execute so adroitly.

For Castiglione is only a beginning; the *Cortegiano* lies at the root of a vast genealogical tree of texts on the topic of nobility and noble identity. It is tempting to divide this tree into two main branches, representing two strains of writing on the topic, the "literary" and the "non-literary," *scriptible* and *lisible*, or even "good" and "bad," and instantly dismiss the latter; this temptation becomes almost overwhelming when one actually reads, for example, *La Guide des Courtisans* of Nervèze. However, as Barthes himself eventually shows, such distinctions tend to be self-negating, since even the least sophisticated of the courtesy manuals is not – and cannot be – purely *lisible*, that is, a completely unselfconscious, rhetorically transparent text. Even these texts are already "about" the reading and rewriting (to one's own advantage) of the performed text of public behavior, whether one's own or that of others, which one is attempting to read through. Moreover, whatever Castiglione's original intent in writing the *Cortegiano*, his book was certainly read by many as a kind of self-help book for the aspiring courtier, and the multitudinous rewritings of it that populate the rest of the sixteenth century tend to present themselves explicitly as instrumental texts, manuals of conduct for the would-be gentleman. The master trope of the theatre, with its associated lexicon of sub-metaphors (the mask, backstage space, staying in character, and so on), suffuses a broad range of texts which, while operating on widely varying levels of sophistication or insight, all share a double concern with (1) the proper interpretation of the courtly theatre of appearances, and (2) perpetuating the system of consensual illusion upon which that theatre depends, by avoiding and concealing the very real historical and logical contradictions at its heart.

Castiglione's artistry allows him to sidestep these contradictions, but even for him they are always and everywhere present, if just under the surface. The less self-conscious texts are not so fortunate; their more straightforward practicality, and in some cases their lesser literary complexity, mean that they can neither conceal nor overcome the internal contradictions of the social world they represent. We find instead a variety of evasions, rhetorical gestures intended to paper over those contradictions, to render them somehow negotiable to their readers, without however coming to terms with what they represent. Even such a sophisticated work as Giovanni della Casa's *Galateo* (1558) avoids calling into question the necessity of courtly theatricality. The beginning of the treatise explicitly announces that, since opportunities for its use are few and far between, Virtue writ large is irrelevant to the question of everyday behavior; far more important are small "virtues," like good manners, since they are needed daily.[35] He does criticize, albeit obliquely, the artificiality of courtly manners, by claiming that they are not native to Italy, but are a pernicious import. Although he does not here state where they come from, he clearly has Spain in mind, and like Castiglione casts an elegiac glance backwards to the good old days when Italians were free to behave as themselves:

La quale usanza sanza alcun dubbio a noi non è originale, ma forestiera e barbara, e da poco tempo in qua, onde che sia, trapassata in Italia: la quale, misera, con le opere e con gli effetti abbassata et avilita, è cresciuta solamente et onorata nelle parole vane e ne' superflue titoli.[36]

[This habit is undoubtedly not original with us, but foreign and barbarous, and only recently brought into Italy from wherever it began; our miserable Italy which, degraded and humiliated in deed and effect, now grows and is honored only in vain words and superfluous titles.]

However, the rest of the treatise avoids such questions, and is concerned instead with practical advice on how to conform to the theatrical demands of this postlapsarian society. Most other works on the subject will omit even this sort of token gesture, preferring instead to remain in the realm of what they conceive to be the purely practical. This reduced ambition produces some peculiar results, as in Cammillo Baldi's *Congressi civili*, first published in 1637.[37] Baldi echoes a great deal of Aristotle, and seems at first glance to be emphasizing the Civil in a Ciceronian sense; it turns out, however, that Baldi's "Uomo dabbene" is instructed not to serve the public good through the *vita activa* but to preserve civil order and tranquillity, on an almost microscopic scale, by being well-mannered towards one's fellow citizens. Another common phenomenon is an explicit, even cheerful, self-contradiction, as in (for example) the same author's *Politiche considerationi* (1625), which advocates and disclaims dissimulation in the same breath.[38] Torquato Accetto's *Della dissimulazione onesta* (1641) offers a bizarre reconciliation of these two positions, drawing upon both biblical[39] and Classical sources to demonstrate that dissimulation, which he conceives of as a persuasive performance, is not only essential to the well-being of the *res publica* but is the crown of all the virtues.[40]

Likewise, in France, innumerable *livres de politesse* [roughly, "manners manuals"] proffer concrete advice to the would-be courtier, for the most part unencumbered by apparent concerns about contradictions within either their own rhetoric or their subject.[41]   These contradictions nevertheless are very near the surface of these texts, and one in particular is both omnipresent and eternally unresolved: namely that in order to lay claim to nobility one must assert that one has always (genetically) been what one claims to be. This is an assertion difficult to sustain for most readers of these manuals, and so Castiglione's deft evasion of the dilemma is not available to them. Outright prevarication is therefore a commonly proposed option. The pragmatic, even cynical, tone of these treatises may also be in part the result of the ever more narrowly defined roles available to the actual or would-be courtier in seventeenth-century France. While early examples of these how-to manuals are often little more than thinly disguised translations or imitations of Castiglione, the genre gradually adapts to its particular situation and audience. Castiglione wrote, albeit in an elegiac tone, for and about an audience of people who were performing, or liked to think they were, in a theatre where the courtier was the primary personage, but the writers and readers of seventeenth-century French courtesy manuals are operating under a different set of circumstances. The courtier is no longer a player in a court where the prince is, or pretends to be, a *primus inter pares*; rather, the courtier now finds himself locked into a pyramidal structure of power, with an increasingly dominant monarch at the apex, to which the courtier must accommodate himself.[42] This narrowing of options produces a variety of responses, which nevertheless share an acceptance of the inevitability of the performative demands of the court. One of the most common responses is that found in the semi-ironically titled *La Guide des Courtisans* (1610) of Nervèze, who attacks the court in general, and court vices such as dissimulation in particular, in the name of a kind of bourgeois neo-Stoic piety. Even he, however, does not entirely reject a certain post-humanist "prudence," a balanced discretion which he is at pains to distinguish from courtly feigning. While describing the duplicitous "personnage, que le Courtisan allors joüe ordinairement sur ce Theatre" ["character that the Courtier ordinarily plays on this Stage"], he insists that one must differentiate between the kind of *faintise* [feigning] "qui trompe sous la bonne foy d'autruy" ["that deceives thanks to others' good faith"] and "celle qui agit prudemment selon le monde" ["that which acts prudently according to worldly custom"].[43] And elsewhere, while insisting that "... Dieu & la Cour sont deux choses contraires qui font agir diversement" ["God and the Court are two contrary things, which produce different behavior"], he goes so far as to praise the *faintise* of those who manage to be devout while still being good courtiers (*Guide*, 42, 42a–43). Even such an ill-humored anti-courtly text as the *Guide* cannot quite manage to reject courtly theatricality entirely; but other works, such as Eustache de Refuge's *Traicté de la Court* (1616), seem to embrace it wholeheartedly, only occasionally gesturing towards more conventional notions of moral behavior in passages that seem simply tacked on.[44] Refuge's well-organized and eminently practical manual has as its governing principle "accortise," a word significantly borrowed from the Italian *accortezza*, which in his hands becomes a kind of mercantile cleverness directed towards maximizing the advantage of its practitioner while minimizing that of others. Refuge makes no effort to pretend that the performance of *accortise* consists of anything except deceiving one's audience, coupled with efforts to penetrate the deception of others,[45] "avec neantmoins un visage ouvert et agreable à tous." ["with, nonetheless, a visage which is open and agreeable to all."] (*Traicté* 96f). The key to maintaining this "Affabilité agréable" is an obstinate averageness, Aristotle's virtuous mean reduced to a flat-footed bourgeois conformity (*Traicté* 4, and 75ff.). That it is a class-specific viewpoint is borne out by the text's anti-aristocratic tone, as well as certain very specific statements, as for example when he characterizes the *noblesse* as "ambitieux, orgueilleux, insolens, ingrats, vindicatifs, arrogantz, ostentateurs & vains, imprudents, avaricieux… " ["ambitious, prideful, insolent, ungrateful, vindictive, arrogant, ostentatious and vain, imprudent, avaricious… "] (*Traicté* 78).

This bourgeois outlook is shared by one of the most successful of the *livres de politesse*, Nicolas Faret's *L'Honeste homme. Ou, l'art de plaire à la Cour*, which first appeared in 1630, and was reprinted and translated many times in the following decades.[46] This work owes much to Castiglione, particularly in its attempts to define nobility and to discuss the question of heredity versus training. However, where Castiglione ironizes or aestheticizes these unresolvable dilemmas, Faret – lacking his master's *grazia* – contents himself with platitudes and vague formulae, while clumsily leaving the contradictions themselves in the open for the reader to stumble over. Like Refuge, he says that the would-be courtier should be *moyen* [average] in all things, and the goal of this relentless mediocrity is, above all, *plaire* [to please] (*L'Honeste homme* 5). Audience reception is all, and therefore every action of Faret's "Honeste homme" will be directed towards producing an appropriate response. To this end, he will present

les principales qualitez que doit avoir celuy qui pretend passer pour Honestehomme devant tant d'yeux dont l'on est éclairé à la Cour, et parmy un si grand nombre d'esprits delicats, à qui les defauts les plus cachez ne le sçauroient estre long temps. (Faret 12–13)

[the principal qualities that one should have in order to pass for an *honnête homme* in front of the many eyes that gaze upon one at Court, and among such a great number of sensitive *esprits*, from whom the most hidden faults cannot hope to remain so for long.]

There is no question of essence or naturalness here; all that matters is that one is able to "passer pour Honeste-homme" before the courtly audience. The worst thing that can befall such a pretender is to be caught pretending:

La principale chose à quoy il prendra garde, c'est qu'il ne paroisse point de dissimulation en son discours, & que son visage ne démente point sa bouche, ny ne destruise pas en un moment ce que son esprit aura bien eu de la peine à inventer. (Faret 143)

[The principal thing he must be careful of, is that no dissimulation appear in his discourse, and that his visage does not belie his mouth, nor destroy in a moment what his mind has taken a great deal of trouble to invent.]

This notion of the courtly self as an entity that needs careful planning, elaborate preparation, and flawless performance is certainly at odds with his assertion, repeated throughout the treatise, that, while one's reputation – and, indeed, existence – as a courtier are dependent upon "opinion," i.e. audience reception, "Le solide fondement de cette opinion est bien la vertu & le merite ..." ["The solid foundation of this opinion is indeed virtue and merit ..."] (Faret 74). But Faret is untroubled by such problems as the tensions between appearance and essence inherent in the idea of nobility. His how-to tract abounds in unreflective self-contradiction, moral confusion, and awkward or absent reasoning. At one point, for example, he claims that religion is essential to the courtly behavior of the "Honeste homme," since "Sans ce principe il n'y a point de probité, et sans probité personne ne sçauroit estre agreable, non pas mesme aux meschans." ["Without this principle there is no probity, and without probity nobody can be agreeable, even to bad people."] (Faret 54–55) The leap from "probité" to being "agreable" is difficult to follow, to say the least, and why one would want to be "agreable ... mesme aux meschans" is left unexplained. As is true for Refuge, probably one of Faret's sources, the gap between the performative imperatives of courtly identity and a kind of pious bourgeois morality remains unbridged, and it will be left for more complex texts to grapple with these problems.

It is therefore hardly fair to subject this courtesy literature to intensive scrutiny, since it reveals to us so plainly, and without much critical persuasion, the main feature of the discourse of nobility in this period: the dominance of the master tropes of theatre and theatricality, as a means of giving metaphorical presence to the tensions and contradictions inherent in the idea of noble identity. We do not need to perform for these works a kind of therapeutic textual psychoanalysis, exorcising the demons of theatrical (self-)deception to cure the neurosis of the text and the society it seeks to represent, or at least to allow the one and the other to live in a "healthy" fashion with that neurosis. Nor is it necessary to undertake a facile deconstruction of texts so transparently blind to themselves that they hardly require any sophisticated theoretico-interpretive intervention in order to be shown for what they are; the texts almost pathetically confess their rhetorical collapse before the reader's eyes. What is important to recognize is that this post-Castiglione literature of noble courtesy and courtly behavior, whatever its limitations, nevertheless sets forth the conditions of possibility for the more sophisticated inquiry of, say, Montaigne. The matrix of terms and gestures these manuals provide, dominated by metaphors of theatricality, constitutes the broad substrate for the more complex literature to which we now turn, literature which is only the tip of the vast iceberg that is the literary discourse of nobility in the late Renaissance and the seventeenth century.

"La plus part de nos vacations sont farcesques. 'Mundus universus exercet histrioniam.'" Few authors know better than Montaigne how to conceal the profound behind the platitude. When he makes this remark in "De mesnager sa volonté," the tenth essay of the third book of his *Essais*, he is perfectly aware that he is recycling a truism already old in the time of Petronius. Indeed, he cites the Roman author's version of this common-place almost as an anti-authority, as if to emphasize the triteness of his own statement. Yet at the same time he does not mean his remark to be merely banal; it provides both Montaigne and his reader with an enormously powerful metaphor, one which functions both as a tool with which to explore the structure of the self and as a figurative vocabulary with which to describe the dynamics of that structure, once discovered. The set of metaphoric images here conjured up – stage, role, performance, mask – permeate Montaigne's language of the self, a language not incidentally appropriated by the majority of his readers.[1] Given the critical attention lavished by such readers as Villey, Friedrich, and Starobinski upon Montaigne's ideas of identity, we certainly shall not attempt here to come up with yet another all-encompassing Theory of Montaigne. Nor will we try to find a definitive answer to another, related problem, similarly overburdened with critical attention: whether or not there is a "true Montaigne" lurking behind the various personæ or masks shown to us by the author of the *Essais*.[2] Our inquiry, while situated in the midst of these major critical debates, will have a more modest scope. Specifically, we will look closely at the intersection of Montaigne's theatrical language of the self with another discursive arena where the dominant metaphor is that of theatre and theatricality: the court. Our aim is to discover how Michel de Montaigne, author of the *Essais*, and Michel de Montaigne, Mayor of Bordeaux, *Seigneur de Montaigne, Chevalier de l'Ordre du Roy & Gentil-homme ordinaire de sa Chambre*,[3] courtier and advisor to kings, are related to one another. These two Montaignes, or two zones of Montaigne, seem to overlap precisely in the realm of theatrical language and metaphor, and it is this realm that seems to hold the key to an understanding of just how

Montaigne constitutes himself as a nobleman at a point in history when noble identity was subject to contestation and redefinition. Before beginning our examination of this aspect of Montaigne, however, it may be useful briefly to survey more general ideas of the structure of the *moi Montaignien*.

Since the seminal work of Pierre Villey,[4] it has been customary to divide "Montaigne" into two domains, an "inner" and an "outer," along what one might call a spatial axis, and into three others, "early," "middle," and "late," along a quasi-temporal axis. Such divisions are arbitrary, potentially misleading, and, to a degree, inevitable. In the first case, Montaigne himself makes much of the distinction between inner and outer, private and public, particularly in such essays as I, 20: "Que philosopher c'est apprendre à mourir," II, 3: "Coustume de l'isle de Cea," I, 40: "Consideration sur Cicéron," and especially I, 39: "De la solitude," where he offers his famous definition of the private *arrière-boutique*.[5] It might therefore seem natural simply to follow Montaigne's own line, as many critics have done, even if – as we shall see – there are substantial reasons to call it into question. The temporal division, although not explicitly set forth by Montaigne himself, is almost as difficult to avoid, given the unique nature of Montaigne's text. The three major layers of text have often been approached by critics as a set of archeological deposits, whose strata have been laid down on top of each other through time; the so-called A, B, and C texts are thus seen as representing different stages in the temporal evolution of Montaigne's thought. Villey, of course, is the primary exponent of this view; the features and problems of his division of Montaigne's intellectual activity into three periods – Stoic, Skeptic, and Epicurean – are sufficiently well-known to need no further comment here. Despite the eagerness of post-Villey readers of Montaigne to distance themselves in one way or another from his rigidly chronological and over-literal interpretation, the three layers of text make it difficult to avoid some kind of tripartite temporal structure. Hugo Friedrich, for example, enumerates what he sees as the three major phases of Montaigne's thought (*der erniedrigte Mensch, der bejahte Mensch, das Ich*) in the chapter titles of his magisterial work, but insists that all three coexist throughout the *oeuvre* of Montaigne; the differences that manifest themselves, he says, are primarily ones of emphasis.[6] Likewise, Jean Starobinski's comprehensive reading proposes a development of Montaigne's consciousness along three "étapes d'un parcours,"[7] steps or stages which in Starobinski's reading are defined primarily with reference to Montaigne's changing interactions with the social world, his own identity, and the text of the *Essais*.[8] Our inquiry will try to avoid assigning particular moments in the text of Montaigne to particular moments in his life, since such correspondences are often not only reductive but unprovable. However, it will of course remain necessary to take into account these issues of chronology and development, keeping a close eye on shifts in emphasis, refinements, or changes in position, not to mention outright contradictions. The multi-layered diversity of the text will be a key to our understanding of Montaigne's theatrical conception of the noble self.

If we accept the idea that Montaigne conceives of the self, in whatever sphere of activity, as a performance, an obvious corollary to this idea is that there exists an audience before whom this performance takes place and for whom it is intended. Again, as with the related problems already mentioned, considerable critical energy has been expended on the question of audience in the *Essais*. Here we have to deal with two intimately related, but not identical, questions: first, for whom is the performance of self that is the *Essais* intended? and second, how does Montaigne conceive of the relationship between Self (performer) and Other (audience) in a larger, more general sense? On the most basic level, Friedrich is surely right to conclude that, given the extreme diversity of the audiences for which Montaigne claims or appears to be writing, the first question does not admit of an exact answer.[9] More recent critics, beginning with Anthony Wilden, have gone beyond the *Publikumsfrage* of Friedrich, tending to see Montaigne as constituting the book of the *Essais* itself as his audience, substituting the text for the absent ideal Other (La Boétie) in a quest for perfect, unmediated communication.[10] For the purposes of the present work, we shall try to understand Montaigne's performances in the context of his attempts at political self-definition in late sixteenth-century France. This was not an easy task for Montaigne; to begin with, his alleged nobility was of extremely recent origin, the estate of Montaigne having been bought by his great-grandfather, a successful Bordeaux merchant, only fifty-five years before the birth of Michel. Michel's father Pierre was the first of the family to give up commercial activity, and Michel himself was the first to follow the aristocratic practice of adopting the name of the estate as his own. Montaigne's vehement and enthusiastic assertion of his own *noblesse* might therefore be seen as an attempt to (over)compensate for his *roturier* background.[11] Moreover, his eagerness to identify with the idea of hereditary nobility is tempered, as we shall see, by his distaste for many of the concrete realities of that class; this is particularly true in the context of the civil wars, where many of the *noblesse d'épée* distinguish themselves through their ignorance,[12] arrogance, rapaciousness, and brutality.[13] Finally, Montaigne finds himself playing a number of other roles incident to his noble identity in the course of his career: courtier, landowner, jurisconsult, public servant, and writer, among others; and he plays these roles before widely disparate audiences: the *noblesse d'épée et/ou de robe*, parents, teachers, aspiring poets, students of history, other public servants, an imaginary or absent friend, himself, his text, and the abstract *lecteur bénévole*. Montaigne therefore has to make constant adjustments to and justifications of his personæ according to the audience(s) he is addressing at any given moment; and our task will be to discover how Montaigne articulates the dynamic relationship between these audiences, his disparate personæ, and his multivalent text, with specific reference to the question of noble identity in late sixteenth-century France.[14] We shall see that the particular problems of self-definition confronting Montaigne as a member of the *noblesse de robe* in this historical moment will have a great deal to tell us about larger questions of identity in the *Essais*.

i.   Stoic posturing

One of the more carefully elaborated personæ we find in the *Essais* seems in many ways to be a direct response to the problems of Montaigne's historical moment. This is the neo-Stoic nobleman who, disillusioned with the ills of the age, accepts the vicissitudes of fortune with equanimity and spends his life preparing to *faire une belle mort*. It should be pointed out at once that this stance is not merely arbitrary. There is a clear linkage between the historical position of the sixteenth-century *noblesse d'épée* – a group which senses its feudal privileges and political strength slipping away as royal power increases, while its military role is being reduced by the changing nature of military strategy (gunpowder, the rise of professional soldiers), and its economic power undermined by the expansion of a trade economy in which it cannot directly participate – and the discursive style it chooses to adopt. To a class thus threatened on all sides with loss of status, both real (politico-economic) and symbolic (honor and prestige *vis-à-vis* the Crown), it is certainly conceivable that an attitude of seeming indifference to the inevitable, and a corollary claim to real fulfillment in some inner realm, might have considerable appeal.[15] Montaigne's position relative to this class and to this model of noble behavior is somewhat more complex, since Montaigne was a *noble de robe* anxious, like most of his counterparts, to be seen as a "true" noble, a *noble d'épée*. Rather than being himself a "real" Stoic, or even presenting this version of the noble self as a model to be emulated, it seems more probable that, even in such essays as "Que philosopher c'est apprendre à mourir" (I, 20), and "De la solitude" (I, 39), Montaigne is setting up something of a straw man, a hypothetical entity to be examined and discussed, but not necessarily imitated.[16] Whether this is true will be investigated more carefully later; in the meantime, straw man or not, the Catonian ideal expressed in these essays is a useful place to begin our delineation of noble identity, just as it seems to have been for Montaigne.

"De la solitude" opens with an ill-humored attack on Ciceronian humanism, with its emphasis on public action, so dear to Erasmus and Italian civic humanists.

[A] Laissons à part cette longue comparaison de la vie solitaire à l'active; et quant à ce beau mot dequoy se couvre l'ambition et l'avarice: Que nous ne sommes pas nez pour nostre particulier, ains pour le publicq, rapportons nous en hardiment à ceux qui sont en la danse... Les mauvais moyens par où on s'y pousse en nostre siecle, montrent bien que la fin n'en vaut gueres. (237)

[Let us leave aside that long comparison between the solitary and the active life; and as for those fine words with which ambition and avarice cover themselves – that we are not born for ourselves, but for the public – let us look boldly to those who are in the dance... The foul means by which people advance themselves in our day and age show clearly that the end is hardly worth it.]

If we are to believe this passage, Montaigne (unlike Bacon, as we shall see in the next chapter) seems not to have been seduced by the republican ideal of the humanist public man. Montaigne associates this ideal and its Ciceronian rhetorical style with the only theatre of political activity available in late sixteenth-century France: the court, where "free" republican debate is out of the question. The Ciceronian mode is therefore linked (via the figure of Cicero himself) to courtly self-advancement. Montaigne is not fooled by "l'ambition et l'avarice" masquerading as disinterested civic virtue; he strips away the mask to reveal the truth, which inspires only disgust. In a world where base self-interest is the sole motor, what is a virtuous man to do? Clearly, the alternatives are limited (238): "[A] Il faut ou imiter les vitieux, ou les haïr." ["One must either imitate the vicious, or hate them."] And yet it does not seem possible to flee into the wilderness; one is compelled to live among humanity, repugnant though such a prospect may be. Therefore, given the necessity of living in society with "les vitieux," an inner attitude of complete detachment from and indifference to worldly concerns appears to be the only solution (241): "[A] Il faut avoir femmes, enfans, biens, et sur tout de la santé, qui peut; mais non pas s'y attacher en maniere que nostre heur en despende."[17] ["We ought to have wives, children, goods, and above all health, if we can; but we shouldn't be so attached to them that our happiness depends on them."] The true sage can rise above such trivial considerations, finding happiness in the private contemplation of pure virtue, while preparing for death, as Montaigne proposes in "Que philosopher c'est apprendre à mourir" (I, 20).[18] And where does this activity of contemplation and preparation take place?

[A] Il se faut reserver une arriere-boutique toute nostre, toute franche, en laquelle nous establissons nostre vraye liberté et principale retraicte et solitude. En cette-cy faut-il prendre nostre ordinaire entretien de nous à nous mesmes, et si privé que nulle acointance ou communication estrangiere y trouve place... Nous avons une ame contournable en soy mesme; elle se peut faire compagnie... [19] (241)

[We should reserve for ourselves a back room entirely our own, entirely free, in which we establish our true liberty and our main retreat and solitude. Here we should have our ordinary conversation with ourselves, so private that no external connection or communication can find a place... We have a soul that can turn back on itself; it can keep itself company...]

So the stage on which the "vraye liberté" of the sage plays itself out is purely internal, wholly independent of and entirely sealed off from any "communication estrangiere"; the sage's self-sufficient "ame" needs no external stimuli whatsoever, and is both player and audience. It is surely not amiss to begin even here to wonder about the practical viability of this particular kind of solitude, or to become suspicious of the degree to which Montaigne actually believes – or hopes to persuade us that he believes – in the possibility of its realization. This is particularly true when we focus on what is perhaps the most intriguing aspect of this self-reflexive theatre-in-the-round: its claim to be able to subsist outside of language, "sans paroles" ["without words"]. It is tempting to seize upon this as a kind of Rousseau-esque yearning for an unspoiled, prelapsarian universe, in which there exists only pure, unmediated interaction between persons, untainted by the corruptions of language.[20] Cave and others have pursued the general implications of such a reading of the *Essais*, and it would be straightforward to show how, in this particular case, the very language in which this ideal of self-sufficiency is enunciated denies the possibility of its realization.

However, we shall focus instead on something more specific. The word "paroles" in this context means not so much language *per se*, but rather an excess of language, a superfluity of words – especially the wrong kinds of words, words that are misleading, confusing, or outright false. Montaigne's self-proclaimed distaste for rhetorical display and deceptive language[21] is manifested in several places, such as "De la vanité des paroles" (I, 51), as well as in the essay immediately following "De la solitude," "Consideration sur Ciceron" (I, 40).[22] There, Montaigne discusses at length the form of "parole" appropriate to a person of his station; the backbone of his argument is the famous Senecan dictum (which he cites in a C-text addition, p. 251): *Non est ornamentum virile concinnitas*. While attacking Cicero (with Pliny the Younger as a corollary figure) for his vanity and ambition in life, and for his correspondingly vain and pompous style of writing, he holds up Seneca (and Epicurus) as a model both of Stoic virtue in life and of concision, directness, and plenitude in letters.

[A] ... encore ne sont ce pas lettres vuides et descharnées, qui ne se soutiennent que par un delicat chois de mots, entassez et rangez à une juste cadence, ains farcies et pleines de beaux discours de sapience, par lesquelles on se rend non plus eloquent, mais plus sage, et qui nous apprennent non à bien dire, mais à bien faire. Fy de l'eloquence qui nous laisse envie de soy, non des choses; si ce n'est qu'on die que celle de Cicero, estant en si extreme perfection, se donne corps elle mesme.[23] (252)

[... still, these are not just empty and fleshless letters, which only sustain themselves by a delicate choice of words, stacked up and arranged in a neat cadence, but rather letters stuffed full of fine discourses of wisdom, by which one renders oneself not more eloquent, but wiser, and which teach us not to speak well, but to do well. Fie on the eloquence which makes us desire itself, not things; unless we say that that of Cicero, being so perfect, gives itself substance.]

For Montaigne, there is a close correlation between character and language; even if he does not completely subscribe, as Defaux claims, to the Erasmian view that "[h]abet animus faciem quamdam suam in oratione velut in speculo relucentem,"[24] at least he is willing to accept its utility on a provisional basis; for, as he remarks in "Des menteurs" (I, 9, p. 36): [B] "Nous ne sommes hommes, et ne nous tenons les uns aux autres que par la parole."[25] ["We are men, and can grasp one another, only through words."] If one's verbal style gives the reader or hearer indications as to one's personal *stile*, then Ciceronian rhetoric, more interested in its own beauty and persuasive power than in conveying solid truth as simply as possible, clearly indicates that its user is not to be trusted; his *parole* is, in every sense, unreliable. In this essay, as well as in "De l'institution des enfans" (I, 26), from which the following citation is taken, Montaigne associates this type of *parler* with a particular group of people, and a particular sphere of activity, namely the court; and he sees such corruption of language as an inevitable consequence of being a *courtisan*:

[C] Un courtisan ne peut avoir ny loi ni volonté de dire et penser que favorablement d'un maistre qui, parmi tant de milliers d'autres subjects, l'a choisi pour le nourrir et eslever de sa main. Cette faveur et utilité corrompent non sans quelque raison sa franchise, et l'esblouissent. Pourtant void on coustumierement le langage de ces gens-là divers à tout autre langage d'un estat, et de peu de foy en telle matiere. (255)

[A courtier can have neither the right nor the will to speak other than favorably of a master who, from among so many thousands of other subjects, has chosen him to sustain and raise up with his own hand. This favor and this utility corrupt, not without reason, his freedom, and dazzle him. Thus one customarily finds the language of these people unlike any other language of a state, and not to be trusted in such matters.]

The *parole* of the courtier is here shown to be unreliable not only because it conceals "l'ambition et l'avarice," but also because it involves a sacrifice of independence and *franchise* (that very *franchise* which is the essential defining quality of the *arrière-boutique*), a sacrifice entailing in turn a loss of the ability to speak freely. It is not just that the courtier cannot speak his own mind; he is no longer able even to speak the same language as the rest of us. Instead, he speaks a language of deception, dissimulation, and concealment; a language which, says Montaigne in "Des menteurs" (I, 9), is worse than no language at all. In the same essay, Montaigne remarks scornfully (36) on "[B] ceux qui font profession de ne former autrement leur parole, que selon qu'il sert aux affaires qu'ils negotient, et qu'il plaist aux grands à qui ils parlent."[26] ["... those who profess to form their words only to further the affairs they are negotiating, and to please the great to who they are talking."] He tells us, in "De la præsumption" (II, 17, p. 647), that nothing is more repugnant to a noble soul (in this case, his own):

[A] Plustost lairrois je rompre le col aux affaires que de tordre ma foy pour leur service. Car, quant à cette nouvelle vertu de faintise et de dissimulation qui est à cet heure si fort en credit, je la hay capitallement; et, de tous les vices, je n'en trouve aucun qui tesmoigne tant de lâcheté et bassesse de coeur. C'est un' humeur couarde et servile de s'aller desguiser et cacher sous un masque, et de n'oser se faire veoir tel qu'on est. Par là nos hommes se dressent à la perfidie: [B] estants duicts à produire des parolles fauces, ils ne font pas conscience d'y manquer. [A] Un coeur genereux ne doit desmentir ses pensées; il se veut faire voir jusques au dedans. [C] Ou tout y est bon, ou aumoins tout y est humein.

Aristote estime office de magnanimité hayr et aimer à descouvert, juger, parler avec toute franchise, et, au prix de la verité, ne faire cas de l'approbation ou reprobation d'autruy.

[A] Apollonius disoit que c'estoit aux serfs de mantir, et aux libres de dire verité.

[I'd rather let affairs break their necks [i.e. come out disastrously] than twist my faith for their sake. For as to this new virtue of feigning and dissimulation which is now so much in fashion, I hate it to death; and of all vices, I cannot find any which demonstrates so much cowardice and baseness of heart. It is cowardly and servile to go off and disguise ourselves, and to hide behind a mask, and not to dare to show oneself as one is. This is the way men train themselves for perfidy; being accustomed to produce false words, they have no scruples about breaking it [their word]. A generous heart should not belie its thoughts; it wants to show itself inside and out. Everything there is good, or at least human.

Aristotle thinks it the duty of magnanimity to hate and love openly, to judge and speak with total freedom, and, for the sake of truth, not to care about the approval or disapproval of others.

Apollonius said that it was for slaves to lie, and for the free to speak the truth.]

Liberté, franchise, magnanimité, générosité; and their inverses, *servilité, bassesse, lâcheté, couardise*; all the code-words are there. Montaigne is enunciating – and carefully aligning himself with – an ideal of the *noblesse d'épée*, combining features of the feudal model with quasi-Stoic elements appropriate to the new, incipiently disenfranchised situation of sixteenth-century nobility.[27] Before discussing in more detail Montaigne's exact relationship to this class ideal, however, let us pursue further his view of language.

Despite the great danger posed to the "free" individual by participation in the world of affairs, Montaigne does not intend that his wise man, in rejecting the deceptions of courtly discourse, should entirely abandon the cultivated use of language. The sage, too, has his characteristic discursive style; his language is as sound and authentic as his actions are disinterested and virtuous. Montaigne describes this mode of using language, whether written or performed, in "De l'institution des enfans":

[A] Le parler que j'ayme, c'est un parler simple et naif, tel sur le papier qu'à la bouche; un parler succulent et nerveux, court et serré, [C] non tant delicat et peigné comme vehement et brusque:
   Haec demum sapiet dictio, quae feriet,
[A] plutost difficile qu'ennuieux, esloigné d'affectation, desreglé, descousu et hardy: chaque lopin y face son corps; non pedantesque, non fratesque, non pleideresque, mais plutost soldatesque, comme Suetone appelle celuy de Julius Caesar; [C] et si sens pas bien pour quoy il l'en appelle.[28] (171–72)

[The speech I like is a simple and naive speech, the same on paper as when speaking; a succulent and strong speech, short and compressed, not so much delicate and well-groomed as vehement and brusque:
   That speech has most taste which is most striking, rather difficult than boring, far from affectation, irregular, disjointed, and bold; every part having its own body; not pedantic, not monkish, not legalistic, but rather soldierly, as Suetonius calls that of Julius Caesar; and yet I don't quite see why he calls it that.]

The practitioners of this style are not courtiers but "real men," whose unconstrained words are at one with their heroic deeds; and Montaigne is extremely eager to be counted as one of their number.[29] An important part of doing so is demonstrating that he is not really a writer, since such an activity is beneath the dignity of a true gentleman. We have already seen how, in "Consideration sur Ciceron," he roundly criticizes Cicero and Pliny not only for their excessive focus on matters of style but also for their unseemly eagerness to be known as men of letters; he uses the examples of Scipio and Laelius to show (249–50) that "la perfection du bien parler" ["the perfection of speaking well"] does *not* "apporter quelque gloire sortable à un grand personnage" ["bring any glory appropriate to a great personage"], and goes on to point out (250) that "[A] [c]'est une espece de mocquerie et d'injure de vouloir faire valoir un homme par des qualitez mes-advenantes à son rang…"[30] ["It's a kind of mockery and insult to praise a man for qualities inappropriate to his rank..."] In fact, he says, being known as a writer is so embarrassing to a man of quality that some persons of his acquaintance will do almost anything to avoid it. Montaigne is himself very eager indeed to avoid the label of "escrivailleur"; it is far more important, he says, to be known as someone who *acts*:

[A] Quel que je soye, je le veux estre ailleurs qu'en papier. Mon art et mon industrie ont esté employez à me faire valoir moy-mesme; mes estudes, à m'apprendre à faire, non pas à escrire. Voylà mon mestier et mon ouvrage. J'ay mis tous mes efforts à former ma vie. Je suis moins faiseur de livres que de nulle autre besoigne.[31]

[Whatever I am, I want to be it somewhere else besides on paper. My art and industry have been employed to make myself better; my studies, to teach me to do, not to write. That's my profession and my work. I have put all my efforts into forming my life. I am less a maker of books than anything else.]

However, since he is, after all, still writing, he goes to even greater lengths to show (again, in "Consideration sur Ciceron") that his own style is as close as possible to that appropriate to the "real man." First, a disclaimer to show that he really doesn't even want to discuss the question of style (251):

[C] Je sçay bien, quand j'oy quelqu'un qui s'arreste au langage des Essais, que j'aimeroye mieux qu'il s'en teust. Ce n'est pas tant eslever les mots, comme c'est deprimer le sens, d'autant plus picquamment que plus obliquement.

[I know well, when I hear someone focus on the language of the *Essays*, that I'd rather he kept quiet about it. It doesn't so much praise the words, as it denigrates the sense, all the more sharply for being more oblique.]

Having thus insulated himself (he hopes) from the kinds of attacks he himself has aimed at Cicero, he goes on to describe, not without immodesty, his own style, both literary and otherwise, carefully aligning it with the Senecan model he has just discussed and praised (in the passage on "lettres vuides et descharnées" cited above). He first mentions, via an uncharacteristically maladroit use of a form of disclaimer familiar to readers of Renaissance texts,[32] that his own letter-writing abilities are not far inferior to those of, say, Seneca: "[B] Sur ce subject de lettres, je veux dire ce mot, que c'est un ouvrage auquel mes amys tiennent que je puis quelque chose." ["On this subject of letters, I want to say this, that it's an area in which my friends say that I am fairly capable."] He then continues:

J'ay naturellement un stile comique et privé, mais c'est d'une forme mienne, inepte aux negotiations publiques, comme en toutes façons est mon langage: trop serré, desordonné, couppé, particulier; et ne m'entens pas en lettres ceremonieuses, qui n'ont autre substance que d'une belle enfileure des paroles courtoises. Je n'ay ny la faculté ny le goust de ces longues offres d'affection et de service. Je n'en crois pas tant, et me desplaist d'en dire guiere outre ce que j'en crois. C'est bien loing de l'usage present: car il ne fut jamais si abjecte et servile prostitution de presentations; la vie, l'ame, devotion, adoration, serf, esclave, tous ces mots, y courent si vulgairement que, quand ils veulent faire sentir une plus expresse volonté et plus respectueuse, ils n'ont plus de maniere pour l'exprimer.

Je hay à mort de sentir au flateur: qui faict que je me jette naturellement à un parler sec, rond et cru qui tire, à qui ne me cognoit d'ailleurs, un peu vers le dedaigneux. [C] J'honnore le plus ceux que j'honnore le moins; et, où mon ame marche d'une grande allegresse, j'oublie les pas de la contenance. [B] Et m'offre maigrement et fierement à ceux à qui je suis. [C] Et me presente moins à qui je me suis le plus donné: [B] il me semble qu'ils le doivent lire en mon coeur, et que l'expression de mes paroles fait tort à ma conception.

[C] A bienvienner, à prendre congé, à remercier, à salüer, à presenter mon service, et tels complimens verbeux des loix ceremonieuses de nostre civilité, je ne cognois personne si sottement sterile de langage que moy. (252–53)

[I have naturally a cheerful and familiar style, but it is all my own, ill-adapted to public negotiations, as is in every way my language, which is too brief, disorderly, abrupt, and personal; and I'm no expert in ceremonious letters, which have no substance other than a fine parade of courteous words. I have neither the talent nor the taste for these long offers of affection and service. I don't believe it, and I don't like saying more than I believe. This is far removed from current usage, for there has never been such abject and servile prostitution of compliments; life, soul, devotion, adoration, servant, slave, all these words are so vulgarly current that, when they want to convey a more sincere and respectful sentiment, they have no way left to express it.

I mortally hate to sound like a flatterer, which means that I naturally throw myself into a dry, direct, raw manner of speaking which, to those who don't know me, tends to sound a little disdainful. I honor most those whom I honor least; and, where my soul goes in a hurry, I forget the steps of ceremony. And I offer myself meagerly, and proudly, to those to whom I really belong; and present myself least to those to whom I have given myself most; it seems to me that they should read it in my heart, and that my words' expression doesn't do justice to my thoughts.

As to welcoming, taking leave, thanking, greeting, offering my services, and suchlike verbose comments imposed by the ceremonious laws of our civility, I know nobody so stupidly sterile in words as myself.]

This long and important passage brings together many of the critical issues we have thus far discussed. Montaigne begins with a focus on literary style, but the focus quickly expands to take in the spoken word and the theatre in which it is deployed. If we find it impossible to separate the written and the spoken, the inscribed and the performed, it merely illustrates the intimate connection between the two in Montaigne's discursive universe. This connection is made most explicit in "De l'institution des enfans," where Montaigne, after counseling the young proto-noble to take his instruction in behavior not from the study of books but rather from "le commerce des hommes," goes on to clarify just which "hommes" he has in mind (156):

"[A] En cette practique des hommes, j'entends y comprendre, et principale-ment, ceux qui ne vivent qu'en la memoire des livres." ["In this association with men, I mean to include, and above all, those who live only in the memory of books."] Literary style and "personal style" are, for Montaigne, one and the same.

As self-evident as this point may seem, it is worth emphasizing, because it has extremely significant ramifications. Montaigne expands the role of language beyond the literary to the social. Language becomes a means not only of communication, of conveying information, but also of defining and revealing social identity. The *franc parler* of Montaigne's hypothetical nobleman defines a class, limiting its membership to "real men" in the sense discussed above, and excluding those whose *parole* does not measure up. It functions as a kind of veil, through which only the initiated may pass; those who are unable to "lire dans [son] coeur," to penetrate through his allegedly inadequate and sterile language, are rigorously excluded. This claim of linguistic inadequacy seems something of a paradox, since the language of the true nobleman is also supposed to be a language of plenitude and transparency. The solution lies in the exact location of that inadequacy; it is a language which is inadequate only and precisely where the language of the court proliferates most overwhelmingly, in the public display of "lettres ceremonieuses," "presentations," and so forth.[33] Like-wise, the language of the true nobleman is perfectly transparent to those not blinded by the smokescreen of courtly discourse, whose prolixity acts as an opaque barrier concealing its own emptiness. This verbal over-luxuriance and opacity is the locus of true linguistic sterility; when the *courtisan* wants to express something real and true, to go beyond his hyperbolic *formules de politesse*, he finds himself without a language corre-sponding to his thoughts. His vocabulary and credibility, linguistic and social, are exhausted. The language of the private sphere, of the *arrière-boutique*, is the revealer of the true self, the carrier of truth; public language, the language of the theatre of the court, can produce only an endlessly self-replicating duplicity.

Throughout this passage, Montaigne strives mightily to distance himself as greatly as possible from the language and persona of the *courtisan*. One strategy he adopts, both here and elsewhere, is a kind of temporal separ-ation. He often associates himself with his favorite figures from antiquity, "ceux qui ne vivent qu'en la memoire des livres," as we have seen him do in comparing himself to Seneca and Epicurus; the implication, of course, is that he (or at least his language) is too noble for such corrupt times as these. He is also fond of situating himself in another historical period, chronologi-cally closer to his own time, but equally remote, in a discursive sense, from the age of the courtier (and indeed from any historical reality that ever existed – a point to which we will return): the "good old days" of the old nobility, when men were men, and discourse was still untainted by the nefarious influence of the Italians.

Montaigne speaks of this time in "Couardise mere de la cruauté" (II, 27), where he decries the new and pernicious fad of fencing and duels. He makes it clear that this fashion is an Italian import (697): [B] "Nous allons apprendre en Italie à escrimer..." ["We go to Italy to learn to fence..."]. (The use of the first person plural pronoun here is no accident; in the *Journal de Voyage*, Montaigne tells us about his own brother's fencing lessons in Italy: "La domenica 15 d'Ottobre la mattina io partii di Roma, e ci lasciai il mio Fratello con 43 scudi d'oro, con i quali si risolveva di poter star là, et imparar la scherma per il tempo di cinque mesi." ["The morning of Sunday 15 October I left Rome, and left my brother there with 43 gold *scudi*, with which he planned to be able to stay there, and spend five months learning to fence."] Apparently the lessons proved useful, as in the present essay (696–97) Montaigne recounts how his brother, during his Roman sojourn, became involved in a duel as a second, and how – "apres s'estre desfaict de son homme" ["after having rid himself of his man"] – he needed the King of France's help to get out of prison. [34] He goes on to claim that it was not always so: [B] "...en mon enfance, la noblesse fuyoit la reputation de bon escrimeur comme injurieuse, et se desroboit pour l'apprendre, comme un mestier de subtilité, desrogént à la vraye et naifve vertu..." ["...in my youth, the nobility avoided the reputation of 'expert fencer' as insulting, and learned it in secret, as an underhand occupation, derogating from true and sincere virtue..."] (There follows a quotation from Tasso's *Gerusalemme Liberata* (XII, 55), describing how, in the combat of Tancredi and Clorinda, the antagonists eschew such craven tactics as parrying and ducking, preferring to bash away at each other with abandon.) Notice, however, that Montaigne does *not* say that the nobility of the previous generation disdained fencing as unworthy of a true nobleman, and therefore scorned to learn how to fence; rather, he says that to be *known* as an expert fencer was an embarrassment, and that as a result one was forced to conceal the fact that one did in fact take fencing lessons. Once again, what counts is not the essence, but the appearance; this seems to undermine any assertion that the nobility of yesteryear were fundamentally different from those of the present day. If anything, one could argue that current-day nobles are *more* straightforward and honest, since at least they don't try to hide the fact that their fencing ability is an acquired skill.

Perhaps sensing this weakness in his argument, Montaigne continues with a slightly different emphasis (698):

Les butes, les tournois, les barrieres, l'image des combats guerriers estoient l'exercice de nos peres: cet autre exercice [duelling] est d'autant moins noble qu'il ne regard qu'une fin privée, qui nous apprend à nous entreruyner, contre les loix et la justice, et qui en toute façon produict tousjours des effects dommageables. Il est bien plus digne et mieux seant de s'exercer en choses qui asseurent, non qui offencent nostre police, qui regardent la publique seurté et la gloire commune.

[Archery, tournaments, jousting, the image of warlike combats were the exercise of our fathers. This other exercise [duelling] is so much the less noble as it regards only a private end, which teaches us to ruin each other, against law and justice, and which in any case always produces damaging results. It is much more worthy and fitting to exercise oneself in things which strengthen, rather than undermine, our government, which regard public security and the glory of all.]

By the time we arrive at the end of this remarkable passage, we find that Montaigne has stood the *épée* ethos on its head; what is truly ignoble turns out to be the noble "privilege" (in the etymological sense) of private violence, while true nobility resides in the subordination of individual impulses to the public good. (Notice, too, that it is not even actual warfare, but "*l'image* des combats guerriers," that constitutes the manly, warlike activity of "nos peres"...) This is the voice not of an assertively independent Old Noble (who neither would nor could use such phrases as "publique seurté"), but of a *noble de robe*, a jurist educated and trained in the civic-humanist tradition. This ironic reversal seals itself with the beautifully oxymoronic formulation "la gloire commune." After all, "la gloire" is nothing if not an individual, private quality, and it is in theory the quality that alone defines the identity of the nobleman; yet here Montaigne incorporates it into a legalistic phrase that not only renders that quality universal but appropriates it to the State. *Mais nous nous devançons...*

To return to Montaigne's move into the imaginary "good old days," we find that the discursive style of this period – a style with which Montaigne is careful to identify his own – is, he tells us, "bien loing de l'usage present." In "De la præsumption," Montaigne reinforces this point, reemphasizing his own unsuitability for the courtly life in particular, and late sixteenth-century France in general:

[A] Les qualitez mesmes qui sont en moy non reprochables, je les trouvois inutiles en ce siecle. La facilité de mes meurs, on l'eut nommée lácheté et foiblesse; la foy et la conscience s'y feussent trouvées scrupuleuses et superstiteuses; la franchise et la liberté, importune, inconsiderée et temeraire. A quelque chose sert le malheur. Il fait bon naistre en un siecle fort depravé; car, par comparaison d'autruy, vous estes estimé vertueux à bon marché. Qui n'est que parricide en nos jours, et sacrilege, il est homme de bien et d'honneur... (646)

[The very qualities which are irreproachable in me, I found useless in this day and age. My relaxed ways would have been called cowardice and weakness; good faith and conscience would have been found over-nice and superstitious; frankness and freedom, importunate, thoughtless, and rash. Misfortune is good for something. It pays to be born in a particularly depraved age; for, in comparison with others, you are considered virtuous at a bargain price. One who, in our days, is merely a parricide and sacrilegious, is a good and honorable man...]

Not only these otherwise unexceptionable virtues but also Montaigne's seemingly unconscious pride in laying claim to them are coded links to an old-nobility, *épée* ideology. Montaigne is, on one level, simply complaining about the barbarousness and corruption of his times; but he is also articulating a specific political position, associated with a particular class to which he is eager to be seen to belong.[35]

That he does not come by this position as naturally as he would have us believe is also apparent in the densely packed passage from "Consideration sur Ciceron." He remarks rather emphatically that he dislikes being perceived as participating in the discourse of the court; therefore, he says, "...je me jette naturellement à un parler sec, rond et cru qui tire, à qui ne me cognoit d'ailleurs, un peu vers le dedaigneux." This *dédain*[36] is meant to be part and parcel of the rude honesty of the true nobleman; and in "De la præsumption," Montaigne expends considerable energy demonstrating that he comes by this quality honestly, naturally, and unconsciously.

[A] Il me souvient donc que, des ma plus tendre enfance, on remarquoit en moy je ne scay quel port de corps et des gestes tesmoignants quelque vaine et sotte fierté. J'en veux dire premierement cecy, qu'il n'est pas inconvenient d'avoir des conditions et des propensions si propres et si incorporées en nous, que nous n'ayons pas moyen de les sentir et reconnoistre. Et de telles inclinations naturelles, le corps en retient volontiers quelque pli sans nostre sçeu et consentement. (632–33)

[I remember, then, that from my earliest childhood, people noticed in me a certain carriage and certain gestures indicating some vain and silly pride. I want to say this first, that it is not inconvenient to have some characteristics and propensities so much our own, and so much a part of us, that we have no way of feeling and recognizing them. And of such natural inclinations the body is likely to retain some imprint, without our knowledge or consent.]

Later in the same essay, he links this allegedly genetic quality to his public behavior, claiming for himself – in phraseology with which we are by now familiar – the qualities of *liberté* and *franchise* which we have been discussing, and insisting that these qualities force him (and/or give him license) to speak the truth-bearing language of the private sphere, the *arrière-boutique*, even in public (649):

[A] Or, de moy, j'ayme mieux estre importun et indiscret que flateur et dissimulé.
    [B] J'advoue qu'il se peut mesler quelque pointe de fierté et d'opiniastreté à se

tenir ainsin entier et descouvert sans consideration d'autruy; et me semble que je deviens un peu plus libre où il le faudroit moins estre, et que je m'eschaufe par l'opposition du respect. Il peut estre aussi que je me laisse aller apres ma nature, à faute d'art. Presentant aux grands cette mesme licence de langue et de contenance que j'apporte de ma maison, je sens combien elle decline vers l'indiscretion et incivilité. Mais, outre ce que je suis ainsi faict, je n'ay pas l'esprit assez souple pour gauchir à une prompte demande et pour en eschaper par quelque destour, ny pour feindre une verité, ny assez de memoire pour la retenir ainsi feinte, ny certes assez de asseurance pour la maintenir; et fois le brave par foiblesse. Parquoy je m'abandonne à la nayfveté et à tousjours dire ce que je pense, et par complexion, et par discours, laissant à la fortune d'en conduire l'evenement.

[C] Aristippus disoit le principal fruit qu'il eut tiré de la philosophie, estre qu'il parloit librement et ouvertement à chacun.[37]

[Now, for my part, I prefer to be importunate and indiscreet rather than flattering and dissembling.

I admit that there may be a bit of pride and stubbornness in keeping myself thus entire and open, without considering others; and it seems to me that I become a little freer where I ought least to do so, and that I chafe against the restraint imposed by respect. It may also be that I let myself go according to my nature, lacking art. Displaying to great men the same freedom of language and bearing that I have at home, I feel how much it inclines towards indiscretion and incivility. But, besides the fact that I'm made that way, my mind isn't supple enough to dodge a sudden question and to escape it by some detour, nor to invent a truth, nor do I have enough memory to retain it once invented, and certainly not enough assurance to maintain it; so I put on a bold face through weakness. Therefore, I abandon myself to naïve honesty and to saying always what I think, both through inclination and through reason, leaving Fortune to govern the result.

Aristippus said that the main benefit he had gotten out of philosophy was that he spoke freely and openly to everyone.]

However, if we return to the passage from "Consideration sur Ciceron" with which we began this discussion, and look more closely at the language he uses to describe his "natural" inclinations, we find a curious twist: "...je me jette naturellement à un parler sec...", he claims; but it is difficult to see how it is possible to *throw* oneself into a particular mode of behavior in a "natural" (spontaneous, unforced, unconscious, instinctual, automatic) way. This peculiar tension between verb and adverb is reinforced by his remark that he (un)consciously chooses/hurls himself into this mode of behavior precisely *because* of his distaste for being perceived as a courtier. If his "parler sec" were as natural and unforced as he claims, surely such external stimuli would be superfluous. Indeed, it is because he is eager to appear to be a non-courtier that he adopts this "natural" mode of behavior. In other words, his protestations against the posturing artificiality of courtly discourse are themselves a pose, and his "nayfveté" resembles not so much *la nature* as the studied *sprezzatura* of Castiglione.[38]

A critical and revealing moment in the *Essais*, one at which this contradiction comes most sharply into focus, is found in "Des récompenses d'honneur" (II, 7). Recall that one of Montaigne's favorite tactics for dissociating himself from courtly discourse is that of temporal separation, through identification either with a fictive version of ancient Rome or with a semi-mythical, quasi-feudal *noblesse d'épée*. In "Des récompenses d'honneur," Montaigne explicitly associates these two imaginary ages with one another precisely when he also gives his most categorically stated definition of nobility:

[A] Mais il est digne d'estre consideré que nostre nation donne à la vaillance le premier degré des vertus, comme son nom montre, qui vient de valeur; et que, à notre usage, quand nous disons un homme qui vaut beaucoup, ou un homme de bien, au stile de nostre court et de nostre noblesse, ce n'est à dire autre chose qu'un vaillant homme, d'une façon pareille à la Romaine. Car la generale appellation de vertu prend chez eux etymologie de la force. La forme propre, et seule, et essencielle, de noblesse en France, c'est la vacation militaire. (384)

[But it is worth considering that our nation gives to valor the first rank among virtues, as its name shows, which comes from "value"; and that, according to our usage, when we say a worthy man, or a good man, in the language of our court and our nobility, it is to say nothing else than that he is a valiant man, in the same fashion as the Romans. For the general term, virtue, has for the Romans its etymology from "strength." The proper, and the only, and the essential form of nobility in France is the military profession.]

This passage has a strangely hollow ring to it, quite aside from the shakiness of its etymological argument. Montaigne's oddly dogmatic tone, combined with his formulaic assertions, gives one the sense that Montaigne is enunciating, not ideas that he has thought out for himself, but rather clichés he feels obligated to parade before the reader as part of an effort to consolidate his own identification with the class in question.[39] Montaigne emphasizes "la vacation militaire" not because he himself is a great warrior – indeed, he himself makes no direct claims on this score, and, after all, his primary interests and talents lie elsewhere – but because it is the mode of life most diametrically opposed to that of the court.[40] The odd formulation "au stile de nostre court et de nostre noblesse" contains a peculiar tension; note that the two terms are presented separately, and not simply assumed to be identical. Does this mean that some at least of the *noblesse* (*d'épée*, presumably) exist outside the court – and, more importantly, that perhaps some of the denizens of the court of Henri III are not (the right kind of) noble? (Recall also that, in his discussion (cited above) of the "parler … soldatesque" in I, 26, Montaigne manifests greater interest in adopting the language of the soldier than in actually performing the activities proper to such persons. We will return to this point later.) That Montaigne himself is hardly convinced of the soundness or veracity of his hyperbolic assertion about the "forme" of French nobility becomes even more evident when we recall that, only slightly earlier in the same essay, he points out that martial valor is actually within the reach of anyone, even the common people, and has in fact become almost (303) "vulgaire: comme il est tres-aysé à voir par l'experience que nous en donnent nos guerres civiles."[41] ["... vulgar; as may easily be seen through the experience of it our civil wars give us."]

It seems clear, then, that Montaigne's model of the nobleman as the man who is literally of his *parole*, who does not hide behind masks or *visages* not his own, who performs no role other than that of his "true self," is an untenable myth; and it seems equally clear that Montaigne's effort to identify himself with this nonexistent class of beings is itself a performance, a mystification, an attempt not at revealing his "true self" (despite his innumerable protestations to the contrary) but at persuading his reader/ audience that he is other than what he is. We are therefore forced to ask the following questions: first, given that he is not the kind of *noble d'épée* he has tried to describe (both because he is not and because the existence of any class conforming to his description is highly problematic), why does he spend so much time constructing this artificial identity, and then trying to perform for us in such a way as to convince us that the identity is his own? Second, if he is not what he says he is, then what is he? What alternate identities are available to him, and to us? In what follows we will try to show that Montaigne recognizes the difficulties and contradictions inherent in his model of the neo-Stoic nobleman, and that – far from simply abandoning it as untenable – he embraces its irreality as a rhetorical and theatrical device, using its purely hypothetical status as a kind of Archimedean standing-place from which to move his own political world. The irony developed as he refines and sophisticates his performance of self becomes a powerful tool to be used in the process of constructing Michel de Montaigne.

ii.   **The style of performance**

Let us first address the question of why Montaigne seems compelled, at least in some instances, to adopt this role, and/or to promulgate its propaganda line. Friedrich says that some of his "Adelsprätension" may have been due to simple vanity, but goes on to suggest that Montaigne may have wished to persuade his readers of the validity of his own noble background in order to enhance the credibility (to non-*nobles d'épée*) and effectiveness (to *nobles d'épée*) of his project of improving the image (and quality) of

contemporary French nobility, which suffered from a not-entirely-unde-
served reputation for illiteracy and uncultured barbarousness. He points
out that Montaigne, even though he was eager to belong to the *noblesse
d'épée*, nevertheless was put off by their violence and anti-intellectualism.[42]
It may also have been something of a moral stance; perhaps Montaigne felt
that such a position enabled him to hold – still within the universe of
political reality – the moral high ground, to retain political power and
status along with a degree of independence, without seeming to cave in to
the corrupting influences of the age. Or, more simply, it may be linked to
his pragmatic conservatism; confronted with the chaotic political and
social situation of France in the 1560's and 1570's, it might seem natural for
someone with Montaigne's horror of change and instability to take refuge
in an ideology of rigor and stasis. However, this is not what Montaigne
actually does in his political life; as we shall see, far from being (or playing
the role of) an isolated country nobleman, shut up on his estate and
avoiding or resisting external authority, Montaigne takes an active part in
the national and local politics of his day, even after his professed "retirement" from the world. Furthermore, in the course of this activity he shows
himself not to be a hard-liner of any kind, Ligueur or Huguenot; instead, he
is a *politique*, an experienced courtier whose judicious adaptability earns
him the respect of both sides, as for example when he acts as mediator in a
dispute between Henri III and the future Henri IV. If anything, Montaigne
is repelled by inflexibility and extremism.[43] Why, then, does Montaigne
bother to articulate this pose of quasi-Stoic detachment, if he feels so little
compelled to act according to its precepts? It may indeed be a persuasive
strategy, as Friedrich suggests, but perhaps not in the sense that Friedrich
has in mind. It may be that Montaigne's efforts to present the old-noble
pose in a convincing manner may be meant to demonstrate the importance
of being able to play a role effectively, even when nobody, including the
actor, really believes in the actor's identity with that role. Montaigne works
very hard at his performance, not necessarily because he believes in it, but
because it is necessary to be able to perform effectively, should the occasion
arise; what counts is the appearance. The ability to play a role effectively is
critical to his *real* project.

To see how Montaigne makes his way from the Stoic nobleman to the
nobleman-as-actor, let us briefly examine the distance that Montaigne
places between himself and this Stoic role even as he enunciates it. He
establishes this distance in two ways: by undermining the "true" Stoic
position, and by claiming that he himself is not suited to its demands. With
regard to the first of these tactics, it is worth recalling that, as we have
already observed, Montaigne's so-called switch to an anti-Stoic line in the
later layers of his text is less a radical repudiation of earlier attitudes than a

refinement or sophistication of a previously existing position. That this is the case may be seen if we examine two versions of Montaigne's famous comparison between Seneca, held up as the Voice of Stoicism, and another of Montaigne's favorite edifying authors, Plutarch, who seems to represent something very different. We have seen how Seneca functions as a crucial model for the Stoic nobleman, both literarily and practically; and yet Montaigne is not unaware of the irony inherent in this choice of exemplar. In this passage from "Des livres" (II, 10), Seneca comes off sounding not like a Stoic sage speaking from the moral safety of his *arrière-boutique*, but rather suspiciously like a courtier:

[A] Plutarque est plus uniforme et constant; Seneque, plus ondoyant et divers. Cettuy-cy se peine, se roidit et se tend pour armer la vertu contre la foiblesse, la crainte, et les vitieux appetis; l'autre semble n'estimer pas tant leur effort, et desdaigner d'en haster son pas et se mettre sur sa targue. [...] Il paroit en Seneque qu'il preste un peu à la tyrannie des Empereurs de son temps, car je tiens pour certain que c'est d'un jugement forcé qu'il condamne la cause de ces genereux meurtriers de Caesar; Plutarque est libre par tout. Seneque est plein de pointes et saillies; Plutarque, de choses. Celuy-là vous eschauffe plus, et vous esmeut; cettuy-cy vous contente davantage et vous paye mieux. [B] Il nous guide, l'autre nous pousse. (413)

[Plutarch is more uniform and constant; Seneca, more undulating and diverse. The latter labors, stiffens, and tenses himself to arm virtue against weakness, fear, and vicious appetites; the former seems not to care so much about their power, and to scorn hurrying or putting himself on his guard. [...] It seems in Seneca that he gives in a bit to the tyranny of the Emperors of his time, since I consider it certain that it is by a forced judgment that he condemns the cause of those generous murderers of Caesar; Plutarch is everywhere free. Seneca is full of points and sallies; Plutarch, of things. The former excites you more and moves you; the latter contents you better, and rewards you more. He guides us, the other pushes us.]

To begin with, there is the peculiar opening sentence, which ascribes to Plutarch the quality we would expect to be most Senecan (that is, if we take Seneca at his word), namely "constancy"; and Seneca is described, oddly (but, as it turns out as we read farther, accurately), as "ondoyant et divers." Montaigne conjures up an image of Seneca rushing about loudly proclaiming his inflexibility and toughness to all and sundry – but adapting his message according to his audience of the moment. Moreover, it seems that even Seneca does not enjoy complete *franchise*; his ability to speak freely and openly is hampered, and his credibility damaged, by his complicity in the tyrannies of Nero. Finally, his writings are not quite as "farcies et pleines de beaux discours de sapience" as one might wish; they too have their stylistic preoccupations, their self-conscious "pointes et saillies" which may obscure the *matière*. Seneca's arm-waving gives him away; his persona is revealed to be not an unforced expression of his true inner self, but a consciously willed performance.

That this comparison with Plutarch occurs not in a C-text portion of one of the essays of the third book but in an essay from the first two books, and in the A-text at that, indicates to us that even prior to 1580 Montaigne is aware of – and uncomfortable with – the contradictions and inconsistencies at the heart of a hard-line Stoic position. By the time this comparison is taken up again in "De la phisionomie" (III, 12), while it is still presented in similar terms, it seems more like an outright condemnation of Seneca, particularly when read in the full context of the essay. Simultaneously, Plutarch is viewed in an increasingly positive light. Montaigne begins the essay by talking about the fundamental unsoundness of our judgment (1037): [B] "Quasi toutes les opinions que nous avons sont prinses par authorité et à credit." ["Practically all the opinions we have, we take on authority and credit."] Even Socrates, that greatest of men (and Montaigne's hero throughout the third book), owes his present reputation not to any merits he may himself have possessed, but simply to the inability of the rest of us to think independently. Our opinions are formed through inertia. He goes on to deplore the opinion-swaying "artifice" and "ostentation" of courtiers and courtly discourse, contrasting these attributes unfavorably with such anti-courtly qualities as "nayfveté" and "simplicité." Montaigne here goes farther than usual in recognizing the power of the former, their moral dubiousness notwithstanding; flashy artifice and glib deceit will sway the mind far more effectively than the plain and naked truth. Perhaps this cannot be helped, he says, but it is nevertheless to be deplored.[44] In this context, he returns to the comparison between Seneca and Plutarch:

[B] L'un [Seneca], plus vif, nous pique et eslance en sursaut, touche plus l'esprit. L'autre, plus rassis, nous informe, establit et conforte constamment, touche plus l'entendement. [C] Celuylà ravit nostre jugement, cestuy-cy le gaigne. (1040)

[The one [Seneca], livelier, pokes us and makes us jump, touches our mind more. The other, more calm, informs, settles, and comforts us constantly, touches our understanding more. The former ravishes our judgment, the latter wins it over.]

Clearly, for Montaigne, a discursive style which "nous pique et eslance en sursaut" achieves these results through meretricious effects, "artifice" and "ostentation," and therefore its integrity is necessarily suspect. Ultimately, Seneca's Stoicism, as presented by Montaigne, sounds like an unsustainable pretense, not a state of inner repose. It may even be empty posturing, or – worse yet – hypocrisy, concealing unpleasant truths through rhetorical display. This is not to say, however, that Montaigne is directly condemning Stoicism *per se*; he is merely saying that Seneca doth protest too much. Excessive carrying on, *à la* Seneca, in support of *any* position tends to weaken that position and make its supporter (or performer) suspect. In other words, Montaigne's critique of Senecan (literary and personal) style is just that: a stylistic critique, and not so much a direct attack on substance.

Meanwhile, Montaigne tries to disqualify himself from the ranks of the "true" Stoics by claiming that he is insufficiently tough. This is evident even in an essay we have been reading as one of the most "Stoic" in the *Essais*, "De la solitude." Here, after describing the Stoic *arrière-boutique* and the corresponding attitude of harsh disdain for the world expected of its occupant, he describes the reading he plans to do ("des livres ou plaisans et faciles, qui me chatouillent, ou ceux qui me consolent et conseillent à regler ma vie et ma mort" ["books either pleasant and easy, which entertain me, or those that console me and teach me to order my life and my death"]) in his own state of retreat from the world, and in a more general sense how he approaches the whole question of retirement:[45]

[A] Les gens plus sages peuvent se forger un repos tout spirituel, ayant l'ame forte et vigoureuse. Moy qui l'ay commune, il faut que j'ayde à me soutenir par les commoditez corporelles; et, l'aage m'ayant tantost desrobé celles qui estoyent plus à ma fantasie, j'instruis et aiguise mon appetit à celles qui restent plus sortables à cette autre saison. (246)

[Those wiser than me can forge for themselves an entirely spiritual repose, having a strong and vigorous soul. Me, I only have a commonplace one; I must sustain myself with bodily comforts, and, age having recently robbed me of those that I liked best, I instruct and sharpen my appetite for those which remain better suited to this other season.]

Even in retreat, Montaigne claims that he is not up to the rigorous Stoic version of solitude; privation and mortification of the flesh are not for him – nor, for that matter, is affliction of the spirit; he wants readings to entertain and console him, not to make him more uncomfortable than he already is. He is, he tells us, simply too weak for that sort of thing.

As a result, Montaigne's place of retirement, far from being an abstract space into which he withdraws to prepare eagerly for death, is rather a specific physical place (his estate), where he surrounds himself in his tower study with physical comforts and with all his best friends, "ceux qui ne vivent qu'en la memoire des livres," most notably Plutarch.[46] In this distinctly non-ascetic retreat,[47] he concentrates his energies not on death but on the proper conduct of life. It may therefore be argued that this territory of retirement, this inner space of the self, is a locus of considerably greater plenitude than the Stoic retreat; and one could conceivably suggest further, *pace* Reiss, Cave *et al.*, that there exists a private self that occupies this space.[48] It may be true that (1) it is not possible to gain direct access to this space, or to this self, via the worldly discourse of masks, and that (2) the primary constituent of this inner self is a kind of continuous flux; but to claim that, because something moves, it cannot be said to exist, is to fall victim to the very mystification Montaigne tries so hard to eradicate. As we shall see, Montaigne argues strongly for the idea of the self as a process, rather than a static entity; likewise, he sees the *Essais* themselves not as a fixed or monolithic representation of the self but as a continuous process of presentation of his continually evolving *moi*.

The real difficulty with the Stoic line, then, is not so much that it is wrong or unsound as that it is impracticable for "les âmes communes" like Montaigne himself.[49] We see, therefore, that this *doubly* oblique undercutting of Seneca renders Montaigne's own position(s) with regard to noble identity, neo-Stoic or otherwise, more sophisticated and complex; Montaigne would have us believe that it also leads towards a more realistic and accurate representation of his state, or rather process, of being. In what follows, we shall try to show that this increasing complexity also makes his positions more directly accessible. To put it another way, Montaigne's performance as a writer before an audience becomes less histrionic and more polyvalent; it is more readily legible because Montaigne offers us more points of access.

This new mode of performance is presented to us, in this comparison, through the exemplar of Plutarch. Far better than the nervous Seneca, Montaigne tells us, is Plutarch's equable calmness, a style which achieves plenitude and density without harshness, obscurity, or deception. Plutarch's rhetoric maintains an easy, measured pace, unruffled by external threats; this in turn bespeaks a solid internal *suffisance*, such as we shall find embodied in Socrates, the practical counterpart to this literary paradigm.[50] As a result, says Montaigne, Plutarch is "libre par tout"; his rhetorical neutrality enables him to avoid the kind of questionable ethical entanglements into which Seneca's more vehement and polemical rhetoric draws him. This accounts for the description of Plutarch as more "constant" than that paragon of Stoic constancy, Seneca; but what about Montaigne's statement that Plutarch also holds opinions "douces et accomodables à la société civile"? This seeming contradiction is resolved when we realize that one who possesses or adopts this kind of serene indifference has as a result a certain liberty, a freedom to maneuver, and is therefore able to adapt to circumstances as they arise. This does not mean that Montaigne has suddenly become a crypto-Machiavellian in his dotage, although, as we shall see, his attitudes do begin to take on more of an Italianate tinge. This "new" ideal of flexibility is actually part of and consistent with Montaigne's revised concept of the human world, as expressed in his famous remark at the beginning of "Du repentir" (III, 2, p. 804): [B] "Le monde n'est qu'une branloire perenne." ["The world is nothing but a perennial movement."] Montaigne applies this idea of constant flux directly to himself and to his project of representing himself through the *Essais* (805): "Je ne peints pas l'estre. Je peints le passage..." ["I don't depict being. I depict passing..."] His self-representation may seem to be inconsistent and unstable, but it is actually all the more accurate for its variability (804): "...les traits de ma peinture ne forvoyent point, quoy qu'ils se changent et diversifient." ["...the lines of my painting do not go astray, even though they change and diversify."] To reduce himself to a single representation, a single persona, would be misleading (if not downright dishonest), since (805) "[l]a constance mesme n'est autre chose qu'un branle plus languissant." ["[c]onstancy itself is nothing other than a slower movement."] Therefore, his mode of self-representation, focusing on the continuous process of being, is, he claims (in a C-text addition), both more accurate and more complete than the traditional approach, which seeks to impose a false stasis on a perpetually moving subject (805): [C] "Les autheurs se communiquent au peuple par quelque marque particuliere et estrangere; moy le premier par mon estre universel, comme Michel de Montaigne, non comme grammairien ou poëte ou jurisconsulte." ["Authors communicate themselves to the public by some particular, extrinsic mark; I am the first to do so by my whole being, as Michel de Montaigne, not as a grammarian or a poet or a jurist."]

This is a far less innocent statement than it first appears to be. It may seem that Montaigne is simply saying that he wants to show all aspects of his identity to his audience, to present a complete, comprehensive, and honest performance, without hiding behind any "marque ... estrangere"; but the very language in which he makes this claim is ideologically loaded. It echoes a similar statement in "De l'institution des enfans" (I, 26), where the place of the term "estre universel" is taken by the word "gentilhomme." Montaigne tells a shaggy dog story ([A] "Allant un jour à Orleans..." ["Going one day to Orléans..."]) whose punchline (168–69) ("Il n'est pas gentilhomme; c'est un grammairien..." ["He's no gentleman; he's a grammarian..."]) betrays an aristocratic scorn (whether "natural" or adopted) for such lowly beings as *grammairiens*. The story is of course situated in the larger context of what the proper attitude of a budding *gentilhomme* should be towards his studies; and the answer is much like that given by Castiglione, advocating a kind of dilettantism for the nobility. Over-specialization is bad because it is unworthy of a *gentilhomme*, a point which Montaigne reemphasizes when he tells us that his mission in "De l'institution des enfans" is to (169) [A] "... former non un grammairien ou logicien, mais un gentil'homme..." ["... form not a grammarian or a logician, but a gentleman..."] Likewise, here in "Du repentir," where his project is to delineate his own persona (or personæ), he wishes to distinguish himself from "les autheurs," and to establish an identity free from such degrading specializations. So the universality that Montaigne both advocates and lays claim to is not a philosophical, abstract, or absolute universality, but rather a kind of practical, even politic versatility *à la* Castiglione. In other words, Montaigne's "estre universel" seems somewhat more class-bound, and hence less "universel," than he would have us believe.

We shall therefore concentrate here on the instrumentality of that peculiarly flexible "estre universel," insofar as it serves Montaigne to enact or perform his identity in specific contexts. Just as the self is no philosophical ideal, so too the circumstances to which Montaigne would have it adapt are not mere abstractions, but concrete aspects of a particular historical context. We shall see that the equable adaptability found in Plutarch's literary style and in the person of Socrates (as represented via Montaigne's readings of Ficino's Latin translations of Plato) becomes, in Montaigne's hands, a tool for his own survival (political, social, and physical) in late sixteenth-century France. Indeed, such performative flexibility is an essential capacity in Montaigne's world as he describes it to us.

So much so, in fact, that Montaigne chooses to close his major discussion of the behaviors appropriate to nobility, "De l'institution des enfans," with an assertion of the value and utility of theatrical activity to a young nobleman. He justifies theatre and theatricality by invoking illustrious aristocratic precedents, while simultaneously claiming for himself, in no uncertain terms, an innate propensity and talent for play-acting.

[B] Mettray-je en compte cette faculté de mon enfance: une asseurance de visage, et soupplesse de voix et de geste, à m'appliquer aux rolles que j'entreprenois? Car, avant l'aage,

Alter ab undecimo tum me vix ceperat annus,

j'ai soustenu les premiers personnages és tragedies latines de Bucanan, de Guerente et de Muret, qui se representerent en nostre college de Guienne avec dignité. En cela Andreas Goveanus, nostre principal, comme en toutes autres parties de sa charge, fut sans comparaison le plus grand principal de France: et m'en tenoit-on maistre ouvrier. C'est un exercice que je ne mesloüé poinct aux jeunes enfans de maison: et ay veu nos Princes s'y adonner depuis en personne, à l'exemple d'aucuns des anciens, honnestement et louablement.

[C] Il estoit loisible mesme d'en faire mestier aux gens d'honneur en Grece: "Aristoni tragico actori rem aperit: huic et genus et fortuna honesta erant; nec ars, quia nihil tale apud Graecos pudori est, ea deformabat." (176–77)

[Shall I talk about this faculty of my childhood: an assurance of *visage*, and flexibility of voice and gesture, in applying myself to the roles I took on? For, before the usual age,

I had just then entered my twelfth year,

I played the leading parts in the Latin tragedies of Buchanan, Guerente, and Muret, which were performed with dignity in our Collège de Guyenne. In this, Andreas Goveanus, our principal, as in all other areas of his job, was without comparison the greatest principal in France; and I was considered a master craftsman. This is an exercise that I do not at all disapprove of for young children of good family; and I have since seen our Princes take part in it in person, following the example of certain of the ancients, honorably and commendably.

It was even praiseworthy for persons of honor to make a profession of it in Greece. "He revealed the matter to the tragic actor Ariston. This man was honorable both in family and in fortune; nor did his art spoil [his honor], since nothing of this kind is considered shameful among the Greeks."]

Montaigne's eagerness to justify this activity, both through contemporary aristocratic precedent and by alleging the unimpeachable example of the ancient Greeks (and not just any Greeks, but the "gens d'honneur" among them), has a curious twist to it. It is only after asserting his own status as a "maistre ouvrier" that he goes on to recommend that "jeunes enfans de maison" follow his example; and the remark that he has "veu nos Princes s'y adonner depuis en personne" contains, at least syntactically, the peculiarly circular (and subversive) suggestion that it is he, Montaigne, that has set the precedent for "nos Princes." This is too shadowy to be pushed very far, but it is at least consistent with Montaigne's frequently observed habit (manifested in the present passage) of aligning himself with "les anciens" in order to buttress his own claims to nobility. That this is here one of Montaigne's main objectives may be seen if we examine the syllogism at the heart of this passage, the first two terms of which Montaigne explicitly sets forth, while the third is left to the reader: (1) Theatricality is a noble attribute. (2) I, Michel de Montaigne, possess this attribute in abundance, and I come by it naturally, without having to work at it. (3) Therefore, I am myself a legitimate member of the nobility (here understood to be the very highest nobility, since its exemplars are "nos Princes" and the "gens d'honneur" among the ancient Greeks).

Having thus established, on the one hand, a set of unimpeachable noble credentials for the practice of role-playing, and on the other hand his own natural propensity for the stage, Montaigne can go on to discuss practical applications in the wider sense. To the charge that he is betraying his previously enunciated quasi-Stoic principles, he might respond as he does in the opening sentences of "De trois commerces" (III, 3):

[B] Il ne faut pas se clouër si fort à ses humeurs et complexions. Nostre principalle suffisance, c'est sçavoir s'appliquer à divers usages. C'est estre, mais ce n'est pas vivre, que se tenir attaché et obligé par necessité à un seul train. Les plus belles ames sont celles qui ont plus de variété et de souplesse.
[C] Voylà un honorable tesmoignage du vieil Caton: "Huic versatile ingenium si pariter ad omnia fuit, ut natum ad id unum diceres, quodcumque ageret." (818)

[We must not nail ourselves so firmly to our humors and dispositions. Our main capacity is to know how to apply ourselves to various practices. It's existing, but not living, to hold oneself stuck and obliged by necessity to a single course. The most beautiful souls are those who have the most variety and flexibility.
    Here's an honorable testimony about the elder Cato: "He had a mind so versatile and adaptable to all things, that whatever he did, you'd say he was born to do that thing alone."]

It is remarkable that Montaigne chooses to illustrate this decidedly anti-Stoic point with the example of the one ancient Roman figure who is ordinarily taken to represent the utmost in intransigent Stoic virtue. Perhaps Montaigne does so merely to show that even Stoics play-act; or possibly he is trying to defuse the suggestion that he is merely making a virtue out of vice, converting what he has previously advertised as his own weakness and flabbiness into the *souplesse* of his "new ideal."[51] But that he should choose Cato the Elder in particular is suggestive of something more. Cato the Elder was renowned not only for his stern and uncompromising morality, but also for his effective adoption of the persona of a barbarous rustic, as one ill adapted to – and impatient with – the niceties of urban social norms. This persona enabled him to act in the urban political arena, and to enforce his conservative views, all the more effectively. Montaigne surely expects his reader to be familiar with this aspect of Cato's story, and we might wonder if Montaigne's use of this particular example is meant to illustrate not just the inevitable failure, both logical and practical, of any attempt to hew to a "pure" Stoic position in the "real" world, but also the specifically utilitarian, politic nature of his own relationship to that philo-sophical position. It also reinforces two aspects of Montaigne's new theatricality to which we have already alluded: (1) that the performer must maintain a critical distance between himself and the role (for, as Montaigne indicates, too-thorough commitment to one role makes it almost impossible to play any other roles effectively); and (2) that this ability to maintain critical distance is in turn contingent on what we have described as an interior *suffisance*, a self-knowledge (and concomitant self-sufficiency) that enables the wise person to avoid a crippling dependency on the externalia of the various roles he adopts.[52]

iii.   **"La faccia sua era faccia d'uom giusto": the mask of *franchise***

Montaigne offers numerous other illustrations of this kind of perfect adaptability, particularly in the course of his discussion, in "De l'institution des enfans," of the value and prudence of courtly conformity. He tells us of a well-traveled acquaintance who followed the politic maxim, "when in Germany, get drunk with the Germans," and goes on to discuss (166–67) a not unrelated ancient example, Alcibiades. But perhaps the most telling instance is found in "De la præsumption" (II, 17), where he describes his great friend, his "other self," Estienne de la Boétie, as the only modern he knows worthy of comparison with the ancients (659): "...c'estoit vrayement un' ame pleine et qui montroit un beau visage à tout sens; un' ame à la vieille marque..."[53] ["...he was really a full soul, and one that showed a handsome face in every direction; a soul of the old stamp..."] Clearly, La Boétie possesses in full the attributes we have been discussing: "un' ame pleine ... [et] ... à la vieille marque," that is to say possessed, like that of Cato the Elder, of an interior plenitude and *suffisance*, which as a result can display "un beau visage à tout sens." Montaigne suggests that the connection between the "ame pleine" and its *beaux visages* may not be automatic and involuntary, governed by a kind of straightforward moral determinism; rather, that connection is consciously willed, and what is seen by the external world is that which the inner *âme* chooses to display. The passage also indicates that the choice of *visage* is intended, to put it bluntly, to make the wearer look as good as possible "à tout sens." Presumably, La Boétie is able to present such an impressive array of *beaux visages* because of his solid internal virtue, but the language of this passage – when considered within the context we have here described – makes it clear that even such a paragon of virtue must somehow engage the external world through a performance, an adaptation or interpretation of that virtue to an audience via the medium of the *beau visage*.

Montaigne goes on to tell us that La Boétie's great potential, despite his transcendent virtue, remained unfulfilled, suggesting that perhaps La Boétie was a little too perfect, a little too well adapted to the Golden Age, to abide in these corrupt times; how convenient, then, that his "other self," his double, Michel de Montaigne, has survived to carry the torch.[54] Indeed, it may be more than convenient; perhaps Montaigne actually possesses certain advantages over his late lamented friend. La Boétie may have had "un' ame ... qui montroit un beau visage," but we are told in the essay "De la phisionomie" (III, 12, p. 1057) of "[C] [l]a laideur qui revestoit une ame tres-belle en La Boitie" ["[t]he ugliness that clothed a very beautiful soul in La Boétie"]; he is compared in this regard to Socrates, the Renaissance's favorite exemplar of an unattractive exterior concealing an interior of great beauty and worth.[55] Unlike Erasmus or Rabelais, however, Montaigne chooses to emphasize, not the relative unimportance of external beauty compared to internal virtue, but rather the misfortune ("injustice", he calls it) suffered by both Socrates and La Boétie, namely that they were saddled with an unattractive physical appearance (1057), "[B] disconvenable à la béuté de [leurs] ame[s]" ["ill-suited to the beauty of [their] soul[s]"]. After all, he tells us, "[B] Il n'est rien plus vray-semblable que la conformité et relation du corps à l'esprit." ["There is nothing more probable than the conformity and relation of the body to the spirit."] For Montaigne, the validity of this "opinion ... Platonique" extends beyond the realm of philosophical abstraction; it has important practical applications as well. He makes it quite clear that he considers external beauty to be an extremely useful commodity:

[B] Je ne puis dire assez souvant combien j'estime la beauté, qualité puissante et advantageuse. [...] Elle tient le premier rang au commerce des hommes: elle se presente au devant, seduict et preoccupe nostre jugement avec grand authorité et merveilleuse impression. (1058)

[I cannot say often enough how much I consider beauty a powerful and advantageous quality. [...] It holds the first rank in the interactions of men; it presents itself first, seduces and pre-empts our judgment with great authority and a marvelous impression.]

We are therefore relieved to find, as we read further in the essay, that Montaigne himself is lucky enough not to be hampered by physical unattractiveness; indeed, if we are to believe what he tells us, the opposite is the case. And it is precisely that aspect of his own allegedly *beau visage*, that it inspires confidence and trust, that he elects to highlight, as if to forestall any skepticism or mistrust on the part of his reader. He even goes so far as to contrast himself directly with Socrates, stopping just short of explicitly asserting his own superiority to his antique model (and, tacitly, to La Boétie):

[B] J'ay un port favorable et en forme et en interpretation,

Quid dixi habere me? Imo habui, Chreme!
Heu tantum attriti corporis ossa vides,

et qui faict une contraire montre à celuy de Socrates. Il m'est souvant advenu que, sur le simple credit de ma presence et de mon air, des personnes qui n'avoyent aucune cognoissance de moy s'y sont grandement fiées, soit pour leurs propres affaires, soit pour les miennes; et en ay tiré és pays estrangieres des faveurs singulieres et rares. (1059–60)

[I have a favorable bearing, both in itself and in others' perception,

> What did I say, "have"? I mean "had," Chreme!
> Alas, you see only the bones of this worn-out body,

and which looks entirely unlike that of Socrates. It has often happened to me that, on the mere credit of my presence and manner, people who didn't know me at all have placed great trust in me, whether for their own affairs or for mine; and from this I have derived, in foreign countries, singular and rare favors.]

It does not seem to be mere physical beauty or attractiveness, nor imposing stature, that make his "presence" so remarkable; indeed, he has told us elsewhere that he is only average-looking, and slightly shorter than most.[56] The strange powers of his "port favorable" must therefore lie elsewhere. Montaigne is of course eager to give a detailed demonstration of these powers in action, and we find this demonstration in the extraordinary twin anecdotes which follow this passage, and which conclude "De la phisionomie."[57] In them, he relates how, on two separate occasions, he was saved from robbery and death by his own honest, confidence-inspiring face and comportment. In the first of these stories, Montaigne finds his house invaded by a number of armed men who, while pretending to seek refuge from imaginary pursuers, actually intend to dispossess Montaigne of his estate and belongings (and, presumably, his life). Now, Montaigne is no fool; he is not so naïve "de nature" that he can fail to be made suspicious by the presence of thirty armed men in his front yard. On the contrary, he tells us that he is well aware of the potential danger (1060): "[B] Je n'ignorois pas en quel siecle je vivois." ["I was not ignorant of the times in which I was living."] Nevertheless, he tells us that *despite his suspicions* he chooses to allow these men, whose leader is one of his acquaintances (and vaguely related to him through marriage), to enter his gate: "[B] je me laissay aller au party le plus naturel et le plus simple, comme je faicts tousjours, commendant qu'ils entrassent." ["I let myself follow the most natural and simple course, as I always do, giving orders for them to come in."] Confronted with an array of choices, Montaigne makes a conscious decision to adopt the role of the simple and trusting person, one who is willing to take the utterances and behavior of others at face value. He is careful to claim that this is a natural tendency on his part:

[B] Aussi à la verité, je suis peu deffiant et soubçonneus de ma nature; je penche volontiers vers l'excuse et interpretation plus douce; je prens les hommes selon le commun ordre, et ne croy pas ces inclinations perverses et desnaturées si je n'y suis forcé par grand tesmoignage, non plus que les monstres et miracles. Et suis homme en outre qui me commets volontiers à la fortune et me laisse aller à corps perdu entre ses bras. De quoy, jusques à cette heure, j'ay eu plus d'occasion de me louër que de me plaindre; et l'ay trouvée et plus avisée [C] et plus amie de mes affaires [B] que je ne suis. (1060–61)

[Besides, in truth, I am not very distrustful or suspicious by nature; I willingly lean towards excuse and more charitable interpretation. I take people according to the common order, and don't believe in perverse or unnatural inclinations unless I'm forced to by hard evidence, no more than in monsters or miracles. What's more, I'm a man who willingly commits myself to Fortune, and I let myself go bodily into her arms. For which, up to now, I have had more occasion to rejoice than to complain; and I have found her both wiser and more a friend to my affairs than I am.]

Montaigne is here performing two movements which, if they do not entirely contradict one another, at least do not coincide as smoothly as Montaigne would have us believe. First, he says that his mind or nature possesses considerable inertial mass; that is, its continuous motion along the straight path of good faith and trust cannot be disturbed except through the application of considerable force. He then says that the inertial mass of his "nature" is actually quite low, since he allows himself to be bounced around continuously by "la fortune." Both cannot be simultaneously true; what actually happens is that Montaigne surreptitiously lowers his inertial mass in the second case, thereby decreasing his resistance to being pushed around. The point is that through this sleight of hand he gives to what he says is his generosity of nature a startlingly passive cast. Surely the presence of thirty armed and hostile-looking men at his door constitutes a sufficiently "grand tesmoignage"; and yet he stubbornly persists in a kind of wilful passivity. This is no accident; nor is it due to simple bull-headedness. Montaigne insists on this odd passivity because he wants the reader (and the armed men confronting him) to believe that he genuinely cannot do otherwise; that his real nature is indeed honest, open, plain-spoken, *franche* – in other words, noble. That this is nevertheless a performance, rather than a pure unveiling of the self, may be seen in what he says of the results of his passivity.

To begin with, his motives for letting Fortune run the show do not seem to be as pure (or as absent) as he claims; after all, he is quick to point out that he finds Fortune, as a decision-maker, to be more "avisée" (something of a contradiction in terms, applied to Fortune) and practically astute ("amie de mes affaires") than he is himself. This conclusion is eventually borne out by the felicitous result of the invasion; the leader of the brigands, disarmed by

Montaigne's relentless good faith, finds himself unable to carry out his dastardly plan (1061): "[B] Souvant depuis il a dict, car il ne craingnoit pas de faire ce compte, que mon visage et ma franchise luy avoient arraché la trahison des poincts." ["He has often said since – for he did not fear to tell this story – that my face and frankness had disarmed him."[58]] Montaigne is saved by his honest (?) face – which is not quite the same thing as his honest nature. The *visage* he presents, that of the nobly honest man, is one which is calculated to disarm aggression – and, more broadly, suspicion – through persuading the onlooker that it is not what it is: that it is not a *visage*, a face presented to the world, a mask, but rather a transparent window into the inner nature of its wearer.[59] This is a special and extremely significant case of what we have all along been arguing about the noble self: that one of the keys to the successful performance of nobility is the ability to persuade the onlooker that what is being presented is not a performance, even and especially when it is precisely that. The other factor to which he owes his deliverance, his *franchise*, is similarly complex. The term as he uses it here, and as we have analyzed it previously, goes beyond simple openness and directness of character: it is freighted with an ideological significance that makes it the exclusive province of a single class. It is also made an instrument of policy; it seems here to be not an omnidirectional openness in tandem with a blithe disregard for context or consequences, but rather a focused performance of persuasion directed to a specific practical end, in this instance saving Montaigne's skin.

The second anecdote follows similar contours, while adding another dimension to this dynamic of self-deployment. Montaigne is traveling during a supposed truce in the Wars of Religion when he is held up by a large party of masked and armed men.[60] They keep him prisoner in a forest for some time, debating whether to kill him or hold him for ransom; suddenly, however, their chief changes his mind and decides to return to Montaigne both his freedom and his possessions. Montaigne professes to be baffled, even in retrospect, at this abrupt and miraculous change of heart (1062):

[B] La vraye cause d'un changement si nouveau et de ce ravisement, sans aucune impulsion apparente, et d'un repentir si miraculeux, en tel temps, en une entreprinse pourpensée et deliberée, et devenue juste par l'usage (car d'arrivée je leur confessay ouvertement le party duquel j'estois, et le chemin que je tenois), certes je ne sçay pas bien encores quelle elle est.[61]

[The real cause of such a sudden change and of this reversal, without any apparent reason, and of such a miraculous repentance, in such a time, in a planned and premeditated enterprise, and one justified by custom (for from the start I openly confessed to them what party I belonged to, and what road I was taking) – I certainly still do not know what it is.]

This claim to ingenuousness seems rather disingenuous when read in the light of the sentence that immediately follows it, wherein Montaigne is told not once but "plusieurs fois," by none other than the chief of his captors, that he owes his salvation, just as in the preceding adventure, to his honest face and to his *franchise*:

Le plus apparent, qui se demasqua et me fit cognoistre son nom, me redict lors plusieurs fois que je devoy cette delivrance à mon visage, liberté et fermeté de mes parolles, qui me rendoyent indigne d'une telle mes-adventure ... (1062)

[The foremost among them, who unmasked himself and told me his name, then repeated to me several times that I owed this deliverance to my face, and to the freedom and firmness of my speech, which made me undeserving of such a misadventure...]

Here, Montaigne's *visage* and *franchise* not only save him, they define his exalted class status. The capacity for free, open, and guileless speech is, as we have seen, the exclusive province of the nobility; therefore, the "liberté et fermeté de [s]es parolles" shows Montaigne to be too noble to be subjected to such indignities as assault and highway robbery. The structure of Montaigne's narration – his own claim to be mystified, coupled to his captor's apparently spontaneous recognition of his inherent nobility – seems to be designed to reinforce in the reader's mind the idea that Montaigne's performance of nobility is involuntary, not to say unconscious.

This second anecdote also shows forth another aspect of Montaigne's remarkable "port favorable," one not present in the first story. It seems that his openness has the power to induce a kind of mimetic reaction in those around him; Montaigne's display of his "real" self, however spurious it may be, inspires in his audience a desire to do the same. His unidentified and masked assailant, having seen Montaigne's *franchise* in action, removes his own mask and names himself to Montaigne – hardly a prudent action for a professional highwayman, since he is now effectively at Montaigne's mercy, should Montaigne choose to denounce him; but he relies on Montaigne's sense of honor as a gentleman to protect his confidence. Note, too, that the person in question is not just any member of this troop of "gentils-hommes masquez," but their leader, significantly described – *before* he removes his mask – as "le plus apparent." In a sense, then, his subsequent revelation of his *visage* merely confirms what Montaigne has already deduced from his bearing. Nobility, it seems, will out, no matter how thoroughly concealed. His *noblesse*, evidently greater than that of his cohorts, also helps to account for his peculiar susceptibility to Montaigne's own noble *franchise*.

This episode neatly demonstrates to the reader the practical utility of Montaigne's self-revelatory performance, showing how his *franchise* enables him to transform even a position of absolute weakness into one of at least equal, if not absolute, strength. On a deeper level, this exchange is also an image of what Montaigne hopes will be the relationship between the author and the reader of the *Essais*. Montaigne aims to inspire in his reader the same reciprocal openness and trust his *franchise* has produced in his would-be assailant – a kind of "you show me yours and I'll show you mine" intimacy. Read in this light, the first sentence of the *Essais* takes on a new dimension. "[A] Cest icy un livre de bonne foy, lecteur." (3) ["This is a book of good faith, reader."] It is a claim that the book is being written and presented to its audience in good faith, i.e. honestly; but it may also be seen as a demand that the reader respond in kind, that he read it in good faith as well. The "Au lecteur" therefore functions not only as a welcome mat but also as a warning, a kind of screening device against *lecteurs de mauvaise foi*, those who are unwilling or unable to read with an open mind, who refuse to allow themselves to be persuaded by Montaigne's performance. One suspects that here, too, ideology is not entirely absent; for clearly, as the two anecdotes we have just examined suggest, only persons of a certain (noble) background possess the capacity for such an open, fearless exchange of identities.

Indeed, this kind of reciprocal self-revelation constitutes an ideal of behavior for Montaigne, one which he sets up in opposition to the self-concealment ordinarily practiced at court. It ultimately comes to be seen as the noble activity *par excellence*, that which defines the noble self, supplanting (while co-opting the rhetoric of) the *vacation des armes*. Even in such physically threatening situations as the two narratives we have just discussed, where we might naïvely expect Montaigne to tell us how he fought his way to freedom through the strength of his sword-arm, discursive fortitude replaces physical prowess; the word replaces the deed. This will become the hallmark of the new nobleman. Montaigne prepares the way even as early as "De la gloire" (II, 10, p. 622), where he argues (directly against Castiglione) that it is both useless and counterproductive to attempt to distinguish oneself through feats of arms on the chaotic modern battlefield. Even more significant is that, in this age of civil and religious wars marked by the advent of firearms and the consequent decline of the mounted knight, mere physical bravery has become the common property of all, and thus no longer distinguishes the noble from the peasant; if anything, the latter may have greater natural fortitude than the former.[62] How, then, is the modern nobleman to distinguish himself, if the battlefield is no longer a stage on which to perform famous feats of arms, but merely a place to get killed alongside everyone else? Montaigne is unwilling to write off completely that traditional theatre of nobility, the *vacation des armes*, but even when he praises it most fulsomely, he emphasizes some rather unorthodox points ("De l'experience," 1096):

[B] Il n'est occupation plaisante comme la militaire; occupation et noble en execution (car la plus forte, genereuse et superbe de toutes les vertus est la vaillance), et noble en sa cause: [...] La compaignie de tant d'hommes vous plaist, nobles, jeunes, actifs, la veue ordinaire de tant de spectacles tragiques, la liberté de cette conversation sans art, et une façon de vie masle et sans ceremonie...⁶³

[No occupation is so pleasant as the military one; an occupation noble both in execution (because the strongest, most generous, and proudest of all virtues is valor) and in cause: [...] You enjoy the company of so many noble, young, active men, the regular sight of so many tragic spectacles, the freedom of that artless conversation, and a manly and unceremonious way of life...]

It seems that what is pleasant and important about this most noble of activities is not so much breaking skulls as being in good company, where men are men and the "conversation" is unfettered by such courtly restraints as "art" and "ceremonie." As for bravery itself, it seems to be available to all and sundry; Montaigne remarks in a C-text addition that Plato even (1096) "en faict part aux femmes et aux enfans" ["makes women and children share [it]"]. In fact, valor seems to be more a question of peer pressure than anything else:

De craindre les hazards communs qui regardent une si grande presse, de n'oser ce que tant de sortes d'ames osent, c'est à faire à un coeur mol et bas outre mesure. La compagnie asseure jusques aux enfans. (1097)

[To fear the common hazards that affect such a big crowd, not to dare what so many kinds of souls dare, this is for a heart weak and base beyond measure. Company reassures even children.]

What, then, is the enterprising nobleman to do? This question has obvious relevance to the *noblesse d'épée*, who are finding themselves displaced from their traditional warrior status both tactically and politically; it is equally pressing to a *novus homo* like Montaigne, who is probably just as happy not to have to go to war too often, but who must nevertheless justify what might otherwise be viewed as cowardice. Hence this dual strategy of (1) making traditional martial valor the common property of all, and (2) substituting for that traditional attribute another distinguishing factor, cloaked in similar rhetoric, but one which can more readily be made the exclusive province of the new class. That distinguishing factor is none other than "cette conversation sans art," described in considerable detail – and in explicitly martial terms – in "De l'art de conferer" (III, 8).⁶⁴ Montaigne describes the experience of conversation in language nearly identical to, and if anything more violent than, that in which we have just seen him describe the experience of war itself:

[B] Si je confere avec une ame forte et un roide jousteur, il me presse les flancs, me pique à gauche et à dextre, ses imaginations eslancent les miennes. La jalousie, la gloire, la contention me poussent et rehaussent au dessus de moy-mesmes. Et l'unisson est qualité du tout ennuyeuse en la conference. (923)

[If I talk with a strong soul and stiff jouster, he presses my flanks, pokes me right and left; his ideas launch mine. Jealousy, glory, competition push me and raise me above myself. And unison is a completely boring quality in conversation.]

The object of this kind of conversation is not to please one's audience, nor to make oneself agreeable to one's company; far from it.[65] What is really at stake, on this new battlefield, is (quasi-)martial honor. However, Montaigne is quick to point out, just as we have seen him do regarding traditional martial valor, that it is both degrading and a waste of time to seek fame and princely favor on this battlefield:

[B] J'ayme à contester et à discourir, mais c'est avec peu d'hommes et pour moy. Car de servir de spectacle aux grands et faire à l'envy parade de son esprit et de son caquet, je trouve que c'est un mestier tres-messeant, à un homme d'honneur. (923)

[I like to argue and discuss, but with few men and for myself. For to serve as a spectacle to the great, and to make a rivalrous display of one's cleverness and chatter, is an occupation I find very unbecoming to a man of honor.]

Clearly, this "conversation sans art" is not meant for everybody, but rather for "peu d'hommes." Certain classes of persons are therefore excluded from Montaigne's ideal conversation, beginning with those too stupid to hold up their end of the conférence; Montaigne says that talking to fools is not only a waste of time, it is also dangerous, because of the risk of contagion. This prejudice is not purely intellectual; when Montaigne approvingly points out (926) that "[C] Platon, en sa republique, prohibe cet exercice [la conférence] aux esprits ineptes et mal nays" ["Plato, in his republic, prohibits this exercise [conversation] to inept and low-born minds"], the categories of (1) stupid people (2) persons of less than exalted birth are essentially identical. Here, for Montaigne, "esprits ... mal nays" are of necessity morally and intellectually inferior; the one inevitably entrains the other. Moreover, Montaigne seems to be expressing more than one kind of anxiety about intercourse with those of lesser status (925): "[B] Je cerche à la verité plus la frequentation de ceux qui me gourment que de ceux qui me craignent. C'est un plaisir fade et nuisible d'avoir affaire à gens qui nous admirent et facent place."[66] ["In truth, I seek more the company of those

that handle me roughly than that of those who fear me. It's a weak and
unhealthy pleasure to deal with people who admire and give way to us."]
There is something degrading about defeating an inferior adversary; hence,
such persons are banished from the ideal conversation, leaving only one's
"equals" as potential interlocutors.[67]

In a more general sense, Montaigne strives to isolate his ideal conversation
from the network of power relationships – or, to speak less anachronistically, the complex of "particulier[s] interest[s]" – at the heart of noble
society. In "De l'incommodité de la grandeur" (III, 7), Montaigne attacks
the issue as it relates specifically to social interaction with "les Princes,"
illustrating the flip side of the problem of intercourse with those of lesser
status. At court, says Montaigne, everyone pretends to be discursively
"weaker" – just as they pretend to be inferior to the royal personage in feats
of arms – so as to avoid giving offense.[68] This is no way, he says, to run a
conversation. Questions of precedence and superiority need to be checked
at the door, if the conversation is really to be a free and open contest of
minds; power relationships, of whatever kind, must remain absent. This is,
as Montaigne recognizes, difficult to achieve:

[B] Il est peu de choses ausquelles nous puissions donner le jugement syncere,
parce qu'il en est peu ausquelles, en quelque façon, nous n'ayons particulier interest.
La superiorité et inferiorité, la maistrise et la subjection, sont obligées à une
naturelle envie et contestation; il faut qu'elles s'entrepillent perpetuellement. (918)

[There are few things about which we can give a sincere judgment, because there
are few in which we do not somehow have a personal interest. Superiority and
inferiority, mastery and subjection, are doomed to a natural envy and competition;
they must perpetually pillage each other.]

It is precisely this kind of contestation that needs to be screened out of
Montaigne's ideal conversation, and not only because it tends to cloud the
issues and taint the discussion. At issue is a more fundamental question of
self-definition, whereby one's identity as a noble (and therefore one's right
to participate in the ideal conversation) is dependent upon one's degree of
independence and autonomy, both political and conversational. One's
franchise must be absolute, in both the discursive and the political senses.
Montaigne even goes so far as to make the subversive suggestion that to
participate in courtly rituals of deference and consequent dissimulation is
degrading and dishonorable, not only for the superior party (in this case,
the prince), but also for the inferior (here, the courtier). Hence, Montaigne
strives to isolate himself from relationships of power (917): "[B] Je suis
desgousté de maistrise et active et passive." ["I am disgusted by mastery,
both active and passive."] Real discursive "pleasure" – and honor – is to be

found in those contests of mind (or body) where such political realities do not intrude:

[B] Il n'est à l'avanture rien plus plaisant au commerce des hommes que les essays que nous faisons les uns contre les autres, par jalousie d'honneur et de valeur, soit aux exercices du corps, ou de l'esprit, ausquels la grandeur souveraine n'a aucune vraye part. (918)

[There is probably nothing more pleasant in human intercourse than the trials that we have against each other, out of jealousy of honor and worth, whether in exercises of the body, or of the mind, in which the grandeur of the sovereign has no real part.]

If defeating a socially inferior adversary is degrading, so too is bowing to a socially superior one out of politic politeness; it is therefore necessary that the ideal conversation take place outside the network of such "particular interests" and its accompanying discursive restraints. Only then can the noble identity reach its full efflorescence, and deploy its cardinal attributes of *grazia*, *générosité*, and so forth, as he remarks in "De la vanité" (III, 9): "[B] Si l'action n'a quelque splendeur de liberté, elle n'a point de grace ni d'honneur." (967) ["If the action doesn't have some splendor of liberty, it has no grace or honor."]

We are therefore not surprised to find, returning to "De l'art de conferer," that Montaigne goes on to exclude another group of potential interlocutors, namely those who aim for concord and pleasure in conversation, and who (924) "[C] parlent tousjours avec dissimulation en presence les uns des autres" ["always speak with dissimulation in each other's presence"] – i.e. those who adhere to the norms of courtly discourse set forth by Castiglione and others – implying that they do so simply because they are not brave enough to stand up to contradiction. Disagreement in conversation is good, he says, because it makes one tough; the most important thing is to say what one thinks, and let the chips fall where they may:

[B] J'ayme, entre les galans hommes, qu'on s'exprime courageusement, que les mots aillent où va la pensée. Il nous faut fortifier l'ouie et la durcir contre cette tandreur du son ceremonieux des parolles. J'ayme une societé et familiarité forte et virile, une amitié qui se flatte en l'aspreté et vigueur de son commerce, comme l'amour, és morsures et esgratigneures sanglantes.

    [C] Elle n'est pas assez vigoureuse et genereuse, si elle n'est querelleuse, si elle est civilisée et artiste, si elle craint le hurt et a ses allures contreintes.

"Neque enim disputari sine reprehensione potest."

[B] Quand on me contrarie, on esveille mon attention, non pas ma cholere; je m'avance vers celuy qui me contredit, qui m'instruit. (924)

[I prefer, among gallant men, that people express themselves courageously, that the words go where the thought does. We must fortify our hearing and harden it against that tenderness of the ceremonious sound of words. I like a strong, virile fellowship and familiarity, a friendship that takes pleasure in the harshness and vigor of its intercourse, as love does in bloody bites and scratches.

It isn't vigorous and generous enough, if it isn't quarrelsome, if it is civilized and artful, if it fears collisions and moves with constraint.

"Indeed, there can be no discussion without contradiction."

When someone opposes me, he gets my attention, not my wrath; I go to meet one who contradicts me, who instructs me.]

This last remark hints that perhaps conversational fortitude is not of itself sufficient, and that there are other qualities necessary to the ideal (conversational) knight. Montaigne expands this thought, pointing out that mere contentiousness is as tiresome in conversation as stupidity or duplicity; conversation ought to be edifying, and to that end one's utterances must be clearly organized, well thought out, and well presented (928): "[B] Tout homme peut dire veritablement; mais dire ordonnéement, prudemment et suffisamment, peu d'hommes le peuvent." ["Anybody can speak truly; but to speak with order, prudently and competently – few men can do that."] This is a two-edged sword, by which Montaigne contrives to exclude not only those members of the *noblesse d'épée* too barbarous and uneducated to speak in an organized fashion, but also professional orators, pedants who persuade not through reason and truth but through obfuscation and deceptive rhetoric.[69] When calling for a clear and organized "moyen de traicter," he says (926), "je ne dis pas moyen scholastique et artistique, je dis moyen naturel, d'un sain entendement." ["I don't mean a scholastic and artificial manner, I mean a natural manner, that of a sound understanding."] It seems, then, that Montaigne's ideal *conférence* is neither courtly "civil conversation," nor the bluff, rude speech of the warrior, nor the over-rhetoricized discourse of the professional. Instead, with its emphasis on clarity, instruction, and the search for truth, it sounds most like the Socratic ideal of enlightened moral, ethical, or philosophical debate. The class of persons that Montaigne considers capable or worthy of participating in such a conversation has become remarkably small: his ideal interlocutor must be his social and intellectual equal, but he cannot be either a courtier, an uneducated *noble d'épée*, or a professional scholar; who does that leave? The answer seems to be the *noblesse de robe*. Only these persons have (or can claim) the social standing requisite for an invitation into Montaigne's circle, together with the humanistic training necessary to hold up their end of the conversation. They turn out to be just like Montaigne himself.[70]

The preferred stage for this theatre of *franchise*, moreover, is none other than Château Montaigne. Montaigne's house, his retreat from the world (and, not coincidentally, the theatre in which the first of the saved-by-*franchise* anecdotes is played out), is revealed to be a kind of anti-court, where all the conventions of courtly discourse and behavior are set aside, and Montaigne and his (numerous) guests can simply be themselves. He describes this stage-set in "Des trois commerces" (III, 3), where, after characterizing his house, not without pride, as "une ... maison des plus fréquentées" ["a house as full of visitors as any"], he gives the stage directions for his play, while assigning to himself the role of an unobtrusive master of non-ceremonies:

J'y voy des gens assez, mais rarement ceux avecq qui j'ayme à communiquer; et je reserve là, et pour moy et pour les autres, une liberté inusitée. Il s'y faict trefve de ceremonie, d'assistance et convoiemens, et telles autres ordonnances penibles de nostre courtoisie (ô la servile et importune usance!); chacun s'y gouverne à sa mode; y entretien qui veut ses pensées: je m'y tiens muet, resveur et enfermé, sans offence de mes hostes. (823–24)

[I see plenty of people there, but rarely those with whom I like to converse; and I reserve there, for myself and for others, an unusual freedom. There is a truce on ceremony, on face-time and meeting and greeting, and other such annoying pre-scriptions of our code of courtesy (oh, what a servile and annoying practice!); everyone there does what they like; whoever wants to, communes with his thoughts; I remain mute, abstracted, wrapped up in my thoughts, without offending my guests.]

Apparently, this is Montaigne's vision of the ideal retreat. Within the confines of his estate, where the only authority is that of the master of the house, the few persons who qualify for admission may behave as they wish, say what they will, and express themselves freely, without "ceremonie ... et ... [les] ordonnances penibles de nostre courtoisie." It seems that, under these conditions of "liberté inusitée," the perfect conversation among friends and equals may be realized, a Symposium *en permanence* around Montaigne's dinner table. The participants are described in terms which will become practically holy writ for the civil society of the next two centuries (824): "[B] Les hommes de la societé et familiarité desquels je suis en queste, sont ceux qu'on appelle honnestes et habiles hommes: l'image de ceux cy me degouste des autres." ["The men whose society and intimacy I seek are those who are called gentlemen of tact and talent; the idea of them ruins my taste for others."] The nature and purpose of the conversation are defined in terms of similar import for posterity:

[B] La fin de ce commerce, c'est simplement la privauté, frequentation et confer-ence: l'exercice des ames, sans autre fruit. En nos propos, tous subjects me sont

égaux; il ne me chaut qu'il n'y ait ny poix ny profondeur: la grace et la pertinence y
sont tousjours; tout y est teinct d'un jugement meur et constant, et meslé de bonté,
de franchise, de gayeté et d'amitié. (824)

[The point of this association is simply intimacy, fellowship, and conversation; the
exercise of souls, without any other fruit. In our conversations, all subjects are the
same to me. I don't care if there is neither gravity nor depth; grace and pertinency
are always there; everything is imbued with a mature and constant judgment, and
blended with goodness, frankness, cheerfulness, and friendship.]

This is a theatre of openness, of *franchise*, of self-presentation rather than
self-representation; masks and role-playing are abandoned; and in this, as
well as in its choice of any conceivable subject matter, it seems to resemble
Montaigne's vision of the *Essais* themselves.

However, this description of his domestic discourse also contains hints of a
slightly different reality, one which is perhaps less than perfect. If "chacun
s'y gouverne à sa mode; y entretien qui veut ses pensées," is there anyone
listening? Is this an ideal conversation, or is it a *dialogue des sourds*?
Moreover, Montaigne's own status within this discursive sphere is far from
unproblematic: even *chez lui*, it seems, he remains in a state of inertial
passivity. Rather than talking with his guests, he sits in a corner, "muet" et
"enfermé," apparently not interacting with them at all. Of course, he does
say that he doesn't necessarily need to talk in order to commune with, or
"discover," his guests (824): "[B] Je connois mes gens au silence mesme et à
leur soubsrire, et les descouvre mieux à l'advanture à table qu'au conseil."
["I know my people by their very silence and their smiles, and probably
find out more about them at table than in council."] Or he may simply
mean that, on the occasions when he doesn't feel like talking, he doesn't feel
obliged to do so. However, it does seem odd that he should focus on his
seeming inability – or refusal – to participate in the ideal discourse he has
taken such pains to construct, precisely when he is articulating that ideal
most definitively. This raises questions about the nature and even the
possibility of an ideal theatre of the noble self: are the participants free and
equal noble souls, sharing between and of themselves, or are they monads,
entities sealed off from their surroundings, whose inner workings are not
observable from without, and who are likewise incapable of absorbing any
information not generated by themselves? Is Montaigne's ideal *conférence*
a meeting of unfettered souls, or a bunch of people shouting at the walls?
And is Montaigne's role therein that of an active participant, whatever that
may be, or is he rather a passive listener and observer?

As is usually the case with Montaigne, the answer is probably "both."
Montaigne clearly wants to preserve for himself as many options as possible; he wants to be able to participate in the conversation at his own

dinner-table, but he wants to do so without irrevocably committing himself to any particular role, since to do so would belie what he sees as the essence of his being: *l'inconstance*. Hence the necessity, even in his own house, of having at his disposal both an array of masks and the complete passivity that implies (but does not necessarily guarantee) an absence of any mask whatsoever. The mask both enables and protects;[71] the same is also true of the absence of the mask. On the one hand, the ability to perform any role he pleases has clear utility in "le commerce des hommes"; on the other hand, his professed dullness and inertia relieves him of the responsibility of having to perform, should he be so inclined. When linked, as it is here, to a kind of ingenuousness, this inertia also enables Montaigne to persuade his audience that he is incapable – and therefore innocent – of any kind of performed deception. The result, evidently, is that Montaigne has an entirely free hand, both within the confines of his estate and without. Inside, he (supposedly) exists in an atmosphere of complete *liberté* and *franchise*; outside, he can also do as he pleases, if he observes certain precautions.

iv.   The grammatical solution

What those precautions are, and in a more general sense how Montaigne puts to work, in the "real" world of politics, the discursive modes here described, will be examined in this the final section of this chapter. In our previous discussion of what Montaigne describes as the qualities necessary for effective political action, we have, like Montaigne, emphasized the idea of adaptive, multivalent performance, played out and governed by an activist consciousness. However, Montaigne also mentions, with specific reference to himself, the attributes of passivity, indecisiveness, inertia[72] – qualities which he has seemed to invoke primarily to disqualify himself from action in the public sphere. Indeed, he claims that these qualities of his manifest themselves most strongly when it comes to "les affaires publiques." We have already examined Montaigne's efforts in "De la præsumption" to distance himself from courtly discourse through claims of ineptitude; later in the same essay, he tries to dissociate himself more generally from civic action, claiming (654) that he is possessed by "l'irresolution," which makes him particularly unsuited to "la negociation des affaires du monde" ["the negotiation of worldly affairs"]. Montaigne goes on to claim that, as a result of his inability to make a decision, he often simply leaves things to chance, and that he is really only a follower, not a leader. But in fact the historical Montaigne did take a considerable part in public affairs, and in so doing held a number of leading roles. How did he manage to do so, while claiming in his *Essais* to do the opposite?

Montaigne addresses himself to the same problem in more detail in the first essay of the third book, "De l'utile et de l'honneste," with similarly paradoxical results. In "les polices" ["polities"] as in human nature, says Montaigne, there exist unsavory and vicious elements, elements which cannot be eliminated. Indeed, vices can in some cases serve a necessary function. Better, therefore, to let those who are naturally talented at such things (read: depraved) defile themselves with the day-to-day realities of political life; the rest of us are thereby relieved of such unpleasant responsibilities. In other words, leave the dirty work to the professionals (courtiers and politicians):

[B] ... il faut laisser jouer cette partie aux citoyens plus vigoureux et moins craintifs qui sacrifient leur honneur et leur conscience, comme ces autres antiens sacrifierent leur vie pour le salut de leur pays; nous autres, plus foibles, prenons des rolles et plus aisez et moins hazardeux. Le bien public requiert qu'on trahisse et qu'on mente [C] et qu'on massacre; [B] resignons cette commission à gens plus obeissans et plus soupples. (791)

[... one must let this part be played by the more vigorous and less fearful citizens, who sacrifice their honor and their conscience, as the ancients sacrificed their lives, for the good of their country; the rest of us, weaker, let us take roles both easier and less hazardous. The public good requires one to betray and lie and massacre; let us resign this commission to more obedient and flexible people.]

Montaigne is eager to separate himself from such persons, persons whose excessive complaisance and performative adaptability make them untrustworthy at best. He describes his own civic *modus operandi* (for, it seems, he has not been able to avoid being saddled with certain civic responsibilities) as naïvely straightforward and direct:

[B] En ce peu que j'ay eu à negotier entre nos Princes, en ces divisions et subdivisions qui nous deschirent aujourd'huy, j'ay curieusement evité qu'ils se mesprinssent en moy et s'enferrassent en mon masque. Les gens du mestier se tiennent les plus couverts, et se presentent et contrefont les plus moyens et les plus voisins qu'ils peuvent. Moy, je m'offre par mes opinions les plus vives et par la forme plus mienne. Tendre negotiateur et novice, qui ayme mieux faillir à l'affaire qu'à moy! (791)

[In what little negotiating I have had to do between our princes, in these divisions and subdivisions that tear us apart today, I have carefully avoided letting them misunderstand me and be fooled by my outward aspect. Professionals keep themselves more hidden, and present themselves as best they can as most moderate and conciliatory. Me, I reveal myself through my strongest opinions and my most characteristic manner. A green and naive negotiator, who would rather fail in my undertaking than fail to be true to myself!]

Not for Montaigne are the stratagems of the "gens du mestier," professional courtiers and diplomats who pretend to be both as "moyen" (unre-
markably average, *à la* Castiglione's courtier) and as "voisin" (near to the
adversary's point of view) as possible. The very idea of being a "professional" is, as the slightly scornful phrase "gens du mestier" indicates,
degrading to a true nobleman like Montaigne. He is a mere amateur,
"[t]endre ... et novice," preferring to remain true to himself above all else.
Unfortunately for Montaigne's claim to naïveté, his own language betrays
him. His self-presentation in these "negotiations" is not automatic or
unconscious. On the contrary, the adverb "curieusement" indicates not
only conscious selection of a *persona*, but also a certain calculating under-
handedness; it is a word implying not ingenuousness but its opposite, and
one which we might reasonably expect to see used in conjunction with the
machinations of "les gens du mestier," rather than Montaigne's own supposedly guileless activities. (Moreover, what he claims to have "curieusement evité" is the possibility that his interlocutors might be baffled or
frustrated by his "masque" – precisely that which he claims not to be
wearing; the military image here combines with the dominant theatrical
metaphor to produce an ironic undercutting of his assertion.) Similarly,
Montaigne makes a conscious choice of *opinions* and *formes* through which
to "offer himself," and does not simply state that for him there are no others
available. Montaigne's claim to naïve openness once again discloses itself
to be a courtly stratagem, an example of *sprezzatura* put to practical use.
For the other half of Castiglione's equation, namely that the noble amateur
is naturally and inevitably more successful than the "professional," is also
present:

C'a esté pourtant jusques à cette heure avec tel heur (car certes la fortune y a
principalle part) que peu ont passé de main à autre avec moins de soubçon, plus de
faveur et de privauté. J'ay une façon ouverte, aisée à s'insinuer et à se donner credit
aux premieres accointances. La naifveté et la verité pure, en quelque siecle que ce
soit, trouvent encore leur opportunité et leur mise. (792)

[Up to now, however, it has been with such good luck (for certainly Fortune has the
major part in it) that few have gone from one side to the other with less suspicion,
more favor, and more privacy. I have an open manner, which easily insinuates itself
and gains credit upon first acquaintance. Sincerity and pure truth, in whatever age,
still find their time and their place.]

The focus shifts from the intrinsic moral value of being open, direct, and
honest, to the instrumental effectiveness of "une façon ouverte" in practical
terms, insofar as it serves to "s'insinuer et ... se donner credit." In the end,
we even see "[l]a naifveté et la verité pure" themselves reduced to merely

another set of stratagems available to the adept courtier. And Montaigne himself, far from being one who has neither interest in nor ability for "les négotiations publiques," has proven to be both highly adept and highly successful at such activities. Moreover, what initially seems, or claims, to be a critique of Castiglione has become a covert confirmation and enactment of his precepts. What Montaigne has endeavored to keep constant through the course of this transformation is the appearance of honesty, because it serves to deflect suspicion and mistrust, no matter what is going on behind the mask (792): "Ma liberté m'a aussi aiséement deschargé du soubçon de faintise par sa vigueur ... et qu'elle a une montre apparente de simplesse et de nonchalance." ["My freedom has also readily freed me from any suspicion of dissimulation by its vigor ... and by its evident simplicity and nonchalance."]

By the time Montaigne takes up the issue again in "De la vanité" (III, 9), he has essentially abandoned even this pretense of good faith in public affairs. We have already alluded to the manner in which, in this essay, Montaigne bewails both the corruption and decadence of his *siècle* and the wretched necessity of dealing with it on its own terms. He concedes that *les affaires du monde* demand adaptability above all, and reluctantly confesses that his vaunted directness and *franchise* is by itself no match for the demands of the real world:

[B] La vertu assignée aus affaires du monde est une vertu à plusieurs plis, encoigneures et couddes, pour s'apliquer et joindre à l'humaine foiblesse, meslée et artificielle, non droitte, nette, constante, ny purement innocente. [...] J'ay autresfois essayé d'employer au service des maniemens publiques les opinions et reigles de vivre ainsi rudes, neufves, impolies ou impollues, comme je les ay nées chez moy ou raportées de mon institution, et desquelles je me sers [C] sinon [B] commodéement [C] au moins seurement [B] en particulier, une vertu scholastique et novice. Je les y ay trouvées ineptes et dangereuses. Celuy qui va en la presse, il faut qu'il gauchisse, qu'il serre ses couddes, qu'il recule ou qu'il avance, voire qu'il quitte le droict chemin, selon ce qu'il rencontre; qu'il vive non tant selon soy que selon autruy, non selon ce qu'il se propose mais selon ce qu'on luy propose, selon le temps, selon les hommes, selon les affaires. (991)

[The virtue proper to worldly affairs is one with many folds, twists, and turns, so as to apply and join itself to human weakness; mixed and artificial, not straight, clean, constant, or purely innocent. [...] I formerly tried to employ in public service opinions and rules for living as rough, raw, unpolished or unpolluted, as I have them either inborn or derived from my education, and which I use, if not conveniently, at least surely in private – a scholastic and novice virtue. I found them inept and dangerous. He who moves in the crowd must swerve, pull in his elbows, step back or advance, even leave the straight path, according to what he encounters; he must live not so much according to himself as according to others, not according to what he proposes but according to what is proposed to him, according to the times, according to men, according to affairs.]

Nobody, not even the most virtuous Stoic, can avoid these demands; those who hope or claim to do so are either fools or liars. Among the most dangerous and most reprehensible of these persons are those (such as Machiavelli, Castiglione, or himself) who arrogate to themselves "l'institution des princes," particularly since they are (1) less likely to be mere fools, and (2) more likely to be in a position to do serious damage; chief among these is one who above all should have known better, Seneca.[73] Montaigne does not, however, underestimate the difficulty of keeping one's hands clean; he points out that, particularly in a time of conflict and chaos such as that in which he finds himself, even the most virtuous are tainted (993): "[B] chacun se travaille à deffendre sa cause, mais, jusques aux meilleurs, avec desguisement et mensonge" ["everyone works to defend his cause, but, even including the best, with feigning and lying"]. What, then, is to be done? Non-participation has been ruled out as impossible; indeed, slightly earlier in the same essay, Montaigne even goes so far as to praise public service, fortifying this position with an apposite quote from Cicero:

[B] Je suis de cet avis, que la plus honnorable vacation est de servir au publiq et estre utile à beaucoup. [C] "Fructus enim ingenii et virtutis omnisque præstantiæ tum maximus accipitur, cum in proximum quemque confertur." (952)

[I am of the opinion that the most honorable vocation is to serve the public and to be useful to many. "Indeed, the fruits of genius, virtue, and all kinds of excellence are best enjoyed when shared with one's fellow."]

Of course, he immediately hastens to add that, since he himself is ill-suited for such activity, he tries to avoid it, "[B]partie par conscience, ... partie par poltronerie" ["partly from conscience, ... partly from cowardice"]. Despite his invocation of Cicero, Montaigne's vision of public service is not Ciceronian but Tacitean, and his protestations of innocent ineptitude are meant to serve primarily as a Tacitean safety valve, an effort to persuade the reader that, even should Montaigne be forced to participate in the "police corrompue" of sixteenth-century France, he would somehow remain detached and therefore untainted.[74] His actual ability to retain that purity is of course just as problematic as that of Tacitus, as he obliquely admits (992): "[C] Platon dict que qui eschappe brayes nettes du maniement du monde, c'est par miracle qu'il en eschappe." ["Plato says that whoever escapes with clean pants from handling worldly affairs, escapes by a miracle."]

Montaigne has, however, a strategy ready to hand, a *modus operandi* that will permit him to have his cake and eat it too. We have already suggested what form this plan might take; Montaigne spells it out for us more explicitly in, among other places, "De mesnager sa volonté" (III, 10), where he provides an epigrammatic formulation worthy of Tacitus himself (1003): "[B] Mon opinion est qu'il se faut prester à autruy et ne se donner qu'à soy-mesme." ["My opinion is that one must lend oneself to others, and give oneself only to oneself."] The language of this sentence reveals not only a desire to avoid moral contamination, but also an effort to maintain independence, the aristocratic *liberté* and *franchise* so dear to Montaigne's heart (and perhaps a more fundamental kind of independence as well – a desire to preserve the self (whatever that may be) inviolate).[75] To "give oneself" to another is a risky and dangerous business; Montaigne seems to feel that it should be avoided unless the circumstances permit of no alternative, and even then one can hope for success only if one's partner in the exchange is one's equal (as, for example, in the anecdotes from "De la phisionomie" examined earlier). He goes on to claim that he has adhered to this maxim in the course of his own civic activities:

[B] Si quelquefois on m'a poussé au maniement d'affaires estrangieres, j'ay promis de les prendre en main, non pas au poulmon et au foye; de m'en charger, non de les incorporer; de m'en soigner ouy, de m'en passionner nullement: j'y regarde mais je ne les couve point. (1004)

[If I have sometimes been pushed to deal with affairs not my own, I have promised to take them in hand, not to heart [lit. "to lungs and liver"]; to take them on, not to incorporate them into me; to take care of them, yes; to become impassioned about them, not at all. I look at them but I do not brood over them.]

Much of the rest of the essay is taken up with his description of a specific case in which he has put these principles of disinterestedness and detachment to practical use, namely his tenure as mayor of Bordeaux. He positions himself, at the beginning of this performance on the public stage, as far from that stage as possible, and even intimates that his election was a kind of sneak attack by the citizens (1005): "[B] Messieurs de Bordeaux m'eslurent maire de leur ville, estant esloigné de France, et encore plus esloigné d'un tel pensement." ["*Messieurs de Bordeaux* elected me mayor of their city, [while] I was far from France, and even farther from such a thought."] After so much talk about the undesirability of involvement in public affairs and the dangers, moral and otherwise, attendant upon such involvement, coupled with Montaigne's repeated and vehement insistence that he is completely ill-suited to such activity, it is natural that he should wish to present himself as indifferent – or even actively hostile – to being saddled with civic office. Indeed, his resistance is such that it requires the intervention of the very highest authority (1005): "Je m'en excusay, mais on

m'aprint que j'avois tort, le commandement du Roy aussi s'y interposant."
["I excused myself, but I was told that I was wrong, as the King's command
also came into play."] Montaigne's refusal may have been a genuine
attempt to avoid the office; or it may have been merely a *pro forma* gesture,
made in the knowledge that it would be of no avail. Perhaps even the royal
command was a simple confirmation of what all those involved, including
Montaigne, knew to be inevitable.[76] It is at least possible that both are
partly true; Montaigne's refusal, while containing a greater or lesser element of sincerity, may have also been a ritual gesture of politeness, one
expected from the future office-holder by those conferring the office, as a
way of allowing them to be sure they were getting the right person for the
job.

Lest this charade of refused refusal be insufficient to convince the reader of
the strength of Montaigne's convictions – he does, after all, take the job –
Montaigne hastens to point out that, even if he does finally accept the
position, it is not because it is especially remunerative. If, as he claims, the
mayoralty is a job whose only compensation is (1005) "l'honneur de son
execution" ["the honor of its performance"], then Montaigne can hardly
be suspected of acting according to any motives other than the most
thoroughly high-minded and noble. This nobility of character apparently
serves him well during his tenure as mayor, since he suggests that it is the
reason for his near-unprecedented reelection. Montaigne accounts for the
doubling of his tenure only indirectly, by associating himself with certain
illustrious predecessors (both Maréchaux de France) who were likewise
returned to office; and their reelections, and by extension his own, seem to
have been the result not of any great deeds or accomplishments while in
office (indeed, if there were any, the reader is kept in the dark as to just what
they might have been), but rather of the exalted nobility of character of the
mayor in question.

As though to preempt any possibility of the quality of his mayoralty being
viewed as the result of any consciously willed action or deed on his part,
Montaigne goes out of his way to describe his approach to his task as one
of passive ineptitude. (In this, he contrasts himself with another of his
predecessors in the office, namely his own father, who seems to have taken
the job entirely too much "au poulmon et au foye" for Montaigne's taste.)
Furthermore, according to Montaigne, his own term as mayor is not
remarkable for occurrences or events of any kind. This is perhaps just as
well, considering that he presents himself to his constituents (and to the
reader) as entirely devoid of any attributes whatsoever. He tells us how,
upon his return to Bordeaux after having been notified of his election, he

offers to "messieurs de Bordeaux" a psychological profile of their new mayor:

[B] A mon arrivée, je me deschiffray fidelement et conscientieusement, tout tel que je me sens estre: sans memoire, sans vigilance, sans experience, et sans vigueur; sans hayne aussi, sans ambition, sans avarice, et sans violence; à ce qu'ils fussent informez et instruicts de ce qu'ils avoyent à attendre de mon service. (1005)

[Upon my arrival, I unfolded myself faithfully and conscientiously, entirely such as I feel myself to be: without memory, without vigilance, without experience, and without vigor; also without hatred, without ambition, without avarice, and without violence; so that they might be informed and instructed as to what they might expect from my service.]

A person possessed of such singular qualifications would not ordinarily be the ideal candidate for the highest office; but in Montaigne's scheme of things, the reverse appears to be true. If Montaigne has no attributes, then he cannot be accused of faking any, since all are equally (un)available to him. If his relationship to his job is one of detached passivity, then he can hardly be held responsible for any untoward events that might occur. If he discharges his duties without internalizing any of them, then he has successfully maintained the integrity of his inner self (whatever that may be). And Montaigne seems to think that he has indeed been successful in playing this double game (1007): "[B] J'ay peu me mesler des charges publiques sans me despartir de moy de la largeur d'une ongle, [C] et me donner à autruy sans m'oster à moy." ["I was able to be involved in public affairs without departing from myself by the width of a fingernail, and to give myself to others without depriving me of myself."] If anything, says Montaigne, throwing oneself into one's (public) work is a distinct disadvantage, because it clouds one's judgment and causes one to act with "beaucoup d'imprudence" ["much imprudence"]. On the other hand, one (1008) [B] "...qui n'y employe que son jugement et son adresse, il y procede plus gayement: il feinct, il ploye, il differe tout à son aise, selon le besoing des occasions..." ["...whoever uses only his judgment and cleverness, he proceeds more cheerfully; he feints, he bends, he defers everything at his convenience, according to the need of circumstances..."] From what seemed earlier to be a vaguely anti-Italianate stance, Montaigne appears to have shifted all the way to the other end of the scale; this last remark might have come from the pen of the Great Satan himself, Machiavelli. Montaigne does seem conscious of this ethical bind into which he has maneuvered himself, and therefore goes on to try to justify his position in terms of *suffisance*, disinterestedness, and practical necessity. He articulates a dual imperative of, on the one hand, conscious role-playing and even deliberate dissimulation, and on the other, the cultivation of an attitude of haughty disinterestedness, a noble disdain or *sprezzatura* for such activities.

[B] La plus part de nos vacations sont farcesques. "Mundus universus exercet histrioniam." Il faut jouer deuement nostre rolle, mais comme rolle d'un person-nage emprunté. Du masque et de l'apparence il n'en faut pas faire une essence réelle, ny de l'estranger le propre. Nous ne sçavons pas distinguer la peau de la chemise. [C] C'est assés de s'enfariner le visage, sans s'enfariner la poictrine. (1011)

[The majority of our occupations are farcical. "The whole world plays a part." We must duly play our role, but as though it is the role of a borrowed character. Of mask and appearance one must not make a real essence, nor turn the foreign into our very own. We cannot distinguish the skin from the shirt. It's enough to make up one's face, without making up one's heart.]

Montaigne insists that he himself has been able to maintain this distance between himself and his various roles (1012): "[B] Le Maire et Montaigne ont tousjours esté deux, d'une separation bien claire." ["The Mayor and Montaigne have always been two, clearly separated."] Provided that one maintains a clear conscience internally, practically anything, even invest-ment banking, seems to be permitted:

[B] Pour estre advocat ou financier, il n'en faut pas mesconnoistre la fourbe qu'il y a en telles vacations. Un honneste homme n'est pas comptable du vice ou sottise de son mestier, et ne doibt pourtant en refuser l'exercice: c'est l'usage de son pays, et il y a du proffict. Il faut vivre du monde et s'en prevaloir tel qu'on le trouve. (1012)

[To be a lawyer or a financier, one must not misunderstand the villainy in such occupations. An honest man is not accountable for the vice or stupidity of his profession, and should not therefore refuse to exercise it; it's the custom of his country, and there is profit in it. One must live in the world and make the best of it, as one finds it.]

It is one thing to say that detached self-control, based upon thorough self-knowledge, and tempered with discernment and prudence, is the key to a succesful performance of the self on the public stage. It is quite another to say, as Montaigne seems to be doing here, that – provided that one maintains the proper attitude of detachment – all kinds of knavery and reprehensible behavior may be undertaken with impunity. Is it really possible to play this double game? Can Montaigne actually sustain this array of seemingly contradictory *visages*? Does he genuinely believe (or hope to persuade the reader to believe) that, in order to combine worldly success with a clear conscience, all that is needed is to maintain deniability? Or has he simply abandoned the advocacy of ethical behavior?

Similar questions also present themselves to the reader concerned with the problem of interpreting the *Essais*. Even the first-time reader of Montaigne cannot help but notice the extraordinary degree to which Montaigne contradicts (or to use his own, more precise, term "adjusts") himself. "Self-adjustment" is perhaps the most appropriate term to use for Montaigne's continuous process of revising himself and his various personæ as he revises the text through which he presents that self. Such lability may make that text/self remarkably accessible at first, since its enormous variety of *visages* insures that every reader will find something familiar, a sentiment or idea which resonates with one of the reader's own. However, that same reader of Montaigne, if she persists, quickly discovers what Cave calls the "duplicity" of the "Montaignian physiognomy,"[77] becoming lost in a maze of real and apparent inconsistencies in the text; and this *jeu de miroirs* presents apparently insuperable difficulties to the interpreter of that text. For every assertion of the form, "Montaigne says X," there is an equally valid assertion of the form, "Montaigne says non-X"; how is one to decide between them?

It is not possible here to attempt to answer these larger questions. Our goal is more modest; we wish merely to examine, and if possible resolve, the single contradiction just described: How is it possible for Montaigne to maintain the integrity of both a private and a public self, or selves, under conditions and constraints he himself describes as impossibly corrupt? In our earlier discussion of Montaigne's notion of the self as process, we saw how the infinite variability of the self offered to the Montaignian subject the possibility of a correspondingly infinite array of *visages*, an array from which individual *visages* could be chosen according to the demands of the moment. Now, however, the problem is more complex; Montaigne needs to be able to deploy several selves simultaneously, and to have those selves coexist without canceling one another out. He needs to be M. le Maire de Bordeaux; Michel, Sieur de Montaigne; Michel de Montaigne, "Chevalier de l'Ordre du Roy & Gentil-homme ordinaire de sa Chambre"; and just plain Michel to his friends (and, presumably, readers). How is this to be accomplished? It will not suffice merely to say, "well, it's all a process"; Montaigne needs a more complex discursive structure within which to deploy these various selves, a structure whose framework and contours permit a number of personæ to exist and to perform with the minimum of mutual interference.

One possibility is raised in "De l'experience" (III, 13), where Montaigne offers the peculiar example of one Perseus, King of Macedonia, an example which, he suggests, may actually be a useful paradigm for "tout le monde." Montaigne tells us that this royal personage so thoroughly disguised himself that none could claim to know him; even Perseus's own ability to know and recognize himself is brought into question. The core of the self seems to disappear, or even evaporate, behind an impenetrable smoke-screen of adaptive performances. Montaigne goes on to say that he has himself seen (1077) "quelque autre de sa taille" ["another of his stature"] (Henri IV?), who above all "affectoit et estudioit de se rendre cogneu par estre mescognoissable" ["affected and endeavored to make himself recognized by being unrecognizable"]. Is this what Montaigne is actually proposing – a self that is all disguise, and thus unknowable, even to the point of uncertainty as to whether there is a self at all? And, as a result, is the reader of the *Essais* simply reduced to saying that the text is so contradictory and inconsistent as to be ultimately unreadable? Perhaps not, but the problem remains: how can Montaigne define and construct a discursive space that allows for the simultaneous performance of several selves? And how can he allow those selves to be at odds with one another within that space without causing it to collapse or disintegrate?

We find this space carefully delineated further on in "De l'experience," where Montaigne discusses his conduct in one of his public roles, that of a courtier and royal advisor – or rather what would have been his conduct, had he ever been called upon to fulfill that role; for Montaigne here goes to great lengths to situate himself at the furthest possible remove from the role of courtier, despite his actually having performed it, off and on, throughout his public career. This deliberate distancing takes place on every possible level.

[B] Quelque fois on me demandoit à quoy j'eusse pensé estre bon, qui se fut advisé de se servir de moy pendant que j'en avois l'aage,

> Dum melior vires sanguis dabat, æmula necdum
> Temporibus geminis canebat sparsa senectus.

– A rien, fis-je. Et m'excuse volontiers de ne sçavoir faire chose qui m'esclave à autruy. (1077)

[Sometimes I used to be asked what I would have thought myself good for, if someone had decided to make use of me while I was still young enough,

> When better blood gave strength, before the snows
> Of envious Time were scattered on my brow.

"For nothing", I said. And I readily excuse myself for not knowing how to do anything that enslaves me to others.]

To begin with, he does not merely say, "I was asked to perform this role, and I refused"; he says that he is asked what he would have done had he been asked, thus interposing an additional layer of question and refusal between himself and the role, pushing it as far as possible into the realm of the hypothetical. He adds to the distancing effect by situating the role in a temporal frame irreversibly remote from the present, making it clear that, whatever might have been done in the past, it is now too late. Furthermore, he responds to the multiply hypothetical question in the negative, saying that he would have been good for nothing – going on to justify this statement through a paradoxically egotistical claim of inadequacy, an assertion that any activity (for example being a courtier) entailing a diminution of his noble *franchise* would be beyond his capabilities and therefore out of the question. Finally, the question, and indeed the entire passage that follows, is presented in the verb tense most remote from temporal and grammatical reality, the pluperfect subjunctive.

This grammatical dodge offers a key to Montaigne's identity as a nobleman. Montaigne proposes for himself the role of a perfect nobleman, dispensing sage advice to his king and protecting him from flatterers, while still retaining the independence and *franchise* central to his noble identity (precisely the condition which Montaigne claims disqualifies him from holding such a position in actuality). He then situates that role in a domain of grammatical irreality, as if to emphasize that such an ideal set of circumstances cannot hope to exist in these corrupt times. If, however, he had been called to the court, this is what he would have done:

Mais j'eusse dict ses veritez à mon maistre, et eusse contrerolé ses meurs, s'il eust voulu. Non en gros, par leçons scholastiques, que je ne sçay point (et n'en vois naistre aucune vraye reformation en ceux qui les sçavent), mais les observant pas à pas, à toute oportunité, et en jugeant à l'oeil piece à piece, simplement et naturelle-ment, luy faisant voyr quel il est en l'opinion commune, m'opposant à ses flateurs. (1077)

[But I would have told the truth to my master, and would have governed his conduct, if he had wanted. Not in general, by pedantic lessons, which I do not know (and I don't see any real reformation coming from those who do know them), but by observing his conduct step by step, at every opportunity, and by judging with my own eyes, piece by piece, simply and naturally, making him see how he stands in public opinion, opposing his flatterers.]

In other words, Montaigne the courtier would have functioned as an anti-courtier, using his *franchise* as his primary weapon, "reading" the king and interpreting to him for his amelioration the erroneous "readings" (= flattery) of other, less independent (= less noble) courtiers around him; all this without being pedantic or over-wise, since this too would demean his noble status. Montaigne claims that, had anyone bothered to ask him, he would have done quite well (1078): "J'eusse eu assez de fidelité, de jugement et de liberté pour cela."[78] ["I would have had enough faith, judgment, and liberty for that."] A little farther on, he describes in more general terms the sort of person he considers most likely to be possessed of this kind of *liberté*, and therefore most likely to be suited to this hypothetical advisory post, saying that he should be (1078) "[B] ... un homme content de sa fortune, *Quod sit esse velit, nihilque malit*, et nay de moyenne fortune" ["...a man happy with his station, 'who wants to be what he is, and wants nothing else,' and born to a middle rank"]. A man content with his status, says Montaigne, is not likely to distort his advice to serve his own self-interest; and a man of "moyenne fortune" is more likely to have the flexibility to adapt to a wide range of circumstances and audiences (1078): "...il auroit plus aysée communication à toute sorte de gens" ["...he would have easier access to all sorts of people"]. Not surprisingly, the circumstances and characterstics of this hypothetical person closely resemble those of Montaigne himself; but in this emphasis on the *moyen* we are also reminded, once again, of one of the primary attributes of Castiglione's courtier, and we are given a foretaste of what will be the essential quality of *l'homme de cour* under Louis XIV.

Montaigne states further that it is advisable to have this advisory power concentrated in one pair of hands (1078): "[C] Je le voudroy à un homme seul, car respandre le privilege de cette liberté et privauté à plusieurs engendreroit une nuisible irreverence." ["I would want it to [belong to] a single man, for to distribute this privilege of freedom and intimacy to many would engender an unhealthy irreverence."] This claim to uniqueness seems designed to avoid not only "une nuisible irreverence," but also any kind of competition; to be effective, the anti-courtier's power must be in some sense absolute. He has to have the last word. Indeed, Montaigne goes so far as to reverse the polarity of the power relationship between the king and his advisor; in his view, the success of the royal personage's performance on the public stage (not to mention that performer's personal safety) is actually dependent upon the wisdom and *franchise* of his counsellor:

[B] Or il n'est aucune condition d'hommes qui ayt si grand besoing que ceux-là [les rois] de vrays et libres advertissmens. Ils soustiennent une vie publique, et ont à agreer à l'opinion de tant de spectateurs, que, comme on a accoustumé de leur taire tout ce qui les divertit de leur route, ils se trouvent, sans le sentir, engagez en la hayne et detestation de leurs peuples pour des occasions souvent qu'ils eussent peu eviter, à nul interest de leurs plaisirs mesme, qui les en eut advisez et redressez à temps. Communement leurs favorits regardent à soy plus qu'au maistre; et il leur va de bon, d'autant qu'à la verité la plus part des offices de la vray amitié sont envers le souverain en un rude et perilleus essay; de maniere qu'il y faict besoing non seulement beaucoup d'affection et de franchise, mais encore de courage. (1078)

[Now there is no sort of man that has such a great need as they [kings] do for true and frank admonitions. They lead a public life, and need to suit the opinions of so many spectators, that, as people have developed the habit of keeping from them anything that distracts them from their plans, they find themselves, without noticing, the object of the hatred and loathing of their people for reasons that they could often have avoided, without any harm even to their pleasures, if someone had warned them and set them right in time. Usually their favorites look out for themselves more than for their master; and this works well for them, since in truth most of the duties of true friendship are hard and dangerous to use on a king; so that one needs not just a great deal of affection and frankness, but also courage.]

Only the truly noble (in all the senses we have heretofore developed) person is suited to this arduous role; only he can save the royal performer from the dangers of bad reviews.

Montaigne also explains that the holder of this uniquely powerful position should not have any official title (1078): "Ce seroit un office sans nom; autrement il perdroit son effect et sa grace." ["It would be an office without title; otherwise it would lose its effect and its grace."] Why? If anything, the reverse would seem to be true, at least on the surface. But Montaigne recognizes that the efficacy of such a position would depend upon his being given an absolutely free hand (hardly a likely circumstance in a royal court), since to define it with a name – to assign to Montaigne a fixed and definite position at court – would be not only to limit his otherwise limitless powers, but to negate the very essence of his role as a wholly independent entity. One cannot simultaneously be courtier and anti-courtier.

Or so it seems. Montaigne quite fairly points out that not everyone is suited to fulfill the demands of this peculiar non-office; however, his reasons are not, perhaps, what one might expect:

[B] Et est un rolle qui ne peut indifferemment appartenir à tous. Car la verité mesme n'a pas ce privilege d'estre employée à toute heure et en toute sorte: son usage, tout noble qu'il est, a ses circonscriptions et limites. Il advient souvant, comme le monde est, qu'on la láche à l'oreille du prince, non seulement sans fruict mais dommageablement, et encore injustement. Et ne me fera l'on pas accroire qu'une sainte remontrance ne puisse estre appliquée vitieusement, et que l'interest de la substance ne doive souvent ceder à l'interest de la forme. (1078)

[And it is a role that cannot belong indiscriminately to everyone. For Truth itself does not have the privilege of being employed at any time and in any way; its use, noble as it is, has its circumscriptions and limits. It often happens, as the world is, that one lets a prince hear it, not only fruitlessly but harmfully, and even unjustly. And nobody will make me believe that a holy remonstrance cannot be wrongly applied, and that the interest of the substance should not often give way to the interest of the form.]

This remark sounds suspiciously Machiavellian, and seems almost to negate what has gone before. Montaigne started out by claiming for his anti-courtier the privilege of what in ancient Greece was known as *parrhesia*, the absolute right to tell the truth, no matter how unpleasant, to the ruler. Now, however, it seems that the anti-courtier has need of certain skills normally considered the exclusive domain of his opposite number; in other words, the use of truth, appropriated to Montaigne's putative class by his choice of adjective ("tout noble qu'il est"), is something to be undertaken with judicious restraint, an eye to opportunity and occasion, and close attention to "l'interest de la forme," even at the expense of "la substance." The problem is that the conditions which demand adjustment of the truth to circumstances are precisely those which make the existence of the anti-courtier impossible. The anti-courtier cannot afford to worry about "comme le monde est"; his ability to speak the truth at all costs, from a position of absolute *liberté*, is the rock upon which he must stand. Deprived of this absolute safety, he is forced into the realm of the pluperfect subjunctive.

Paradoxically, however, this enforced irreality of the noble ideal does not render it meaningless; on the contrary, its unique grammatical position makes it supremely useful to the aspiring nobleman in the real world. It becomes a theatrical resource: a fund of gestures, poses, attitudes and masks upon which the courtier may draw when he wishes to adopt the role of an independent nobleman, as well as a kind of moral and ethical high ground or stage from which that role may be performed. Personæ may be adopted on this imaginary stage, and pronouncements may be made from it, all without compromising the performer's status as a participant in the world of "les affaires publiques" and the court. Indeed, thanks to the protection offered by this role, its performer may freely engage in such non-noble activities as adjusting the truth to suit the circumstances, so long as appearances are kept up. For it is clear that the role is indeed primarily appearance, illusion, an image without substance.[79] As we observed earlier, Montaigne sees clearly that the myth of the *noblesse d'épée*, which claims for that class an intrinsic, hereditary superiority and independence extending back into the indefinitely remote past, is indeed mostly a myth, and bears relatively little relation to the real state of that class. Now, however, he also sees the utility of that myth to "New Men" like himself; laying claim to an exalted pedigree, to an estate associated with that pedigree, and to the status – however imaginary – concomitant to that role, provides him with an identity, a place from which to speak, however specious it may be. Adopting that role enables the "New Man" to participate actively in public life, and especially in that most dangerous of arenas, the court. The court is the most threatening theatre of public performance because its overwhelming exigencies of conformity and deference menace most directly the autonomy, ethical, political, and personal, of the participant. The would-be courtier, therefore, if he is to defend the frontiers of his *moi* against the threat presented by the court, must have recourse to an ideological system that allows him to lay claim to an absolute independence and autonomy.[80] At the same time, however, he must not be so tied to this ideology that it prevents him from taking action in the real world; and what I have called the "grammatical dodge," situating the noble identity in a realm of syntactical and practical irreality, provides the perfect escape. Rendered thus non-real, the mask of nobility becomes a more practical tool than it might otherwise be; acknowledging its theatricality gives the actor the flexibility of self he needs to exist in history.

This, then, seems to be the provisional, if not entirely stable, accommodation reached by Montaigne at the end of the *Essais* with regard to noble identity. On the one hand, one must admit the necessary existence of a corrupt reality, and act accordingly; on the other hand, one may simultaneously proclaim (in the pluperfect subjunctive, naturally) the superiority of the imaginary alternative, establishing in that realm a kind of *arrière-boutique*, preserving an uncorrupted inner space (however unreal it may be) against the ravages of reality. Ultimately, Montaigne wants to have it both ways; the entire array of performative strategies he has evolved, ranging from active role-playing and theatricality to absolute passivity, is designed to enable him both to participate in "le commerce des hommes" and to sit in a corner, "enfermé," protecting his *arrière-boutique* from prying eyes. If he reveals himself, Montaigne wants it to be on his own terms; his performances are a series of half-silvered mirrors, surfaces through which he can observe "le commerce des hommes," while the audience on the other side can see only the reflection of its own *visage(s)*. Montaigne seems to hope that only those readers not winnowed out by the series of rhetorical and performative screens he sets up for that purpose will be likely to get a glimpse of the shadowy image of Montaigne himself.

Whether he succeeds in this effort at simultaneous self-revelation and self-concealment is an open question. It does seem clear, at any rate, that Montaigne is able to present to his audience an infinite variety of *visages*, and the one displayed at any given moment is in some sense a product of the viewer's gaze itself. On the public stage, Montaigne is the Mayor of Bordeaux; at court, he is the sagacious counsellor of Henri III and Henri IV; presiding over his own dinner-table, he is Michel de Montaigne; and to the reader, he is *l'auteur*, and/or any or all of the preceding, in addition to the innumerable other guises he adopts. Which one he is at any particular moment in his performance depends both on the mask he himself chooses to don, and upon the light in which his audience chooses to observe him; and the event of observation itself plays a role in determining which mask is seen by the observer. Montaigne is now a particle, now a wave, depending on how the observation is made.

Clearly, this is a rather delicate balance to maintain. Montaigne is constantly struggling to keep the two mutually exclusive alternatives in equilibrium, and to persuade his audience that he is doing so successfully. His attempts at persuasion, as we have seen, often do more harm than good; in particular, hints of courtly casuistry creep in to undermine his *épée* rhetoric. In the next chapter, we will see how a more restrictive set of political circumstances combines with a very different authorial personality to make even this fragile equilibrium wholly untenable.

The *Essais* of Montaigne and the *Essayes* of Sir Francis Bacon are often
linked, albeit superficially, in histories of Renaissance literature; but one
who comes to the *Essayes* for the first time after having read Montaigne,
expecting to find Anglicized echoes of "Des cannibales" or "De l'amitié,"
will be sorely disappointed and not a little baffled. While Bacon does seem
to have read Montaigne, he appears to have had little interest in following
in the footsteps of his illustrious predecessor. Montaigne's writings are
loquacious, diffuse, extended, often wandering great distances from their
starting points and ostensible subjects; Bacon's are brief, compact, and
appear to be tightly focused and organized around their titles. Montaigne
never shies away from talking about himself; indeed, whatever the alleged
topic of a given essay, the subject matter is equally Michel de Montaigne,
his consciousness, his thoughts, his kidneystones. Bacon speaks mostly in
abstract, third-person observations; he seems reluctant to speak of himself
when discussing historical, moral, and political themes. On the rare occasions when he does use the first person, it is usually only to express an
opinion on an aesthetic point, as in the linked essays "Of Building" and "Of
Gardens." In place of Montaigne's ingratiating charm and generosity we
seem to find an impersonal and legalistic sententiousness, occasionally
punctuated with grim irony.

This contrast between Montaigne's "subjective" style and the apparently
"objective" style of Bacon parallels the contrast between their respective
political styles. As we saw in the previous chapter, Montaigne is anxious to
show that, although he had the option of being a courtier, he rejected that
option, resisting the demands of a nascent absolutist system in an effort to
preserve a certain subjective autonomy.[1] For Bacon, however, the situation
is quite different. To begin with, unlike Montaigne, he is quite anxious to
play the courtly game, and perfectly willing to admit it; furthermore, under
the more developed absolutist system of Elizabeth and James, he cannot
avoid being thrust onto the stage in some way or another, whether he
wants to be or not. As he says in the *Advancement of Learning*: "... in this
theatre of man's life it is reserved only for God and Angels to be lookers

on."² Bacon sees resistance to the performative demands of this court as simply too dangerous. Thus, for him, the question becomes not one of whether or not to step on the stage, but rather one of the degree of control one will be able to exercise over the role(s) that one is called upon to play. This semi-enforced public role-playing, and Bacon's consequent avoidance of Montaignian subjectivity – partly from choice, partly from necessity – ultimately calls into question the very possibility of a private self apart from its public roles.³ The absence of self-indulgence à la Montaigne in Bacon's *Essayes* may simply mean that, for the sometime Lord Chancellor, there is no self to indulge.

Even the point of greatest apparent similarity between the two collections, namely their common title, manifests this divergence. The full title of the *Essayes*, as given on the title page of the 1625 edition, is: *The Essayes or Counsels, Civill and Morall, of Francis Lord Verulam, Viscount St. Alban.* Bacon seems here to be announcing a specific project, very different from that of Montaigne; he appears to be taking up not the genre of personal observation/revelation created by the latter, but rather the tradition of the "Advice to Princes," especially as exemplified in the work of Bacon's favorite author, Machiavelli.⁴ Many critics have examined Bacon's filial relationship with Machiavelli, particularly the long shadow cast by the *Discorsi* (much more than the *Principe*) over Bacon's writing; Bacon repeatedly holds up the Florentine's readings of Livy as a model of historical scholarship and political insight.⁵ I will refrain from going over this well-traveled ground; I wish merely to reinforce the point that to Bacon, swimming against the generally anti-Machiavellian current of thought of the period, Machiavelli was an essential model for the formulation and expression of political ideas.

Nevertheless, Bacon's political writings do differ from those of his mentor in ways which are at first deceptive and confusing. Again, as with Montaigne, a reader coming from the *Discorsi* to the *Essayes* may initially be disappointed. Machiavelli's remarks on statecraft and politics have shocked and appalled some, but few accuse him of shallowness or triviality; yet some have found precisely these faults in Bacon's observations on the same subjects. Machiavelli's incisive readings of history and of the motives of the actors on its stage are replaced by apparently commonplace remarks on "human nature"; at times Bacon seems to be doing nothing more than stringing together proverbs. Indeed, some readers have felt that Bacon was merely doing what so many of his less gifted contemporaries were also doing at the time: reducing Machiavelli's maxims on the government of nations to apply to the petty world of intramural machinations at court, and cranking out yet another collection of stale platitudes on the subject of How to Get Ahead in Society.⁶ This assertion that Bacon's writings on

what he called "civil knowledge" represent a simple transfer of Machiavellian precepts from "public" to "private" life, without at least a clearer idea
of what such categories might have meant to Bacon or his audience, is
problematic at best. In discussing Bacon's relationship to Machiavelli, it
seems most accurate to say that, as the comparison with Montaigne also
shows, the entire notion of "private life" or a "private sphere," as opposed
to a "public" or "political" sphere, is radically questioned by the *Essayes*.

There are those who go still further in their denigration of the *Essayes*,
seeing the collection as a mere grab-bag of commonplaces, altogether
unworthy of serious examination; C. S. Lewis, for example, dismisses the
Essayes in a famous, if unjust, remark: "...it is a book for adolescents."[7]
William Blake is equally dismissive, and even less charitable; in his mar-
ginal notations to his copy of the *Essayes*, he says: "I am astonishd how
such Contemptible Knavery & Folly as this Book contains can ever have
been calld Wisdom by men of Sense..."[8] While such misjudgments can
safely be disregarded, one cannot ignore the apparent simple-mindedness
presented upon first reading by many of the *Essayes*. Bacon's little sayings
do seem to have a familiar ring to them, and sometimes go beyond the
familiar to the painfully obvious. However, even at their most banal, they
resist a superficial reading. The reader who attempts to peruse the *Essayes*
as though they were in fact a collection of commonplaces, skimming
through them at high speed while pausing only long enough over each
sentence to "recognize" it as something supposedly familiar before moving
on to the next, will quickly become lost. There is more going on than meets
the eye; the tension between the text's various nodes of familiarity generates
a resistance to easy reading. Hazlitt felt this disturbance beneath the
surface: "His sayings have the effect of axioms, are at once striking and
self-evident..."[9] In what follows I will attempt to show how and why the
Essayes are considerably more "striking" than "self-evident," and to demonstrate how that "striking" quality is intimately connected with their
purpose.

That purpose is not immediately obvious, despite many critical attempts
to clarify Bacon's aims in writing the *Essayes*, and to develop from those
ostensible aims a reading that accounts for some of their anomalies.[10]
While it does seem clear that some sort of didactic intent is lurking behind
the scenes, critics disagree as to its exact nature, its degree of explicitness, its
univocality, and its content. There is a division between those who see the
Essayes as a work promulgating a specific program for the sociopolitical
behavior of its readers, and those who argue that Bacon is both more
devious and less single-minded. Among the former, Lisa Jardine argues
that the *Essayes* have a clear and univocal didactic purpose. "The essays
are ... carefully constructed to put across practical precepts which Bacon

believed to be of value to men of all intellectual backgrounds. The essay
form is used as a 'method' for projecting these precepts in an appealing and
readily acceptable form."[11] To others, however, this reading is too optimistic, failing to account for ambiguities and contradictions present in the text.
Stanley Fish, for example, says that "the essays advocate nothing (except
perhaps a certain openness and alertness of mind); they are descriptive, and
a description is ethically neutral..."[12] He goes on to claim that Bacon sets
for his reader a number of traps, designed systematically to undermine the
reader's confidence in the apparent simplicity both of the text and of its
subject matter.[13] He suggests further that, having fallen into those traps, the
reader finds himself in a state of dissatisfied confusion, which state nevertheless will open his eyes to any further traps that may be lying in wait,
whether in the text at hand or in the world of phenomena. Pushed to the
limit, Fish's deconstructive argument would imply that the *Essayes* in fact
say nothing at all to anyone, a conclusion patently at odds with Bacon's
clearly stated method and purpose in several of his other works, namely to
bring forth and make clear empirically verifiable truth. Fish therefore
hedges his bets, concluding his essay by saying that the *Essayes* are not so
much self-consuming as "self-regulating," and that, rather than evaporat-
ing into the dialectical void, they remain present to provide "helps" (in the
form of "method") to the reading mind.[14]

Both Fish and Jardine seem to agree that some sort of program is being put
forth, but neither is clear on what that program might be. Jardine declines
to state exactly what "practical precepts" Bacon offers to his readers,
perhaps because they are not to be found; Fish proposes that Bacon is
supplying his reader with a method for reading and evaluating ethical
problems, but sidesteps the question of what is to be done with the
problems once they have been read. Both critics insist on the presence of a
"method," but differ radically on what constitutes that "method." Given
Bacon's own careful use (and suspicion) of that word, it is perhaps worth
trying to define more closely Bacon's "method" in the *Essayes*, and to ask
careful questions about the nature and existence of whatever "truth" Bacon
is supposedly trying to bring to light. Moreover, neither critic gives us
much information about just who the readers of the *Essayes* are. To say
that they are "men of all intellectual backgrounds" is perhaps to accept a
mystification that the *Essayes* sponsor, while remaining too general (and,
possibly, ahistorical) to be helpful; and Fish, despite his insistence that
Bacon's writing is "reader- rather than information-oriented,"[15] is remarkably vague as to the specifics of that reader's existence. We are therefore left
with several questions. First of all, who is reading the *Essayes*, and why?
What information is Bacon trying to convey (or not, as the case may be)?

How is he presenting that information? If the *Essayes* are related to Bacon's overall project as expressed in his other works, what role do they play? More specifically, what effect(s) is Bacon trying to produce in the consciousness of his reader, and to what end? Without embarking on a potentially futile quest for "authorial intent," I do think that it is worth asking whether the *Essayes* are performing a didactic function, and if they are, what the mechanism and content of that function might be.

I shall attempt to demonstrate that the *Essayes* are indeed a kind of manual, and are intended for a specific audience, that of persons like Bacon himself. Bacon is writing both for and about a specific reader in a specific sociohistorical context; not a hypothetical blank-slate reader, nor the average man in the street of 1625, but rather a reader of a specific category to which he himself belongs: male, wealthy, urban by necessity if not choice, and actively engaged in the political, legal, and social life of the Jacobean court – or desirous of being so engaged. In the 1625 dedication of the *Essayes* to the Duke of Buckingham, he reminds us of what he sees as the special pertinence of the *Essayes* to this group: "I doe now publish my *Essayes*; which, of all my other workes, have beene most Currant: For that, as it seemes, they come home, to Mens Businesse, and Bosomes."[16] However, the *Essayes* do not function as a simple how-to tract; they do not offer to the reader a collection of straightforward precepts. Rather, they present the reader with a series of deceptive surfaces, designed to fool the reader initially, as Fish suggests, while simultaneously inviting him to inquire further and to discern the truth(s), or absence thereof, behind those surfaces. This process of reading that the *Essayes* attempt to induce in the reader, I shall argue, mirrors Bacon's conception of the way an aspiring courtier ought to "read" his world; the court and its denizens are to be read, and read through, in the same way as the *Essayes*. Finally, I hope to show that the structure of Bacon's version of the noble self, the performed identity that a courtier constructs for himself, is likewise represented in the structure and rhetoric of the *Essayes* themselves.

The various dedicatory epistles with which the successive editions of the *Essayes* (1597, 1612, 1625) were delivered to their readers are a reasonable place to begin. It is worth recalling that dedications in the Renaissance often functioned not as carriers of specific information regarding the superlative virtues of their subjects, but rather as coded sociopolitical gestures, in which their authors signaled their dependence on the dedicatees and solicited their patronage and support (financial, social, political, or any combination of the three). Now, despite the numbingly conventional nature of most dedicatory epistles, it is unwise simply to dismiss Bacon's efforts in this area as simple sycophancy. As we shall see, no one in Renaissance England was more sharply attuned to the resonances of such conventional gestures than Francis Bacon, and his control of even such an apparently rigid and one-dimensional form as the dedicatory epistle clearly demonstrates that sensitivity. One of the most revealing of these letters is that written to Henry, Prince of Wales, originally intended to accompany the 1612 edition of the *Essayes*, but abandoned upon the untimely death of the prince. To appreciate its significance, it is worthwhile to compare it with the letter prefacing the first (1597) edition, a letter both more modest and more unselfconsciously commonplace. The content of the 1597 letter is pure literary convention; Bacon offers the standard excuse for printing the *Essayes*, namely that someone else has procured a copy of the manuscript and published an unauthorized and corrupt version, and that therefore he is obliged to publish in order to prevent "any further disgrace." This is hardly innovative.[17] The direction of the conventional gesture is slightly more interesting: recall that, as a result of a gaffe four years prior to the date of this letter, Bacon had been pushed off the political fast track, and had in the intervening years been trying vainly to regain the Queen's favor.[18] The 1597 letter is addressed to his brother Anthony, a high official in Elizabeth's government; it may therefore be read as an appeal to Anthony, not only for approval of his literary effort, but also for him to put in a good word (again?) for Francis at court. But this appeal, too, while demonstrating Bacon's awareness of the real function of epistles dedicatory, is not particularly unusual.

When we turn to the letter to Henry, however, we find a more complex appreciation of the possibilities inherent in the form. The Prince seems already, by the time of this letter, to have made some use of Bacon's considerable talents, for example by appointing him to be his solicitor; it seems likely that Bacon hoped that further advancement would be forthcoming from this quarter, especially as Henry was heir to the throne. Therefore, Bacon will be eager not just to demonstrate his general worthiness, but to display his specific suitability for a position as counselor to a prince in matters of state. And it is not even enough for Bacon merely to assert that his experience in matters political makes him a worthy advisor; he presents his case in a way calculated to persuade his princely reader, while also preparing the mind of that reader for the action of the *Essayes* themselves. The first sentence of the letter shows this process at work: "Having devided my life into the contemplative, and active parte, I am desierous to give his M[ajesty], and yor H.[ighness] of the fruites of both, simple thoughe they be." (317) Bacon begins by reminding his reader that he is anything but unfamiliar with the machinery of state, having had considerable hands-on experience; in this he wishes to distinguish himself from other, less practically qualified offerers of advice. He simultaneously refuses to play down the worth of his scholarly endeavors, echoing a point he makes at considerable length in the first book of the *Advancement of Learning*: that the best and most sagacious advisors in matters of state are those (not coincidentally, like Bacon himself) who combine book-learning with worldly experience.[19] It is a point Bacon will reemphasize in the *Essayes*, particularly (and unsurprisingly) in an essay which appeared for the first time in the 1612 edition, namely no. XX, "Of Counsell":

> ...it is one thing to understand Persons, and another thing to understand Matters; For many are perfect in Mens Humours, that are not greatly Capable of the Reall Part of Businesse; Which is the Constitution of one, that hath studied Men, more than Bookes. Such Men are fitter for Practise, then for Counsell; And they are good but in their own Alley: Turne them to New Men, and they have lost their Ayme... (69–70)

"Practise" seems to be used here in the Renaissance sense of "intrigue, conspiracy, base scheming." Bacon is saying that the average sort of courtier-politicians, without the benefit of sound humanist training such as his own, are good for nothing but petty scheming and gossip; the bowling metaphor brings out the frivolity and shallowness of this kind of activity, as contrasted with the gravity of "Counsell" on weighty matters of state. Yet Bacon, in this dedicatory letter, indicates his desire to return to active service, to the world of political counsel, but also of "Practise." We shall find this double impulse over and over again in the *Essayes*, although rarely expressed so nakedly. This passage is perhaps the closest Bacon comes to Montaigne's explicit (if disingenuous) rejection of the life of the courtier in "De l'experience"; more often, Bacon is content to allude, in an obscure or backhanded way, to the sordid triviality of court life, and then go on to embrace that life enthusiastically. We will have more to say later about the reasons for, and consequences of, this move.

His use of the active voice in this passage ("Having devided my life...") suggests that he is trying to assert some retrospective authority over his not-entirely-voluntary concentration on scholarly pursuits in his recent past. One might even read into this first clause a slight trace of bitterness, since Henry could not help but be aware that Bacon considered his non-employment in matters political to have been forced upon him. (In this he is once again following in the footsteps of Machiavelli, who like Bacon was forced to retire from the world of political activity, and who did not fail, in the dedication of the *Principe*, to remind his princely dedicatee that he felt his exclusion from political life to be unjust.) Bacon's offering of the fruits of his labors to the King first, and to the Prince second, is perhaps required by protocol, but it is also a demonstration of his awareness (as well as a reminder to the Prince, and to all other readers) of the ultimate

source of power and patronage in the Jacobean court. It may also be
Bacon's tactful way of asserting a certain importance for the insights he is
about to offer. Finally, Bacon's claim that the "fruites" he offers are
"simple," while again a *pro forma* gesture, is typically disingenuous. Nothing could be further from the truth; and yet it is essential, as we shall see,
to Bacon's rhetorical strategy that the reader be told (if not entirely
persuaded) that what he is about to read is indeed "simple."[20]

The last sentence of the dedication reinforces the hints laid down in the
first, and discreetly suggests a solution to the problems implied there.
Having in the second sentence alluded, not without irony, to the temporal
demands placed upon him by his "continuall Services," he offers the
Essayes to the Prince, asking him "to conceive that if I cannott rest, but
must shewe my dutifull, and devoted affection to yor H: in theis thinges w[ch]
proceed from my self, I shalbe much more ready to doe it, in performance of
any yor princely Commaundementes; And so wishing yor H: all princely
felictye I rest…" In other words, the *Essayes* are a job résumé. Bacon uses
this letter of dedication to point out his fitness for a position as princely
advisor; not only does he explicitly suggest his availability and suitability
for the job, but he also intimates that the works introduced by the letter
demonstrate that fitness. The letter functions as a kind of advance guard,
clearing a path in the princely reader's mind for the persuasive action of the
Essayes themselves.

In this connection, let us return to Bacon's claim to simplicity. Having
once made it, he reinforces it with another disclaimer, one calculated to
appeal to the busy man of affairs: "To write just Treatises requireth leasure
in the Writer, and leasure in the Reader…" neither of which, he says, is the
case here. Therefore, as one busy man of state to another, he offers a
different sort of information-packaging: "… certaine breif notes, sett downe
rather significantlye, than curiously, w[ch] I have called *Essaies*." Brevity,
naturally, seems to imply straightforward efficiency, a compact and dense
presentation of vital information, in which the content-to-volume ratio is
maximized. "Curiously," then, would indicate at least a more extended
presentation, if not something downright Ciceronian – which would have
been, to Henry and his contemporaries, the "normal" form the writings of a
professional humanist on such matters would take.[21] Bacon is here claiming that he has renounced the procedures of at least one kind of standard
humanist literary form, and that he is producing instead a work which will
present to its reader crucial data unadorned by the superfluities of rhetoric.
These "dispersed Meditacions," he asserts, will place fewer untoward demands on the reader than the more conventionally systematic, "curiously"
wrought treatises of the professional humanist (a class to which Bacon,
despite his posturing, cannot deny that he belongs). What is Bacon seeking

to accomplish by rejecting the tools of his humanist trade? Is he really just trying to make things easier for his preoccupied and possibly distracted reader, by presenting a fast-food version of "How to Be a Man of State," conveniently pre-packaged in bite-sized chunks?

Let us examine more closely the meaning of the word "significantlye." Bacon thoughtfully supplies us with a crucial clue when he offers to Henry an example, in the form of a classical precedent, of the type of literary endeavor in which he is engaged; he says that his own "*Essaies*" are like those of another anti-Ciceronian moralist, namely Seneca. More specifically, the mode of signification adopted by Bacon for his "breif notes" is here being aligned with that found in Seneca's *Epistolae*. Bacon himself describes this prose style in the *De Augmentis*, where, after outlining the main features (and criticizing the excesses) of Ciceronian style, he goes on to say of its opposite number (I: 452):

Paulo sanius est aliud styli genus (neque tamen ipsum omnino vanitatis expers), quod copiae illi et luxuriae orationis tempore fere succedit. Illud totum in eo est, ut verba sint aculeata, sententiae concisae, oratio denique potius versa quam fusa; quo fit, ut omnia per hujusmodi artificium magis ingeniosa videantur quam revera sint. Tale invenitur in Seneca effusius, in Tacito et Plinio Secundo moderatius; atque nostri temporis auribus coepit esse non ita pridem accommodatum. Verum hoc ipsum mediocribus ingeniis gratum esse solet (adeo ut dignitatem quandam literis conciliet); attamen a judiciis magis limatis merito fastiditur, et poni possit pro intemperie quadam doctrinae, cum sit verborum etiam et eorum concinnitatis aucupium quoddam.

[Somewhat sounder is another form of style – yet neither is it innocent of some vain shows – which is likely to follow in time upon this copious and luxuriant oratorical manner. It consists wholly in this: that the words be sharp and pointed, sentences concised, a style in short that may be called "turned" rather than fused; whence it happens that everything dealt with by this kind of art seems rather ingenious than lofty. Such a style is found in Seneca very freely used, in Tacitus and the younger Pliny more moderately; and it is beginning to suit the ears of our age as never before. And indeed it is pleasant to subtle and low-ranging minds (for thereby they conciliate the honor due to letters); however, better-trained judgments disapprove it; and it may be looked upon as a distemper of learning, insofar as it is accompanied by a chasing after mere words and their concinnity.][22]

Bacon here describes his own prose style quite accurately, simultaneously demonstrating that he is far from unaware of the potential shortcomings of that style. In typical Baconian fashion, however, he does not explicitly signal his own relationship to the style he describes; neither does his apparent disapprobation amount to much, when closely examined. He does not say that it *is* "intemperie doctrinae," "a distemper of learning"; he says only that it "may be looked upon" as one, *if* or *insofar as* ("cum sit") it brings with it "verborum ... et eorum concinnitatis aucupium," "a chasing after mere words and their concinnity." The danger is that a style which ought to convey information concisely may, if wrongly handled, do the opposite; that is, it may act to empty itself out, to reduce itself to "mere words." But this is an aberration, not a necessary attribute of the style. As usual, Bacon is hedging his bets, distancing himself from a literary movement of which he is actually one of the primary exponents, while remaining close enough to use that stylistic trend as a tool, insofar as it suits him to do so.

Now, rejecting Ciceronian style in favor of some sort of supposedly unbiased reporting is one thing; rejecting it in favor of another, clearly defined, opposing stylistic convention is something else again. This move into the camp of Seneca and Tacitus carries with it a whole array of literary and ideological consequences. Just what these consequences are has been the subject of considerable critical debate, much of it conditioned by the influential essays of Morris Croll.[23] Many critics have made greater or lesser adjustments to features of Croll's schema, while still adhering to its basic lineaments.[24] F. J. Levy, for example, in an article on the 1597 version of the *Essayes*, follows Croll's paradigm, while claiming that Bacon's own development as a politician and writer traces a move from Ciceronianism to Tacitism; specifically, he suggests that Bacon's apparent rejection of his humanist training may be a response to his own political failure of the early 1590s.[25] Alluding to the Tacitean phrase, *difficilia quae pulchra*,[26] Levy argues that the 1597 *Essayes* represent an extreme of Stoic gnomicity, and that this aesthetic of deliberate obscurity functions as a kind of screen, keeping the unqualified reader (the "mass of humanity") from understanding the deep secrets – the tricks of policy and statecraft – of the text, while revealing those secrets only to the qualified few – in this case, "those ... who, like Bacon himself, had passed through the Elizabethan political system."[27] Specifically, Bacon was trying to demonstrate to these readers the bankruptcy of traditional civic-humanist discourse, not only through explicit statements, but also through a disruptive and potentially confusing method of presentation. Levy, following Fish, says that this presentation forces the reader to work out the meaning or meanings for himself, in the process becoming aware of the traps, rhetorical and political, held out to ensnare the unwary reader. The 1597 *Essayes*, in the traditional view, are the most disjointed and difficult of the three versions, and therefore seem to fit Levy's argument best. We shall later have cause to question whether this traditional view is entirely accurate; for the moment, it is enough to see that Bacon's 1612 claims to transparency and directness are perhaps somewhat more double-edged than they initially seem.

Bacon's prefatory insinuations (and Croll's apparent acceptance of similar proposals at face value) notwithstanding, then, we may safely assert that Bacon's turn away from Ciceronian style, whether literary or civic, is not a turn away from imitation, or self-conscious literary artifice, in favor of a more "natural," "rational," "true" mode of expression.[28] It remains, at least at this stage, a conscious imitation, following good Renaissance literary practice, of an ancient model, one which itself makes no claims to being anti-literary; certainly Bacon himself had no illusions on this score. However, that it differs at all from the norms of humanist political discourse, and that Bacon expends so much energy on convincing the reader of this difference, should draw our attention to questions of stylistic choice. Why does Bacon consider this style of writing, as he describes it both in his dedicatory letter to Prince Henry and (in similar terms) in the passage from the *De Augmentis* quoted above, to be appropriate to his project? Simultaneously, why might he feel it necessary to camouflage the nature of his prose style, and give potentially misleading statements about its supposed or intended effect on the reader? In order to understand what is at stake, we need to examine more closely Bacon's ideas on just how information is conveyed through language, and on the ways in which the method of presentation affects the information delivered.

Bacon's concern with the problem of how best to convey information is not confined to the letter to Prince Henry, nor even to the *Essayes* alone; it is one of the major preoccupations to be found in all of Bacon's writings. Whether he is writing about "civill Businesse"[29] or natural philosophy, he is always concerned with presenting material in a way that facilitates its assimilation; witness, for example, this remark in the preface to the *Novum Organum* (I: 154):

Nos certe cogitationem suscepimus et curam adhibuimus, ut quae a nobis proponentur non tantum vera essent, sed etiam ad animos hominum (licet miris modis occupatos et interclusos) non incommode aut aspere accederent.

[I have on my own part made it my care and study that the things which I shall propound should not only be true, but should also be presented to men's minds, how strangely soever preoccupied and obstructed, in a manner not harsh or unpleasant. (IV: 42)]

Bacon's preferred method of presentation, the one which he considers most effective and least "incommode aut aspere" (paradoxically enough, considering that his main classical models, Tacitus and Seneca, are precisely that), is the aphorism. We have already discussed some of his justifications for this stylistic choice, particularly as applied to the *Essayes*. I would like to turn here to a brief consideration of the more general claims he makes, in several of his other works, for the utility of the aphorism as a means of communication. Bacon's central project is the development of an inductive method of reasoning, based on the accumulation of individual data points, which he proposes as an antidote to what he sees as the excesses of scholastic reasoning from first causes. This program is set forth most succinctly in the *Novum Organum* (itself written in the form of a series of aphorisms), where Bacon discusses the dangers of systematic ideas in the realm of natural philosophy, and proposes a purely inductive method of the accumulation of particulars as a superior alternative. Speaking of traditional methods of deductive reasoning, he says (I: 161):

Rationem humanam qua utimur ad naturam, *Anticipationes Naturae* (quia res temeraria est et praematura), at illam rationem quae debitis modis elicitur a rebus, *Interpretationem Naturae*, docendi gratia vocare consuevimus.

[The conclusions of human reason as ordinarily applied in matters of nature, I call for the sake of distinction *Anticipations of Nature* (as a thing rash or premature). That reason which is elicited from facts by a just and methodical process, I call *Interpretation of Nature*. (IV: 51)]

He comments further on the potential effects of these "Anticipationes" (I: 161): "Anticipationes satis firmae sunt ad consensum; quandoquidem si homines etiam insanirent ad unum modum et conformiter, illi satis bene inter se congruere possent." ["Anticipations are a ground sufficiently firm for consent, for even if men went mad all after the same fashion, they might agree with one another well enough." (IV: 51)] But Bacon is after more than mere agreement. In fact, he regards this kind of system-based universal consent as not only empty but dangerous; in the famous series of aphorisms where he enumerates and describes (I: 163) the "[q]uatuor ... genera Idolorum quae mentes humanas obsident" ["four classes of Idols which beset men's minds" (IV: 53)], he warns against one kind of Idol in particular, that which produces belief in an illusion, a performance, rather than reality itself (I: 164):

Sunt denique Idola quae immigrarunt in animos hominum ex diversis dogmatibus philosophiarum, ac etiam ex perversis legibus demonstrationum; quae Idola Theatri nominamus; quia quot philosophiae receptae aut inventae sunt, tot fabulas productas et actas censemus, quae mundos effecerunt fictitios et scenicos.

[Lastly, there are Idols which have immigrated into men's minds from the various dogmas of philosophies, and also from wrong laws of demonstration. These I call Idols of the Theatre, because in my judgment all the received systems are but so many stage plays, representing worlds of their own creation after an unreal and scenic fashion. (IV: 55)]

For Bacon, the false coherence of such *fabulae* is particularly dangerous, because it so effectively persuades an audience to believe in illusions. However, as we shall see, he is perfectly willing to use this kind of specious consent as a tool, a sort of way-station on the path to the truth, but his ultimate goal is something more profound. He wishes to teach his reader to go beyond the façade of mere consent, to look behind the scenes to discover what is really going on, whether it be in the realm of natural philosophy or of "Businesse"; and particulars are the means to this end.

When speaking of natural philosophy, Bacon meant by "particulars" specific individual facts, from which larger ideas could be produced, after painstaking evaluation of all the available data, by pure induction, uncontaminated by preconceived ideas. Much has been written about the weaknesses, not to say the impossibility, of this method of pure induction, and of Bacon's consequent failure to make any real advance towards so-called "modern scientific method."[30] What is important here is that his emphasis on particulars and his suspicion of general rules are not limited to the realm of natural philosophy; this attitude is a consistent presence throughout Bacon's work, and informs nearly every sentence he utters, not only on scientific and philosophical discovery, but also on education, learning, and the uses of rhetoric.[31] It is therefore germane to ask how Bacon thought such an inductive method might function in the realm of "civill Businesse," and to examine how such procedures manifest themselves in the *Essayes*.

Allied with Bacon's interest in methods of presentation is a concern for the appropriateness of the method, both to the material being presented and to the audience for whom it is intended. The rhetorical method may in fact vary according to the subject, but an author must always be thoroughly aware of the way in which his presentation affects what he is presenting. This is especially important since, as we have already seen Bacon suggest, careless use of rhetoric will at best undermine its own effectiveness, and may carry with it more serious negative consequences. With regard to the method appropriate to "civill Businesse," Bacon has this to say in the *Advancement of Learning*:

I cannot likewise be ignorant of a form of writing which some wise and grave men have used, containing a scattered history of those actions which they have thought worthy of memory, with politic discourse and observation thereupon; not incorporate into the history, but separately, and as the more principal in their intention; which kind of Ruminated History I think more fit to place among books of policy ... (III: 339)

This is the technique used in treating of such matters by Bacon's great model, that wise and grave man, Machiavelli:

And therefore the form of writing which of all others is fittest for this variable amount of negotiation and occasions is that which Machiavel chose wisely and aptly for government; namely, *discourse upon histories or examples*. For knowledge drawn freshly and in our view out of particulars, knoweth the best way to particulars again. (III: 453)[32]

This last sentence is vital. Bacon will insist that unique examples, "particulars," must be emphasized in a "book of policy," such as the *Principe* or the *Discorsi*, and such as the manual Bacon says he is writing, since such a work concerns itself not with philosophical or even ethical abstractions, but with the widely varying specifics of individual real-world experiences. (In this, of course, Bacon's theory – if not, perhaps, his practice – resembles not so much that of Machiavelli as that of another Florentine both wise and grave, Machiavelli's great rival Guicciardini, who insists on the uniqueness of historical "particulars," and therefore heaps scorn on Machiavelli's attempts to draw general inferences from them.[33]) One would further expect that such a move might entail a corresponding move away from the abstract, systematizing rhetoric of the Ciceronian humanist, a move that, as we have seen, Bacon seems to be making quite self-consciously. This interest in particulars is, moreover, entirely consistent with Bacon's emphasis on "facts" in the passages from the *Novum Organum* discussed above. It is therefore hardly surprising that the form of prose utterance that dominates the *Essayes* is the aphorism, which combines terseness, wit, and "significance" (in the sense in which Bacon uses the word in his letter to Prince Henry) into a small and neat package; and it seems that this small package is the particular of the discourse of "civill Businesse."[34] However, we may legitimately question whether the correspondence between the "particular" of natural philosophy and the "particular" of what Bacon calls "negotiation and occasions" is an exact one. Does the aphorism provide the reader with a genuine Baconian "fact," that is, a piece of concrete and specific information, about the human world?

Consider, as one example among many, Essay LIV, "Of Vaine-Glory." Bacon opens this piece with a proverb he erroneously attributes to Aesop, makes a few deprecatory remarks, throws in another proverb (rhymed, this time), and then goes on to discuss (161) the "Use of this Qualitie, in Civill Affaires." He provides the reader with numerous *sententiae* such as the following:

In Militar Commanders and Soldiers, *Vaine-Glory* is an Essentiall Point; for as Iron Sharpens Iron, so by *Glory* one Courage sharpneth another. In Cases of Great Enterprise, upon Charge and Adventure, a Composition of *Glorious* Natures, doth put Life into Businesse... (161–62)

And further:

Certainly *Vaine-Glory* helpeth to Perpetuate a Mans Memory; And Vertue was never so Beholding to Humane Nature, as it received his due at the Second Hand. Neither had the Fame of *Cicero, Seneca, Plinius Secundus*, borne her Age so well, if it had not been joyned, with some *Vanity* in themselfes: Like unto Varnish, that makes Seelings not onely Shine, but Last. (162)

If we take at face value such generalized utterances, and assume that they represent concrete truths about the world of human affairs, we run the risk of becoming C. S. Lewis's "adolescents", especially when, only a few lines further on, at the conclusion of the essay, we find the equally authoritative-sounding maxim, "*Glorious* Men are the Scorne of Wise Men; the Admiration of Fooles; the Idols of Parasites; And the Slaves of their own Vaunts." (162) – which tends to undermine the remarks that precede it. It certainly seems here as if Bacon has sacrificed truth, not to mention logical continuity, on the altar of *concinnitas verborum*. Once we are through being dazzled by his varnished ceiling, we are left with the questions: Are all of these so-called "facts" true? If so, what then? If not, how are we to decide among them?

The problem manifests itself in subtler ways as well. Let us allow for a certain degree of contradiction within the text, rather than using one statement to cancel out another and leaving ourselves with nothing. Our provisional hypothesis, then, is that Bacon supplies us with a range of possible truths which, taken together or at least in larger aggregations, will offer us a reasonably clear idea of where the truth (assuming it is possible to speak of "truth" in this context) of "civill Businesse" lies. Such an approach would enable us to salvage the view that the *Essayes* function according to Bacon's rules for "magistral" discourse, a view espoused by Jardine:

Bacon's *Essays* fall squarely under the heading of presentation or "method of discourse." They are didactic, in Agricola's sense of presenting existing knowledge to someone in a form in which it may be believed and assimilated. Whatever methods they employ must therefore be 'magistral' as opposed to 'initiative.'[35]

However, this approach seems no more effective in disposing of the problem. To begin with, how do we decide which of the assorted chunks of "existing knowledge" Bacon offers is the correct one? Do we add up the numbers of aphorisms on each side of an issue, and go with the larger total? Do we decide based on what we think we know about Bacon's life, personality, and political activities? Do we pick whichever alternative seems to us more persuasive? More attractive? Or do we simply make an arbitrary choice? The real issue is whether this kind of "evaluation" can be made at all, and a close examination seems to indicate that it cannot. These alleged facts, or units of knowledge, are neither; they are vague generalizations, containing no real particulars or specific information whatsoever.

Therefore, Bacon cannot really be said to be "presenting existing knowledge," in the sense that Jardine seems to intend; or, if he is, it is knowledge of an entirely useless kind. For what are these sententious maxims but neat repackagings of received truth, commonplaces already generally known? Worse yet, is not this type of knowledge, according to Bacon's own criteria, not only useless but pernicious, closing people's minds and blinding them to real, factual knowledge?

We are thus confronted with a paradox. Whether or not aphoristic utterances actually contain specific "facts" pertaining to human interaction (and, as we have seen, the opposite tends to be true of any given individual aphorism), it is clear that Bacon intends them to function as the inductive building blocks of Civil Knowledge. In the *Advancement of Learning*, he has this to say about the utility of aphorisms (III: 405): "...Aphorisms, representing a knowledge broken, do invite men to enquire farther; whereas Methods, carrying the shew of a total, do secure men, as if they were at furthest." And this is precisely the effect that he hopes the *Essayes* will have on their princely reader (317): "But my hope is, they may be as graynes of salte, that will rather give you an appitite, then offend you wth satiety."[36] And yet it seems that any given aphorism, such as "Vertue was never so Beholding to Humane Nature, as it received his due at the Second Hand," or (from the same essay) "They that are *Glorious*, must needs be *Factious*; For all Bravery stands upon Comparisons," functions not according to the laws he lays down for aphorisms, but rather in conformity with what he says about methods – that is, providing a predigested, self-contained pseudo-truth about human experience, one that satisfies the reader (perhaps "consumer" would be more accurate) and discourages further thought.[37] It is therefore difficult to see how the *Essayes* can be read as purveying specific quanta of useful information, or as functioning according to Bacon's rules for methodical or "magistral" discourse. Such a view is undermined by, on the one hand, Bacon's assertion that aphoristic discourse, as pioneered by Machiavelli, is ideally suited to a discussion of "civill Businesse," and, on the other hand, his explicit statement that he intends the *Essayes* to provoke inquiry, not put an end to it. The paradox, then, may be stated thus: how can Bacon open the reader's mind with tools designed to do the opposite?

We have already seen the speciousness of Bacon's attempts to present the *Essayes* as unadorned by rhetoric; the reverse is in fact the case. Indeed, whether Bacon is aligning himself with the Ciceronian rhetorical tradition or the Tacitean is almost irrelevant; they have in common with each other, and with Bacon's efforts, the function that defines rhetoric, namely that of persuasion. Bacon's introductory epistles announce this function, even as they enact it themselves. The aphorism itself is, so to speak, a unit of persuasion; it presents information in an easily comprehensible (and therefore persuasive) form. Thus, we may state, at the risk of belaboring the obvious, that the *Essayes* function, at least on one level, according to the laws of rhetoric. In this context, we mean merely that rhetoric acts to persuade, without necessarily assigning to that persuasion the nefarious ends ascribed to it by Fish in his discussion of the Platonic differentiation between rhetoric and dialectic.[38] All rhetorical persuasion is not necessarily deceptive; or, if it is, the deception is not necessarily damaging or permanent. Bacon, in the *Advancement*, sees it as a means to a particular end (III: 409–10):

The duty and office of Rhetoric is *to apply Reason to Imagination* for the better moving of the will. [...] And therefore as Plato said elegantly, *That virtue, if she could be seen, would move great love and affection*; so seeing that she cannot be shewed to the Sense by corporal shape, the next degree is to shew her to the Imagination in lively representation: for to shew her to Reason only in subtility of argument, was a thing ever derided in Chrysippus and many of the Stoics; who thought to thrust virtue upon men by sharp disputations and conclusions, which have no sympathy with the will of man.[39]

The thought is further refined in the *De Augmentis* (I: 671–72): "Finis denique Rhetoricae phantasiam implere obversationibus et simulachris, quae rationi suppetias ferant, non autem eam opprimant." ["The end of rhetoric is to fill the imagination with manifestations and images, to second reason, not to oppress it." (IV: 456; trn. modified)] Bacon wants rhetoric to induce an appetite in the mind of the audience, to direct the will to move in a particular direction; and he sees that this task may be most easily and efficiently accomplished by methods which at least appear to have "sympathy with the will of man" – i.e. those which make it easier rather than more difficult for the mind to accept the information offered. The *De Augmentis* revision of the passage goes further; it indicates the potential dangers of rhetoric, and warns against abuse of the power that rhetoric confers upon the rhetorician. Educated thought, not thought control, is his stated purpose. However, there seems to be no way to avoid a certain degree of untruth in verbal communication between persons; in the *Novum Organum*, Bacon speaks of the "Idola Fori," the "Idols of the Market-Place," which, he says, are most problematic in this regard (I: 170–71):

At Idola Fori omnium molestissima sunt; quae ex foedere verborum et nominum se insinuarunt in intellectum. Credunt enim homines rationem suam verbis imperare; sed fit etiam ut verba vim suam super intellectum retorqueant et reflectant; quod philosophiam et scientias reddidit sophisticas et inactivas. Verba autem plerunque ex captu vulgi induntur, atque per lineas vulgari intellectui maxime conspicuas res secant. Quum autem intellectus acutior aut observatio diligentior eas lineas transferre velit, ut illae sint magis secundum naturam, verba obstrepunt.

[But the *Idols of the Market-place* are the most troublesome of all: idols which have crept into the understanding through the alliances of words and names. For men believe that their reason governs words; but it is also true that words react on the understanding; and this it is that has rendered philosophy and the sciences sophistical and inactive. Now words, being commonly framed and applied according to the capacity of the vulgar, follow those lines of division which are most obvious to the vulgar understanding. And whenever an understanding of greater acuteness or a more diligent observation would alter those lines to suit the true divisions of nature, words stand in the way and resist the change. (IV: 60–61)].

How, then, is this resistance of words and men's minds to truth to be overcome? It seems that this will be an enormously difficult task. For

Intellectus humanus illis quae simul et subito mentem ferire et subire possunt maxime movetur; a quibus phantasia impleri et inflari consuevit; reliqua vero modo quodam licet imperceptibili, ita se habere fingit et supponit, quomodo se habent pauca illa quibus mens obsidetur; ad illum vero transcursum ad instantias remotas et heterogeneas, per quas axiomata tanquam igne probantur, tardus omnino intellectus est et inhabilis, nisi hoc illi per duras leges et violentum imperium imponatur. (I: 166)

[The human understanding is moved by those things most which strike and enter the mind simultaneously and suddenly, and so fill the imagination; and then it feigns and supposes all other things to be somehow, though it cannot see how, similar to those few things by which it is surrounded. But for that going to and fro to remote and heterogenous instances by which axioms are tried as in the fire, the intellect is altogether slow and unfit, unless it be forced thereto by severe laws and overruling authority. (IV: 56–57)]

In the *Novum Organum*, Bacon seems to think that it is possible, despite the evident persuasive power of rhetoric, to develop such "duras leges," "severe laws," and to apply them in such a way as to constrain the human mind to follow them. In the *Essayes*, however, especially in the later versions, he seems to have adopted a more subtle set of tactics. This is perhaps due to the nature of the matter to be treated; it may also be due to a loss of confidence in the efficacy of brute force in the shaping of a reader's mind. In any event, he seems more willing to swim with the current, as he defines it (and criticizes it) in the *Advancement of Learning* (III: 403–04):

For as knowledges are now delivered, there is a kind of contract of error between the deliverer and the receiver; for he that delivereth knowledge, desireth to deliver it in such form as may be best believed, and not as may be best examined; and he that receiveth knowledge desires rather present satisfaction, than expectant inquiry; and so rather not to doubt, than not to err...[40]

Therefore, while it remains true that in the *Essayes* Bacon is delivering up information to be examined, not to be passively absorbed, he is perfectly willing to enter into a provisional "contract of error" with his audience. In fact, it is essential that the reader be persuaded, at least initially, that the *Essayes* are what they pretend to be (superficial, facile truisms about "civill Businesse"), if Bacon's rhetorical strategy is to succeed. We may see this process of persuasion in action if we return once more, briefly, to the letter to Prince Henry (a letter which, it will be remembered, was replaced with another, more modest one, addressed to Sir John Constable, when the death of Prince Henry rendered the original letter inappropriate). After defining the *Essayes* as "dispersed Meditacions," he insists both on the real-world particularity of those "Meditacions," and on his care in making them palatable to the reader:

And althoughe they handle those things wherein both Mens Lives, and theire pens are most conversant, yet (What I have attained, I knowe not) but I have endeavoured to make them not vulgar; but of a nature, Whereof a Man shall find much in experience, litle in bookes; so as they are neither repetitions, nor fansies. (317)

This peculiarly convoluted passage, with its baffling array of qualifying conjunctions ("... althoughe ... yet ... but ... but ... neither ... nor..."), presents us with a great deal of information, if we have the patience to sort it out. Bacon is saying that the material he will discuss, the ways of the court world, is painfully familiar to every member of his audience, because it has been not only experienced but also written and read about *ad nauseam*. Yet Bacon has tried to make the particulars of his subject "not vulgar," that is, not commonplace, so that the reader will keep reading and not put the book down. His desire to avoid "vulgarity" and "repetitions," though, is meant not only to hold the reader's interest; Bacon is also attempting to render the familiar unfamiliar, so that it may be looked at anew – but without the reader's being aware of it until it is too late. He wishes to lead the reader to the difficult and demanding task of the examination of particulars through persuading him that he is doing the opposite. Rhetorical persuasion is a means to an end; Bacon will deceive his reader temporarily, if there is no other way to undeceive that reader permanently. Beneath any disguise, Bacon's method and ultimate goal remain the same (I: 162):

Restat vero nobis modus tradendi unus et simplex, ut homines ad ipsa particularia et eorum series et ordines adducamus; et ut illi rursus imperent sibi ad tempus abnegationem Notionum, et cum rebus ipsis consuescere incipiant.

[One method of delivery alone remains to us which is simply this: We must lead men to the particulars themselves, and their series and order; while men on their side must force themselves for a while to lay their notions by and begin to familiarize themselves with facts. (IV: 53)]

Bacon's apparent glibness and superficiality are therefore only apparent; his aphorisms persuade easily, the better to lead the unwary reader to the precipice of contradiction and shove him off. These "dispersed Meditacions," the *Essayes*, are intended not as neat, easily assimilable packages of knowledge, handy hints to be memorized and applied to whatever situations happen to arise, but rather as points of resistance, whose density and disjunction will inspire (if not force) their reader to go beyond the easy and obvious and to confront the particulars of human interaction in all their nakedness.

Bacon leads off the *Essayes* proper with a piece whose title ("Of Truth"), at least, would lead us to believe that it is a kind of statement of method and purpose, intended to set the tone for the rest of the collection. The title also seems to hint that the *Essayes* may be linked with Bacon's other works in his great project of The Search For Truth. Both the essay's position at the beginning of the book and the fact that it appears for the first time in the 1625 edition seem to indicate that one might read it as a kind of anticipatory commentary upon what will follow. However, when we turn to "Of Truth," we discover that it delivers a somewhat more ambiguous message. Where the reader might expect an authoritative, direct opening sentence of the form "Truth is...," followed by a series of defining statements, he finds instead a quoted question (7): "*What is Truth*; said jesting *Pilate*; And would not stay for an Answer." Nor does Bacon stay for an answer, and we are left wondering whether he is condemning Pilate's irreverence, or jesting along with Pilate at our expense. After indulging himself in a cheap pun aimed at the Skeptics, he goes on to talk at some length about truth's opposite number. Speaking in language that echoes that of the *Novum Organum* and the *De Augmentis*, he says,

But it is not onely the Difficultie, and Labour, which Men take in finding out of *Truth*; Nor againe, that when it is found, it imposeth upon mens Thoughts; that doth bring *Lies* in favour: But a naturall, though corrupt Love, of the *Lie* it selfe. (7)

He goes on to explain the peculiar attraction the lie holds for the human mind:

This same *Truth*, is a Naked, and Open day light, that doth not shew, the Masques, and Mummeries, and Triumphs of the world, halfe so Stately, and daintily, as Candlelights. *Truth* may perhaps come to the price of a Pearle, that sheweth best by day: But it will not rise, to the price of a Diamond, or Carbuncle, that sheweth best in varied lights. A mixture of a *Lie* doth ever adde Pleasure. (7)

In the *Novum Organum*, Bacon claims that the susceptibility of the human mind to false systems of thought, combined with the duplicity of language, places barriers in the path of the seeker of philosophical truth; here, he discusses the same problem as it applies to the realm of human society. If the scholar is befuddled by the false Idols of the Theatre, "fabulas productas et actas ... quae mundos effecerunt fictitios et scenicos" ["stage plays, representing worlds of their own creation after an unreal and scenic fashion"], so too may the courtier be led astray by the pleasures of untruth, fooled by "the Masques, and Mummeries, and Triumphs of the world," which nevertheless cannot stand up to the harsh light of Truth. Obviously, Bacon is not speaking only of those court performances that are literally theatre; nor is he simply putting forth a vague metaphor for all human interaction, although both of these elements are present in his formulation. The image focuses at the point at which the literal and figurative meanings intersect: the "stage plays" of the court world are the entire range of courtly behavior. All interaction at court is a performance, one which gives pleasure to the beholder, but which nevertheless is a lie.

Bacon does not, however, go on to condemn the pernicious influence of this duplicity in civil affairs; his crusade to eradicate error from philosophy does not extend to the realm of social interaction. To be sure, the entire middle section of the essay is devoted to demonstrating (8) that truth "is the Soveraigne Good of humane Nature"; but this demonstration, couched as it is in language borrowed now from the Bible, now from Lucretius, seems to have little to do with everyday reality, or indeed with the rest of the essay. It is all very well to love truth, he says with a hint of irony (8): "Certainly, it is Heaven upon Earth, to have a Mans Minde Move in Charitie, Rest in Providence, and Turne upon the Poles of *Truth*." In the real world, however, things are different. Bacon abruptly shifts from this Ptolemaic vision of a truth-centered universe to a new paragraph, which rather chillingly begins: "To passe from Theologicall, and Philosophicall *Truth*, to the *Truth* of civill Businesse..." Clearly divine truth and human truth are two different things; there is no question here of the Divine Mind being mirrored in the doings of men. In the realm of "civill Businesse," utility rather than veracity is the overriding concern. To be sure, part of truth's lack of appeal is linked to the "pleasure" (read: safety) offered by the lie; after all, if people were forced to regard themselves and their fellows in that "Naked, and Open day light" of truth, says Bacon, imagine the consequences (7):

Doth any man doubt, that if there were taken out of Mens Mindes, Vaine Opinions, Flattering Hopes, False valuations, Imaginations as one would, and the like; but it would leave the Mindes, of a Number of Men, poore shrunken Things; full of Melancholy, and Indisposition, and unpleasing to themselves?[41]

Therefore, in order for people to feel happy and go about their business, they must be permitted a certain amount of leeway; in other words, they must be allowed to fool themselves, to be taken in by their own vanity. Presented in this way, it seems harmless enough. He continues (7): "One of the Fathers, in great Severity, called Poesie, *Vinum Daemonum*; because it filleth the Imagination, and yet it is, but with the shadow of a *Lie*."[42] This recalls his earlier remark in the *Novum Organum*, cited above, in which he decries the fact that the "human understanding is moved by those things most which strike and enter the mind simultaneously and suddenly, and so fill the imagination"; it also suggests once again that Bacon's attitude towards such linguistic prestidigitation is perhaps not as severe as that of the ill-humored Church Father in question. Bacon sees the language-based "contract of error" on which human interaction depends as noxious, but also as necessary; indeed, he even seems willing to exculpate that great producer of falsehoods, language, insofar as it acts merely to generate pleasure in human affairs.[43]

However, as Bacon begins his discussion of the role of truth, and untruth, in civil society, we see a more sinister note emerge. He moves beyond an apparently almost harmless aesthetic pleasure in falsehood, and also leaves behind the similar, if slightly more dangerous, indolent comfort of deceptive oversimplification in matters philosophical. The Lie is useful not merely because it keeps people from having to face uncomfortable truths; there is something more powerful, and more unpleasant, about it (8):

> To passe from Theologicall, and Philosophicall *Truth*, to the *Truth* of civill Businesse; It will be acknowledged, even by those, that practize it not, that cleare and Round dealing, is the Honour of Mans Nature; And that Mixture of Falshood, is like Allay in Coyne of Gold and Silver; which may make the Metall worke the better, but it embaseth it. For these winding, and crooked courses, are the Goings of the Serpent; which goeth basely upon the belly, and not upon the Feet. There is no Vice, that doth so cover a Man with Shame, as to be found false, and perfidious.

We now find ourselves in the domain of *Realpolitik* pioneered by Bacon's mentor Machiavelli. Bacon may seem at first glance to be advocating the application of the principles of his "Heaven upon Earth" to everyday reality; but a closer reading shows us that the opposite is true. "[C]leare and Round dealing" may indeed be "the Honour of Mans Nature," and it costs nothing to acknowledge the idea – so long as one is not constrained to "practize" such an irrelevant and useless precept. (The very word "practize" is in this context oxymoronic. Furthermore, as we shall see, Baconian "Honour" is a concept more dependent upon opinion and the perception of others than upon any ideas of interior virtue. Therefore, the apparent praise which Bacon here bestows upon "cleare and Round dealing" is somewhat less substantial than it initially seems.) The currency of "civill Businesse" is an impure one, and it is that impurity which renders possible not only coinage but also circulation. These "winding, and crooked courses" may be base, but they are nonetheless unavoidable. Bacon justifies intimate practical knowledge of "the Goings of the Serpent," showing that such knowledge is both desirable and necessary, in the *Advancement of Learning* (III: 430–31):

For it is not possible to join serpentine wisdom with the columbine innocence, except men know exactly all the conditions of the serpent; his baseness and going upon his belly, his volubility and lubricity, his envy and sting, and the rest; that is, all forms and natures of evil. For without this, virtue is open and unfenced. Nay, an honest man can do no good upon those that are wicked, to reclaim them, without the help of the knowledge of evil.[44]

Straightforward virtue unalloyed with at least a thorough working knowledge of vice is not only ineffectual and impractical; it may actually be dangerous. Hence, even if one's only goal is to reform the world and lead it to the path of virtue, it is still necessary to be able to lie and cheat with the worst of them (to use "that Mixture of Falshood ... like Allay in Coyne of Gold and Silver; which may make the Metall worke the better..."), should the occasion call for it. Bacon does point out that untruthfulness carries with it negative repercussions; but what counts is not the evil itself, but rather the appearance of evil. To be a liar may or may not be a bad thing, but in this context it is almost irrelevant. What is really unacceptable is "to be *found* false, and perfidious" [emphasis mine], and the dire consequences of such a discovery take the form not of religious or moral anathema, nor even of legal punishment, but rather of shame in the eyes of one's fellows.

In the court society of which Bacon is writing, this kind of public mortification is the worst possible fate, because one's existence is based on, and defined by, the perceptions of others; if those perceptions are in some way disrupted, one ceases to exist. To be more specific: Bacon posits that social intercourse functions according to rules similar to those he lays down for rhetoric, that is to say through the purveying of pleasing falsehoods or pseudo-truths in order to persuade one's interlocutor.[45] The Lie, as the pleasure-producing agent, the sugar-coating that makes the world palatable, is the fundamental currency of social intercourse. Therefore, society functions smoothly only so long as that currency is accepted by all as valid. Should its validity be called into question, the stability, if not the very existence, of the society itself is jeopardized; and this is precisely what happens when one of the members of the society is unmasked as a liar, a purveyor of false currency, a counterfeiter. This person poses a threat precisely because he is of course no more a liar than anyone else – and thus it is not his personal veracity that is really at stake, but rather the integrity of the entire lie-based social fabric. Hence, in order to prevent a run on the social bank, anyone who is thus unmasked must be excised from society.

We may explore the further ramifications of this phenomenon by switching Baconian metaphors, moving from the economic back to the theatrical. We have already seen how Bacon adapts the commonplace equation of the court with a theatre. The unmasking of the courtly performer as a liar, then, may be seen as the failure of that person's performance to convince and to persuade. The mask has slipped, revealing (at best) a discrepancy between the mask and what lies behind it. The result is a literal loss of face; one's identity – one's courtly persona, as defined by the collective regard of the other members of the court – simply evaporates. One of Bacon's principal preoccupations in the *Essayes*, then, will be to discover how to go about saving face – that is, how to sustain a convincing and persuasive perform- ance in the theatre of the court. One of the most detailed treatments of the problem, in which Bacon's attention is closely focused on social perform- ance in the arena of the Jacobean court, is to be found in the sixth essay of the 1625 edition, "Of Simulation *And* Dissimulation." Fish's discussion of this essay shows how Bacon repeatedly sets up seemingly moral poses, often (as in the opening of the essay) expressed in ringing *sententiae*, only to undermine them immediately.[46] But Fish's reading, for all its strength, nevertheless seems to presume perhaps too much of an obsessively linear, insect-like consciousness on the part of his hypothetical reader. Moreover, Fish's emphasis on Bacon's self-cancelling rhetoric seems to leave that reader with little or nothing after having read the essay. I hope to show that this tension between rhetorical pose and quasi-practical message, rather than simply neutralizing whatever content might be present in the essay, augments that content through enacting it, ultimately sharpening its effect upon the reader. The beginning of the essay is vintage Bacon:

Dissimulation is but a faint kind of Policy, or Wisdome; For it asketh a strong Wit, and a strong Heart, to know, when to tell Truth, and to doe it. Therfore it is the weaker Sort of Politicks, that are the great Dissemblers. (20)

Read carelessly, this sounds as though Bacon is repudiating dissimulation as a practice unworthy of the wise and politic man; but when we look at what those strong persons who eschew dissimulation are supposed to do instead, we notice that their "Policy, or Wisdome" consists merely in the adept and selective manipulation of information. "Cleare and Round dealing" is not their defining characteristic; rather, it is only one weapon in the arsenal of the politic courtier. As to "the weaker Sort of Politicks," they turn out, in the next paragraph, to be nearly everyone.

These Properties of *Arts* or *Policy*, and *Dissimulation* or *Closenesse*, are indeed Habits and Faculties, severall, and to be distinguished. For if a Man, have that Penetration of Judgment, as he can discerne, what things are to be laid open, and what to be secretted, and what to be shewed at Half lights, and to whom, and when, (which indeed are Arts of State, and Arts of life, as *Tacitus* calleth them) to him, A Habit of *Dissimulation*, is a Hinderance, and a Poorenesse. But if a Man cannot obtaine to that Judgment, then it is left to him, generally, to be Close, and a *Dissembler*. For where a Man cannot choose, or vary in Particulars, there it is good to take the safest and wariest Way in generall; Like the Going softly by one that cannot well see. (20)

Clearly, mastering these Tacitean "Arts of State, and Arts of life" is a tall order, and those capable of doing so are few and far between. However, as the present essay makes clear, such omniscience is not given to mere mortals; we are all like the "one that cannot well see," and must therefore learn to dissemble. Besides, even the wisest and cleverest are not so much morally superior as they are merely better at persuading others of that superiority, specious though it may be:

Certainly the ablest Men, that ever were, have had all an Opennesse, and Francknesse of dealing; And a name of Certainty, and Veracity; But then they were like Horses, well mannaged; For they could tell passing well, when to stop, or turne: And at such times, when they thought the Case indeed, required *Dissimulation*, if they then used it, it came to passe, that the former Opinion, spred abroad of their good Faith, and Clearnesse of dealing, made them almost Invisible. (20)

It is not veracity, but the name and reputation thereof, that leads to worldly success. The successful courtier or statesman is one who, through training and practice, is able to dissimulate while persuading his audience that he is doing the opposite; hiding behind a mask of good opinion, the courtier's true visage becomes "almost Invisible." Bacon here implements one of his standard procedures for dealing with potentially troublesome ethical questions as they apply to the real world: First, he locates the ideal of moral perfection beyond human capacity and outside of the human world, thereby making that ideal irrelevant; and second, he demonstrates that even those humans that seem to have achieved moral or ethical superiority are merely more adept than the rest of us at prevarication and chicanery. Having thus debunked any impractical notions of so-called ethical behavior, Bacon can turn to the real business at hand, that of supplying "helps" to the reader desirous of making his way in the treacherous world of human affairs.[47]

Bacon's method of getting to this point is revealing. We have seen how he begins with an arrangement of *sententiae* whose meanings, whether taken singly or collectively, prove to be the opposite of what the reader initially expects. He uses the attention-grabbing (and assent-commanding) power of the aphorism to start the reader moving in a particular direction, but that direction turns out to be the wrong one; the real goals are elsewhere. This process of persuasive deception is presented as the matter of the essay while it is enacted in the essay's rhetoric; Bacon means for the reader to read both the mask ("dissimulation is reprehensible and a sign of weakness") and the face (or mask) behind it ("dissimulation is necessary and unavoidable"), and to experience the tension between them. I do not think that this tension neutralizes whatever message or content a given essay might claim to deliver; rather, the ultimate result for the reader is (or should be) something slightly different: a global, synchronic view of the whole, in which the movement of pretense and the movement of grim practical reality are simultaneously present in a state of permanent but dynamic suspension. The experience of this tension should, first of all, render the reader wary of simple answers; second, thus enlightened, Bacon's reader ought to be able to grasp another important point: the critical necessity of adaptability. Just as the rhetoric of a text must be controlled so as best to persuade the reader, so too must one's behaviors be adapted to the specifics of the situation and the persons at hand. Viewed in this light, apparently contradictory utterances or visages presented to one's interlocutors or audience need not be seen as mutually exclusive, nor is it necessary that one be "true" and the other "false"; rather, each is completely valid, given the appropriate situation, and the reader's job is to learn how to decide what is proper to a given set of circumstances, literary or social.

Once armed with this discipline, the reader is prepared to absorb more concrete particulars on the problems of simulation and dissimulation, and Bacon is free to discuss those problems unencumbered either by naïve ethical misconceptions or by naïve readers. He makes what may be over-nice distinctions among the various types of self-concealing activity (21):

There be three degrees, of this Hiding, and Vailing of a Mans Selfe. The first *Closenesse, Reservation,* and *Secrecy;* when a Man leaveth himselfe without Observation, or without Hold to be taken, what he is. The second *Dissimulation,* in the *Negative;* when a man lets fall Signes, and arguments, that he is not, that he is. And the third *Simulation,* in the Affirmative; when a Man industriously, and expressly, faigns, and pretends to be, that he is not.[48]

Regarding the first category, secrecy, Bacon remarks that

...assuredly, the *Secret* Man, heareth many Confessions; For who will open himselfe, to a Blab or a Babler? But if a man be thought *Secret,* it inviteth Discoverie; As the more Close Aire, sucketh in the more Open... (21)

This is a crucial point. Ultimately, Bacon means for the reader to become adept in two related areas: (1) reading through the masks presented to him by those around him, discerning what lies behind them and what the true motivations of their owners are; and (2) manipulating his own mask or masks in such a way as to deceive (or persuade; it amounts to the same thing) his audience, manipulating his interlocutors to his ends while preventing them from reading behind those masks. Here Bacon links together both of these practices in a single movement; the veiling of one's self leads to the self-unveiling of others. The degree to which one is able to discover the true visages of others is directly proportional to the degree to which one is able to conceal one's own.[49] He goes on to justify this secrecy, somewhat sheepishly, on aesthetic grounds; but the language in which he does so, echoing passages we have examined above, reminds us that the aesthetic in question is one of utility, where pleasure serves the interests of persuasion.

Besides (to say Truth) *Nakednesse* is uncomely, as well in Minde, as body; and it addeth no small Reverence, to Mens Manners, and Actions, if they be not altogether Open. As for Talkers and Futile Persons, they are commonly Vaine, and Credulous withall. For He that talketh, what he knoweth, will also talke, what he knoweth not. Therfore set it downe; *That an Habit of Secrecy, is both Politick, and Morall.* And in this Part, it is good, that a Mans Face, give his Tongue, leave to Speake. For the Discovery, of a Mans Selfe, by the Tracts of his Countenance, is a great Weaknesse, and Betraying; By how much, it is many times, more marked and beleeved, then a Mans words. (21)

Despite Bacon's seemingly rigorous and logical construction, it is difficult to understand his justification of "*an Habit of Secrecy*"[50] as "*Morall*"; it is, however, easy to see how he construes such behavior/garb as "*Politick*," especially since – as he points out – behavior is less likely to be disbelieved, and is therefore more persuasive, than speech. The essential factor, for the Baconian man, is that adroit manipulation of *externalia* confers great freedom to maneuver. In this regard, essay LII, "Of Ceremonies and Respects," is worth a brief detour, as it emphasizes a crucial element in that manipulation of masks, namely Castiglione's *sprezzatura*: appearing as though one's actions and manners are natural, even and especially when they are most studied and artificial. It opens with yet another iteration of the jewel motif we encountered at the beginning of "Of Truth," reemphasizing that, as naked human nature is too unpleasant to behold, it needs to be dressed up somehow if social commerce is to become possible.[51] Bacon goes on to point out both that formal, even artificial behaviors are necessary to one's social existence, and that inept, over-studied manners can be more revealing and therefore dangerous than no pretense at all (157–58):

Therefore it doth much adde, to a Mans Reputation, and is, (as Queene *Isabella* said) *Like perpetuall Letters Commendatory*, to have good *Formes*. To Attaine them, it almost sufficeth, not to despise them: For so shall a Man observe them in Others: And let him trust himselfe with the rest. For if he Labour too much to Expresse them, he shall lose their Grace; Which is to be Naturall and Unaffected. Some Mens Behaviour, is like a Verse, wherein every Syllable is Measured: How can a man comprehend great Matters, that breaketh his Minde too much to small Observations?[52]

There is a strange double movement here; the courtier is advised not to "despise" (*sprezzare*) good manners, but in so doing he must nevertheless appear to be doing exactly the opposite. Nothing is more inimical to the successful carrying off of correct behavior than the appearance of effort, of showing an active interest in "good *Formes*," so Bacon's reader must simultaneously despise and not despise them. What counts is the external effect; what goes on internally is, so long as it is unobservable, irrelevant. (One might also see this passage as a self-conscious comment upon the aesthetic technique of the *Essayes* themselves. Each essay, like the aphorisms of which it is constructed, is carefully orchestrated and "Measured," but Bacon continually strives to persuade the reader that the opposite is the case, and – as an examination of critical responses to the *Essayes* shows – he has largely succeeded.) The essay continues with a discussion of how one's manners are to be adjusted according to the particular persons with whom one has to deal, with one's own advantage as the governing principle. Bacon makes no show here of advising his reader to act in accordance with any "inner self" which might be lurking behind the masks (still less does he bother with moral abstractions); such considerations are irrelevant. The final sentence sums it up (159): "Mens Behaviour should be like their Apparell, not too Strait, or point Device, but Free for Exercise or Motion."[53] Behavior, like clothing, is socially necessary, but bears no essential relation to the wearer; one may change one's persona as easily as one changes one's doublet.

If this is true, then it begins to look as though all behavior is a kind of deception, in that no one set of actions is any more or less "true" or authentic than any other. To a reader already imbued with the spirit of adaptability, this will hardly come as a surprise; but Bacon seems still to be wrestling with this problem when, in "Of Simulation *And* Dissimulation," he seems unable to establish clear distinctions between his three kinds of behavioral prevarication. Having discussed the necessity of secrecy, he goes on to show how it inevitably entails a certain degree of dissimulation (21–22):

For the Second, which is *Dissimulation*. It followeth many times upon *Secrecy*, by a necessity: So that, he that will be *Secret*, must be a *Dissembler*, in some degree. [...]

So that no man can be *secret*, except he give himselfe a little Scope of *Dissimulation*; which is, as it were, but the Skirts or Traine of *Secrecy*.

Once again, he speaks in terms of behavior as a garment which, properly tailored, gives one sufficient room to operate. He continues:

But for the third Degree, which is *Simulation*, and false Profession; That I hold more culpable, and lesse politicke; except it be in great and rare Matters.

Here, in a typically Baconian maneuver, he pretends to deplore outright lying (which is nevertheless difficult to distinguish from "dissimulation" as he defines it in the passage quoted earlier) as a reprehensible action, but then undermines that moral pose by also mentioning that simulation is less politic – and finally demolishes any pretense whatsoever of ethical anxiety with his *caveat*, "except it be in great and rare matters." In other words, express falsehood is a perfectly acceptable tactic, given the appropriate situation. It is to be avoided not because it is more wicked but because it is more dangerous; there is a greater risk of getting caught. Those that most often resort to simulation are not the most iniquitous; they are merely the most inept, insufficiently clever to get by with the subtler strategies of secrecy and dissimulation. He goes on to explain, in terms we have already begun to approach, that

The great *Advantages* of *Simulation* and *Dissimulation* are three. First to lay asleepe Opposition, and to Surprize. For where a Mans Intentions, are published, it is an Alarum, to call up, all that are against them. The second is, to reserve to a Mans Selfe, a faire Retreat: For if a man engage himselfe, by a manifest Declaration, he must goe through, or take a Fall. The third is, the better to discover the Minde of another. (22)

Again, efficiency in attaining one's ends and safety for oneself while doing so are paramount, along with the emphasis on reading others while avoiding being read oneself. He counterbalances these three advantages with three "*Disadvantages*, to set it even"; but it seems as if this neat symmetry is there only for the sake of making the structure of the essay more tidy. Indeed, the first two objections[54] seem rather feeble, and Bacon makes little or nothing of them; and when he arrives at the third, which he asserts is more substantial (as in fact it seems to be), he simply leaves it hanging, moving directly from it to the aphoristic closing sentence of the essay (22):

The third, and greatest is, that it depriveth a Man, of one of the most principall Instruments for Action; which is *Trust* and *Beleefe*. The best Composition, and Temperature is, to have *Opennesse* in Fame and Opinion; *Secrecy* in Habit; *Dissimulation* in seasonable use; And a Power to faigne, if there be no Remedy.

Examined more closely, the juxtaposition of these two sentences neutralizes the first of them, or at least makes its moral message more ambiguous.

Granted, it is useful, if not essential, to have the *"Trust* and *Beleefe"* of others in order to attain one's worldly ends, but is not such trust generated and guaranteed by the very *"Opennesse* in Fame and Opinion" in which this essay teaches its reader to cloak himself? And if this is true, then simulation and dissimulation (if properly employed), far from depriving the Baconian man of the instrument of trust, serve rather to ensure its availability to him.

The final sentence of the essay has other, more ominous consequences as well. The "Composition" it proposes of the social man is peculiar in that it has no interior. "Fame and Opinion" are, by definition, external attributes; and the other three categories are also masks or disguises, surfaces to present to the outer world. The presence of a disguise naturally implies that there is something behind it to be kept hidden, but that something always seems here to be absent, or at best negatively defined. Nowhere in the essay is there any question of a conflict or even a discrepancy between the inner self and the outer shell; the focus is exclusively on the latter. Moreover, this emphasis on the external, to the point of a virtual elimination of any question of an internal self, is not restricted to this essay alone; it is in fact a dominant theme of the entire collection.[55] Bacon seems to conceive of the self, particularly the noble or courtly self, as an array of masks or exterior shells, carefully orchestrated to please and thereby persuade the self's various audiences, and which conceal an ultimately irrelevant – if not nonexistent – interior. That this is the case may be seen if we turn, briefly, to a consideration of some of the other essays which amplify Bacon's ideas on the externality of selfhood, and finally to a reading of the essay that, almost alone of all the collection, actually raises the question of the "inner self": essay XXVII, "Of Frendship."

It is worth recalling here that Bacon's subjects and audience (members of a particular class of persons resembling himself: ambitious actual or would-be office-holders and statesmen, courtiers in the orbit of Elizabeth and James), about and for whom he writes, are not actually part of the so-called "old nobility," persons whose claim to a court position is based upon heredity and *de facto* historical presence at the court. On the contrary, the Baconian Man is what Bacon himself calls the "New Man," someone who is not automatically entitled to high station by birth and must therefore find other means to attain such a position; and Bacon's concern in the *Essayes* is to discover those means to his audience of presumed "New Men."[56] His particular examples thereof, drawn from observations of "civill Businesse," find their way back to particulars again in several essays such as "Of Envy," "Of Great Place," "Of Nobility," "Of Counsell," "Of Cunning," and so on. Here, he reiterates and refines many of the ideas we have already discussed, giving particular points new color through what seem to be case-specific applications. On closer examination, these refinements often turn out to be just clever aphoristic repackagings – which, however, in Bacon's universe, *are* case-specific applications after all, given what we have described as the priority he assigns in his writing to effective rhetorical presentation. Recall that this priority is the same as the emphasis he places on persuasive self-presentation in the substantial realm of politics and the court; each activity parallels and (re)enacts the other. Even when Bacon is discussing a concrete problem of court life, he is less interested in offering sage (or specific) advice on how to deal wisely, justly, or even practically with the substance of particular situations than in how one should appear while doing it.

Nowhere is this more true than when Bacon discusses the intimately connected concepts of power and nobility. For Bacon, as for so many other Renaissance minds, these two entities exist in a kind of paradoxical interdependence; each implies and necessitates the other, but in such a way that each is the necessary precondition of the other. To be noble is (by definition – at least according to the official line) to have political power, and perhaps even more true (in a practical sense) is this rule's corollary: that it is impossible to have power in the court without the status of nobility. At the same time, it seems impossible, for those not favored by accident of birth, to achieve noble status without first exercising considerable power to get there. The goal of the "New Man" is therefore a complex one: on the one hand, to gain and wield political power in the court; on the other hand, to create a persona (of nobility, of course) for himself such that he (1) appears naturally to deserve his desired position and (2) appears to have occupied that position always, and never to have held any status inferior to that to which he aspires. Hence the necessity of effective persuasion, which we have already discussed, and the equal necessity of a correspondingly effective concealment of one's true[57] status and motives.

Given this double impulse, then, it will be instructive to examine just how Bacon defines "nobility," and further how he proposes that the "New Man" arrive at a status which by definition is theoretically unattainable to those not already possessed of it. In essay XIV, "Of Nobility," he discusses nobility (41) "first as a *Portion* of an *Estate*"; without defining what he means by the term "nobility," he makes some remarks along Machiavellian lines regarding the place and utility of the nobility as a class in the composition of a state. He then goes on to discuss nobility as applied to the condition of individuals:

As for *Nobility* in *Particular Persons*; It is a Reverend Thing, to see an Ancient Castle, or Building not in decay; Or to see a faire Timber Tree, sound and perfect: How much more, to behold an Ancient *Noble Family*, which hath stood against the Waves and weathers of time. (42)

The sight (once again, Bacon relies on the language of the visual) of an Ancient Family inspires in the beholder a kind of aesthetic respect. He continues by contrasting the old with the new: "For new *Nobility* is but the Act of Power; But Ancient *Nobility* is the Act of Time." This sentence is apparently meant to show the intrinsic superiority of "Ancient *Nobility*," but, despite its utterly conventional sound, it does so in a subtly underhanded way; if Old Nobility is created by and in time, then it has a beginning, a point in time earlier than which it did not exist. Now, what is supposedly reverend about Old Nobility is that it seems always to have existed, not merely that it began earlier than its competitors; therefore, to assert, however faintly, that it is in this way contingent seems to reduce the main distinction between Old and New from a qualitative level to a quantitative one. So Bacon may perhaps be seen here as beginning to nudge Old Nobility off its pedestal of absolute superiority to the New.

Or he may not; this sentence alone is not enough to force the reader in that direction, and we may feel that we are simply reading a conventional apologia for the natural superiority of the old aristocracy. However, if we read on, we find that the nudge has become a shove, radically destabilizing the idea of Old Nobility, which now seems ready to topple from its pedestal:

Those that are first raised to *Nobility*, are commonly more Vertuous, but lesse Innocent, then their Descendants: for there is, rarely, any Rising, but by a Commixture, of good and evill Arts.[58]

Here is confirmation that Nobility, New or Old, does not exist in some sort of timeless eternity, but has a starting point in time. Moreover, not only do all strains of nobility start somewhere, but it seems that they arise from impure roots. Bacon's use of the word "Vertuous" is here diabolically double-edged. The first part of the sentence may lead us to believe that he is merely repeating and reinforcing the familiar line that those who are ennobled deserve it because of their inherent superiority in a kind of *moral* (even Christian) virtue; but the remark that they are "lesse Innocent" ruthlessly undercuts this notion. We now realize that moral virtue is, in this case, only a smokescreen; the real "virtue" in question is more like *virtù* in the Machiavellian sense. What counts is not some abstract moral superiority, but rather superiority in the ability efficiently to advance one's own ends by whatever means available, not excluding outright villainy. The idea that nobles are intrinsically "better" than the rest of humanity begins here to look a little shaky; Bacon hints that they may, if anything, be worse. He continues: "But it is Reason, the Memory of their vertues, remaine to their Posterity; and their Faults die with themselves."[59] Note first that it is "the Memory of their vertues," and not the virtues themselves (dubious though they may be) that are passed on to the descendants of the founders of a noble line; so it seems that, despite the institutionalized belief to the contrary, heredity alone is not enough to ensure even that one is as "Vertuous" as one's noble forebears. Moreover, this sentence puts in a new light Bacon's earlier remark that "... Ancient *Nobility* is the Act of Time." Apparently Time's real function in the creation of Old Nobility is to erase the memory of its base origins.

Having thus demolished standard notions of hereditary Old Nobility, all the while pretending to do the opposite, Bacon returns to the comparison between the Old and the New: "*Nobility* of *Birth*, commonly abateth Industry: And he that is not industrious, envieth him, that is." In other words, the Old Nobility is not only degenerate but slothful, and thus is both genetically and practically inferior to – who else? – the New Nobility, the "New Men," people like Bacon himself: zealous, energetic, and laying claim only to those "virtues" they themselves actually possess. It is nevertheless true that envy is a more complex phenomenon than this sentence indicates, as Bacon continues: "Besides, *Noble Persons*, cannot goe much higher; And he that standeth at a stay, when others rise, can hardly avoid Motions of Envy." Why is this true? In essay IX, "Of Envy," he explains (28):

Men of Noble birth, are noted, to be *envious* towards New Men, when they rise. For the distance is altered; And it is like a deceipt of the Eye, that when others come on, they thinke themselves goe backe.[60]

This seemingly self-evident observation carries considerable importance. Bacon's choice of another visual simile is not happenstance. Given Bacon's conception, already demonstrated, of the world of human interaction as dependent solely and entirely upon the perceptions of others, without any relation or connection whatsoever to some reality or truth lying beyond those perceptions, it follows naturally that the essence of nobility resides not in some quality intrinsic to the subject, but rather in the perceived relative distance between subject and object. The optical illusion that gives rise to envy in the mind of the noble beholder is no illusion. It is the truth; there is no other. We will have more to say about the significance of Bacon's visual language in a moment; but let us first return to "Of Nobility." After his remark on the sloth of those that are born noble, Bacon continues, rather cryptically: "On the other side, *Nobility* extinguisheth the passive Envy, from others towards them; Because they are in possession of Honour." It is initially unclear how the "possession of Honour" might preclude the possibility of envy; but this curious remark becomes less obscure when we connect it to the opening paragraph of essay LV, "Of Honour and Reputation":

The Winning of *Honour*, is but the revealing of a Mans Vertue and Worth, without Disadvantage. For some in their Actions, do Wooe and affect *Honour*, and *Reputation*: Which Sort of Men, are commonly much Talked of, but inwardly little Admired. And some, contrariwise, darken their Vertue, in the Shew of it; So as they be under-valued in opinion. If a Man performe that which hath not been attempted before; Or attempted and given over; Or hath beene atchieved, but not with so good Circumstance; he shall purchase more *Honour*, then by Effecting a Matter of greater Difficulty, or Vertue, wherein he is but a Follower. If a Man so temper his Actions, as in some one of them, hee doth content everie Faction, or Combination of People, the Musicke will bee the fuller. A man is an ill Husband of his *Honour*, that entreth into any Action, the Failing wherein may disgrace him more, then the Carying of it through can *Honor* him. *Honour*, that is gained and broken upon Another, hath the quickest Reflection; Like Diamonds cut with Fascets. And therefore, let a Man contend, to excell any Competitors of his in *Honour*, in Outshooting them, if he can, in their owne Bowe. Discreet Followers and Servants helpe much to *Reputation*: *Omnis Fama à Domesticis emanat*. Envy, which is the Canker of *Honour*, is best extinguished, by declaring a Mans Selfe, in his Ends, rather to seeke Merit, then Fame: And by attributing a Mans Successes, rather to divine Providence and Felicity, then to his owne Vertue or Policy. (163–64)

Honor is here defined not as something due to a person based on his natural deserts, but rather as a perception induced in one's audience by adroit self-presentation, which must above all be accomplished "without Disadvantage." Furthermore, it is as this sort of effective persuasion that honor helps to neutralize "the passive Envy" referred to in the sentence just quoted from "Of Nobility."[61] The essay "Of Nobility" concludes by saying:

Certainly Kings, that have Able men of their *Nobility*, shall finde ease in imploying them; And a better Slide into their Businesse: For People naturally bend to them, as borne in some sort to Command.

This final remark on the utility of the nobility to the Crown, like the sentences that precede it, seems ultimately to undermine the proposition it initially appears to advance. The nobility are effective in implementing the will of their King not because they are in fact worthy of being obeyed; Bacon does not say "...*because* they are borne to Command," or "...*for* they are borne to Command," but rather "...*as* borne *in some sort* to Command." In other words, "as if" or "as though," rather than "because"; and the clause is further weakened by the vague qualifying phrase "in some sort." What makes the nobility useful instruments of royal will, then, is not any quality they themselves possess, but rather the perception of the "People" that the nobility ought to be obeyed.

We see, finally, that we have come a long way from the "Reverend Thing" that Ancient Nobility was supposed to be. While supposedly attempting to support that traditional notion, Bacon has in fact demonstrated the opposite. In his revisionist view, Old Nobility is: (1) finite and contingent; (2) tainted with baseness and villainy; (3) inferior, both genetically and practically, to New Nobility, and (4) false and hollow anyway. Now, Old Nobility having been thus hurled from its pedestal, the question arises: Where does this leave the "New Man"? Given that the purpose of the "New Man" is to gain and hold power in the court, it would seem that he stands in a position of considerable advantage relative to his Old-Nobility competitiors, or at least has weapons with which to offset the traditional prerogatives of the latter group. His awareness (no doubt gained through a careful reading of the *Essayes*) that the traditional notion of Nobility is empty and illusive liberates him from dependence upon such chimeras. Coupled with the knowledge, set forth in the sentence concluding "Of Nobility," that it is honor or the *appearance* of "nobility" (whatever that now means) that carries with it real power, he is then free to use that appearance as another mask to gain his ends. It would not perhaps be too strong to say that Bacon conceives of Nobility purely as the exercise of the art of seeming (what one is not);[62] indeed, he appears to define it as *the* category of human life in which this activity is paramount. If this is so, then who is better suited to participate in this activity than Bacon's "New Man"?

This leap into the void is not without its dangers. If, as Bacon seems to be asserting, the field of human interaction is dominated, or even defined, by the activities of Simulation and Dissimulation, and if in this realm there are no absolute intrinsic truths (or at least none that are relevant to the quest for and exercise of power), then in some sense everything is permitted; and thus the "New Man," the aspirant to political power and Great Place, finds himself endowed with tremendous liberty of action. In a world where truth is what you persuade others it is, the key to success is, as we have seen, the aptitude and flexibility to adapt one's personæ to the random fluctuations of one's surroundings and audience. The ability to persuade confers enormous power; for, as Bacon remarks in "Of Vaine-Glory" (161), "... it often falls out, that *Somewhat* is produced of *Nothing*: For Lies are sufficient to breed Opinion, and Opinion brings on substance." Opinion, in the Baconian world, is Truth; and he who controls opinion therefore controls his destiny.[63] However, this is a sword that cuts both ways. If there is no truth except that generated by Opinion, then one becomes completely dependent upon that Opinion for one's own existence. In a sense, the "New Man" becomes the victim of his own too-effective persuasive abilities; once others are persuaded by his performance, he himself is constrained to behave as though his mask were his real visage. Throughout the *Essayes*, Bacon reiterates the necessity and utility of controlling and manipulating appearances to one's own advantage; but in the opening of essay XI, "Of Great Place," he talks about the consequences:

Men in *Great Place*, are thrice *Servants*: Servants of the Soveraigne or State; Servants of Fame; and Servants of Businesse. So as they have no Freedome; neither in their Persons; nor in their Actions; nor in their Times. It is a strange desire, to seeke Power, and to lose Libertie; Or to seeke Power over others, and to loose Power over a Mans Selfe. (33)

This passage stands out in stark contrast to most of what we have seen thus far. It is unusual, first, in that it raises the possibility of a self other than a public one, and precisely in the context of an essay concerned with defining the self as a public entity. Second, it asserts that the public self must be at odds with the private self, to the point of mutual exclusion. Coming from one whose work in the main has been concerned with demonstrating the importance of the public self and the irrelevancy – to the point of nonexistence – of the private self, this is, to say the least, surprising. The final phrase is perhaps the most striking; we have been persuaded, up to now, that it is through gaining power over one's self, through acquiring the ability to control absolutely the performance of the self, that one gains power over others and is able to "Worke" them to one's ends. And yet here it seems that power over others, once attained, deprives one of control of one's self; indeed, the two seem to exist in inverse proportion to each other. The actor on the public stage becomes a prisoner of his role, controlled not by his own will but by the perceptions of his audience. Throughout the *Essayes*, this public stage is represented as a terrifying array of traps and pitfalls, where the slightest slip or miscalculation – the wrong mask at the wrong moment – is fatal;[64] but this is one of the few places where Bacon begins to give us a sense of what the *internal* consequences of error or misjudgment might be for the actor himself.

Furthermore, it seems that it is precisely those persons most successful in controlling the opinion of others who are most dependent upon the resulting audience perceptions for their own self-definition:

Certainly Great Persons, had need to borrow other Mens Opinions; to thinke themselves happy; For if they judge by their owne Feeling; they cannot finde it: But if they thinke with themselves, what other men thinke of them, and that other men would faine be as they are, then they are happy, as it were by report; When perhaps they finde the Contrary within. (34)

As we have seen, it is unusual enough for Bacon to suggest the existence of a "within" of the self at all, much less that there is a potential conflict between "within" and "without"; but here he goes further, and gives that notion special poignancy. Given that such a conflict exists, in spite of the "New Man's" best efforts to ignore it, how then is it to be resolved? What steps can be taken to alleviate this tension?

In perhaps the most important essay of the collection, number XXVII ("Of Frendship"), Bacon confronts this problem directly. The essay exists in two entirely different versions, the first appearing in 1612, and the second in the 1625 edition.[65] The less familiar early version, quoted here in its entirety, seems rather more direct, and certainly less cynical, than much of what we have so far examined; it displays a kind of guileless optimism rare in Bacon, a hope that, in spite of everything, some form of genuinely disinterested human interaction is still possible:

There is no greater desert or wildernes then to bee without true friends. For without friendship, society is but meeting. And as it is certaine, that in bodies inanimate, union strengthneth any naturall motion, and weakeneth any violent motion; So amongst men, friendship multiplieth joies, and divideth griefes. Therefore whosoever wanteth fortitude, let him worshippe *Friendship*. For the yoke of *Friendship* maketh the yoke of *fortune* more light. There bee some whose lives are, as if they perpetually plaid upon a stage, disguised to all others, open onely to themselves. But perpetuall dissimulation is painfull; and hee that is all *Fortune*, and no *Nature* is an exquisit *Hierling*. Live not in continuall smother, but take some friends with whom to communicate. It will unfold thy understanding; it will evaporate thy affections; it will prepare thy businesse. A man may keepe a corner of his minde from his friend, and it be but to witnesse to himselfe, that it is not upon facility, but upon true use of friendship that hee imparteth himselfe. Want of true friends, as it is the reward of perfidious natures; so is it an imposition upon great fortunes. The one deserve it, the other cannot scape it. And therefore it is good to retaine sincerity, and to put it into the reckoning of *Ambition*, that the higher one goeth, the fewer true friends he shall have. Perfection of friendship, is but a speculation. It is friendship, when a man can say to himselfe, I love this man without respect of utility. I am open hearted to him, I single him from the generality of those with whom I live; I make him a portion of my own wishes. (80n.)

One passage particularly strikes the eye, and sounds suspiciously familiar: "There bee some whose lives are, as if they perpetually plaid upon a stage, disguised to all others, open onely to themselves. But perpetuall dissimulation is painfull; and hee that is all *Fortune*, and no *Nature* is an exquisit *Hierling*." This resembles nothing so much as the Baconian Man himself, the type we have been describing all along as the consummate courtier into which Bacon has been endeavoring to transform his reader. Yet here Bacon seems to be condemning exactly that sort of person, and exhorting his reader in no uncertain terms to avoid becoming merely a performance in the gaze of others. Bacon goes further; he decries the turning of friendship itself to purely utilitarian ends (although he does admit that a friend can help to "prepare business"), and proposes that his reader keep in reserve a sort of internal *arrière-boutique*. This is intended not to protect himself against betrayal, but rather to reassure himself of the purity of his own motives: "A man may keepe a corner of his minde from his friend, and it be but to witnesse to himselfe, that it is not upon facility, but upon true use of friendship that hee imparteth himselfe." This "true use," as defined in the last two sentences of the essay, is a far cry from standard Baconian comportment as defined elsewhere in the *Essayes* and as we have described it in the course of our argument. Bacon does not go so far as to claim that ideal friendship actually exists in this world ("Perfection of friendship, is but a speculation"[66]), "but he does seem to think that a reasonable approximation of it can be made to work, and that it can operate "without respect of utility." What, then, are we to make of this apparently irreconcilable discrepancy between this essay and the weight of the others?

If this essay were Bacon's only utterance upon the subject, and/or if he had left this essay intact in the 1625 edition, we should be left with a contradiction impossible to resolve; we should also be left with a popular image of Bacon considerably less unflattering than the one now commonly held. However, the 1612 version of the essay undergoes a radical transformation for the 1625 edition, becoming an entirely different piece in the process. The first version is, for Bacon, optimistic almost to the point of naïveté; the final version, couched in language of considerably greater rhetorical sophistication, is more subtle, less direct, and apparently more in keeping both with the mature Bacon's ideas on the power and uses of persuasive rhetoric and his similar conclusions regarding human nature. The first was written while Bacon was on the way up in the world; the second after Bacon had been to the top and fallen. It may therefore be legitimate to read the second version as the thoughts of one whose high hopes have been dashed, or at least tempered, through long and not entirely pleasant experience.[67] Bacon is now considerably more suspicious with regard to the possibilities of "true friendship"; and both his rhetoric and the material it presents reflect this new skepticism. Witness, for example, his opening sentence (80): "It had beene hard for him that spake it, to have put more Truth and untruth together, in few Words, then in that Speech; *Whosoever is delighted in solitude, is either a wilde Beast, or a God*." Bacon's professed esteem for the laconically effective rhetoric of his Aristotelian aphorism (esteem which, interestingly, is expressed without regard to the truth-carrying value of the rhetoric) is not entirely disinterested; Bacon himself, as he is well aware, is a master at putting "Truth and untruth together, in few Words," and surely he is here expressing admiration for himself as well as for Aristotle. At any rate, this involuted, ambiguous, and self-referential opening is very different from the straight-forward assertion that opens the 1612 version, and it sets the tone for what is to follow. As we read on, we find a denunciation of solitude which, while not dissimilar to that in the earlier version of the essay, is both more focused and more vehement (81): "But little doe Men perceive, what *Solitude* is, and how farre it extendeth. For a Crowd is not Company; And Faces are but a Gallery of Pictures; And Talke but a *Tinckling Cymball*, where there is no *Love*."[68] Bacon's elaboration of his earlier thoughts seems to refer specifically to that world of self-interest and manipulative perform-ance with which he has long acquaintance; the "Faces [that] are but a Gallery of Pictures" are the masks that populate the court – hardly distinguishable from the paintings lining the walls of the palaces in which they congregate – where surely "there is no *Love*" to be found. The biblical echo serves to heighten the contrast between the Christian ideal, here presented as hopelessly out of reach, and the grim actuality of the court.

As the essay continues, several subtle shifts in emphasis from the earlier edition become apparent, shifts which, taken together, leave the reader with an entirely different impression from that produced by the 1612 version. First, there is the methodical enumeration of the "*Fruits*" of friendship, as though the benefits to be gleaned from association with a friend were enumerable and quantifiable in the same way as, for example, the three "great *Advantages* of *Simulation* and *Dissimulation*" (not to men-tion the "three *Disadvantages*, to set it even"). Second, there is the rather over-material characterization of friendship as a kind of spiritual medic-ament, acting as a purgative upon the troubled conscience; the friend becomes a sort of personified Valium, or at least aspirin, for the courtier. Third, there is the emphasis, entirely consistent with what we have de-scribed as the intended readership of the 1625 version of the *Essayes*, on friendship as it exists in and is applied to a context of statecraft and the court. We see this emphasis displayed in his piling up of examples of friendships between Great Persons taken both from ancient and from contemporary history, with pithy comments thereon – a procedure, it will be recalled, which Bacon has defined as most appropriate for "books of policy," and "fittest for this variable amount of negotiation and occasions." Moreover, these examples, despite their seemingly beneficial intent, actual-ly produce a subversive effect, verging on the sinister; most of the examples, it turns out, are negative, illustrating not so much the benefits of true friendship as the dangers of its antithesis. Finally, as the essay progresses, Bacon gradually moves away even from talking about abstract or spiritual benefits that accrue to the person endowed with a friend, and focuses instead upon more practical concerns, such as "*Manners*":

Reading good Bookes of *Morality*, is a little Flat, and Dead. Observing our faults in Others, is sometimes unproper for our case. But the best Receipt (best (I say) to worke, and best to take) is the Admonition of a *Frend*. It is a strange thing to behold, what grosse Errours, and extreme Absurdities, Many (especially of the greater Sort) doe commit, for want of a *Frend*, to tell them of them; To the great dammage, both of their Fame, and Fortune. (85)

This seems to be paramount; for what can be of greater importance, in Bacon's world, than to avoid those dangerously revealing slips and errors that are so detrimental to one's "Fame" – and, therefore, one's social existence? So if a friend can help one to adjust one's various personæ, thereby averting this kind of socioexistential disaster, he is indeed of great utility. A friend in this connection functions, like other persons, as an audience to one's performances, but a slip in front of this audience – unlike all others, at least theoretically – is not necessarily fatal.

Bacon continues by showing how handy friends are as reliable counselors in that familiar realm, "*Businesse*." And he closes the essay with a discussion of (86) "the last *Fruit*; which is like the *Pomagranat*, full of many kernels; I meane *Aid*, and *Bearing a Part*, in all *Actions*, and *Occasions*." What Bacon means by this is that the friend can function as a kind of proxy, an auxiliary identity, to accomplish worldly ends inaccessible to any persona one could deploy oneself:

How many Things are there, which a Man cannot, with any Face or Comelines, say or doe Himselfe? A Man can scarce alledge his owne Merits with modesty, much lesse extoll them: A man cannot sometimes brooke to Supplicate or Beg: And a number of the like. But all these Things, are Gracefull in a *Frends* Mouth, which are Blushing in a Mans Owne. So againe, a Mans Person hath many proper Relations, which he cannot put off. A Man cannot speake to his Sonne, but as a Father; To his Wife, but as a Husband; To his Enemy, but upon Termes: whereas a *Frend* may speak, as the Case requires, and not as it sorteth with the Person. But to enumerate these Things were endlesse: I have given the Rule, where a Man cannot fitly play his owne Part: If he have not a *Frend*, he may quit the Stage. (86–87)

In other words, the friend enables the Baconian Man both to avoid unseemly and shameful discovery and to gain access to an entire range of alternate identities otherwise beyond his reach. To "alledge his owne Merits," or "to Supplicate or Beg," would for the Baconian Man involve an unacceptably dangerous degree of self-revelation, since such activities consist precisely in the unmasking of his true motivations: greed, desire for power, and general self-interest. Furthermore, it seems that no matter how adept one is at shifting masks, there are always some constraints, forced upon one, as we have seen, by one's public identity or identities; but the friend is, according to Bacon, infinitely adaptable (a quality which, it will be recalled, is at a premium in the Baconian social universe): ". . . a *Frend* may speak, as the Case requires..." The friend offers to the Baconian Man a flexibility of identity otherwise unachievable, and thereby appears to provide a way out of the trap described in "Of Great Place." But at what cost? We have come a considerable distance from the 1612 edition, and even from the expectations we might have had at the beginning of the present version; true, solitude does seem to be an unbearable burden, but not perhaps for the reasons we originally thought. It is not the spiritual desert into which one is cast by solitude that frightens the Baconian Man, but rather (1) the absence of an outlet for the frustration engendered by the strain of keeping up one's various (and possibly contradictory) public identities, and (2) the limitations imposed by solitude on the efflorescence of those identities. Likewise, friendship does seem to offer an escape from solitude, but, rather than being an end in itself, "without respect of utility," it seems to be just another tool, if perhaps the most important, in the tool-chest of the Baconian Man, a tool which enables him to transcend even his own formidable powers of performance and to extend the deployment of his array of masks beyond the limits of his public self. Bacon seems to have abandoned completely even the suggestion, made in 1612, of an ideal friendship, a connection between internal selves without interest as the dominating factor. Instead, he seems to have settled for a utilitarian solution, in which the role of a friend is not so much to offer complete relief from the burden of one's public masks as to offer practical help in sustaining them. In the earlier essay there seems to exist for the self a genuine internal identity, albeit beleaguered on all sides by the demands of external social reality; furthermore, it seems possible that individuals can forge bonds of friendship between their respective private identities, without depending upon the mediation of any external masks. By 1625, however, Bacon has given up hope of finding, much less making, such connections, and to have reduced friendship to a practical relationship entered upon so that one may more easily sustain the external fictions upon which one's social existence depends. The barriers erected by the self to prevent its own discovery by and to others at inopportune moments, to protect others from reading behind the mask, to prevent exposure of the illusion, ultimately function also to preclude the possibility of unmediated, disinterested interaction between two selves, i.e. "true" friendship. All that is left is a kind of simulacrum of the genuine item, where both sides serve each other's interests, mutually agreeing to pretend to believe the other's impostures so as to prevent exposure of their own.[69] In a court world governed by ruthless self-interest, in which illusion, through persuasive performance, becomes the only reality, there is no room for an identity existing apart from the theatre of persuasion. The internal self, if indeed it still exists, seems condemned to a pathetic kind of isolation-through-irrelevance. His grim closing metaphor sums it up: "I have given the Rule, where a Man cannot fitly play his owne Part: If he have not a *Frend*, he may quit the Stage." Indeed, without a sympathetic audience (whose (self) interest overlaps the "New Man's" own) the performance of Baconian Man cannot succeed, and *à la limite* must evaporate into nothingness.

4   Noble Romans: Corneille and the theatre of aristocratic revolt

By the time of the appearance of the final version of Bacon's *Essayes*, in 1625, their author had been in involuntary retirement from the theatre of the Jacobean court for some time, and would quit a larger stage for good only a year later. The *Essayes* may indeed seem to represent both the apogee and the endpoint of a certain trajectory within the larger problem of noble identity in the literature of the late Renaissance; however, their appearance by no means signals an end to literary explorations of what we have called the "theatre of nobility." On the contrary, the crisis of noble identity is one of the dominant themes of Continental writing after 1600. We see this crisis reflected both in the popularity of the *Essayes* themselves (to say nothing of the many reeditions of Montaigne, Castiglione, Guazzo, and others), and in the proliferation of imitations of these works in the first half of the century in both England and France. We have already seen how these works, whether offering helpful advice on how to get ahead, or fulminating against the amorality and hypocrisy of the court and its denizens, are dominated by the master trope of theatre. We have also seen how these works, in Italy and England but also in France, constitute a kind of substrate for more complex literary versions of the discourse of nobility. I wish now to turn to the specific problem of theatricality "onstage," as it were; therefore, my focus will shift from the semi-private stage of the essayist to the public stage of the theatre itself, and from England back across the Channel to France. In the work of Pierre Corneille, the intersection between theatre *per se* and the metaphorical theatre of nobility is most strongly displayed; indeed, the question of the performance of noble identity dominates his entire *oeuvre*, and is addressed repeatedly throughout his career – with, one senses, results increasingly distressing to the playwright.

Few texts are as intimately linked with their historical context as those of Corneille. The settings of his plays, no matter how apparently remote – even alien – in time and place, are inevitably variations on the historical situation of Corneille and his audience. Mediæval Spain, ancient Greece, ancient Rome, all seem to be seventeenth-century France in rather thin disguises.[1] The precise nature of the connection between Corneille's various texts and their historical context has, however, been a source of considerable critical debate. Georges Couton has marshaled immense erudition and detailed historical knowledge in an effort to demonstrate close connections between the plays and contemporary issues and events.[2] Others, such as André Stegmann, have tended to reject any such identification of particular characters or events with the "real world," preferring instead to see the plays as more abstract representations of certain ideas or problems which, while perhaps present in the political and social life of the seventeenth century, find their true significance only when considered from a more "universal," less consciously "historical" perspective.[3] Serge Doubrovsky is unwilling to go this far, but nevertheless rejects what he sees as Couton's tendency to make the plays into barely concealed allegories of contemporary events and persons, claiming instead that Corneille both reflects and mythologizes history; he sees Corneille's theatre, in the context of his own Hegelian-existentialist reading, as "un déchiffrement symbolique de l'histoire" ["a symbolic deciphering of history"].[4] Bernard Dort, in a brief but intriguing study (to which Doubrovsky acknowledges a considerable debt), posits a Corneille whose dramatic perspective is inevitably conditioned by his historical situation as a provincial functionary and successful commercial playwright. While sometimes coming close to a reductive materialism, Dort's reading of Corneille's relationship to history is, on the whole, nuanced and suggestive.[5] More recently, Jean-Marie Apostolidès has offered a reading of the theatre of Corneille that draws upon history, anthropology, psychoanalysis, and literary theory to situate the texts within a larger politico-historical context, that of a theatrical model of absolutism.[6] Another point of view is to be found in the work of Michel Prigent, who offers a detailed and comprehensive reading of Corneille's political tragedies that rejects what Prigent sees as extratextual matters in favor of a renewed focus on the text, considered as a self-sufficient entity, and its literary sources. Dismissing Doubrovsky as anachronistic and Dort as dogmatically Marxist, he endeavors instead to understand Corneille on what he sees as the playwright's own terms. This Aristotelian reading, despite its clarity, intelligence, and conscientious thoroughness, nevertheless seems at times too willing to accept at face value political concepts and categories (*gloire*, *noblesse*, etc.) proposed by the texts.[7] It seems to me that one must not only understand but also question the ahistorical essentialism of seventeenth-century political theory if we are to penetrate beyond that essentialism to the problems raised by Corneille's theatre. Still more recently, Marc Fumaroli, in a wide-ranging collection of essays, shows how Corneille's theatre works within and against the ethical and rhetorical teachings of his Jesuit schoolmasters.[8]

Rather than attempting, like Doubrovsky or Prigent, to account for all elements of Corneille's *oeuvre*, this study will focus on the single problem of the construction and performance of noble identity as it is treated in a few key plays, plays which seem to represent distinct stages in the development of Corneille's concept of nobility. They all attempt to respond not only to the problem of the nature of "true nobility," but also to what, for Corneille, is the more agonizing problem of what is, or can be, the role(s) of nobility in the context of a court society.[9] Specifically, how can the noble self adapt to the rapidly shifting power relations of the court, relations which increasingly take on the guise of a refractory absolutism? It should be stated at the outset that the very notion of "development" with regard to Corneille's vision of nobility is perhaps a misleading one; indeed, throughout his entire *oeuvre*, Corneille's idea of nobility is remarkably uniform. Less constant, though, are the structures of power surrounding his version of the noble self; both the conditions of possibility for the deployment of noble identity and the performative strategies which the possessor of that identity is compelled to adopt are in a state of constant change. In fact, the courtly universe of Corneille's plays appears to develop in a linear and essentially irreversible fashion. Its structures of power become ever more rigidly unidirectional; as a result, the inhabitants of that court become progressively more isolated from one another in ever-greater mutual incomprehension, and are increasingly polarized along an axis defined at one end by the noble courtier and at the other by the holder of royal authority.

One may, somewhat arbitrarily, distinguish three phases or nodes in this progression, represented by three plays (although others could also be chosen): *Le Cid*, *Cinna*, and *Suréna*. The first of these sets forth the essentials of Corneille's vision of the noble self, together with the fundamental structures of the conflict between throne and noble which will be the central problem of the plays that follow, without however pushing that conflict to what will come to seem its inevitable conclusion. The second proposes a transcendent resolution to the conflict, one which, however, proves to be both incomplete and illusory. The third, not incidentally Corneille's final play, presents a kind of *cas limite* of the conflict, demonstrating nothing so much as the ultimate impossibility of the full realization of the noble identity or role in an absolutist context.

i.   **"La haute image": *Le Cid***

Le Cid is perhaps the most extensively commented-upon play in the history of French theatre. It may therefore be redundant to offer yet another "reading" of the play as a whole. However, as *Le Cid* offers to the spectator the prototype (in triplicate) of the "héros cornélien," some observations on the configuration of the noble self as posited by this play may nevertheless be in order. For Doubrovsky, the *héros cornélien* is virtually identical to the existential hero of the 1950s.[10] Less arbitrarily, Paul Bénichou describes the *héros cornélien* in general as being a kind of ultra-egotist, a self with no social limits.[11] This is not mere Nietzschean anachronism; Bénichou is careful about placing the *héros cornélien* before its seventeenth-century audience. He says of such characters as Don Diègue and Don Gomès that "leur seul devoir est d'être dignes d'eux-mêmes, de porter assez haut leurs visées, et de donner aux petits des exemples suffisamment édifiants de leur grandeur" ["their sole duty is to be worthy of themselves, to aim sufficiently high, and to give to lesser beings sufficiently edifying examples of their greatness"].[12] Bénichou is no doubt correct to insist on the essential *outrance* of the character; however, he seems to ascribe to it (and here he does perhaps slip into anachronism) a unity and coherence that may not be present.[13] To be sure, the *héros cornélien* predictably and invariably manifests such attributes as martial prowess, courage, and *générosité*; moreover, those attributes are always present in their purest, most absolute, most extreme form.[14] However, it is less clear that the *personnage* is anything more than the sum of these unitary attributes; indeed, it often seems to be somewhat less. I am not, of course, merely accusing Corneille of failing to produce "convincing," "rounded" characters; to do so would be to fall into simple-minded anachronism.[15] But neither is it true that the composite nature of Corneille's characters is only a seventeenth-century theatrical convention. On the contrary, it is both peculiar to and essential to the nature of the *héros cornélien*.[16] We will try to show that the character may be viewed as the point of intersection of certain ideological strands, a nexus of maximum tension in the field of forces acting in the dramatic universe of Corneille.

In the first scene of *Le Cid*, Don Gomès says of his youthful soon-to-be rival that "Don Rodrigue surtout n'a trait en son visage / Qui d'un homme de coeur ne soit la haute image"[17] ["Don Rodrigue, above all, has nothing in his lineaments / That is not the very image of a man of courage"], and goes on to discuss him in terms which make it clear that Rodrigue is indeed

> Th'expectancy and rose of the fair state,
> The glass of fashion and the mould of form,
> Th'observ'd of all observers...

The emphasis on externality (the "visage") is significant, but more so is the fact that the attributes (bravery, martial prowess, etc.) which define Rodrigue's soon-to-be realized character are precisely those for which Rodrigue's father, Don Diègue, is already known, and likewise are those which

Don Gomès attributes to himself[18] when he confronts Don Diègue:

> Si vous fûtes vaillant, je le suis aujourd'hui,
> Et ce bras du Royaume est le plus ferme appui;
> Grenade et l'Aragon tremblent quand ce fer brille,
> Mon nom sert de rempart à toute la Castille,
> [...]
> Chaque jour, chaque instant, entasse pour ma gloire
> Laurier dessus laurier, victoire sur victoire: (I, iv, 189–96)

> [If you were valiant, I am so today,
> And this arm is the realm's staunchest support;
> Granada and Aragon tremble when this steel shines,
> My name is a rampart for all Castille,
> [...]
> Every day, every instant piles up laurels upon laurels,
> Victory upon victory, for my glory:]

In the midst of Don Gomès's vaunting, we notice that he is nevertheless perfectly willing to admit that Don Diègue was at one time the possessor of the honored title of Bravest Man in Castille.[19] This act of magnanimous acknowledgment reveals to us the following consequences: (1) If Don Diègue and Don Gomès are interchangeable in this way, then the position Don Gomès now holds must be in some sense arbitrary. Indeed, since the attribute (or complex of attributes) in question is an abstract absolute, unchanging in form and content no matter who possesses it at any given time, it is in some sense external to its possessor, rather than being an intrinsic virtue unique to a particular person. (2) If the position is arbitrary, it is also temporary. Since this complex of attributes consists in a set of uniquely superlative virtues (the best, bravest, strongest, etc.), there can be only one Bravest Man at any given time. If they are interchangeable, and the younger man may supplant the older, then (as in fact happens) Don Gomès himself may be supplanted as well, which is not, however, a consequence that seems to be foremost in Don Gomès's mind. (3) Finally, this complex of superlative attributes appears to be the sole defining factor in a noble's identity; note that once Don Diègue is deprived of his title, his entire being seems simply to evaporate.[20]

Don Gomès's failure to understand his own contingency is, of course, his fatal flaw. In every other way he seems identical to his predecessor, Don Diègue, and to his future posthumous son-in-law, Rodrigue. What sets him apart – and makes his removal both inevitable and necessary – is his blind insistence that he *personally* is essential to the well-being of the State. "Sans moi, vous passeriez bientôt sous d'autres lois, / Et si vous ne m'aviez, vous n'auriez plus de Rois." (I, iv, 193–94) ["Without me, you would soon be subject to other laws, / And if you did not have me, you would have no more Kings."] This is in some sense true, but he does not realize that the "moi" he considers so indispensable is not he himself, but rather the role he plays in the theatre of the State. He takes his role too seriously and too literally; he identifies with it too closely, and places what in the context of this play is an excessive emphasis on the absolute and superlative side of the role. His too-close identification with his role makes him a dangerously destabilizing force; he must therefore be eliminated.

Don Gomès's error is actually rather subtle, and therefore almost (but not quite) forgivable. After all, as his remarks on Rodrigue make clear, one of the most fundamental attributes of his noble role, at least officially, is its genetic component.[21] That is, the virtues he possesses are supposedly not acquired, but inherent; they need not, and in fact cannot, be learned or practiced, but are always already present *in toto*. Rodrigue himself announces his adherence to this belief, not coincidentally when confronting Don Gomès:

> Je suis jeune, il est vrai, mais aux âmes bien nées
> La valeur n'attend pas le nombre des années.
> [...]
> Mes pareils à deux fois ne se font pas connaître,
> Et pour leurs coups d'essai veulent des coups de maître. (II, ii, 407–12)

> [I am young, it is true, but to well-born souls
> Valor does not wait upon years.
> [...]
> Those like me do not need two chances to make themselves known,
> And for their first blows deliver master strokes.]

However, as we shall see, Rodrigue differs from Don Gomès precisely in his understanding and use of this aspect of his role, and this is what makes his presence in the court both more useful and less destructive than that of Don Gomès. Don Gomès fails to recognize that the inherent, quasi-automatic nature of noble *valeur* is not in itself sufficient to justify his status as primary *soutien* of the State. It is all very well to possess those genetic traits, but until the King recognizes and confirms their presence they are not only meaningless but dangerous. Don Diègue, crabby, intransigent old man that he is, nevertheless recognizes that his own *gloire* and *renommée* are dependent on the good will of his king. Of course, he may only be willing to admit this fact because he has just been the beneficiary of that good will as the play opens, but it remains true that he is more aware of the existence of a certain mutual dependence than Don Gomès. This failure of comprehension is evident in Don Gomès's conversation with Don Arias, when the latter attempts to persuade him to moderate his transports:

> Don Gomès: Monsieur, pour conserver ma gloire et mon estime
> Désobéir un peu n'est pas un si grand crime.
> Et quelque grand qu'il [Don Diègue] fût, mes services présents
> Pour le faire abolir sont plus que suffisants.
>
> Don Arias: Quoi qu'on fasse d'illustre et de considérable
> Jamais à son sujet un Roi n'est redevable:
> Vous vous flattez beaucoup, et vous devez savoir
> Que qui sert bien son Roi ne fait que son devoir.
>
> Don Gomès: Je ne vous en croirai qu'après l'expérience. (II, i, 367–75)
>
> [Don Gomès: Sir, to preserve my glory and esteem
> A small disobedience is not such a great crime.
> And however great he [Don Diègue] was, my present services
> Are more than sufficient to excuse my action.
>
> Don Arias: No matter what illustrious and important action one performs,
> A King to his subject is never indebted;
> You flatter yourself greatly, and you ought to know
> That who serves his King well is only doing his duty.
>
> Don Gomès: I'll believe it when I see it.]

The first two lines cited indicate the crux: Don Gomès, despite his claim to be the principal defender of the realm, is in fact more concerned about his "gloire" (his public reputation) and his "estime" (his own vision of himself) than with the good of the state. He fails to recognize that his *gloire*, at least, is dependent less on himself or his deeds than on the royal power that authorizes it. He goes on to discuss the degree of his own necessity to the State:

> Don Arias: Vous devez redouter la puissance d'un Roi.
>
> Don Gomès: Un jour seul ne perd pas un homme tel que moi.
> Que toute sa grandeur s'arme pour mon supplice,
> Tout l'État périra plutôt que je périsse.
>
> Don Arias: Quoi? vous craignez si peu le pouvoir souverain?
>
> Don Gomès: D'un sceptre qui sans moi tomberait de sa main?
> Il a trop d'intérêt lui-même en ma personne,
> Et ma tête en tombant ferait choir sa couronne. (II, i, 377–84)

[Don Arias: You ought to fear the power of a King.

Don Gomès: A single day cannot destroy a man like me.
Let all his grandeur arm itself for my punishment;
The whole State will perish before I do.

Don Arias: What? you fear the sovereign power so little?

Don Gomès: [The power] of a sceptre which, without me, would fall from his hand?
He has himself too much interest in my person,
And my head, in falling, would bring down his crown.]

Ironically, Don Gomès is partly right; the state, as presented by Corneille, does in fact depend on him, or at least on some person fulfilling the role he currently plays. He is probably not wrong to overestimate the importance of his role; he is wrong to attribute that importance to himself, rather than to his role, and his greatest mistake is to articulate that importance publicly.[22] Rodrigue later fulfills exactly the same state-sustaining function, but he is more prudent in choosing the audiences to whom he articulates his awareness of this fact. When Rodrigue's discourse most closely approaches that of Don Gomès[23] – "Paraissez, Navarrais, Mores, et Castillans" (V, i, 1568–74) ["Appear, Navarrese, Moors, and Castillians"] – he is speaking to an empty stage.

Corneille, in the 1660 *Examen*, raises the general question of how best to deal with the question of disagreement with one's sovereign, saying that not only is it indiscreet at best to articulate publicly such conflict, but that even silence can be dangerous:

> Je sais bien que le silence passe d'ordinaire pour une marque de consentement; mais quand les Rois parlent, c'en est une de contradiction: on ne manque jamais à leur applaudir quand on entre dans leurs sentiments; et le seul moyen de leur contredire avec le respect qui leur est dû, c'est de se taire, quand leurs ordres ne sont pas si pressants qu'on ne puisse remettre à s'excuser de leur obéir lorsque le temps en sera venu, et conserver cependant une espérance légitime d'un empêchement qu'on ne peut encore déterminément prévoir. (*OC* I: 701)

> [I know well that silence usually passes as a sign of consent; but when Kings speak, it is a sign of contradiction. One never fails to applaud them when one agrees with them; and the only way to contradict them with due respect is to be silent, when their orders are not so pressing that one may not rely on excusing oneself from obeying when the time comes, and meantime retaining a legitimate hope for an obstacle that one cannot yet definitely foresee.]

The convoluted syntax of the latter portion of this sentence may be Corneille's effort to enact in his own discourse the protective self-concealing discretion he describes; he seems to be suggesting that the best way to disagree with one's sovereign, tactically or syntactically, is through procrastination and obfuscation, laying down a smokescreen behind which one waits and hopes for an obstacle that will prevent one from having to fulfill the obligation in question.

Such maneuvers hardly seem to be in keeping with the character of a true *généreux* like Rodrigue; it is therefore fortunate that his discretion is never put to such a severe test. Indeed, even such discretion as he does exhibit may not be entirely his own doing. Events offer him the opportunity to demonstrate through concrete actions his absolute necessity to the security of the crown; as a result, he is spared the obligation of asserting his own worth too strongly, since his sovereign conveniently does it for him. Before examining the crucial scene in which this occurs, however, it is worth taking a closer look at the figure of the king, Don Fernand, to see what it is that makes it possible for him to participate in this exchange without dwindling into complete insignificance.

It is clear from the outset that Don Fernand is no Louis XIV, nor even a Louis XIII. In Don Fernand's Castille, the king and his nobles are on a more or less level playing field; we are still in a feudal realm, where the King is merely *primus inter pares*. Corneille himself makes this point in the *Examen*, responding to Scudéry's criticism that the King should have acted more forcefully to prevent Don Gomès and Rodrigue from fighting:

> ... on peut considérer que Don Fernand étant le premier Roi de Castille, et ceux qui en avaient été maîtres auparavant lui n'ayant eu titre que de Comtes, il n'était peut-être pas assez absolu sur les grands Seigneurs de son royaume pour le pouvoir faire. (*OC* I: 703)

> [... one may consider that Don Fernand, being the first King of Castille, and those who had been its masters before him having only had the title of Counts, he was not perhaps sufficiently absolute over the great Lords of his realm to be able to do it.]

Corneille even contrasts this realm with that of "ce temps-ci, où l'autorité Royale est plus absolue" ["the present time, when Royal authority is more absolute"]. How, then, is the King to assert any authority at all? What will enable him to make good his threat (II, vi, 568–70) to punish Don Gomès? As the king's conversation with the youthful and rather silly Don Sanche demonstrates, what enables him to maintain his position as the chief noble among so many of his putative equals is precisely his superior understanding of the language of nobility. Like his nobles, he speaks that language, understands its code, and is able to work within it; but he has a privileged access to certain areas or subsets of that discourse, an access denied to those not performing the royal role. This becomes manifest precisely when Don Sanche tries to justify Don Gomès's actions according to the code of nobility, saying that Don Gomès's behavior stems only from his superlatively noble nature:

> ...une âme accoutumée aux grandes actions
> Ne se peut abaisser à des submissions:
> Elle n'en conçoit point qui s'expliquent sans honte,
> Et c'est contre ce mot qu'a résisté le Comte.
> Il trouve en son devoir un peu trop de rigueur,
> Et vous obéirait s'il avait moins de coeur.   (II, vi, 585–90)

> [...a soul accustomed to great actions
> Cannot abase itself to submissions;
> It cannot conceive any that can be explained without shame,
> And it is against that word that the Count resisted.
> He finds in his duty rather too much rigor,
> And would obey you if he were less courageous.]

Don Fernand has a counter-argument ready to hand, one based not on arbitrary use of power but rather on his role as the one noble who, while still acting within the constraints of the code of nobility, must protect all the others (from themselves and each other, as will be seen later).[24] He starts by reminding Don Sanche that he is out of line, but demonstrates his superior *générosité* by giving Don Sanche the benefit of the doubt; attributing the latter's disrespect to an excess of youthful zeal, Don Fernand forgives him immediately. He continues by pointing out that his own role is in fact different from that of a subject, no matter how noble:

> Un Roi dont la prudence a de meilleurs objets
> Est meilleur ménager du sang de ses sujets.
> Je veille pour les miens, mes soucis les conservent,
> Comme le chef a soin des membres qui le servent.
> Ainsi votre raison n'est pas raison pour moi;
> Vous parlez en soldat, je dois agir en Roi,
> Et quoi qu'il faille dire, et quoi qu'il veuille croire,
> Le Comte à m'obéir ne peut perdre sa gloire.   (II, vi, 597–604)

> [A King who has more important things to worry about
> Is a better husband of the blood of his subjects.
> I watch over my own, my concern keeps them safe,
> As the head takes care of the members that serve it.
> So your reason is not reason for me;

> You speak as a soldier, I must act as a King,
> And whatever he may say, and whatever he wants to think,
> The Count, in obeying me, cannot lose his honor.]

The discourse of royalty is here presented as subsuming and transcending that of nobility. Don Sanche's "raison" may be enough for Don Sanche, but Don Fernand's greater responsibility requires a more comprehensive "raison"; his role demands more of him than mere individual nobility as it is defined and understood by Don Sanche. As *Horace* and especially *Cinna* will demonstrate, there is another step that must be taken, one that goes beyond and in fact sacrifices the *gloire* of the individual to that of the collective. The last two lines, in particular, indicate the king's willingness to exchange *gloire* for obedience. Don Fernand here also reminds Don Sanche (and us) that the entire notion of a self-sufficient individual *gloire* is itself suspect; the last two verses make it clear that *gloire* is finally dependent not on any characteristic of the individual possessing it (or not) but rather on its audience. "Grandes actions" may be a critical element of noble identity, but they are not, in themselves, enough; it is the authorizing gaze of the king-as-beholder, and not the deeds, words, or thoughts of the performer, that ultimately confers *la gloire*.

Don Fernand's royal status means that he must keep a vigilant watch not only on his subjects' honor but also on his own, or rather that of his royal role. If he is the "chef" of the state, then any affront to any of its "membres" is also an affront to himself, and must be dealt with accordingly, if the health of the body politic is not to be endangered. And this is precisely the situation created by Don Gomès's audacity:

> D'ailleurs l'affront me touche, il a perdu d'honneur
> Celui que de mon fils j'ai fait le Gouverneur,
> Et par ce trait hardi d'une insolence extrême
> Il s'est pris à mon choix, il s'est pris à moi-même.
> C'est moi qu'il satisfait en réparant ce tort. (II, vi, 605–09)

> [Moreover, the affront touches me; he has impugned the honor
> Of him whom I have made the tutor of my son;
> And by this rash deed of extreme insolence,
> He has attacked my choice, he has attacked me myself.
> It is I whom he satisfies in redressing this wrong.]

Corneille offers a different version of lines 607–08 from 1652 on, a version which – by replacing the "moi" of Don Fernand with his political person, the state itself – makes the point even clearer: "S'attaquer à mon choix, c'est se prendre à moi-même, / Et faire un attentat sur le pouvoir suprême" ["To attack my choice is to insult me, / And to assail the power of the throne"]. In other words, Don Gomès's action is no longer only a private affront, or a simple *affaire d'honneur*; "un attentat sur le pouvoir suprême" is nothing less than the capital crime of *lèse-majesté*, high treason. This political-legal dimension adds to the gravity of the affront, without, however, obliterating the initial question of honor. As Don Fernand's words make clear, Don Gomès's action is still an affront to his honor within the code of nobility. Throughout the passage, Don Fernand persists in using the language of honor (particularly in the first version of the text: "C'est moi qu'il satisfait...") to describe what is at once a problem of private honor and of *le salut public*. Don Fernand is still operating within the discourse of honor and nobility, a discourse he shares with Don Diègue, Don Gomès, Rodrigue, and the rest of his court. His willingness to do so keeps the lines of communication open, and indeed helps to minimize the intensity of the conflict; however, mere participation in a common discourse is not in itself sufficient to resolve conflicts within the all-or-nothing discursive structure of nobility. Therefore, Don Fernand must combine a capacity to speak a common language with his nobles with a capacity to transcend that discourse when necessary; only thus may solutions to conflict be found. As will be seen, this ability also accounts for the fundamental necessity of Don Fernand's presence in the quasi-feudal court depicted in *Le Cid*.

Don Gomès's arrogant indiscretion prevents him from playing the unique role that would otherwise be his by right; Rodrigue, however, combines the requisite superiority of *coeur* with a certain courtly (and suspiciously un-*généreux*?) tact or prudence, and it is this pairing of seemingly incompatible attributes that enables him to play the role of Primary Defender of the Realm with great effectiveness. Ultimately, his prudence will make him a greater threat to Don Fernand than Don Gomès could ever have been; before discussing this seeming paradox, however, we will examine a critical scene of the play, one in which the ideal of nobility and the exigencies of political reality confront one another most directly. In Act IV, scene iii, Corneille strikes a delicate balance between these two entities, a balance dependent solely upon the ability of the scene's participants to sustain their roles, to avoid "breaking character." The King and his (new) chief noble play out their public roles in an elaborate ritual of mutual admiration, simultaneously acknowledging their reciprocal dependence on one another and asserting their individual worth as uniquely necessary elements of the State.

The setting is itself supremely theatrical; no stage directions are given, but it seems clear that the scene is set in the throne room of Don Fernand, where he is holding court. All the primary characters are present in their official, political personæ. The King opens what we may safely call the play-within-a-play by addressing Rodrigue with a formal, even Ciceronian, exordium:

Généreux héritier d'une illustre famille
Qui fut toujours la gloire et l'appui de Castille,
Race de tant d'aïeux en valeur signalés
Que l'essai de la tienne a si tôt égalés,
Pour te récompenser ma force est trop petite,
Et j'ai moins de pouvoir que tu n'as de mérite.   (IV, iii, 1219–24)

[Generous heir of an illustrious family
Which has always been the glory and the support of Castille,
Race of so many ancestors famed for valor
Equaled so soon by the trial of your own,
My strength is too little to compensate you,
And I have less power than you do merit.]

The seemingly conventional vocabulary of the first three lines actually carries considerable weight; by intoning certain critical code-words, Don Fernand formally attaches them to the persona of Rodrigue and confirms the status they announce. "Généreux," "illustre," "gloire," "race," "valeur"; Don Fernand rhetorically links Rodrigue to his genetic heritage, confirming the formal heritability and public continuity of the role he now occupies. In a sense, Don Fernand may be seen as establishing the legitimacy of Rodrigue's descent,[25] and thus his right to the public role formerly held by his father. Don Fernand is simultaneously asserting his monopoly on the conferral of these qualities; the opening of this speech seems to indicate once again that such attributes as *générosité* and *gloire* mean nothing *on the public stage* (even if – as is the case here – they have already been performed on that stage) until their presence has been authorized (in the etymological sense) by the King.

That the King needs to assert this authority is borne out by the remainder of this first speech, which shows just how precarious his position is. We find that Rodrigue has attacked and defeated "les Mores" without waiting for orders from his king, and that as a result the defeated enemy has hailed Rodrigue – not his employer, Don Fernand – as their new lord. What is worse, this act of submission comes not from the *foule* of enemy troops, but from their leaders – not one, but *two* kings. Adding insult to injury, they have done so in the presence of Don Fernand himself:

Mais deux Rois, tes captifs, feront ta récompense,
Ils t'ont nommé tous deux leur Cid en ma présence,
Puisque Cid en leur langue est autant que Seigneur,
Je ne t'envierai pas ce beau titre d'honneur.   (IV, iii, 1231–34)

[But two Kings, your captives, will compensate you,
They have both named you their Master [*Cid*] in my presence;

Since Cid in their language means Lord,
I shall not envy you that fine title of honor.]

Don Fernand hastily assures Rodrigue that he will not contest the latter's new status, but he then moves to appropriate to himself the naming power exercised by his Moorish counterparts.[26] The King wishes to show that deeds performed on the battlefield must still be confirmed in the theatre of the court; he attempts to exercise control over the assignment of status by transforming the apparently spontaneous recognition by the Moorish kings of Rodrigue's intrinsic superiority into a ritual gesture within the court context. Under the King's direction, the entire scene becomes a formal investiture, whereby old or pre-existing roles are confirmed and new ones are created and assigned; Don Fernand's opening speech culminates in his granting to Rodrigue a new and unique title of nobility. Don Fernand deftly integrates the confirmation of Rodrigue's hereditary status with the recognition of Rodrigue's new title (that conferred by his exploits). This title could call into question the King's own status, but the King's appropriation of naming power acts to neutralize the threat.

> Sois désormais le Cid, qu'à ce grand nom tout cède,
> Qu'il devienne l'effroi de Grenade et Tolède,
> Et qu'il marque à tous ceux qui vivent sous mes lois
> Et ce que tu me vaux et ce que je te dois.   (IV, iii, 1235–38)

> [Be henceforth the Cid, let all give way before this great name,
> Let it become the terror of Granada and Toledo,
> And let it show to all those who live under my laws
> Both what you are worth to me and that which I owe you.]

The closing couplet reasserts the King's authority; the "lois" are his, not Rodrigue's, and "ce grand nom" is paradoxically designated as a reminder not of the intrinsic worth of Rodrigue himself but of his worth *to the king*; in other words, it is only in relation to the royal beholder (that is, as a result of the act of royal contemplation/confirmation) that Rodrigue's deeds and title have any worth at all.

However, Don Fernand is not out of the woods yet. He does close with an acknowledgement of his debt to Rodrigue; and recall that, in the second half of his first sentence, Don Fernand insists (with what he may hope is a certain degree of irony) on his absolute inability to compensate Rodrigue for his transcendent exploits, exploits which have assured the safety of the realm and of his own position at its head. He emphasizes the smallness and insufficiency of his own power, particularly with respect to Rodrigue's "mérite." This statement is of course true, but in the context of this ritual performance Don Fernand intends it to be interpreted, on at least one level, as false; that is, he hopes that it will be seen not as a statement of fact but as a courtly gesture of politeness, whose true significance is the opposite of its explicit content. This is a calculated risk; there is a chance that Rodrigue will agree with him (as Don Gomès would certainly have done). However, fortunately for Don Fernand, the gamble pays off, as Rodrigue reads the gesture aright and performs a corresponding, reciprocal gesture of ritual self-denigration in response.

> Que Votre Majesté, Sire, épargne ma honte,
> D'un si foible service elle fait trop de compte,
> Et me force à rougir devant un si grand Roi
> De mériter si peu l'honneur que j'en reçois.
> Je sais trop que je dois au bien de votre empire
> Et le sang qui m'anime et l'air que je respire,
> Et quand je les perdrai pour un si digne objet,
> Je ferai seulement le devoir d'un sujet. (IV, iii, 1239–46)

> [Let Your Majesty, Sire, spare my shame,
> Of such feeble service you make too much,
> And force me to blush before such a great King,
> To merit so little the honor that I receive of you.
> I know too well that I owe to your power
> Both the blood that animates me and the air that I breathe,
> And when I will lose them for such a worthy object,
> I will only be doing the duty of a subject.]

These assertions are meant to be seen, on one level, as the ritual gestures of submission required of the good subject; but they are also meant to reassure Don Fernand, and moreover are not without a certain irony. Rodrigue's contrafactual declarations that he has done virtually nothing; that his "mérite" is negligible; that he owes it all to his sovereign anyway; and that besides he was only doing what any good subject would have done in his place – all are meant to indicate to Don Fernand that, despite Rodrigue's obvious superiority, Don Fernand need have no fear for his position as king. Rodrigue indicates that he understands the exigencies of his role in the play of the court, and will not depart from the script or break character, since such a break would lead to chaos. (Perhaps he has learned from the experience of Don Gomès.) Everyone watching this performance is of course aware that what Rodrigue says is untrue, just as the truth of Don Fernand's preceding statement is self-evident. Nevertheless, each party is willing to sustain the illusion, since the ritual structure of the protestations of personal insignificance and mutual dependence allows each party to "save face," in a literal sense – Don Fernand and Rodrigue are each able to preserve both their *honneur* and the integrity of their respective roles.

Don Fernand's effort to orchestrate the courtly performance, to be the arbiter whose judgment determines significance and status, is not mere self-aggrandizement. His nominal role as king, even if he is only *primus inter pares*, forces upon him certain responsibilities for the collective well-being of the rest. This aspect of his role comes into sharpest focus, and its necessity is most clearly demonstrated, when a dispute arises between various contenders for the position held successively by Don Diègue, Don Gomès, and Rodrigue. Such disputes threaten the stability of the entire system, as we have seen in the case of Don Gomès; thanks to Rodrigue (and to Don Gomès's own indiscretion), however, the king's authority is in this case never really put to the test. Even so, it seems clear that the king's ability both to operate within the discourse of nobility and to transcend it on occasion is essential to his role, in that it makes it possible for him to prevent his nobles from killing one another off in an endless series of duels.[27] Corneille presents this recourse to a transcendent authority as the only way out of what would otherwise be a cycle of perpetual violence; the only way to prevent conflict over the role of Chief Defender of the Realm is to make the possession of that role dependent not upon purely intrinsic qualities of the individual but upon the authorizing gaze of a royal *personnage*, one which both recognizes and legitimizes those intrinsic qualities as they are enacted on the stage of the court.

In *Le Cid*, however, Don Fernand still finds it difficult to impose his authority, however well-grounded it may be in the language of nobility. He meets a formidable adversary in Chimène, who insists on satisfaction according to the old feudal code. Initially he rejects her demands, saying that the need of the State transcends her need for private vengeance; this is the same argument, "abolition," that will enable Tulle to avoid executing Horace. Here, however, it is unsuccessful, as Don Diègue also complains that not only will Don Fernand be violating established court custom, but that such apparently arbitrary exoneration will not sell well with "votre peuple," who will think that Don Fernand is merely providing an excuse for Rodrigue not to appear "Où tous les gens d'honneur cherchent un beau trépas" (IV, v, 1430). "Don't do him any favors," he says:

> Sire, ôtez ces faveurs qui terniraient sa gloire,
> Qu'il goûte sans rougir les fruits de sa victoire.
> Le Comte eut de l'audace, il l'en a su punir,
> Il l'a fait en brave homme, et le doit soutenir. (IV, v, 1431–34)

> [Sire, take away these favors that would tarnish his glory;
> Let him taste, without blushing, the fruits of his victory.
> The Count had audacity, he was able to punish him for it,
> He did it like a brave man, and should uphold it.]

This last is the real point, and the one that forces Don Fernand to give in. He appeals to the king's desire to protect the honor of his main "appui"; and since that honor is, by extension, that of the king himself, it is an argument he can hardly refute.[28] He is therefore forced to concede to the exigencies of the noble code, but he does so unwillingly, and warns Chimène that it will be the last time (1442): "Mais après ce combat ne demande plus rien" ["But after this combat, ask nothing more"]. He also refuses, significantly, to dignify the spectacle with his authorizing presence:

> Mais de peur qu'en exemple un tel combat ne passe,
> Pour témoigner à tous qu'à regret je permets
> Un sanglant procédé qui ne me plut jamais,
> De moi ni de ma Cour il n'aura la présence. (IV, v, 1460–63)

> [But lest such a combat become an example,
> To demonstrate to all that I unwillingly permit
> A bloody proceeding that has never pleased me,
> Neither I nor my court will be present.]

Not only will the King be absent, but so, too, will the court; this scene from the theatre of nobility, thus excised from the script, will play to an empty house. Indeed, the bloodless "duel" between Rodrigue and the hapless Don Sanche takes place offstage, and the audience only finds out about it later, when Don Sanche recounts the tale to the court; nor can we ascribe this absence merely to dramaturgical discretion on Corneille's part. While les bienséances prohibited actual bloodletting from being represented on stage, there was no rule against the representation of duels manqués, as the scene between Don Diègue and Don Gomès (I, iv) clearly demonstrates. Perhaps Corneille felt that two such scenes in one play would be excessive, although he might equally well have been attracted by the symmetry, contrasting Rodrigue's magnanimité with Don Gomès's arrogance. More likely, he simply saw the opportunity for a coup de théâtre afforded by having Don Sanche appear with the sword.

At any rate, even if Don Fernand is not yet able to impose his will unconditionally, he is at least able to signal his disapproval, and fortunately for him the outcome is one that reinforces rather than undermines his stance. Had the duel taken place, that is had one of the participants actually killed the other, then (even if Rodrigue had won) the king's effort to make public status – la gloire – depend on royal approval rather than arbitrary violence would have been thwarted. Don Fernand thus manages to deflect yet another threat to his fragile authority, and as a result may proceed to orchestrate the conclusion of the play. Rodrigue is absolved of his "crime," Chimène will finally marry him, and Don Fernand will remain king; all the characters are in some sense brought to heel, finally constrained to behave according to their roles in the theatre of Don Fernand's court. It remains true, however, that the stability and indeed the very existence of Don Fernand's royal status is still wholly dependent upon the *bras* of Rodrigue.

This dependency, combined with Rodrigue's adept performance at court, confirms our earlier suspicion that Rodrigue might in some sense pose an even greater threat to the stability of the realm than did Don Gomès. Don Gomès's failure to comprehend the difference between the necessity of his role and the contingency of his person made him a relatively easy target for Don Fernand. Perhaps more dangerous to Don Fernand's fragile proto-royal status, and therefore more threatening to the balance of the court system as a whole, would be a noble who, while performing the essential role of Primary Defender of the Realm, avoids articulating openly the absolute dependency of that realm on his role, allowing instead his audience to draw its own conclusions. L'Infante remarks to Chimène that the larger audience of the realm has in fact already done so: "Rodrigue maintenant est notre unique appui, / L'espérance et l'amour d'un peuple qui l'adore" (IV, ii, 1186–87) ["Rodrigue is now our only support, / The hope and the love of a people that adore him"].[29] Rodrigue's very (public) discretion, combined with his perhaps not entirely disinterested willingness to let his actions speak for themselves, makes him paradoxically more of a threat to Don Fernand, a fact that both of them seem to recognize. Don Fernand's enormous and very visible debt to the invincible Rodrigue is entirely beyond his ability to repay, and this dependence creates an unacceptable tension. In many of Corneille's later plays, this tension breaks into open conflict; here, however, Don Fernand is able to continue to do what he does best, that is deflect and defer conflict, in this case by sending Rodrigue forth to conquer other enemies, thereby keeping him literally off the scene.[30] Any real resolution of the potential conflict between them remains finally unresolved within the framework of *Le Cid*.

This is underscored by the final line of the play, addressed by the king to Rodrigue (V, vii, 1866): "Laisse faire le temps, ta vaillance, et ton Roi." ["Let time, your valor, and your King act."] While Don Fernand does have the "last word" of the play, it is a word of deferral rather than conclusion, one which, while asserting royal authority over the action of the play of the court, nevertheless puts off a final resolution of that action indefinitely, referring it instead to an indeterminate time beyond the fifth-act curtain.[31] A complete resolution of the conflict is not yet within the grasp of royal authority; such a resolution, only implicit in *Le Cid*, must be deferred until such time as the royal *personnage* can itself be said to occupy the role here played by Rodrigue. Such a moment, unique in the theatre of Corneille, is found in *Cinna*.

ii.   "Je le suis, je veux l'être": *Cinna*

Le Cid presents to Corneille's audience the problem of noble identity in a court context, without perhaps offering any definitive solutions to that problem; in *Cinna*, the same problem is again presented, this time under slightly different conditions, and with accordingly different answers. What was in the earlier play only virtual or potential conflict becomes in *Cinna* a more genuine and substantial threat to the seat of political authority. To this sharpening and actualization of conflict corresponds a more unequivocal statement of its solution. If, in *Cinna*, the danger to central authority is considerably greater than in *Le Cid*, that danger is also far more effectively eliminated by the end of the later play. Indeed, the more serious nature of the threat in *Cinna* renders Don Fernand's pseudo-resolution unavailable to Auguste; mere neutralization through deferral is no longer possible, since Auguste has a gun pointed at his head. A more concrete solution is needed; fortunately for Auguste, he is up to the task. To be sure, the disruptive tension in *Cinna*, like that in *Le Cid*, is primarily linguistic; after all, the conspirators never progress beyond words to deeds, and the struggle between the protagonists ultimately centers around control of certain key words.[32] This is not to say that the struggle is a trivial one, nor that the consequences are insignificant. The question that *Cinna* seeks to answer is this: Who will set the discursive rules by which everyone must play? The lives of the protagonists, not to mention the future of Rome, depend on the answer.

It has been traditional to see in *Cinna* a kind of historical allegory of the 1630s and early 1640s, describing the various plots and conspiracies against the crown and/or its principal agent, Richelieu.[33] Couton, while less historically specific than is his wont, is undoubtedly right to characterize the play, not as a reflection of a particular incident, but rather as a reflection upon a general historical mood. He points out that the form – or, more precisely, the "look" – of the conspiracy in *Cinna* echoes that of the conspiracies of the reign of Louis XIII.[34] One might use this parallel to show that Cinna's conspiracy can at no point be taken seriously, since its principals are lightweights and their motives narrow and selfish. However, there are reasons to reject this view. First, the arguments advanced by Cinna and even Emilie are not without merit, at least at the beginning, especially insofar as they serve to remind the audience that Auguste has himself gained power through violent usurpation. In this sense, as Cinna will point out, Auguste is no different from, and certainly not morally superior to, the conspirators themselves. Second, the conspirators may indeed be flawed, but their flaws are not in and of themselves sufficient to insure the failure of their scheme; nor would such a self-induced failure justify the position of Auguste.[35] To demonstrate the ultimate validity of Auguste's seizure of power, the conspiracy against him must have both practical credibility and moral force, so that Auguste's final triumph over the conspirators may be seen as more than just a hollow victory over unworthy adversaries. It therefore seems most accurate to suggest that the conspiracy is doomed not (just) because the conspirators are impotent or inept, but because they are (and must be) rendered such in the course of the play by Auguste.

Moreover, it seems a misapplication of categories to describe the motivations or actions of the conspirators as "private" or "selfish," since, as has been already suggested above, it is difficult if not impossible to speak of a genuinely "private" self in Corneille. Even the most overtly "selfish" character, Emilie, functions not as an independent and self-sufficient monad but rather as an element within a specific code of public performance, a code she herself is careful to articulate. Emilie is no post-romantic individualist; she does not and cannot conceive of herself or her relations to Cinna, Auguste, and the rest except through a specific conceptual (and linguistic) vocabulary, that of the Old-Nobility code of honor. Even her amorous relationship with Cinna exists and is given structure and meaning only within a publicly performed matrix of political and social ties that define each individual's identity and relationship to the other(s). Therefore, rather than ascribing Emilie's desire for retribution to her own selfishness, or even to a simple familial vendetta, it should be read in the context of a larger structure of public meaning.

Emilie herself insists on this reading. When, for example, her "confidente" Fulvie quite sensibly points out that since Auguste's brutality has inspired so much public animosity, his downfall is inevitable, and that therefore Emilie should not risk involving herself in dangerous revolutionary schemes, Emilie is indignant (I, ii, 97): "Quoi, je le haïrai sans tâcher de lui nuire?" ["What, I shall hate him without trying to harm him?"] For her, there is nothing worse than (100) "une haine obscure, et des voeux impuissants" ["an obscure hatred, and impotent vows"]; the demise of Auguste will be wholly unsatisfying unless it is simultaneously perceived as public retribution for the death of her father. She huffily rejects any suggestion that she leave the dirty work to others:

> C'est une lâcheté que de remettre à d'autres
> Les intérêts publics qui s'attachent aux nôtres.
> Joignons à la douceur de venger nos parents
> La gloire qu'on remporte à punir les Tyrans,
> Et faisons publier par toute l'Italie,

"La liberté de Rome est l'oeuvre d'Emilie,
On a touché son âme, et son coeur s'est épris,
Mais elle n'a donné son amour qu'à ce prix." (I, ii, 105–12)

[It is cowardice to leave to others
The public interest when it coincides with our own.
Let us join, to the pleasure of avenging our parents,
The glory that one gains from punishing tyrants,
And make it known throughout Italy,
"The liberty of Rome is the work of Emilie;
Her soul has been touched, and her heart captured,
But she has only given her love at this price."]

Her quest for vengeance is a quest for *gloire*, a public confirmation of her
noble identity. Now, Emilie's motives may here be said to be "personal" in
that she desires for herself the public acclaim of having restored to Rome its
former "liberté," but even here the self in question is not an individual one.
She speaks in the first person *plural*, which would seem to indicate that it is
her family – and perhaps by extension her class, the senatorial class
displaced by Auguste – for which and in the person of which she speaks.[36]
She makes even her love for Cinna explicitly conditional upon the fulfillment of her public, political ends. Moreover, when discussing this love,
even though she does revert to speaking of herself in the singular, it is in the
third person. Thus, precisely when we might expect her to speak most
revealingly of her *own* concerns, she speaks instead from the point of view
of the audience, *son public*, as though quoting a review of her performance;
she becomes for herself an object of public contemplation, a performer on a
stage.[37]

The role she is here performing is that of a Roman nobility which, jealous
of its *franchise*, sees itself as the guardian of "la liberté romaine," and which
therefore hates above all else the idea of a king ruling Rome. Witness, for
example, Emilie's tirade when Cinna begins, later in the play, to suspect
that being Auguste's subject may not be the worst of all possible alternatives:

Souviens-toi de ton nom, soutiens sa dignité,
Et prenant d'un Romain la générosité,
Sache qu'il n'en est point que le Ciel n'ait fait naître
Pour commander aux Rois, et pour vivre sans maître. (III, iv, 999–1002)

[Remember your name, uphold its dignity,
And taking the generosity of a Roman,
Know that there is none that Heaven has not caused to be born
To command Kings, and to live without a master.]

(This is, of course, one of Corneille's favorite historical commonplaces, one which appears repeatedly in his Roman plays;[38] in *Cinna* it is Maxime who articulates this viewpoint most clearly.[39]) One of the performative strategies proper to this role is the aligning of its particular interests with more universal concerns; here, for example, Emilie explicitly links her specific ends with those of "Rome" in the largest sense. Just as when she refers to the conspiracy as serving (I, iii, 155) "[l]'intérêt d'Emilie, et celui des Romains" ["the interest of Emilie, and that of the Romans"], her rhetoric is here meant to show that her interests are not just those of the group which actually stands to lose most by the accession of Auguste to absolute power, but those of all Romans. This effort to make the private appear public may of course be seen as an effort to avoid the charge of "selfishness," a charge which would tend to negate whatever legitimacy the aristocratic revolt might otherwise possess. (Emilie also strikes a pose of noble self-sacrifice, as when she professes to disdain as "une lâcheté" the delegating of her revenge to others – yet this is precisely what she actually does in getting Cinna to perform the deed.) This kind of bad faith, whereby the interests of a particular class are pseudo-generalized, through a rhetorical perform-ance, into a public good, undoubtedly acts to undermine the revolt. How-ever, as already suggested, this does not seem sufficient, either logically or dramatically, to justify its failure; and I wish to argue in what follows that the real weakness of the conspiracy, and the flaw that allows Auguste not just to defeat the conspirators but also to demonstrate convincingly his own superiority *on their terrain*, is in fact the reverse: the conspirators insist on keeping to themselves a rhetoric that is actually community property, and are unwilling to "go public" with a mode of performance that ought to be deployed on a civic stage.

This rhetoric, consisting of a repertoire or vocabulary of verbal strategies and performed behaviors, is the rhetoric of nobility. We have already seen, in our discussion of *Le Cid*, how this vocabulary tends to absolutes: there can be only one Bravest Man at a time. Here, similarly, when Emilie lays claim to certain Noble Attributes (*générosité, franchise, courage, vertu*, etc.) she seems to believe that they are valid only as absolute quantities, and that nobody else can share or participate in them. While she is conscious of her nobility (and that of her co-conspirators, which she seems to see as an extension of her own) as a performance, the relation between performer and audience is, for her, entirely unidirectional. Her acting out of her noble role has a straightforward linear structure: (1) she performs; (2) the audi-ence is *ébloui*; (3) curtain. The idea of a mutual exchange between audience and performer is entirely absent. This performance is also unidirectional in another sense, having to do with temporality or history. As we have already seen, such unconditional nobility locates the noble entirely outside the continuum of history, where the only alternative to successful, that is complete and instantaneous, self-realization is death, preferably self-induced. Emilie herself discovers this unpleasant truth when, her plans having been foiled, she finds herself with no other option; and, as the following passage shows, it is precisely and exclusively at this moment that her *vertu*, *courage*, and so forth are most fully realized:

> Si l'effet a manqué, ma gloire n'est pas moindre,
> N'ayant pu vous [son père] venger je vous irai rejoindre;
> Mais si fumante encore d'un généreux courroux,
> Par un trépas si noble, et si digne de vous,
> Qu'il vous fera sur l'heure aisément reconnaître
> Le sang des grands Héros dont vous m'avez fait naître.   (IV, iv, 1309–14)

> [If the attempt has failed, my glory is yet no less,
> Not having been able to avenge you [her father], I will go to meet you;
> But so hot still from a generous wrath,
> By such a noble death, and one so worthy of you,
> That it will make you instantly and easily recognize
> The blood of the great heroes from whom you and I are descended.]

Even her death is conceived of as a performance, a spectacle displaying and confirming her *gloire*, and directed at a specific audience. Here, however, the audience in question is not the court, Cinna, Auguste, or anyone else on Earth, since it is the baseness of the world that has driven her to this pass; no, the only audience worthy of viewing the grand sacrificial ritual of her death is an otherworldly one, in this case her late father. She spells out the exact effect that the spectacle is to have on this quasi-divine onlooker; she hopes, or rather knows, that her performance will make him "sur l'heure aisément reconnaître" her superlative nobility, equal only to his own.

It seems, then, that such absolute nobility has the inevitable effect of driving its possessor out of history and ultimately out of existence. At the very least, the noble is forced out of the present and into the future (as when Rodrigue goes off to conquer the Moors at the end of *Le Cid*) or the past, as here when Emilie plans to rejoin an ancestral ideal. The values she espouses belong to another, earlier time, an extinct moment no longer accessible except through self-extinction. And yet she sees herself as belonging still to that period; she insists that, even if the circumstances have changed after the rise of Auguste, she herself has not (I, ii, 72, 78): "Je demeure toujours la fille d'un proscrit. [...] Je suis ce que j'étais..." ["I still remain the daughter of one banished. [...] I am what I was..."] She appears to recognize that the values of nobility (in the form that she gives them) are not applicable to the less-than-ideal present in which she finds herself. The rules by which she plays – or claims to play – are not those by which the game is now played; she therefore proposes to quit the game entirely.

If Emilie could be taken at her word – that is, if she were as purely noble as she claims to be – then she would be a truly formidable adversary, and Auguste would be in serious trouble, as would the entire notion of absolutism. Ironically, however, Emilie undermines her own claims to absolute title over the ideology of nobility and its attendant vocabulary when, even as she makes those claims, she stands these quantities on their heads.[40] As early as the first two scenes of the first act, Emilie indicates that she intends to attain her ends "by any means necessary," and (I, ii, 83) that "[p]our qui venge son père il n'est point de forfaits" ["for one who avenges one's father there is no infamy"]. These are familiar tropes of the vulgarized Machiavel of Renaissance drama, and as such already begin to undermine Emilie's position. In III, iv, this stance is pushed even farther, when Cinna tries to convince Emilie that he is honor-bound not to assassinate Auguste, since Auguste has been so generous both to him and to Emilie. Emilie, irate, insists first of all on her own complete independence; Auguste may be King of the World, "[m]ais le coeur d'Emilie est hors de son pouvoir" (III, iv, 943) ["but the heart of Emilie is beyond his power"].[41] Cinna begs her not to force him to behave in a dishonorable way towards Auguste, since

> Une âme généreuse et que la vertu guide
> Fuit la honte des noms d'ingrate, et de perfide,
> Elle en hait l'infamie attachée au bonheur,
> Et n'accepte aucun bien aux dépens de l'honneur. (III, iv, 969–72)

> [A generous soul, and one guided by virtue,
> Flees the shame of the names of ingrate, and betrayer,
> It hates the infamy thus attached to happiness,
> And accepts no good at the expense of honor.]

It is the negative public perception of such a performance that makes it such an unattractive alternative; perfidious deeds may be bad enough, but it is the "noms" such deeds and their perpetrators are given, the public "infamie" that follows, that are anathema to a noble soul like Cinna. (Cinna here begins to sound like nothing so much as the Baconian "New Man," one who recognizes the absolute importance of appearance as it is perceived by one's public, as well as his total dependence on the monarch as the ultimate arbiter of language and appearance. We will have more to say about this later.) Emilie, meanwhile, refuses the idea that any audience reaction other than her own can have any importance whatsoever, and insists, à la Humpty Dumpty, that words mean what she says they do:

Je fais gloire pour moi de cette ignominie,
La perfidie est noble envers la Tyrannie,
Et quand on rompt le cours d'un sort si malheureux,
Les coeurs les plus ingrats sont les plus généreux.

Cinna: Vous faites des vertus au gré de votre haine.

Emilie: Je me fais des vertus dignes d'une Romaine. (III, iv, 973–78)

[I make this ignominy into glory for myself;
Perfidy is noble against tyranny,
And when one puts a stop to such a wretched state of affairs,
The most ungrateful hearts are the most generous.

Cinna: You make virtues to suit your hatred.

Emilie: I make myself virtues worthy of a Roman.]

Cinna sees perfectly well that Emilie is claiming absolute title to the traditional categories of nobility, and that she is perfectly willing to invert the meaning of its vocabulary (*gloire = ignominie*; *perfide = noble*; *ingrat = généreux*), if that is what it takes to retain control. Emilie insists in return that she is merely forging virtues for herself according to the paradigm of the Virtuous Roman Citizen; but it is clear that this "Romaine" is a citizen of a Rome no longer extant, if indeed it ever existed, and that such wilful commandeering of what I hope to show is a public vocabulary can only be perceived, in the present, as the work of an ignoble Machiavel. Emilie's error, like that of Don Gomès, is ultimately a historical one. She fails to read history aright, in that she has not caught up with the Novus Ordo of the age of Auguste. One can even argue that the consequences of her error are the same as they are for Don Gomès; she does survive, in a sense, but only after a complete transformation of her personality. When, at V, iii, 1726, Emilie announces of her former hatred for Auguste: "Elle est morte..." ["It is dead..."], surely it is not stretching a point to say that the Emilie of the first four-and-a-half acts is also dead.

This is not to say, of course, that Emilie is the only character who undergoes some kind of alteration; on the contrary, the radical transformation of Emilie differs more in degree than in kind from the various conversions undergone by the other principals in the play. Her conversion is so drastic because of her previous (if more or less logically consistent) extremism; but everyone in *Cinna*, including Auguste, needs to have her or his attitude adjusted to some degree to conform to the exigencies of the new absolutist order. What separates Emilie from the others is this: while she claims exclusive rights to the performative rhetoric of nobility, Cinna (and Auguste) are willing to recognize that the performance is in fact common property, and is actually an exchange, where the reaction of the audience conditions and helps to determine the significance of the performance. It thus functions not as a mechanism of exclusion but as a medium of exchange between one group and another, a way of channeling and regulating both power and its perception.

This may be seen if we examine the conversation between Emilie and Cinna which takes place early in the play and in which they discuss the potential success or failure of their plot. Emilie is confident that the key is the death of Auguste, and shows little concern for or interest in what might happen afterwards. Cinna, however, is more aware of possible complications, and therefore less sure that his action, even if "successful," will have the desired results. He recognizes that it is not so much what he does, or why he does it, as how it is perceived after the fact that counts:

> Demain, j'attends la haine, ou la faveur des hommes,
> Le nom de parricide, ou de libérateur,
> César, celui d'un prince, ou d'un usurpateur.
> Du succès qu'on obtient contre la Tyrannie
> Dépend, ou notre gloire, ou notre ignominie,
> Et le Peuple inégal à l'endroit des Tyrans,
> S'il les deteste morts, les adore vivants. (I, iii, 250–56)

> [Tomorrow, I await either the hatred or the favor of men,
> The name of parricide, or of liberator;
> Caesar, that of a prince, or of a usurper.
> On the results we obtain against tyranny
> Depends, either our glory, or our ignominy,
> And the people, inconstant about tyrants,
> If they hate them dead, they adore them living.]

The actual motivations for his action, no matter how pure or disinterested, are irrelevant, and play no part in determining his eventual status; all that counts is that Auguste be well and truly killed, and the audience response to that deed. If Cinna makes a clean job of it, he will be perceived as a liberating hero; if he fails, Auguste will be the hero, and Cinna the villain, quite independently of Cinna's putative inner state of selfless civic high-mindedness (or, for that matter, Auguste's alleged villainy). The "gloire" or "ignominie" of an action are not necessary consequences of the inner state of the performing subject, but rather contingent phenomena dependent upon the perception of a public before which that action is performed. It is the "nom," assigned by the audience, and based upon that audience's perception of external results, that counts. Cinna's view here, that meaning is determined retroactively by (perceived) success, will turn out to be the key to the political universe of the play.[42]

Nowhere is this clearer than in the debate between Cinna and Maxime, with Auguste as mediator and interested audience, on the advisability of Auguste's resigning his position. Cinna suggests that for Auguste to reject the Imperial throne would be to delegitimize in retrospect both the very idea of "le pouvoir suprême" and the violent means used by both Auguste and his illustrious predecessor, model, and source of legitimacy, Julius Caesar, to attain it.

> C'est ce que fit César, il vous faut aujourd'hui
> Condamner sa mémoire, ou faire comme lui.
> Si le pouvoir suprême est blamé par Auguste,
> Caesar fut un tyran, et son trépas fut juste,
> Et vous devez aux Dieux compte de tout le sang
> Dont vous l'avez vengé pour monter à son rang.   (II, i, 427–32)

> [This is what Caesar did; today you must
> Condemn his memory, or do as he did.
> If supreme power is condemned by Augustus,
> Caesar was a tyrant, and his death was just,
> And you owe an accounting to the Gods of all the blood
> Through which you have avenged him, to climb to his rank.]

Since this (de)legitimization occurs after the fact, the events themselves obviously do not change; it is only the perception thereof that changes. Cinna, recognizing that how the action will appear is what counts, argues from political expediency. If you abdicate, he says, history will be rewritten in a way that is unfavorable, not to say fatal, to you: if, however, you retain power, the opposite will be true. Auguste will be in a position to control the perception of both inscribed past and performed present in such a way as to maximize his own power and security, not to mention that of Rome. Abdicating, on the other hand, would expose him (and, as Cinna later suggests, the State) to terminal danger. Cinna is saying that if Auguste wants to look good – and stay alive – he has no choice but to stay in charge. Auguste may be "maître de l'Univers" (II, i, 440), but he is nevertheless a prisoner of his role.

Governing, for Auguste, thus becomes an act of persuasion, an attempt to put on a convincing performance, one that proffers its own interpretation of itself, and whose purpose is to persuade its audience that that interpretation is the correct one. The critical question facing Auguste, then, is: What are the best *means* of persuasion? Note that Cinna refuses even to ask the question of whether or not Auguste "belongs" in his present position; following Bodin and other political theorists of the late Renaissance, Cinna takes for granted that power, however acquired, is self-legitimizing. There are two main reasons for this, both of which are touched upon by Cinna in his speech. The first is Divine Right: he who holds the *imperium* does so because it is the will of God. Cinna alludes to this when he points out to Auguste that he must be under the protection of a divinity, since no fewer than ten attempts upon his person have failed.[43] One of the most important consequences of this view, and one which would presumably have been familiar to any seventeenth-century audience, is that it renders sinful and sacrilegious any rebellion whatsoever against any ruler, no matter how tyrannical.[44] The second reason, while certainly less exalted, is perhaps more immediately practical; it concerns what Bodin calls "droit de guerre."[45] Power gained through conquest is just as legitimate as any other kind, says Cinna, and hence there is no injustice in Auguste's present position, and no reason for him to be ashamed of it or to contemplate abdication; indeed, to do so would be a shameful and destabilizing error:

> On ne renonce point aux grandeurs légitimes,
> On garde sans remords ce qu'on acquiert sans crimes,
> Et plus le bien qu'on quitte est noble, grand, exquis,
> Plus qui l'ose quitter le juge mal acquis.
> N'imprimez pas, Seigneur, cette honteuse marque
> A ces rares vertus qui vous ont fait Monarque;
> Vous l'êtes justement, et c'est sans attentat
> Que vous avez changé la forme de l'Etat.
> Rome est dessous vos lois par la droit de la guerre
> Qui sous les lois de Rome a mis toute la Terre,
> Vos armes l'ont conquise, et tous les conquérants,
> Pour être usurpateurs, ne sont pas des Tyrans.
> Quand ils ont sous leurs lois asservi des Provinces,
> Gouvernant justement ils s'en font justes Princes...   (II, i, 413–26)

> [One does not renounce legitimate grandeur;
> One keeps without remorse what one acquires without crime,
> And the more noble, grand, and exquisite are the goods we leave behind,
> The more the one who dares to leave them judges them ill-gotten.
> Do not, Seigneur, stamp this shameful mark
> On those rare virtues which have made you the Ruler;
> You hold your position justly, and without violence
> You have changed the form of the State.
> Rome is ruled by you through the right of war
> Which has placed the entire world under the rule of Rome;
> Your arms have conquered it, and not all conquerors,
> Even if usurpers, are tyrants.
> When they have subjugated provinces to their rule,
> By governing justly they make themselves just Princes...]

The answer to the question posed earlier is clear: governing justly and magnanimously is the best, not to say the only, means of persuading the governed of the justice and right of one's position. Performing the role of a wise and just ruler literally (re)makes the performer in the image of such a ruler, simultaneously rewriting the past so as to bring it into conformity with a present "noble, grand, [et] exquis."[46]

There is, as always, a catch. Maxime unwittingly zeroes in on it when he attempts to counter Cinna's argument with an appeal to Auguste's higher instincts. He, too, grants that Auguste has gained power legitimately, but argues that it is more noble to give up power than to retain it:

> Suivez, suivez, Seigneur, le Ciel qui vous inspire,
> Votre gloire redouble à mépriser l'Empire,
> Et vous serez fameux chez la Postérité
> Moins pour l'avoir conquis que pour l'avoir quitté.
> Le bonheur peut conduire à la grandeur suprême,
> Mais pour y renoncer, il faut la vertu même,
> Et peu de généreux vont jusqu'à dédaigner,
> Après un sceptre acquis, la douceur de régner. (II, i, 473–80)

> [Follow, follow, Seigneur, Heaven that inspires you,
> Your glory redoubles when you scorn the Empire,
> And you will be famous to Posterity
> Less for having conquered it than for having left it behind.
> Good fortune may lead to supreme grandeur,
> But to renounce it demands virtue itself,
> And not many *généreux* will go so far as to scorn,
> Having acquired the sceptre, the pleasure of ruling.]

Maxime here brings to bear all the key concepts of nobility: *gloire, vertu, générosité, mépris, renommée,* etc. He calls upon Auguste to out-noble everyone, by demonstrating, in the ultimate act of *sprezzatura,* his complete indifference to "la grandeur suprême"; in this way, says Maxime, your *gloire* – that is, the positive perception of your performance in the public eye – will be even greater than if you were Emperor. Besides, he continues, because of Rome's consummately noble spirit, every self-respecting Roman hates kings, no matter what they're called; he reminds Auguste that

> ...vous régnez dans Rome,
> Où, de quelque façon que votre Cour vous nomme,
> On hait la Monarchie, et le nom d'Empereur,
> Cachant celui de Roi, ne fait pas moins d'horreur.
> Ils passent pour Tyran quiconque s'y fait maître,
> Qui le sert, pour esclave, et qui l'aime, pour traître,
> Qui le souffre a le coeur lâche, mol, abbatu,
> Et pour s'en affranchir tout s'appelle vertu. (II, i, 481–88)

[...you rule in Rome,
Where, no matter what your Court calls you,
Monarchy is hated, and the name of Emperor,
Hiding that of King, is no less repugnant.
They call whoever makes himself master a tyrant,
Who serves him, a slave, and who loves him, a traitor,
Who puts up with him has a heart cowardly, weak, and servile,
And to liberate themselves from him, any deed is virtuous.]

Here, once again, we see an almost single-minded emphasis on naming and labels. In Maxime's model, there are two naming agencies at work: first, the Court, whose efforts to control perception and determine interpretation are here foiled by the superior hermeneutic power of the second naming agency, the Roman citizenry. This last, intransigently jealous of its *franchise*, tolerates no opposition, reserving for itself the power of assigning definitive labels and values to all the roles played on its political stage. Maxime's last statement, intended as a warning to Auguste, actually supplies to Cinna the crucial opening that enables him to demolish Maxime's entire argument; and indeed as the play proceeds we will see Maxime's position undercut in several critical ways. To begin with, Maxime himself becomes less convincing as a spokesman for supposedly noble points of view as we discover that his participation in the conspiracy is actually motivated by a desire to supplant Cinna as Emilie's lover,[47] and when he is suborned by the irredeemably base and ignoble Euphorbe into betraying his co-conspirators his stock drops to zero. Moreover, the rhetoric of inversion with which this passage closes wrongly arrogates to the citizenry the arbitrary power to call vice virtue – in the name of *franchise*, says Maxime, "tout s'appelle vertu." This is the same mistake, it will be recalled, that Emilie commits when she insists that words such as *gloire*, *vertu*, and *générosité* mean only what she wants them to mean. Emilie privatizes this vocabulary, refusing to recognize it as a medium of exchange; Maxime, in an equally one-sided way, assigns the exclusive rights to that vocabulary to the citizenry, again failing to recognize that it is – or at least must needs be perceived as – a means of communication rather than of coercion.[48] Cinna recognizes that such attempts at privatizing the necessarily public must lead to chaos; liberty, he says, is

...un bien imaginaire,
Plus nuisible qu'utile, et qui n'approche pas
De celui qu'un bon prince apporte à ses Etats.
Avec ordre et raison les honneurs il dispense,
Avec discernement punit et récompense,
Et dispose de tout en juste possesseur,
Sans rien précipiter de peur d'un successeur.

Mais quand le Peuple est maître, on n'agit qu'en tumulte,
La voix de la raison jamais ne se consulte,
Les honneurs sont vendus aux plus ambitieux,
L'autorité livrée aux plus séditieux. (II, i, 502–12)

> [... an imaginary good,
> More harmful than useful, and which is nowhere near
> That which a good prince brings to his State.
> With order and reason he dispenses honors,
> With discernment punishes and rewards,
> And disposes of all as a just possessor
> Without precipitating anything for fear of a successor.
> But when the people are master, there is only tumult,
> Nobody listens to the voice of reason,
> Honors are sold to the most ambitious,
> And authority delivered to the most seditious.]

For Cinna, the alternative is clear; and his reasons are extremely signifi-cant. Why is a monarchy superior? Because names, labels, public status, and in particular "honneurs," are assigned, not according to the demands of short-sighted private *intérêt*, but rather with *justesse* and *raison*, thanks to the clear, disinterested vision of the "bon prince." This prevents any confusion or disorder, and ensures, among other things, that the truly noble need have nothing to fear either from the prince or from the baser sort (the "plus ambitieux" and "plus séditieux").[49] Cinna finally insists, in good Aristotelian fashion (II, i, 521): "Le pire des Etats c'est l'Etat popu-laire" ["The worst of States is a Democracy"].

Even if Maxime's stance were not weakened in these ways, however, his argument would necessarily fail. This is because the most important way in which he undercuts his own position, and the one which represents the "catch" referred to above, is that Maxime is appealing to a particular kind of noble *gloire*, invoked earlier by Emilie, a strictly private *gloire* which is not only purely selfish but no longer even available in the Rome of the present, least of all to Auguste. "Selfish," because it refuses to recognize any perception other than that of the noble subject, and "no longer available," since – as we have seen – its realization necessitates an exit from history, which is what Maxime is really asking Auguste to do.[50] However, as Cinna has argued, such an exit would have catastrophic consequences not only for Auguste but also for Rome. Cinna recognizes, as Maxime does not, Auguste's dependence on his role, and sees that, for Auguste, retreat into an illusory private sphere is no longer possible. Moreover, if Auguste needs his role to ensure his personal safety, that role is in turn necessary to the stability of the State. Cinna paints a vivid picture of the violent chaos into which Rome will collapse without Auguste at the helm, and pleads with him to take command (II, i, 589–90): "Seigneur, pour sauver Rome il faut qu'elle s'unisse / En la main d'un bon Chef à qui tout obéisse." ["Seigneur, to save Rome it must be united / under a good Ruler whom all obey."] This seems at last to push Auguste over the edge:

> N'en délibérons plus, cette pitié l'emporte,
> Mon repos m'est bien cher, mais Rome est la plus forte,
> Et quelque grand malheur qui m'en puisse arriver,
> Je consens à me perdre afin de la sauver. (II, i, 621–24)

> [Let us deliberate no longer, this pity wins out,
> My repose is dear to me, but Rome is the stronger,
> And whatever great misfortune may befall me,
> I consent to give myself up to save [Rome].]

Auguste thus decides to sacrifice Octave for the sake of Caesar, a sacrifice of self which will come to be seen, in the political context of the play, as the supreme act of *générosité*. Auguste will in fact out-noble everyone else in the play, but not in the solipsistic, regressive way that Maxime proposes and that Emilie attempts to enact. Instead, his submission to the demands of history will constitute a new paradigm for nobility, one which sacrifices individual *franchise* (ultimately characterized as both disruptive and illusory) in favor of a purely public self which masquerades, at least, as the incarnation of the public will.[51]

We have not yet addressed the complex question of Cinna's relationship to the sentiments he utters in this conversation with Maxime and Auguste. It may seem to us, as it does to Maxime in II, ii, that Cinna is simply selling out. Given that Cinna's words to Auguste directly contradict his previously proclaimed ardor for the Cause, his attempt to defend his actions by claiming that he was merely trying to insure that Auguste remained in his position long enough to be assassinated, rather than foiling the plot by abdicating before the conspirators could get to him, may seem to be nothing but a lame rationalization. It is already clear at this point to the play's audience, if not yet to Maxime, that Cinna is at least partly motivated by a desire to prove his manhood to Emilie in what seems to be the only way acceptable to her. We may therefore wonder if this sort of duplicity – lying to Auguste in order to win the heart of his lover – is not an act of dissimulation unworthy of a Noble Roman. However, this would be out of keeping with what we have seen thus far of Cinna's character, and in fact it might be argued that his insistence that Auguste remain onstage in his role as *Imperator* is of a piece with Cinna's understanding of the public, performative nature of the entire situation. To Cinna, the removal of Auguste from his position will be worth nothing if it, too, does not occur in the most public manner possible; the last thing he wants is for Auguste to get off the hook via (II, ii, 658) "un lâche repentir" ["a cowardly repentance"]. Here, too, though, we might suspect that Cinna is motivated as much by private lust as by public high-mindedness.

However, as the scene progresses we see that, if anything, Maxime seems to be the more prone to moral equivocation. To his dubious suggestion that, to one proposing to overthrow an alleged tyrant, anything is permitted, he now adds further evidence of a willingness to act basely if he feels the need. What counts is that Auguste is removed; the means by which that removal is accomplished are irrelevant. Better that Auguste should remove himself, foiling the conspirators' desire for the *gloire* of a public revenge, than that the conspiracy should run the risk of failure. He rejects Cinna's insistence on the original plan for the solution to their problem:

> Maxime: Vous la voulez sanglante, et la rendez douteuse.
>
> Cinna: Vous la voulez sans peine, et la rendez honteuse.
>
> Maxime: Pour sortir de ses fers, jamais on ne rougit.
>
> Cinna: On en sort lâchement si la vertu n'agit. (II, ii, 681–84)
>
> [Maxime: You want it to be bloody, and make it uncertain.
>
> Cinna: You want it to be easy, and make it shameful.
>
> Maxime: To throw off our chains, we never blush.
>
> Cinna: We throw them off cravenly, if we do it without virtue.]

Maxime here begins to show what will prove to be his true colors. He may be striving for the moral high ground, accusing Cinna of hypocrisy, but in fact we see that Maxime is the duplicitous one. His speech to Auguste, which may have seemed to be merely the sincere expression of a republican political philosophy, is now seen to have been merely a practical stratagem to persuade Auguste to abdicate. Our impressions will be confirmed in the very next scene, where we find that Maxime, too, is motivated by a desire for Emilie. In itself, while it shows him to be less selflessly dedicated to "liberté" than we might have thought, it does not necessarily make him any worse than Cinna. However, where Cinna's nobility of character renders him ultimately unwilling to sacrifice principle for Emilie, Maxime's desire proves too strong for him, and makes him vulnerable to being suborned by that base-born "âme de boue" ["soul of mud"], Euphorbe. Thus corrupted, he will ignobly betray not only the trust placed in him by Auguste, but also his best friend and the object of his affections.[52]

This gives Auguste's unintentionally ironic remark (II, i, 628), "Je vois trop que vos coeurs n'ont point pour moi de fard" ["I see clearly that your hearts hide nothing from me"] a new twist. Auguste believes that both Cinna and Maxime are speaking to him with perfect *franchise*, in every sense of the word, and that neither is concealing from him their true feelings. However, we, the audience, think we know better, since we have already seen that Cinna is planning to overthrow him; and we are equally convinced that Maxime is merely saying what he really thinks about empire. Now, though, we begin to see that Auguste is in fact wrong about Maxime, and that – even more ironically – he is, or will be, correct about Cinna. I would suggest that the question of whether or not Cinna "believes" what he says to Auguste is ultimately irrelevant; the fact is that he is converted by his own performance, or at least the public effect is the same. Cinna may in a sense be said to be trapped by his public role, that of *defensor imperii*, in the same way that Auguste is trapped by his role of *imperator*. Having presented such a convincing case for empire, he finds himself compelled – perhaps honor-bound – to behave accordingly. Indeed, the next time we see him (III, ii), it is already clear that it is only (814) his "serment exécrable" ["vile oath"] to Emilie that prevents him from abandoning the conspiracy altogether; and two scenes later, Emilie's arbitrary inversion of the key terms of the noble code,[53] on which his *serment* depends, destroys the very basis of his loyalty to her.

Cinna is neither the fool nor the weakling that some have made him out to be.[54] Initially dominated by Emilie, he comes to recognize (and to represent) the values of a new, public nobility, over and against the appeal of an illusory private version. Thanks both to his consistently "noble" character and to Emilie's unconscious undermining of her own cause, he is able to reject the demands of a spurious private sphere, as represented by Emilie, in favor of the authentic claims of the *res publica*, as represented by Auguste. As we have seen, this consistency makes it possible for him to "convert" to the role of a worthy subject of Auguste without any radical change, since in a sense he has been "converted" from the beginning.

We have already suggested that Auguste is the prisoner of his role, and that Cinna's argument for absolutism is sound in the context of the play not only because it is consistent with seventeenth-century political theory on the subject but because Auguste does not in fact have any other choice available to him. This would seem to make moot the tired question of whether the clemency of Auguste is *politique* or *généreux*.[55] Livie understands this perfectly well when she counsels Auguste on the proper course of action in IV, iii. Her approach initially seems purely pragmatic; she suggests that, since adopting the role of a brutal and repressive dictator has thus far proven ineffective, why not try the opposite tack? Auguste doesn't want to hear it, and says that he will simply quit, retiring to the country. Livie insists, as we have already seen Cinna do, that this option is no longer available, if indeed it ever was; personal, private satisfaction, of any kind, simply does not exist for someone in Auguste's position. She recognizes that the key to success, for Auguste, is to seize control not of the persons of the conspirators but of the discourse of nobility that they inhabit. His role demands that he out-noble those around him, in a radically transcendent gesture of self-sacrificing *générosité* (IV, iii, 1243–44): "C'est régner sur vous-même, et par un noble choix / Pratiquer la vertu la plus digne des Rois" ["It is to reign over yourself, and by a noble choice / Practice the virtue most worthy of Kings"].[56] By ruling over himself – that is, wholly effacing that self behind its public role – Auguste will demonstrate his fitness to rule over others, to become the embodiment of the State. The persuasive success of this performance depends on whether or not it is completely opaque; if it is truly transcendent, if the audience is so dazzled by it that it can see nothing of Auguste's "private self" behind it, then its opacity leaves Auguste free to impose the interpretation of his choice.[57] Whether or not Auguste is truly the Great Man he hopes to be, or merely another efficient politician, making the right moves at the right time in an effort to maintain power, is finally irrelevant.[58] In order for Auguste's actions to be effective within the world of the play, his "motivations" must remain concealed behind the mask of his performance, and the question of what he "really" thinks is not only naïve but immaterial. What matters, as Livie recognizes, is what is seen, the visible "marque" (IV, iii, 1265–66): ". . . enfin la clémence est la plus belle marque / Qui fasse à l'Univers connaître un vrai Monarque" ["... finally clemency is the finest sign / Which makes a true King known to the Universe"]. Ultimately, of course, the performer becomes the performance; as we have been insisting, for Auguste above all others there is and can be no distinction between himself and his public role. Precisely because his performance consists in the permanent eclipse of himself, he *becomes* his role whether he "wants" to or not.

This is not to say that the transition is an easy one; yet, as the action of the play demonstrates, it is not until that transition is complete that his power is confirmed, and the safety of the Roman state assured. When he confronts Cinna with his knowledge of the conspiracy, he attempts to assert his power – his superior *noblesse* – over Cinna by claiming that the latter's noble identity, his public role on which his hopes for success depend, is wholly contingent on his (Auguste's) good will:

> Ma faveur fait ta gloire, et ton pouvoir en vient,
> Elle seule t'élève, et seule te soutient,

C'est elle qu'on adore, et non pas ta personne;
Tu n'as crédit, ni rang, qu'autant qu'elle t'en donne,
Et pour te faire choir je n'aurais aujourd'hui
Qu'à retirer la main qui seule est ton appui.   (V, i, 1527–32)

[My favor makes your glory, and your power comes from it,
It alone elevates you, and alone sustains you,
It is that which is adored, and not your person;
You have neither credit, nor rank, except insomuch as it is granted to you,
And to make you fall today, I would have only
To take away the hand which alone is your support.]

This will be true later, but it is not yet so; Auguste is probably right to assert that Cinna is not fit to exercise the *imperium*, but he has yet to prove that he, Auguste, is any better. Cinna, although dumbfounded, therefore refuses to surrender; all may be lost, but he is still a Noble Roman, and thus he admonishes Auguste (1551–52): "N'attendez point de moi d'infâmes repentirs, / D'inutiles regrets, ni de honteux soupirs" ["Don't expect from me any disgraceful repentance, / Useless regret, or shameful sighs"]. Auguste is frustrated (1557): "Tu me braves, Cinna, tu fais le magnanime..." ["You defy me, Cinna, you are acting the *magnanime*..."] Auguste does not yet have exclusive control of the vocabulary of nobility; Cinna is still able to make use of it according to his own wishes, to define his noble identity independently of the will of Auguste or anyone else.[59] For a moment Auguste forgets all about clemency, and allows his private desire for revenge to take over; he tells Cinna (1561): "Fais ton Arrêt toi-même, et choisis tes supplices" ["Pronounce your own sentence, and choose your tortures"]. Fortunately, before Cinna can respond, he is interrupted by the arrival of Livie, Emilie, and Fulvie, and Auguste is confronted with the realization that even Emilie, his adopted daughter, was in on the scheme. Cinna and Emilie then proceed to vie with one another in claiming sole responsibility for the plot, each of them thus trying to demonstrate his or her own *générosité* in two ways: by sacrificing him- or herself for the other, and through taking credit for the plan. Finally they resolve to share equally, using all the critical words of the vocabulary of nobility to push that nobility – here, obviously, Emilie's atavistic version – to its logical endpoint, death:

En ce noble dessein nos coeurs se rencontrèrent,
Nos esprits généreux ensemble le formèrent,
Ensemble nous cherchons l'honneur d'un beau trépas,
Vous vouliez nous unir, ne nous séparez pas.   (V, ii, 1653–56)

[In this noble plan our hearts were united,

Our generous spirits formed it together,
Together we seek the honor of a fine death,
You wanted to unite us, do not separate us.]

Auguste is now finding it even more difficult to assert control over the discourse of nobility, and moves from the pseudo-*générosité* of allowing Cinna to choose his own penalty to the outright nastiness of deciding for himself that the punishment of the conspirators will be the most unpleasant he can devise. He tells Emilie and Cinna (V, ii, 1660–62):

Il faut bien satisfaire aux feux dont vous brûlez,
Et que tout l'Univers, sachant ce qui m'anime,
S'étonne du supplice aussi bien que du crime.

[Your ardor must be satisfied,
And the whole Universe, knowing what motivates me,
Must be as appalled by the punishment as by the crime.]

Auguste is about to commit a fatal error, that of demonstrating to "l'Univers" already mentioned by Livie not his superior *noblesse* but a base and selfish vengefulness unworthy of the ruler of Rome. However, a final fortuitous interruption prevents him from immediately carrying out his plan, when Maxime enters to confess his own guilt. This is, finally, the last straw, the decisive push that sends Auguste over the edge – not into a kind of monstrous vengefulness, such as will be seen later in such figures as the Cléopâtre of *Rodogune* or *Suréna*'s Pacorus, but rather into a genuinely transcendent *générosité*, one so blinding that it reduces his erstwhile opponents to helpless nullities. This is not, however, accomplished without a struggle; as we have seen, as the fifth act builds, Auguste is tempted ever more strongly to surrender to the temptations of a private vengeance, made possible by the physical *empire* he holds over his would-be assassins. At last, however, he recognizes that his only hope for success lies in dominating the discourse of nobility on which his antagonists base their opposition, and that he can only arrive at this dominance through a corresponding domination of himself, a complete renunciation of Octave in favor of Auguste:

Je suis maître de moi comme de l'Univers.
Je le suis, je veux l'être. O Siècles, O Mémoire,
Conservez à jamais ma dernière victoire,
Je triomphe aujourd'hui du plus juste courroux
De qui le souvenir puisse aller jusqu'à vous.[60] (V, iii, 1696–1700)

[I am master of myself as of the Universe.
I am, I wish to be. O Time, O Memory,

Preserve forever my final victory;
I triumph today over the most just wrath
Which can ever be recorded in the annals of history.]

He then proceeds immediately to overwhelm Cinna and the rest with his superlative *générosité* (1707–08): "Tu trahis mes bienfaits, je les veux redoubler, / Je t'en avais comblé, je t'en veux accabler" ["You betray my kindnesses, I want to redouble them, / I had laden you with them, I want to overwhelm you with them"]. At last, there is nothing left for the conspirators but complete and utter surrender; Emilie, Auguste's most implacable opponent, is the first to capitulate, in the manner we have discussed above.[61] Cinna, too, recognizes that Auguste's claim to exclusive control of the discourse of nobility has now been realized; Auguste has demonstrated his command of a "vertu" beyond the reach even of a Roman as noble as Cinna (1731–32): "O vertu sans exemple! ô clémence qui rend / Votre pouvoir plus juste et mon crime plus grand" ["O unexampled virtue! o clemency which renders / Your power more just and my crime greater"].

This last remark of Cinna's, even though it indicates his total capitulation, reminds us that the problem is not completely solved; there is still the little matter of that "crime." Auguste may be willing to forgive and forget, but Corneille is not. The potential for violent conflict must somehow be completely excised from the system if everyone is to live happily ever after; and it is for this reason that Euphorbe exists. It seems unlikely that Auguste's *clémence* will extend beyond the circle of those with whom he shares a common vocabulary, the discourse of nobility; Euphorbe, being base-born, is rigorously excluded from that circle, and since, as we have already seen, he is made the play's carrier of the virus of villainy, it is highly probable that Auguste will heed Maxime's request (1687): "Faites périr Euphorbe au milieu des tourments" ["Cause Euphorbe to perish in the midst of torments"].

Rather than being killed or otherwise driven out of existence, then, the conspirators are transformed into ardent supporters of their erstwhile enemy; and, while they launch their rebellion in the name of a particular idea of nobility, it is precisely the conspirators' nobility that ultimately renders them susceptible to (and worthy of) being converted to the cause and viewpoint of Auguste. This conversion is possible only because both Auguste and his adversaries still speak the same language, the language of nobility, and comprehend it in more or less the same way. Auguste and Cinna can arrive at an understanding because they are both willing to abide by the same set of discursive rules; even Emilie, whose use of the vocabulary of nobility does some violence to that set of rules, can be brought around, although not without a reversal of polarities in her character. The language of the revolt is articulated around certain key terms of nobility; and it is upon precisely these terms that Auguste builds his new edifice of power. Auguste may have gained power through acts of physical violence, but he can only retain and legitimize it through pre-emptive acts of discursive authorization. The honor of all parties concerned is preserved, but in the process, the honor of all is in some sense re-inscribed, in that it is made wholly dependent upon the *magnanimité* of one. This dependency means that Auguste has done more than simply meet and defeat the Roman nobility on its own terms; he has not only appropriated those terms, he has transcended and transformed them, establishing a kind of linguistic *imperium* in which he and he alone dominates the discourse of nobility. The theatre of nobility has become, if not a solo performance, at least a show with a single star, whose supporting characters double as a uniformly appreciative audience.

This is, ultimately, the point of Corneille's absolutism – a retrospective neutralization and re-inscription of opposition, whereby all such energy is revised out of existence, or made to seem meaningless from the start. Octave/Auguste wins, so he gets to decide, retroactively, what the rules will be. This is how Octave becomes Auguste, how he converts Cinna and Emilie, how he makes their threat a non-threat, how he imposes after the fact his own reading of the language, his own interpretation of the performance. Does this mean that, if Emilie were to come out on top, her version of nobility would become the dominant one? Perhaps not; the play goes to some lengths to show that the question of who wins is not a matter of indifference, and that its answer is not arbitrary. Nevertheless, one can at least question whether this is not in itself a mystification. It is true that Auguste is shown to be right, but the play also makes clear that Auguste's rightness has a degree of arbitrariness not easily ignored. Even the view that the rebellion is doomed because any rebellion against a monarch, no matter how villainous he may be, is unacceptable, might perhaps be called into question; at the very least it ends up being justified less through divine right than through simple *de facto* pragmatism. On the one hand, Auguste's power is shown to be genuinely absolute; even that most indignantly independent resister of his *bienfaits*, "le coeur d'Emilie" – which, it will be recalled, its owner has stoutly insisted "est hors de son [Auguste's] pouvoir" – now gives in (1726): "...ce coeur devient Sujet fidèle..." ["...this heart becomes a faithful Subject..."] On the other hand, as Livie says to Auguste in her prophecy (1764), "Vous avez trouvé l'art d'être maître des coeurs" ["You have found the art of being master of hearts"]. Auguste may have managed to gain control over the *coeurs* of his subjects, but it is not automatic, and does not inhere in his person; it is rather an *art* that must be found and exercised with effort and prudence, and it is this rhetorical process of *inventio* and performance that the final act of the play lays before us in careful detail.

Livie's strange prophecy at the close of the play, both in its insistence on the totality of Auguste's success[62] and in its effort to situate the source of that success outside the contingent realm of history, therefore seems to emphasize not the security but rather the fragility of the *pax Augusti*. This is particularly true when we couple this prophecy with her remarks in the preceding scene:

> Tous ces crimes d'Etat qu'on fait pour la Couronne,
> Le Ciel nous en absout, alors qu'il nous la donne,
> Et dans le sacré rang où sa faveur l'a mis,
> Le passé devient juste, et l'avenir permis.
> Qui peut y parvenir ne peut être coupable,
> Quoi qu'il ait fait, ou fasse, il est inviolable,
> Nous lui devons nos biens, nos jours sont en sa main,
> Et jamais on n'a droit sur ceux du Souverain.   (V, ii, 1609–16)

> [All those crimes of State that one commits for the Crown,
> Heaven absolves us of them, when it gives us [the Crown],
> And in the sacred rank where its favor has placed him
> The past becomes just, and the future permitted.
> Who can attain it cannot be guilty,
> Whatever he has done, or does, he is inviolable,
> We owe him what we have, our days are in his hand,
> And we never have a right to those of the Sovereign.]

The justification for Auguste's arbitrary seizure of power must be situated outside of history precisely because his actions are finally unjustifiable from within history; and, as we have seen, it is only by jettisoning his past actions and identity that Auguste can operate in the present. His new role forces him to rewrite not only the past of others but also, and especially, of himself; in the end, it is not Auguste "himself" (indeed, the very notion of "himself" is rendered meaningless) but *Augustus Imperator*, the role enacted on the public stage, that takes over. It is not "Octave" or even "Auguste" but "le Souverain," a faceless, person-less Power, that rewrites identity and history to justify and sustain its existence.

One of the primary attributes of this quasi-autonomous role is that it attempts to present itself as a decisive and final solution to the problem of nobility in a monarchical setting, pre-empting all other solutions by removing even the possibility of alternatives. However, the apparent totality of its triumph is both fragile, as we have just seen, and ultimately illusory, since its institution through fiat conceals without eliminating the tension beneath the surface. Auguste may wish to have his triumph universalized, but he owes his success to a unique, irreproducible circumstance: the coincidence of the roles of King and Chief Noble in the same *personnage*. Likewise, he hopes that his moment of supreme triumph will be indefinitely perpetuated – a goal which Livie attempts to further in her strange prophecy, a vision including the entire submission of the most recalcitrant subjects, the total elimination of opposition, and at last (V, iii, 1772) "une place entre les Immortels" ["a place among the Immortals"].[63] And yet the play ends, as it must, precisely at the crucial defining moment, the single instant at which Auguste demonstrates his claim to the title of Noblest of All. We are denied the opportunity to see what happens next, to see the results in history of this critical moment, perhaps because it is literally impossible to go on, except in the extra-historical prophetic vision of a Livie. In other words, Auguste makes of himself a rather hard act to follow; what can he possibly do for an encore?

iii.   A brief detour via *Nicomède*

This is a question that Corneille leaves unanswered. The fragile equilibrium of *Cinna*, dependent as it is upon a fortunate confluence of attributes in a single *personnage*, breaks down, to be replaced by a grim struggle between the doomed ideals of a spotless *noblesse* and the cynical pragmatism of *la raison d'Etat*. The plays that follow *Cinna* deal for the most part with a postlapsarian world in which conflict – generally stemming from royal ingratitude – inevitably occurs between a noble paragon of virtue and a royal figure of at best imperfectly noble character. One important version of this scenario is *Nicomède* (1651), whose political structure has many similarities with *Le Cid*, most notably in the dependence of the play's royal figure on the martial prowess of his chief noble for the maintenance of his reign; but, where in *Le Cid* any conflict between these two figures remains only potential, deflected and defused in the manner we have outlined in our discussion of that play, in *Nicomède* certain obstacles to conflict are deliberately removed by the playwright. The royal figure, the unfortunate Prusias, is made not only ungrateful but weak and pusillanimous, while to Nicomède himself are given not only the usual noble attributes of perfect *générosité, franchise*, and so forth, but also the status of legitimate heir to the throne. The tension between Prusias and Nicomède is thus greatly sharpened relative to that which exists only in a virtual sense between Don Fernand and Rodrigue in the earlier play. Couton has shown that these "adjustments" are neither arbitrary nor coincidental, given the political situation in France around the time of the play's première; the parallels between Nicomède and Condé are surely deliberate.[64] Even Stegmann is compelled to admit that *Nicomède* is Corneille's most overtly political play.[65]

However, it should be pointed out that the identity between the France of 1650 and the Bithynie of Corneille's play is not perfect, and that the points of divergence are significant. One has already been mentioned: Nicomède is the eldest son of the reigning king, and therefore the genuine *héritier présomptif* to the throne; hence, he does not constitute a threat to the presumed legitimacy of that throne in the same way that Condé – of royal blood, but nevertheless definitely not the heir apparent – did under French law. The second is that the official inciter of the rebellion in the play, Laodice, is *not* (again, unlike the *Frondeurs*) a subject of the King against whom she rebels, but rather an equal and independent sovereign. She is, therefore, perfectly within her rights in fomenting rebellion against her adversary, as she herself points out to Arsinoé near the end of the play.[66] The play diverges from its putative model precisely when Corneille needs unambiguous justification of apparently seditious acts, a justification not present in the Fronde itself.[67]

In any event, it is not my intention here either to repeat or to criticize Couton's examination of the historical allegory of the play;[68] nor does it seem necessary to characterize in detail the ways in which the play demonstrates Nicomède to be a paragon of noble virtue. I wish rather to focus on the peculiarly self-conscious theatricality of *Nicomède*, and on its literal representation of political history as a public, theatrical discourse, particularly as it is manifested in the figure of Nicomède himself. What is peculiar about this play's theatricality is the nature of the audience-within-the-play for whom the performance of nobility is given. As in *Le Cid* and *Cinna*, great emphasis is placed upon the capacity of public perception to define and render valuable the performance of nobility. In the earlier works, however, the "public" within Corneille's plays, the audience for whom the theatre of nobility is performed, seems to consist primarily of other nobles, themselves actors on the same stage. Even in *Cinna*, where Auguste succeeds in converting the entire cast of the play into pure audience, all the members of that audience are of noble birth; the only exception, Euphorbe, is not just kept off the stage, he is killed off. Here, however, such a unanimity of audience is no longer possible – or at least not until the end of the play, where even the utterly villainous Arsinoé converts to virtuous and noble behavior; and, as Corneille himself points out, such a happy ending comes about only through doing considerable violence to the material. He announces to us in the "Au lecteur" that he has in fact thoroughly sanitized the play relative to its model in ancient history (and, presumably, relative to the events contemporaneous with its first performances):

> ...et pour la fin, je l'ai réduite en sorte que tous mes personnages y agissent avec générosité, et que les uns rendant ce qu'ils doivent à la vertu,

et les autres demeurant dans la fermeté de leur devoir, laissent un exemple assez illustre, et une conclusion assez agréable. (*OC* II: 640)

[. . . and for the ending, I have reduced it so that all my characters act with generosity, and so that, some doing what they ought in accordance with virtue, and others remaining firm in their duty, [they] offer a sufficiently illustrious example, and a sufficiently pleasant conclusion.]

Throughout every scene but the last one, however, this "exemple assez illustre" of collective nobility is nowhere to be found. On the contrary, the play is dominated by an atmosphere of mutual incomprehension and mistrust. Where in *Le Cid* and *Cinna* nobility was perceived as a public commodity, a currency agreed upon by consensus, a medium of performative exchange between parties, in *Nicomède* that consensus is absent. This not only makes the exchange impossible but also makes the possession of too much of that currency downright dangerous.[69] Nicomède, in the Bithynie of Prusias and Arsinoé, is too noble for his own good, because he no longer shares the discourse of nobility with his weak father and wicked stepmother. Where Nicomède speaks the originary language of nobility with total *franchise*, Prusias speaks a debased, corrupted version, cleverly prompted and encouraged by yet another of those villainous underlings, Araspe. Prusias uses the vocabulary of nobility, yet cannot help but twist and undermine the meanings of its terms, making of Nicomède's exemplary behavior as the Perfect Subject a challenge to his own shaky authority:

> . . . il m'a trop bien servi,
> Augmentant mon pouvoir, il me l'a tout ravi,
> Il n'est plus mon Sujet, qu'autant qu'il le veut être,
> Et qui me fait régner en effet est mon maître. (II, i, 413–16)

> [. . . he has served me too well,
> Augmenting my power, he has taken it all from me,
> He is no longer my subject, except insofar as he wants to be,
> And who makes me rule is really my master.]

The mean-spirited Prusias is constitutionally incapable of understanding Nicomède; he assumes that Nicomède is motivated by the same base impulses that motivate him, and therefore simply cannot believe that Nicomède is not conspiring against him.

> Car je dois craindre enfin que sa haute vertu
> Contre l'ambition n'ait en vain combattu,
> Qu'il ne force en son coeur la Nature à se taire. (405–07)

[For I must finally fear that his exalted virtue
May have struggled in vain against ambition,
And in his heart he may force Nature to be silent.]

This contrasts with Auguste, who could not believe that persons he thought to be noble (that is, like himself) *were* conspiring against him. However, Prusias's flaw is not so much outright villainy as a kind of moral flabbiness that makes him easy prey for the *mauvais conseiller* Araspe. This may remove some of his responsibility for his actions, and it makes his final conversion, if not convincing, at least less resoundingly unlikely than that of his spouse, Arsinoé, who has no such excuse available.

If Prusias speaks a debased version of the language of nobility, Arsinoé speaks a completely different (if more straightforward) language: a language of absolute villainy, one which inverts the values of the terms of nobility – or, more generally, dissociates those terms (together with all others) from their supposed meanings, arbitrarily defining and redefining them to suit its needs. She wishes to assert a kind of absolute power over systems of signification, a linguistic *imperium* similar in structure, if not in intent, to that of Auguste; but there is a crucial difference. Auguste arrives at his discursive control, as we have seen, only through a complete sacrifice of private *intérêt* to the needs of the (noble) collectivity; and he owes that control to his acceptance of the key terms of the discourse in question. Arsinoé, however, wants to have her semantic cake and eat it too. She wants to gain absolute control of the lexicon of the public sphere, and of the state itself, but only so that she may place it in the service of her private ambition. This implies, in contrast to Auguste, a rejection of the correspondences between those terms and the behaviors they describe. In other words, she must completely sever the consensual link between signifier and signified, between performance and reception. It does not matter whether there is any essential connection between *noblesse* and its various performed manifestations; what counts is the public perception of those performances. What Arsinoé must therefore do is disrupt the consensus of interpretation; she wants – and needs – to establish a kind of hermeneutic dictatorship if her project is to succeed. A necessary precondition for this is a breakdown in communications, the sowing of a kind of semantic confusion, and she seems to have attained this goal insofar as the court itself is concerned. Laodice, for one, is baffled (III, iv, 977–78): "Les mystères de Cour souvent sont si cachés, / Que les plus clairvoyants y sont bien empêchés" ["The mysteries of the Court are often so hidden, / That the most clear-sighted are quite hampered"]. The greatest threat to this destabilization of the discourse of nobility, and the thing that Arsinoé therefore hates and fears most, is the *franchise* of such persons as Nicomède and his half-brother, her son Attale; when the latter returns from Rome, she worries that he will make her nefarious designs misfire:

> Je crains qu'à la vertu par les Romains instruit,
> De ce que je prépare il ne m'ôte le fruit,

Et ne conçoive mal qu'il n'est fourbe, ni crime,
Qu'un Trône acquis par là ne rende légitime.[70] (I, v, 289–92)

[I fear that, instructed in virtue by the Romans,
He may deprive me of the fruits of my plan,
And that he may ill understand that there is no villainy or crime
That a throne, acquired thereby, does not render legitimate.]

What may in Attale prove inimical to her plans is his *vertu*-induced inability to understand her discourse, and to be persuaded that villainy is in the eye of the beholder. She therefore tries, and fails, to persuade him that his studies in Rome have left him ignorant and ill-equipped to deal with reality, and that his *franchise* is a handicap rather than a help in her domain (III, viii, 1113): "Vous êtes peu du Monde, et savez mal la Cour" ["You are unworldly, and don't know the Court well"].[71] However, the failure of learning is ultimately her own; she does not seem to have understood her Machiavelli as well as she ought, and this is what will ultimately bring about her defeat. In the meantime, however, she remains far more dangerous than the relatively ineffective Prusias, since to one as absolutely corrupt as she, everything is indeed permitted. In particular, there are no limits on what roles she may adopt to further her ends; having rejected, as she thinks, the validity of the rules of the discourse of nobility, she is not bound by Nicomède's code of *franchise* to any one persona, and can therefore, like Bacon's "New Man," adopt whatever mask she chooses. Perfect dissimulation, perfect hypocrisy are her most formidable tools. This is made abundantly clear when, in IV, i–ii, she pulls a Tartuffe on her hapless husband, playing so convincingly the role of the innocent, aggrieved stepmother that even the *franchise* of Nicomède is temporarily powerless against her performance.[72]

As a result, the Court, where the performance of Nicomède's superlative nobility might expect to find its audience, turns out to be a wholly inappropriate environment for that performance, either uncomprehending or resolutely hostile. Laodice announces this to him in the opening speech of the play (I, i, 9–10): "...mon coeur amoureux / Trouve la Cour pour vous un séjour dangereux" ["...my enamored heart / Finds the Court a dangerous place for you"]. Nicomède is therefore forced to look elsewhere for an audience, and in this play that audience turns out to be *le Peuple*. This is a dangerous step. Ordinarily, in Corneille's universe, those who are not themselves nobles cannot understand, much less participate in, the discourse of nobility, since one of that discourse's fundamental premises is that "it takes one to know one." Here, however, those whom one would normally expect to be active participants in the discourse of nobility are, as we have just seen, disqualified; therefore, the only audience left is "everyone else," the masses, *le Peuple*. Laodice tells Nicomède to leave the court, where he can expect only a hostile reception, and to return to the safety of the army (96): "Ne montrez à la Cour que votre Renommée" ["Show only your renown at the Court"]. Nicomède says that even the army is no longer safe, as his stepmother has filled it with assassins; what option is left? Laodice has the answer (115–16): "Le Peuple ici vous aime, et hait ces coeurs infâmes / Et c'est être bien fort que régner sur tant d'âmes" ["The People here loves you, and hates those infamous hearts / And to reign over so many souls is to be strong indeed"].[73] The masses thus become not only the sole audience left for Nicomède's performance, but also a critical source of power.

Laodice reinforces this view later on when she is confronting the Roman emissary Flaminius, who has been encouraging her to go along with Rome's plans for Bithynie and Arménie. In a revealingly contradictory speech, Flaminius appeals to Laodice to temper her noble *vertu* with *prudence*, a combination which for her is of course a contradiction in terms.

> J'ose donc, comme ami, vous dire en confidence
> Qu'une vertu parfaite a besoin de prudence,
> Et doit considérer pour son propre intérêt
> Et les temps où l'on vit, et les lieux où l'on est.
> La grandeur de courage en une âme Royale
> N'est sans cette vertu qu'une vertu brutale...   (III, ii, 815–20)

> [I dare therefore, as a friend, to tell you in confidence
> That a perfect virtue needs prudence,
> And should consider, in its own interest,
> The times in which we live, and the place where we are.
> Greatness of courage in a Royal soul
> Is only, without this virtue, a clumsy virtue...]

Flaminius's appeal to "intérêt," and his quasi-Jesuitical argument for the necessity of adaptation to particular circumstances shows that he has read Book II of the *Cortegiano* (and that he is an ancestor of Tartuffe), but not that he has understood Laodice. Genuine *vertu*, as exemplified by Nicomède and Laodice, naturally excludes even the possibility of "son propre intérêt." The essence of such *vertu* is precisely its uncompromising purity; "tempering" it with this kind of *prudence*,[74] far from making it more effective, would negate it entirely.

This is not to suggest that Laodice is naïve; far from it. She recognizes not only the ethical desirability but also the practical utility of *vertu* as a public commodity, insofar as it may form a power base for Nicomède. She responds to Flaminius (832) that her "prudence n'est pas tout à fait endormie" ["prudence is not entirely asleep"], meaning by "prudence" not

Flaminius's techniques of compromise or concealment, but rather the reverse: a forthright and public utilization of the resources placed at her (and Nicomède's) disposal by *vertu*. Foremost among these resources is *vertu*-inspired public support:

> Seigneur, dans sa Cour même, et hors de l'Arménie
> La vertu trouve appui contre la tyrannie,
> Tout son Peuple a des yeux pour voir quel attentat
> Font sur le bien public les maximes d'État,
> Il connaît Nicomède, il connaît sa marâtre,   (847–51)

> [Seigneur, in his [Prusias's] very court, and outside Armenia
> Virtue finds support against tyranny,
> His entire People has eyes to see what an assault
> Maxims of State make against the public good,
> It knows Nicomède, it knows his stepmother,]

and therefore, she argues, thanks to the support of his faithful audience, Nicomède is ultimately proof against whatever machinations Rome and its tool Prusias can throw against him.[75]

This is not mere wishful thinking on Laodice's part; Prusias himself recognizes and fears this popular support. He pleads abjectly with Nicomède to behave, at least in public, as though he, Prusias, is the real power in the realm, so that nobody else will get any ideas about seizing that power for him- or herself:

> Le Peuple qui vous voit, la Cour qui vous contemple
> Vous désobéiraient sur votre propre exemple.
> Donnez-leur-en un autre, et montrez à leurs yeux
> Que nos premiers Sujets obéissent le mieux.   (II, ii, 511–14)

> [The People that sees you, the Court that contemplates you
> Would disobey you on your own example.
> Give them another, and show them
> That our first Subjects obey the best.]

Corneille is careful, however, to avoid assigning too much power to the defining gaze of *le Peuple*; it can only act after having been acted upon (or in front of), after having had an example presented to it. Hence, according to Prusias, it is up to Nicomède to be sure that *le Peuple* are given an appropriate example, one that will keep it in line. Prusias's fears seem to be borne out later on in the play, when the revolt is in full swing, and Flaminius observes that the rebelling *Peuple* would be less of a threat without leaders (V, iv, 1571–72): "Si ce désordre était sans Chefs, et sans conduite, / Je voudrais, comme vous, en craindre moins la suite" [If this disorder was without leaders, and without leadership, / I would like, as you do, to fear the consequences less"], but, says Flaminius, such is not the case, and besides it is now too late.

In the end, of course, it is only the irreproachable example of Nicomède that will calm the storm. Just as all seems to be lost for Prusias, Arsinoé, and the rest, Nicomède enters, saying that the situation is under control (V, ix, 1779–80): "Tout est calme, Seigneur, un moment de ma vue / A soudain apaisé la Populace émue" ["All is calm, Seigneur, a moment of my view / Has suddenly pacified the excited populace"]. This most crucial of Nicomède's performances is a literally stunning success, as le Peuple is instantly neutralized by the appearance of its Leader. What is interestingly unclear, however, is the direction of that "vue." Whose is the gaze? Who is doing the looking? Is the crowd simply struck dumb upon seeing Nicomède, or does he actually have to go so far as to look at it, for example silencing them with a stern glance, or perhaps giving them a cheerful, reassuring wave? What is clear is that le Peuple is instantly able, without the mediation of even a single word, much less a speech, to recognize the significance of Nicomède's performance; he is indeed the perfect example for which Prusias had asked. The ambiguity in the direction of the gaze, meanwhile, seems to reinforce the mutual dependency of performer and audience. It is evident, both from what has gone before and from this offstage performance recounted to us by its star, that the audience, "la Populace," is helpless without a "chef"; but it is equally evident that Nicomède can exercise no power except as it is conferred and confirmed by that audience. He cannot intervene in this final scene – that is, perform upon the internal stage of la Cour[76] – until he has first assured himself of support by having played successfully on the larger, external stage of le Peuple.

However, the courtly audience for which he now performs – Prusias, Arsinoé, et al. – has been so debased by the poisoned atmosphere of mistrust and confusion in which it has been living that it is wholly unable to rise to the same level of interpretive perspicacity as the crowd. Nicomède therefore immediately clarifies, as we have seen Rodrigue do under less pressing circumstances, precisely where he stands; indignantly refusing (1782) the label of "Rebelle" ("C'est un nom que je n'aurai jamais" ["That's a name I will never have"]), he spells out exactly what role he is playing:

> Je ne viens point ici montre à votre haine
> Un captif insolent d'avoir brisé sa chaîne,
> Je viens en bon Sujet vous rendre le repos
> Que d'autres intérêts troublaient mal à propos. (1783–86)

> [I do not come here to show to your hatred
> A captive insolent from having broken his chains,

> I come as a good subject to render you the peace
> That other interests were inopportunely troubling.]

The "d'autres intérêts" are, of course, the hidden ones of Arsinoé, since (in the carefully chosen vocabulary of Nicomède) only such a person as she could have any *intérêts* – by definition selfish, inimical to the *bien public* – at all. Nicomède's surpassing *générosité* – after taking this single oblique shot at Arsinoé, he ascribes to her the most generous motive he can think of, maternal love, and then offers to renounce his right to the throne in favor of Attale – overwhelms even Arsinoé as she is compelled to admit (1811): "Contre tant de vertu je ne puis le [mon coeur] défendre" ["Against so much virtue I cannot defend [my heart]"].

The way in which Nicomède overwhelms his audience – whether that audience be merely dangerously disorganized (*le Peuple*) or overtly hostile (Prusias, Arsinoé *et al.*) – through a dazzling theatrical display of *générosité, à la* Auguste, finally comes full circle back to the play's author. In the "Au lecteur" with which Corneille justifies the publication of *Nicomède*, he describes the effect the play, and specifically the *vertu* of its protagonist, is meant to have on its audience; and the "fermeté des grands coeurs" is clearly meant to be as much Corneille's as Nicomède's. Speaking of how he, Corneille, has audaciously modified standard tragedy-writing procedure, he says:

> Ce héros de ma façon sort un peu des règles de la tragédie, en ce qu'il ne cherche point à faire pitié par l'excès de ses malheurs; mais le succès a montré que la fermeté des grands coeurs, qui n'excite que de l'admiration dans l'âme du spectateur, est quelquefois aussi agréable, que la compassion que notre art nous commande de mendier pour leurs misères. Il est bon de hasarder un peu, et ne s'attacher pas toujours si servilement à ses préceptes, ne fût-ce que pour pratiquer celui-ci de notre Horace:
>
> *Et mihi res, non me rebus, submittere conor.*
>
> Mais il faut que l'événement justifie cette hardiesse, et dans une liberté de cette nature on demeure coupable à moins que d'être fort heureux. (*OC* II: 641)

> [This hero of my making is a little outside the rules of tragedy, in that he does not try to induce pity through his excessive misfortunes; but the result has shown that the firmness of great hearts, which excites only admiration in the soul of the spectator, is sometimes as pleasant as the compassion which our art commands us to beg for our miseries. It is good to take a few chances, and not always to attach ourselves so servilely to our precepts, even if it is only to practice that of our Horace:
>
> And I seek to make things submit to me, not myself to things.

But the result must justify this daring, and in [taking] this sort of liberty
we remain culpable, unless we are quite lucky.]

The "fermeté" or "hardiesse" in question is surely the same as the "grandeur de courage" referred to earlier,[77] which operates "à visage découvert";
and clearly, if Nicomède is a practitioner of this style of performance, so too
is Corneille.[78] The "succès" to which Corneille refers is that of the play, but
it is also that of Nicomède himself within the play; and the last sentence,
with which the "Au lecteur" closes, reconfirms Corneille's belief in the
dependency of the performer on his audience. If Nicomède fails to impress
le Peuple, he is carted off to Rome in chains, or worse; if Nicomède fails to
impress le Peuple, the result for Corneille is figuratively identical. However,
since Corneille, like Nicomède (and Auguste), is speaking from a position of
already-confirmed popular success, he can claim with a considerable degree of both safety and truth that his daring, like that of his hero, has been
retroactively justified (in the theological sense, that is, "rendered just") by
the theatrical results.

iv.   Le dernier des Justes: *Suréna*

The difficulty that Corneille experiences in bringing *Nicomède* to "une
conclusion assez agréable" prefigures the utter impossibility of arriving at
such a solution that we find in Corneille's last play, *Suréna, général des
Parthes* (1674). This play represents both a distillation and a summing up of
all that has gone before. The basic outlines of the scenario are by now
numbingly familiar: conflict, both potential and real, between a paragon of
noble virtue on the one hand and a less-than-ideal ruler on the other. All
the usual elements are present: in addition to the two (mutually dependent)
primary adversaries, the play provides the standard assortment of siblings,
princesses, and rivals, not to mention the obligatory villainous counsellor,
in this case Sillace. Traditional interpretations of this play have quite
naturally emphasized the grimness of the play's vision of the world of the
court. Couton sees the Plutarchan source story as offering to Corneille "un
cas exemplaire d'ingratitude royale" ["an exemplary case of royal ingratitude"],[79] providing the playwright with yet another chance to discourse
upon one of his favorite themes: "le non-généreux ne saurait comprendre le
généreux" ["the non-*généreux* cannot understand the *généreux*"]. Suréna,
in this view, is simply the victim of what Couton calls "un tragique de la
bassesse" ["a tragedy of baseness"]. Likewise, Stegmann sees the story of
Suréna as "un des plus tristes exemples du triomphe de la raison d'Etat"
["one of the sorriest examples of the triumph of reason of State"].[80] Others,
while adhering to this basic schema, have seen the play as representing

Corneille's embittered view of a world that has passed him by, both theatrically and politically; or as a veiled and not entirely positive commentary upon the absolutism of Louis XIV; or as an attempt by the aged playwright to enter the claustrophobic, passion-dominated universe of Racine;[81] or as some combination of the above. All of these readings have some truth to them; and all seem to emphasize, I think rightly, a prevailing atmosphere of frustration and failure. However, there are aspects of this "failure" that seem to need further elucidation. First, to what should this "failure" be attributed? It seems insufficient to argue that Suréna is simply a victim, and that Orode is merely ungrateful and villainous.[82] These two *personnages* may be familiar types, and indeed they are in some ways simply more extreme versions of characters already encountered, but I do not think that they are quite so one-dimensional. Second, what is actually different about *Suréna*? What, if anything, sets it apart from its predecessors? Perhaps it is merely a slightly more pessimistic rewrite of earlier plays; but the issue seems to me to be a more complex one. It is at least worth asking whether this play does not in some fundamental respect differ from those that have gone before.

One thing that makes the play unusual, if not perhaps unique, in the Corneillean canon is what is *not* present. What is entirely lacking from *Suréna* is a solution to the dilemma, a way out, a reconciliation between hero and ruler – or, failing that, at least a dignified exit for the hero too noble for this world. The latter case is found in for example *Polyeucte martyr* and *La Mort de Pompée* (where, indeed, the "protagonist" exits heroically before the play even begins); the former, as we have just seen, is exemplified in *Nicomède*, where the *généreux* Nicomède, trapped in a claustrophobia-inducing court full of deception, mistrust, and *intérêt*, is saved only by the availability of an escape route, an alternative audience for the performance of nobility. Suréna is not so lucky. The court-world of this play is sealed; there is no outside, no other audience to which the noble protagonist can appeal. When Suréna is shoved off the stage, he is shoved off the edge of the known world, and even his death – the traditional last act of the too-noble protagonist – is performed (and performed upon, rather than by, the main *personnage* involved) before an audience of only one, the *suivante* Ormène.

This radical scission between the court-world of the play and any larger audience external to that court does not just surface at the end of the play; it is already present at the beginning, and indeed persists throughout. Where previous avatars of the noble protagonist rushed about doing things – Rodrigue defeating the Moors and saving Castille, Auguste winning civil wars and quelling conspiracies, even Nicomède rebelling/not rebelling –

Suréna is wholly passive. He *does* nothing; he only talks, in the vain hope that his speech (a particularly ingenuous version of the discourse of nobility) will ward off any more material threats from those less noble than himself. Whatever deeds of renown he may have performed exist on a different temporal plane, thoroughly dissociated from the world of the play. They are located in a past seemingly without relation to the present; all that remains of them is (1) the bare assertion that Suréna is the "appui" of Orode, and (2) the *gloire* that accrues to him as a result. More than any other Corneillean hero, Suréna is reduced to a simple bundle of superlative attributes, a hollow façade of catch-phrases. In I, i, Ormène asks Eurydice whether Suréna is a king; she replies:

> Il ne l'est pas,
> Mais il sait rétablir les Rois dans leurs États.
> Des Parthes le mieux fait d'esprit, et de visage,
> Le plus puissant en biens, le plus grand en courage,
> Le plus noble, joins-y l'amour qu'il a pour moi,
> Et tout cela vaut bien un Roi qui n'est que Roi.   (I, i, 59–64)

> [He is not,
> But he can reestablish Kings in their States.
> Of the Parthians [he is] the brightest, the handsomest,
> The richest, the bravest,
> The noblest; add to that the love he has for me,
> And all that is well worth a King that is only a King.]

"... le mieux ... le plus ..." Suréna is here presented as being stultifyingly perfect, without being particularly interesting in any way; he seems to constitute a paradigm so completely ideal as to be nearly empty. This description typifies the language of the play; the process of distillation we have described leads to *Suréna* as a limit-case where the characters become hollow types or symbols manipulated to prove a point. To put it another way, Suréna has been so completely taken over by his role, that of the Noblest of All, that he is only capable of asserting over and over again his absolute possession of the virtues concomitant to that role. He can neither say nor do anything else.

I do not think, however, that this process of distillation is merely a rehashing of tired formulas, whereby Corneille inadvertently demonstrates that he has at last beaten his one idea literally to death. On the contrary, it seems to be a conscious process of reduction and diminution, a systematic elimination of superfluous materials so that the problem may be presented in its purest form; and one of the necessary elements of this systematization is a methodical elimination of options for the protagonist. One by one, as we shall see, doors are slammed, whether by Orode, by his evil son/twin

Pacorus, or by Suréna himself, until finally even the door marked "exit" is removed from the scenery.

Suréna may be the ultimate in *héros cornéliens* – the supreme paradigm of courage, *générosité*, and so forth – but he is also in some ways less perfect than his predecessors. Orode's court is permeated by secrets and silences, thoughts and intentions unspoken and unheard. This is hardly the ideal environment for "une grande âme"[83] like Suréna, whose *franchise*, as the defining attribute of his character, can brook no bounds; and indeed he is forced in this environment by his very *franchise* to engage in behaviors diametrically opposed to those demanded by his nominal role. He is forced by circumstance to conduct himself, not "à visage découvert," but rather as though he had something to hide. This comes about because, in II, i, Pacorus (having, of course, his own hidden agenda) asks Suréna what he thinks of Eurydice. Suréna declines to answer, thus entering *malgré lui* into the web of concealment and dissimulation that dominates the entire play. Later on, when Orode offers him his daughter's hand in marriage as compensation for services rendered, Suréna dissimulates once again; he declines the offer, adducing reasons which, although perhaps intrinsically valid, are not his real reasons for turning down the hand of the princess. Orode, if imperfect, is at least no fool; he sees through Suréna's game, and calls him to task for it (III, ii, 881–82): "Je n'examine point si ce respect déguise, / Mais parlons une fois avec pleine franchise" ["I'm not asking if this respect is hiding anything, / But for once let us speak with perfect frankness"]. Suréna's "respect" does indeed *déguiser* his real (illicit, because private) motives, and that Suréna should be recalled to *franchise* by the supposedly ignoble Orode indicates that the division in this play between "généreux" and "non-généreux" is not as clear-cut as one might think. Ironically, Suréna – by participating in the courtly game of dissimulation and deceit – conspires to bring his doom upon himself.

Moreover, even and especially when he insists most strongly upon his own *franchise*, he commits the same critical mistakes that we have already seen made by other too-noble (or, more accurately, inappropriately noble) figures, particularly Emilie and Don Gomès. His refusal to answer the questions of Pacorus and Orode is motivated by an Emilie-like belief that, even in his role as perfect subject of the king, his *coeur* – that is, his relationship with Eurydice – is not subject to the will of that king. Near the end of the play, he complains (V, ii, 1519–20) that Orode "... tâche à s'ériger par l'offre, ou par la peur, / De Roi que j'ai fait, en tyran de mon coeur" ["... is trying to make himself, through bribery or fear, / Not just the King that I made, but the tyrant of my heart"], and insists that his "private life" is his own (1523–24): "Je lui dois en sujet tout mon sang, tout mon bien, / Mais si je lui dois tout, mon coeur ne lui doit rien" ["I owe him, as a subject, all my blood, all that I have, / But if I owe him everything, my heart owes him nothing"]. In fact, in a healthy absolutist state, Orode ought to be the *tyran de son coeur*, and if he is not it is only because Orode, unlike Auguste, is not strong enough to impose his authority. Suréna forgets that his role is only a public one, and that it necessitates the entire erasure of the illusory private sphere. And like Don Gomès, he is rather too aware that he is the sole *appui* of the state, again attributing his success in that role not to the role itself but rather to himself personally. Like Rodrigue and Don Fernand, both Suréna and Orode know quite well who is the Noblest of All, and upon whom the safety of the realm depends; but unlike the earlier couple, they cannot perform on the same stage, for they do not speak the same language. Suréna speaks the purest form of the language of nobility, but Orode speaks the language of a practical, if debased, historical reality; and where Rodrigue and Don Fernand were able to agree upon a kind of mutual discursive dependency, neither Suréna nor Orode is able, much less willing, to cross over into the discursive territory of the other.

Here, the fault is double; if Suréna is rather too aware of his own worth, Orode is equally conscious of his own lack thereof, and feels acutely his own inadequacy in the face of Suréna's list of superlative virtues. Borrowing a thought from Emilie, he remarks (III, i, 704–05) that "Un service au-dessus de toute récompense / A force d'obliger tient presque lieu d'offense"[84] ["A service beyond all compensation / By imposing such obligation is almost an offense"], and goes on to speak of the involuntary resentment he feels as a result of Suréna's success in keeping him, Orode, in power. He recognizes and laments his inferiority to Suréna, and wishes for the stature of an Auguste, the capacity to combine the roles of chief noble and ruler in a single *personnage*:

> Qu'un Monarque est heureux, quand, parmi ses sujets,
> Ses yeux n'ont point à voir de plus nobles objets,
> Qu'au-dessus de sa gloire il n'y connaît personne,
> Et qu'il est le plus digne enfin de sa couronne.   (723–26)

> [A Monarch is fortunate, when, among his subjects,
> He can see no more noble objects,
> When above his glory he knows of nobody,
> And when he is finally the most worthy of his crown.]

Orode seems here to speak with more resignation than rancor; when this play's nefarious underling, Sillace, hints that, if Suréna is such a problem, he should be dispensed with, Orode indignantly rejects the suggestion in the name of an ideal of noble kingship:

> ...ce mot seul me fait pâlir d'effroi,
> Ne m'en parlez jamais, que tout l'Etat périsse,

Avant que jusque-là ma vertu se ternisse,
Avant que je défère à ces raisons d'Etat,
Qui nommeraient justice un si lâche attentat!   (740–44)

[... that word alone makes me blanch with horror,
Never speak of it to me; let the entire State perish,
Before my virtue debases itself to that point,
Before I defer to those reasons of State,
That would call such a cowardly attack justice!]

Perhaps it is genuine pangs of conscience that make Orode react so violently; or perhaps it is the knowledge that, unlike Auguste, he simply is not powerful enough to impose his own interpretation on events, to make *whatever* he does "justice." In the following scene, in any event, he attempts to meet Suréna upon the latter's territory, to acknowledge and repay his debt to the Defender of his Realm; but he is too maladroit, and his own suspicions (like Prusias, he is unable to conceive of anyone acting according to any motives unlike his own, base ones) get in the way. He therefore fumbles the opportunity, insisting on offering to Suréna material and practical compensation up front, rather than the *gloire* which is the only currency Suréna recognizes. Suréna tries to set him straight, to get him to say the lines proper to the royal role in such a situation:

Quand je vous ai servi, j'ai reçu mon salaire,
Seigneur, et n'ai rien fait qu'un sujet n'ait dû faire,
La gloire m'en demeure, et c'est l'unique prix
Que s'en est proposé le soin que j'en ai pris.   (III, ii, 789–92)

[When I served you, I received my salary,
Seigneur, and I have done nothing that a subject should not have done;
The glory of it remains to me, and it is the sole price
Which my efforts have sought.]

Orode persists, offering to him, as we have already discussed, the hand of his daughter, all the while growing more baffled and fearful at Suréna's apparent unwillingness to speak what he, Orode, conceives to be the language of nobility. At last, annoyed beyond his limits by Suréna's oblique refusal of his offer, he insists – at the worst possible moment – upon complete *franchise*: "Je n'examine point si ce respect déguise, / Mais parlons une fois avec pleine franchise." Suréna, as we have seen above, has been trying to conceal the answer to a question that should never have been asked in the first place, and when he is caught and accused of the worst sin a nobleman can commit, he is both embarrassed and insulted. Orode goes on to be inappropriately frank himself; he admits not only his dependence on Suréna, but also his suspicions that Suréna may be tempted to take advantage of that dependence. He acknowledges Suréna's exemplarity, but only to insult him by warning him against acting according to motives baser than he could ever dream of harboring (889–90): "Ils vous ont jusqu'ici suivi comme fidèle, / Et quand vous le voudrez, ils vous suivront rebelle" ["They have followed you up to now as a loyal subject, / And when you wish it, they will follow you as a rebel"]. What Orode does not realize is that Suréna, when speaking of his pleasure in being the king's subject, is speaking with perfect *franchise*; more importantly, he does not realize that, at the least, Suréna's words must be received as if they were spoken in perfect *franchise* if the compact between subject and ruler is to remain intact. That Orode makes manifest his doubts as to Suréna's purity of intention, ascribing to him what would be his own ignoble motives in such a situation, breaks the bond of trust, and makes further communication impossible. Suréna expresses shock and amazement (901–02) that Orode would thus doubt his word and accuse him of harboring such base intentions ("Par quel crime, Seigneur, ou par quelle imprudence / Ai-je pu mériter si peu de confiance?" ["By what crime, Seigneur, or by what imprudence / Have I merited so little confidence?"]), but Orode continues:

> Suréna, j'aime à voir que votre gloire éclate,
> Tout ce que je vous dois, j'aime à le publier,
> Mais quand je m'en souviens, vous devez l'oublier.
> Si le Ciel par vos mains m'a rendu cet Empire,
> Je sais vous épargner la peine de le dire,
> Et s'il met votre zèle au-dessus du commun,
> Je n'en suis point ingrat, craignez d'être importun. (906–12)

> [Suréna, I like to see your glory displayed,
> All that I owe you, I like to make known,
> But when I remember it, you should forget it.
> If Heaven, via your hands, has given me this empire,
> I am able to spare you the trouble of saying so,
> And if it places your zeal above the common level,
> I am not ungrateful for it; fear to be importunate.]

His admonition here seems both unfair and unnecessary. Suréna, as the exemplary subject, surely knows better than to remind his sovereign of debts owed – and yet he has just begun to do so, perhaps because Orode's unjust accusation of rebellious intent has pushed him over the edge. In any event, later in the play Suréna will demonstrate that he no longer feels bound to keep his mouth shut, and will assert openly what Rodrigue had the good sense to pretend not to know. In this, as we have seen, he approaches the indiscretion of Don Gomès, as for example when he speaks of the "Roi que j'ai fait." Near the end of the play, it has become clear to him that his very *noblesse* is what has made him *persona non grata* to his sovereign:

Mon crime véritable est d'avoir aujourd'hui
Plus de nom que mon Roi, plus de vertu que lui,
Et c'est de là que part cette secrète haine
Que le temps ne rendra que plus forte, et plus pleine.
Plus on sert des ingrats, plus on s'en fait haïr,
Tout ce qu'on fait pour eux ne fait que nous trahir,
Mon visage l'offense, et ma gloire le blesse,
Jusqu'au fond de mon âme il cherche une bassesse... (V, ii, 1511–18)

[My real crime is to have today
More fame than my King, more virtue than he,
And this is the source of that secret hatred
That time will only make stronger and fuller.
The more we serve ingrates, the more we make them hate us;
All that we do for them only betrays us,
My face offends him, and my glory wounds him,
In the depths of my soul he seeks some vileness...]

He understands, or seems to understand, that his very nature, his very existence offends a sovereign unable to comprehend the *vertu* and *gloire* upon which his subject's identity is based. Moreover, he recognizes that the inevitable consequence of this incomprehension is his death (V, iii, 1653–54): "Plus je les servirai, plus je serai coupable, / Et s'ils veulent ma mort, elle est inévitable" ["The more I serve them, the more culpable I am, / And if they want my death, it is inevitable"]. And yet, in the end, Suréna seems unable to comprehend what he has just said; he cannot bring himself to believe that Orode does not and cannot speak his language, cannot interpret aright the performance of his noble identity.

Le Roi n'a pas encore oublié mes services,
Pour commencer par moi de telles injustices,
Il est trop généreux pour perdre son appui. (1593–95)

[...]
Mais Dieux, se pourrait-il qu'ayant si bien servi
Par l'ordre de mon Roi le jour me fût ravi?
Non, non, c'est d'un bon oeil qu'Orode me regarde,
Vous le voyez, ma soeur, je n'ai pas même un garde,
Je suis libre. (1663–67)

[The King has not yet forgotten my services
So far as to start being so unjust to me.
He is too generous to lose his support.
[...]
But Gods, could it be that having served so well
I should be doomed by the order of my King?
No, no, Orode looks on me with benevolence,
You see, my sister, I don't even have a guard,
I am free.]

This is not unlike what was earlier seen as the fatal error of Don Gomès; but there are some differences. To begin with, Suréna thinks himself safe because he seems still to believe in the *générosité* of the King, a belief that at once demonstrates his own *générosité* (which in this play looks more like a kind of pathetic naïveté) and throws the blame onto a king unable to live up to that ideal. Moreover, even if Suréna, like Don Gomès, thinks himself indispensable, Suréna nevertheless seems less culpable than Don Gomès, if only because the *personnage* of Suréna has been so thoroughly reduced to its essential noble attributes, and those in the most absolute form possible – he is literally nothing but the *appui* of the State – that one could hardly accuse him of pursuing private ends at the expense of the State. Yet he is not entirely guiltless of this charge. He does rebuff the King's claim to sovereignty over his *vie sentimentale*, and even when he insists, in response to the threats of Pacorus, that he, Suréna, is still the perfect subject, he makes this claim in a way that tends to undermine itself (IV, iv, 1357–58): "J'ai vécu pour ma gloire, autant qu'il fallait vivre, / Et laisse un grand exemple à qui pourra me suivre" ["I have lived for my glory, as much as I had to live, / And I leave a great example to anyone who will be able to follow me"]; has he been living for his sovereign, or for his own *gloire*? The fact that the two interests diverge in the corrupt world of this play is perhaps the real culprit, if there is one to be found. In the Séleucie of Orode, a place governed by incomprehension, mistrust, and subterfuge, it is hardly surprising that there is no room for "une grande âme" like Suréna. He is forced against his will both to betray his ideals, however slightly, and to go to the wall for them, with fatal results.

The final irony of the play is that Suréna is denied even the honor of performing his exit, his *belle mort*, in a way befitting his role. He leaves the stage in the tragically false belief that he is "libre," only to be shot down in the street (V, vi, 1714) by an invisible "main inconnue" ["unknown hand"]. The death of Suréna, inevitable from the beginning (and the only "event" in the play), occurs not only literally offstage (this is simply in keeping with the *bienséances*) but also off the court-stage of the play. The only witness, Ormène, tells us (1713) that "A peine du Palais il sortait dans la rue" ["He had hardly left the palace for the street"], when he was suddenly struck down; that is, having left the world of the court, the known universe, he ceased to exist. Suréna dies because he no longer has an audience before which to perform his noble role; he dies, in fact, in search of that audience, his "Suite"[85] which he hopes fruitlessly to rejoin. Even his death, the final act of his performance, is performed upon rather than by him, and performed not by his enemies in person but by a nameless, faceless assassin. Orode and Pacorus are absent from the scene. Perhaps it is because they are too craven to show their faces; or perhaps it is because they, too, find themselves overpowered by the debased discourse they have set in motion, unable to wield the power they have unleashed. It is possible to see Orode muttering in a dark corner of the palace, wishing he were more *vertueux*, unable now to control or even speak the language of Death to which he had earlier refused to listen.

Indeed, *Suréna, général des Parthes* seems finally to enact a larger death, the death of a particular model of noble theatricality. As the play closes, the principal antagonists, having been systematically reduced to bare essentials, have been swept off the stage, and are either absent, dead, or both. The play has taken on a life of its own, speaking a language independent of and incomprehensible to its characters, noble or otherwise. In earlier plays, even if certain *personnages* spoke mutually incomprehensible dialects of the language of nobility, the plays themselves moved towards the domination and clarification of that language by the noble protagonists; now, however, we find that none of these *personnages*, even those that manage to understand one another, speak the language of the play itself. The women, too, experience this communicative frustration; Eurydice dies, Ormène tries futilely to drag her off the stage, and Palmis rails helplessly against the tyranny that has brought them to this pass.[86]

Ultimately, then, the play is about failure, a failure of theatricality (but not merely – for example – the failure of Corneille to adapt to a new model of play-writing). Corneille's model of the noble self involves a particular kind of theatricality, one which presupposes a free and open discursive field, one where the noble self need perform no role other than its "own." That role, however, is a static, atemporal, ahistorical one, a dimensionless point-source of virtue, a univocal moment outside of time; and it is therefore ultimately incompatible with the demands of the temporal flow of history. Corneille's model of aristocratic selfhood is viable only as long as some accommodation, some escape from history is possible. Rodrigue must leave the stage to go fight more battles, while Don Fernand gets on with the business of governing. Auguste's solution-by-fiat works only because he is both Chief Noble and King, and even then, as we have seen, it, too, rejects history, existing only for a fleeting, supreme moment in the vision of its audience. Moreover, all these solutions are dependent upon a shared belief – whether willingly entered into or coerced – in the performance of nobility, a discursive consensus between performer and audience. In the grubby post-Auguste world of historical reality, this volatile consensus evaporates; there is no more room for the *héros cornélien*, and he is finally forced off the stage and into the street to meet his ignoble and anonymous death.

5 La Bruyère and the end of the theatre of nobility

Death provides an aesthetically convincing and pragmatically effective exit for the noble subject anxious to leave a courtly world grown too corrupt and debased to hold him. However, its unequivocal finality, both artistic and practical, makes it a performative strategy more suited to Corneille's theatre of absolutes than to the metaphorical theatre of late seventeenth-century court life at Versailles. Unlike the actor playing an entirely imaginary Suréna on Corneille's stage, a real-life nobleman choosing this kind of definitive exit will not be able to resurrect himself for the next performance; and there will always be a next performance, or rather the current one will never end. At Versailles, the curtain does not come down at the end of the fifth act, bringing all to a tidy close; instead, the show never stops. There is no opportunity for neat closure, either aesthetic or ethical. Survival is therefore a rather more popular option among the players on this stage, and so a different set of theatrical strategies must be evolved, meant not so much to exemplify virtue as to insure self-preservation. Suréna will have few imitators at Versailles.

In the last half of the seventeenth century, the imperative of self-preservation takes on a special urgency. The machine of royal power set in motion by Richelieu and Louis XIII has, for better or worse, triumphed over the particularizing energies of its noble subjects. The failure of the various aristocratic attempts at resistance and reaction, culminating in the spectacle of the Fronde, and the subsequent solidification of the absolute power of Louis XIV, work to impose restraints upon the kinds of public identity, and arenas of performance, available to the nobility, eventually narrowing the choice to Versailles or nothing. I would suggest that these constraints seem to force upon the noble subject, at least as constituted in literature, a kind of *renfermement* or inward turn. This trend is reflected in the rise of a new genre alongside that of the *livre de politesse*, one more rarefied, circumspect, and hermetic: the aphoristic works of the *moralistes*. The *livre de politesse* is an essentially optimistic text, meant to provide its reader with concrete advice, practical skills to be deployed by the ambitious and status-conscious (whether nobles or would-be nobles) in a field of more or less open competition. The *moralistes* likewise offer social advice to the reader, but complicate the picture by refracting that advice through the lens of satiric commentary on the double vanity of social competition: the universal vanity proclaimed by the Preacher, but also the specifically practical vanity of hoping for any advancement or prestige other than that channelled through and conferred by the royal centers of power. Negotiating these practical and moral problems, particularly when they are (and the *moralistes* tend to suggest, in their several ways, that they always are) in tension with one another, requires considerable finesse; the texts of the *moralistes* therefore both demand from and exemplify to the reader the interpretive and performative skills needed to operate in court society. As we have seen with Bacon, aphorisms "do invite men to enquire farther," and the elliptical invitations of the *moralistes* are offers which, given the stakes, the reader cannot refuse. The weight given to the respective elements (moral, political, pragmatic, even religious) of this often paradoxical discourse will vary with the author, but it is the last of the major *moralistes*, La Bruyère, whose text lies closest to the practical roots of the genre. He himself points out at the beginning of his project that, while he is interested in examining the inner workings of the (social) self, he is neither a Pascal nor a La Rochefoucauld; in the *Discours sur Théophraste*, after alluding to the *Pensées* and the *Maximes*, he says of his own work that "il est tout différent des deux autres ... moins sublime que le premier et moins délicat que le second, il ne tend qu'à rendre l'homme raisonnable, mais par des voies simples et communes ... sans beaucoup de méthode... "[1] ["it is entirely different from the other two ... less sublime than the first and less refined than the second, it merely tries to make men reasonable, but by simple and common means ... without much method..."] Pascal and La Rochefoucauld represent more abstract versions of this inward turn; for both of these authors, the conundrums of the social self (considered in a generalized religious and ethical context by Pascal, linked specifically to the game of the court by La Rochefoucauld) are seen to be rooted in more fundamental problems of human nature, an entity considered by both authors to be inevitably and fatally flawed. Pascal, focusing on the Big Questions, is not directly concerned with the trivial problems posed by court society; and La Rochefoucauld, while certainly preoccupied with the court, is more interested in demonstrating its complete and utter corruption than in exploring avenues of accommodation or compromise. This is not to say that his condemnation of the post-Fronde court is motivated purely by lofty moral standards. The *intérêt* he so mercilessly attacks is not absent from his own discourse; his overt rejection of the court and its theatrics, and his scorn for its denizens, betrays a certain anxiety about the stability of his own noble identity. Despite his own seemingly unassailable hereditary claim to the most exalted noble status, La Rochefoucauld sees the influx of "New Men" as bad for the nobility market; what will his own title be worth when everyone can have one just like it? His response, *à la* Suréna, is to see the world of "New Men" as having no place for himself and those like him. However, his Old-Nobility, *épée* heritage does provide him with an alternative of sorts; strictly speaking, as he does not depend upon the court to define and confirm his own noble identity, he is not obliged to participate. It might be more accurate to say, of course, that he is obliged *not* to participate; but even so, his claim to noble status is, at least in a practical if not in a metaphysical sense, qualitatively the same as – and thus just as incontrovertible as – that of the King himself. The same cannot be said for "New Men" like La Bruyère, and much of his audience, whose identities as "noble" are more visibly contingent. Hence, while the sociopolitical shift we have been describing does not leave even a La Rochefoucauld untouched, the problem of noble identity, as it has thus far been presented, does not possess for him the same kind of urgency that it will for La Bruyère.

La Bruyère's vision is one which shies away from both the shattering paradoxes of a Pascal and the corrosive, world-weary bitterness of a La Rochefoucauld. La Bruyère, less exaltedly and securely noble than the latter, cannot afford to dismiss the court-world so unequivocally (although at times he will adopt a pose of virtuous semi-detachment), and, as La Bruyère himself is the first to point out, he is not in the same league as Pascal. Indeed, many readers, starting with his contemporaries, have seen the disclaimer just cited merely as a confirmation of what one might interpret as a certain timidity or even shallowness in the text of the *Caractères*. In a letter to Pierre Bayle, written shortly after the death of La Bruyère, Mathieu Marais describes La Bruyère as "ce Montaigne mitigé" ["this mitigated Montaigne"].[2] Robert Garapon, in the introduction to his edition of the *Caractères*, points out La Bruyère's uncritical borrowings from and echoes of Descartes and Pascal, as well as his lack of any systematic philosophy.[3] Roland Barthes, too, in his famous essay on the *Caractères*, remarks at length on La Bruyère's restraint,[4] and Louis van Delft opens his 1971 treatise on La Bruyère with a survey of those critics who have accused La Bruyère of being derivative, superficial, or worse, citing such august figures as Taine, Faguet, and Michaut.[5] Van Delft goes on to launch a spirited defense of his subject as an intelligent and subtle didactic moralist, a claim I will not here contest. La Bruyère is certainly not a fool, and van Delft is probably right to insist that what many readers have found to be shortcomings of La Bruyère's work are the inevitable consequences of his conscious effort to produce a text with an immediate practical application: the improvement of the reader's moral state.[6] However, the apparent avoidance of profound anthropological or philosophical questions, while it may in part be a case of deliberate authorial restraint, or even an admission of incapacity, may also be seen as a function of La Bruyère's political and aesthetic conservatism. In some ways, La Bruyère's conservatism is similar to that of Montaigne, in that both authors share a dislike of disruptive change, and a corresponding fondness for established order; however, they differ over the question of what the basis of that order should be. As we saw in the first chapter, Montaigne rejects the notion that any given order (political, religious, or otherwise) is intrinsically superior to any other, claiming instead that all systems of order are equally arbitrary; as a result, he says, that order is best which has existed the longest, simply because it is most likely to be stable and to remain so. La Bruyère, however, despite his general eagerness to align himself with Montaigne, cannot bring himself to follow this radical line of reasoning; for him, political order must be grounded in a higher order, one ordained by the Catholic Christian God. Hence his intense dislike of freethinkers,[7] and his enthusiastic approval of the revocation of the Edict of Nantes.[8] Hence also his praise of Louis XIV[9] and of his children and close relatives,[10] as well as of the high nobility, in particular La Bruyère's sometime employer, the Prince de Condé.[11] A modern reader may wonder how such an incisive social critic as La Bruyère could have failed to bring his wit and skill to bear on such an obvious target as the monarchy, and may be led to ask whether La Bruyère was reactionary, cynical, or just silly, but it is well to remember that – as Barthes points out – for La Bruyère, as for many of his contemporaries, belief in divinely ordained political order was just a fact, or at least a practical necessity.[12] It would therefore be anachronistically unfair to suggest that La Bruyère was willfully ignorant, deliberately choosing to avoid questions he nevertheless knew to be fundamental; nor would it be just to say that La Bruyère was nothing more than a cynical sycophant, doing whatever was necessary to get ahead. La Bruyère did not question the basis of the existing monarchical order because it was not an option available to him.[13]

This does not mean, however, that the modern reader is absolved of the responsibility to understand the textual consequences of this apparently alien mentality. Whether this limitation of vision is deliberate, unconscious, or both, it will have an effect both on what La Bruyère chooses to represent and how he chooses to present it. In the *Discours sur Théophraste* (15), he claims that he differs from his putative model in that, while Theophrastus focuses on externalia, moving from effects to causes, his own text does the reverse, showing first the inner workings of men, so that consequently "... l'on prévoit aisément tout ce qu'ils sont capables de dire ou de faire, et [l']on ne s'étonne plus de mille actions vicieuses ou frivoles dont leur vie est toute remplie" ["... one easily predicts everything they are capable of saying or doing, and is no longer surprised by the thousand vicious or frivolous actions of which their life is entirely full"]. However, even a cursory reading of the *Caractères* will show that, while La Bruyère may occasionally gesture towards general principles of ethics or philosophy, he spends far more time and energy concentrating on the minute particulars of social existence, and on representing them as carefully and accurately as possible to the eye of the reader/viewer. He says further that it is up to that reader to draw appropriate inferences from the data he has assembled: "Il [le public] peut regarder avec loisir ce portrait que j'ai fait de lui d'après nature, et s'il se connaît quelques-uns des défauts que je touche, s'en corriger"[14] ["The public may regard at its leisure this portrait I have made of it from life, and if it recognizes in itself some of the faults I mention, correct itself"]. While this passage clearly reflects the Horatian imperative to instruct while entertaining, La Bruyère does not himself attempt to produce systematic conclusions and then force them upon the reader; to do so would, he claims, be not only pedagogically ineffective, but also beyond his powers. It is the reader that must *se corriger*. At the end of the *Préface* to the *Caractères*, he says that his work consists of observations, not conclusions:

Ce ne sont point au reste des maximes que j'aie voulu écrire: elles sont comme des lois dans la morale, et j'avoue que je n'ai ni assez d'autorité ni assez de génie pour faire le législateur... Ceux enfin qui font des maximes veulent être crus: je consens, au contraire, que l'on dise de moi que je n'ai pas quelquefois bien remarqué, pourvu que l'on remarque mieux.[15]

[Moreover, these are not maxims that I have tried to write; they [maxims] are like moral laws, and I admit that I have neither enough authority nor enough genius to play the legislator... Finally, those who produce maxims want to be believed; I allow, on the contrary, that someone may say of me that I have sometimes not observed well, provided that someone observes better.]

But La Bruyère refuses to "faire le législateur" not just because he is incapable of doing so, but because he believes it is unnecessary. He does not need to construct a theoretical framework for his observations because that framework already exists, having been established by an authority infinitely greater than his own, that of the divine *Législateur*. La Bruyère does not ask certain questions because he believes both that they should not be asked and that they need not be asked, since the answers are (or ought to be) clear to everyone; as a result, he believes, a book on such questions would be short and perhaps a little dull. "La raison tient de la vérité, elle est une; l'on n'y arrive que par un chemin, et l'on s'en écarte par mille. L'étude de la sagesse a moins d'étendue que celle que l'on ferait des sots et des impertinents."[16] ["Reason is like Truth, it is unique; one only gets there by a single road, and one departs from it by a thousand. The study of wisdom is of smaller extent than that which one might make of fools and idiots."] He therefore concentrates on describing and classifying the "sots" and "impertinents," confident that his readers, if they are sufficiently humble and attentive, will draw the appropriate conclusions.[17]

This focus on detail, on representing the particulars of human existence "d'après nature," is also driven by La Bruyère's aesthetic conservatism. He is an unswerving *ancien*, firm in his belief that the ancients got it right, and that imitation and emulation of ancient models is the only proper path to literary achievement. "Tout est dit, et l'on vient trop tard depuis plus de sept mille ans qu'il y a des hommes et qui pensent."[18] ["Everything has been said, and we are seven thousand years' worth of thinking men too late."] That this announcement, clichéd though it may be, opens the *Caractères*, is an important clue to La Bruyère's approach to his work. Thus Barthes states, after citing this passage: "... oui, sans doute; mais on ne vient jamais trop tard pour inventer de nouveaux langages."[19] ["...yes, of course; but one is never too late to invent new languages."] As the remarks already quoted from the *Discours* and from the *Préface* show, this is indeed precisely what La Bruyère will attempt to do: give a new twist to old truths (and for him they are indeed truths), to defamiliarize the familiar so that its veracity – and moral import – may be more effectively demonstrated. It is, moreover, exactly this skill for which his contemporaries will praise him; speaking before the Académie shortly after the death of La Bruyère, one of his colleagues says of the ability of that "génie extraordinaire" to present important truths:

Avec quelles expressions, avec quelles couleurs ne les a-t-il point dépeints! Ecrivain plein de traits et de feu qui, par un tour fin et singulier, donnait aux paroles plus de force qu'elles n'en avaient par elles-mêmes, peintre hardi et heureux qui, dans tout ce qu'il peignait, en faisait toujours plus entendre qu'il n'en faisait voir.[20]

[With what expressions, with what colors did he not depict them! A writer full of [skilful] strokes and fire who, with a fine and singular twist, would give to words more power than they had by themselves, a daring and fortunate painter who, in all he painted, caused more to be understood than he caused to be seen.]

La Bruyère's conviction that the verities expressed by the ancients are indeed eternal, that "le plus beau et meilleur est enlevé"[21] ["the finest and best has been taken"], leads him to concentrate on the "couleurs" of his representations, the dazzling *tours* that seize the attention of the beholder. In this, of course, he is to some extent merely conforming to the aesthetic of aphoristic discourse, as expressed by Quintilian: "ne plus dicatur quam oporteat" ["say no more than is necessary"].[22] But the very choice of an aphoristic style may here be read as a manifestation of the conservative stance of the true *ancien*, since to do otherwise – to offer a systematic and comprehensive exposition of general principles – would in this context be presumptuous, if not sacrilegious.

The aphoristic fragmentation of the text may also be seen as a reflection of what La Bruyère takes to be the fragmented, inconstant nature of his subject, rushing frantically from one excess of vice to another:

Les hommes n'ont point de caractères, ou s'ils en ont, c'est celui de n'en avoir aucun qui soit suivi, qui ne se démente point, et où ils soient reconnaissables. Ils souffrent beaucoup à être toujours les mêmes, à persévérer dans la règle ou dans le désordre; et s'ils se délassent quelquefois d'une vertu par une autre vertu, ils se dégoutent plus souvent d'un vice par un autre vice.[23]

[Men have no characters, or if they do, it is that of not having any which is followed through, which does not belie itself, and in which they can be recognized. They suffer greatly being always the same, persevering in order or disorder; and if they sometimes relieve their boredom by replacing one virtue with another, more often they become disgusted with one vice through another.]

In the context of this fragment, the word "caractère" here implies a kind of permanence or fixity, an attribute wholly absent from the subject here described.[24] "L'homme" is here nothing more than a random and unconnected assortment of attributes, a motley assemblage whose vicious sloth renders it incapable of pulling itself together into some semblance of a coherent whole. La Bruyère claims that the only constancy of which man is capable is itself a kind of inconstancy, an Augustinian absence of virtue:

Les hommes en un sens ne sont point légers, ou ne le sont que dans les petites choses. Ils changent leurs habits, leur langage, les dehors, les bienséances; ils changent de goût quelquefois: ils gardent leurs moeurs toujours mauvaises, fermes et constants dans le mal, ou dans l'indifférence pour la vertu.[25]

[In one sense, men are not frivolous, or they are so only in little things. They change their clothes, their speech, their exterior, their customs, they sometimes change their taste; they always keep their morals bad, firm and constant in evil, or in indifference to virtue.]

So the interior of "les hommes" is merely a void, papered over by a constantly changing array of surfaces. It is simply too difficult for this fallen being to overcome its inertia and to string together two or more moments of its existence, and so it is passively borne along on a tide of random variation. The result, says La Bruyère, is not really "un homme" at all:

Un homme inégal n'est pas un seul homme, ce sont plusieurs: il se multiplie autant de fois qu'il a de nouveaux goûts et de manières différentes; il est à chaque moment ce qu'il n'était point, et il va être bientôt ce qu'il n'a jamais été: il se succède à lui-même. Ne demandez pas de quelle complexion il est, mais quelles sont ses complexions; ni de quelle humeur, mais combien il a de sortes d'humeurs. Ne vous trompez-vous point? est-ce *Euthycrate* que vous abordez? aujourd'hui quelle glace pour vous! hier il vous recherchait, il vous caressait, vous donniez de la jalousie à ses amis: vous reconnaît-il bien? dites-lui votre nom.[26]

[An inconsistent man is not one man, he is several; he multiplies himself as many times as there are new tastes and manners. At each moment he is what he was not, and he will soon be what he has never been; he succeeds himself. Don't ask what sort of person he is, but what sorts of persons; nor what his humor is, but how many kinds of humors he has. Aren't you mistaken? Is that *Euthycrate* you approach? Today, how cold he is to you! Yesterday he was looking for you, he was caressing you, you were making his friends jealous; does he recognize you? Tell him your name.]

The inconstancy of a Euthycrate presents the author with a severe problem of representation. "Les couleurs sont préparées, et la toile est toute prête; mais comment le fixer, cet homme inquiet, léger, inconstant, qui change de mille et mille figures?"[27] ["The colors are prepared, and the canvas is ready; but how to fix him, this man, unstable, inconsistent, inconstant, with a thousand changing faces?"] La Bruyère will try to answer this question by attempting to represent his subject "d'après nature," that is, to focus on each "figure" in turn, as it presents itself to the eye of the beholder, and to reproduce it as faithfully as possible. This is not unlike Montaigne's project of representing the process of his being; however, where Montaigne's text does in fact become a representation of process, of movement, the fragmentation of La Bruyère's text as a whole, coupled with the sharp-edged particularity of each fragment, causes that text to function more like a disjunct series of frozen moments. The *caractères* and portraits are like movie stills, glittering instants which, while perhaps excised from a larger process, are so radically different from one another that the observer cannot tell whether the same actor appears in more than one shot, or even whether the images come from the same film. La Bruyère is less concerned with establishing continuity than with being sure that he gets the picture right; and indeed he argues against the possibility of establishing any kind of continuity at all.[28]

La Bruyère's representational approach, then, governed by what we have defined as his aesthetic and political conservatism, entails two specific formal consequences for the text: a focus on surfaces, and a radical fragmentation of those surfaces.[29] These consequences are not, however, merely formal. The fragmented and surface-oriented text clearly demands some kind of extra-textual resolution, and La Bruyère confidently appeals, both explicitly and implicitly, to various kinds of transcendent interpretive authority (royal, Divine, Antique) to complete and make coherent sense of his observations. His discourse does not and cannot, as he himself points out, contain its own explanation; the reader must step outside its world to complete its meaning. This is particularly so given its claims to be a kind of corrective satire. If the reader is to *se corriger*, he must perforce do so from an interpretive standpoint outside the world represented, and ironized, in the text. However, as will be seen, not only is that standpoint nowhere to be found within the text proper, but the text tends to prove above all the impossibility of locating, much less occupying, any such extra-textual interpretive space. We will find instead that the text enacts and demonstrates nothing so much as the persuasive success of this play of putatively false surfaces, since – in the absence of any privileged interpretive position – those surfaces cannot ultimately be distinguished from what they pretend to be. We will see further that La Bruyère's supposedly objective "on" is inevitably implicated as spectator-participant in the performance from which it tries, and fails, to extricate itself.

For La Bruyère, the main stage on which this performance takes place is, of course, the court. The portrait of Euthycrate may be taken as exemplary in this regard; in it, La Bruyère moves from the realm of moral generalization to a specific application in a particular social context, that of the court. The person to whom the sarcastically questioning voice addresses itself is one seeking to find his way in the maze of courtly social relations; Euthycrate is not just any inconstant man, but a courtier whose behavior requires careful interpretation according to the procedures La Bruyère will lay down for the reader. The problem is one of recognition, of identifying *visages* and acting accordingly, of reading aright the incessantly varying surfaces of courtly behavior.[30] This focus on surfaces is perhaps the most salient characteristic of La Bruyère's text, and one which many critics have cited as evidence of his "superficiality" as an author. However, others, such as Jules Brody, have recognized that La Bruyère's focus on surfaces, far from being a sign of ineptitude, is a natural sequel to La Bruyère's reading of his world.[31] This courtly play of surface and appearance pervades the text, so much so that virtually any text chosen at random from the entire collection would show it at work; but we may narrow our focus by following the trajectory indicated in the portrait of Euthycrate, and concentrating on those *caractères* which manifest most explicitly the link between a fragmented externality and the theatrical nature of the court.[32] Let us begin with a famous example: Ménippe, *l'homme-spectacle*, a personage composed entirely of borrowed surfaces, wholly devoid of any interior, and indeed of anything resembling self-consciousness.

Ménippe est l'oiseau paré de divers plumages qui ne sont pas à lui. Il ne parle pas, il ne sent pas; il répète des sentiments et des discours, se sert même si naturellement de l'esprit des autres qu'il y est le premier trompé, et qu'il croit souvent dire son goût ou expliquer sa pensée, lorsqu'il n'est que l'écho de quelqu'un qu'il vient de quitter. C'est un homme qui est de mise un quart d'heure de suite, qui le moment d'après baisse, dégénère, perd le peu de lustre qu'un peu de mémoire lui donnait, et montre la corde. Lui seul ignore combien il est au-dessous du sublime et de l'héroïque; et, incapable de savoir jusqu'où l'on peut avoir de l'esprit, il croit naïvement que ce qu'il en a est tout ce que les hommes en sauraient avoir: aussi a-t-il l'air et le maintien de celui qui n'a rien à désirer sur ce chapitre, et qui ne porte envie à personne. [...] Sa vanité l'a fait honnête homme, l'a mis au-dessus de lui-même, l'a fait devenir ce qu'il n'était pas. L'on juge, en le voyant, qu'il n'est occupé que de sa personne; qu'il sait que tout lui sied bien, et que sa parure est assortie; qu'il croit que tous les yeux sont ouverts sur lui, et que les hommes se relaient pour le contempler.[33]

[*Ménippe* is the bird decorated with various feathers not his own. He does not speak, he does not feel; he repeats sentiments and discourses, uses so naturally the intelligence of others that he is the first one fooled, and he often thinks he is talking about his taste or explaining his thought, when he is only the echo of someone he has just left. He is a man who holds it together for a quarter of an hour at a time, who the moment after falls, degenerates, loses the little luster that a little memory gave him, and shows the string [that was holding him up]. He alone is ignorant of how far below the sublime and heroic he is; and, incapable of knowing how much intelligence one can have, he naïvely believes that what he has is all anyone could have; so he has the air and carriage of one who has nothing more to wish for in that department, and who envies nobody. [...] His vanity has made him an *honnête homme*, has placed him above himself, has made him become what he was not. One would say, in seeing him, that he worries only about his person; that he knows that everything looks good on him, and that his outfit is as it should be; that he believes that all eyes are upon him, and that people stand in line to look at him.]

The unfortunate Ménippe goes to all this trouble to convince what he takes to be his audience that he is what he is not, wholly unaware that he seems to be the only person fooled by his performance. His efforts are, we are told, doomed to failure; he is weighed in the balance by the loftily pitiless "on" of La Bruyère's text, and found wanting. Ménippe may believe that he is "Th'observ'd of all observers," but he is nothing but "le premier trompé." He cannot even sustain his performance for any length of time; the maximum he can handle is "un quart d'heure de suite," and then the performance breaks down, apparently revealing the nothingness behind.

Another case in point is that of Philémon, he of the talented tailor. La Bruyère's imaginary interlocutor enumerates at some length the marvels of Philémon's wardrobe, to which the *sage* (about whom more in a moment) finally replies: "Vous m'inspirez enfin de la curiosité; il faut voir du moins des choses si précieuses: envoyez-moi cet habit et ces bijoux de Philémon; je vous quitte de la personne."[34] ["Finally, you make me curious; I must at least see such precious things; send me that suit and those jewels of Philémon; you can keep the person."] Philémon is nothing more than a

clothes-rack, holding up various dazzling bits of a fragmented and ultimately alien exterior; his nullity quickly becomes evident when "on" goes
to work on him:

Tu te trompes, Philémon, si avec ce carrosse brillant, ce grand nombre de coquins
qui te suivent, et ces six bêtes qui te traînent, tu penses que l'on t'en estime
davantage: l'on écarte tout cet attirail qui t'est étranger, pour pénétrer jusques à toi,
qui n'es qu'un fat.

[You are mistaken, Philémon, if with that flashy carriage, that great number of
knaves that follow you around, and those six beasts that drag you, you think that
one esteems you the better; one takes away all that paraphernalia that is alien to
you, to penetrate to you, who are just a fool.]

La Bruyère could easily have stopped here, as he seems to with Ménippe;
and indeed the fragment, thus truncated, would seem to enact precisely the
kind of penetrating vision the text appears to be attempting to inculcate in
its readers. It could be argued that the fragmented surfaces of the text
mirror those of the noble subject, squeezed and shattered by the pressures
of the court, and therefore that La Bruyère's didactic intent is to teach
those who must act on the courtly stage (as well as those who would merely
watch) how best to interpret the performances thereon enacted, according
to something like the following schema: Beware of dazzling surfaces, and
watch out for the all-revealing twist at the end. Many of the fragments of La
Bruyère's text, whether portraits, aphorisms, or maxims, have precisely this
structure, and what the final one-liners claim to reveal is often just this sort
of vacuum, be it intellectual, moral, or spiritual.[35] In this famous passage
from *De la cour*, La Bruyère presents the court as a theatre of false
appearances, where brief gestures and grimaces, appropriately timed, take
the place of a sustained discourse of *franchise*:

La cour n'est jamais dénuée d'un certain nombre de gens en qui l'usage du monde,
la politesse, ou la fortune tiennent lieu d'esprit, et suppléent au mérite. Ils savent
entrer et sortir; ils se tirent de la conversation en ne s'y mêlant point; ils plaisent à
force de se taire, et se rendent importants par un silence longtemps soutenu, ou tout
au plus par quelques monosyllabes; ils payent de mines, d'une inflexion de voix,
d'un geste et d'un sourire: ils n'ont pas, si je l'ose dire, deux pouces de profondeur; si
vous les enfoncez, vous rencontrez le tuf.[36]

[The court is never devoid of a certain number of people in whom worldly manners,
politeness, or fortune take the place of intelligence, and replace merit. They know
how to go in and out; they keep themselves out of conversation by not getting
involved in it; they please by keeping silent, and make themselves important by a
long-sustained silence, or at most by a few monosyllables; they get by with faces, an
inflection of the voice, a gesture and a smile. They don't have, if I may say so, two
inches of depth; if you poke them, you'll find the stuffing.]

Here La Bruyère encourages the reader to push beyond the deceptive surfaces of "l'usage du monde," as deployed by these *courtisans*, in order to discover what lies behind; and he seems confident that, if only the reader will push, the truth will out. La Bruyère seemingly wants to show that reading the one (text) is much like reading the other (performance), and that the ultimate goal of such reading is to strip away the superficies to reveal the unflattering truth.

However, becoming this kind of astute reader will prove to be more difficult than the text may initially seem to suggest. The first catch is that the portrait of Philémon does not stop with labeling him as "un fat," but continues (and closes) with a grudging admission of the effectiveness of precisely the kind of imposture the text seeks to expose.

Ce n'est pas qu'il faut quelquefois pardonner à celui qui, avec un grand cortège, un habit riche et un magnifique équipage, s'en croit plus de naissance et plus d'esprit: il lit cela dans la contenance et dans les yeux de ceux qui lui parlent.

[It's not that we must sometimes pardon one who, with a great train, a fancy suit and a magnificent coach and four, thinks himself better born and smarter; he reads that in the countenance and in the eyes of those who speak to him.]

We here encounter a paradox: the impostor is to be blamed only if his imposture fails utterly, only if the only person fooled is the impostor himself. If, on the other hand, the imposture is to some degree successful, the fault becomes more widely distributed; the audience, dazzled and taken in by the borrowed but glittering surfaces of the performer's costume, becomes not just the dupe of the performer but also his partner in crime. In fact, it could even be argued that the roles are here reversed, and that the courtly performer here becomes in some sense the dupe of his audience; it is the gaze of that starry-eyed audience, reflecting back to him his own brilliant performance, that persuades him of the "truth" of his own imposture.

This is, as we have just seen, precisely the belief held by Ménippe, who believes that, thanks to his carefully arranged borrowed plumage, he is the center of attention. La Bruyère goes to considerable effort to demonstrate that this belief is a delusion, and that the truth lies elsewhere. He presents portraits of such *personnages* as Ménippe and Philémon with the intent of stripping away the borrowed feathers, the fancy clothes, the makeup and masks and wigs,[37] in order to reveal the void that lies behind; but he finds this to be a more difficult task than he anticipates – for even the hapless Ménippe is being watched, if only by the faceless "on" of the text; and, as has just been demonstrated, the fact of being watched seems to confer upon the person watched a kind of confirmation-by-acclamation of the identity he seeks to project, no matter how spurious. The very act of stripping away the layers of disguise, even as it reveals the "truth," serves also to emphasize the effectiveness of the original imposture:

A mesure que la faveur et les grands biens se retirent d'un homme, ils laissent voir en lui le ridicule qu'ils couvraient, et qui y était sans que personne s'en aperçût.[38]

[Insofar as favor and great riches draw away from a man, they allow to be seen in him the ridiculousness that they were covering, and that was there without anyone having noticed.]

Just as with Philémon, the "fat," or Ménippe, "le premier trompé," what is at the core of this nameless victim is "le ridicule"; nevertheless, even though it was there all along, nobody notices until the layers of disguise are forcibly removed.

In the meantime, as long as the masks and costumes remain in place, the courtly impostor is overwhelmingly successful. Think, for example, of the theatrical Théognis, whose fraudulent performance should, according to La Bruyère, be transparent to all, but who nevertheless manages to fool most of the people most of the time:

Théognis est recherché dans son ajustement, et il sort paré comme une femme; il n'est pas hors de sa maison, qu'il à déjà ajusté ses yeux et son visage, afin que ce soit une chose faite quand il sera dans le public, qu'il y paraisse tout concerté, que ceux qui passent le trouvent déjà gracieux et leur souriant, et que nul ne lui échappe. Marche-t-il dans les salles, il se tourne à droit, où il y a un grand monde, et à gauche, où il n'y a personne; il salue ceux qui y sont et ceux qui n'y sont pas. Il embrasse un homme qu'il trouve sous sa main, il lui presse la tête contre sa poitrine; il demande ensuite qui est celui qu'il a embrassé.[39]

[*Théognis* is careful in his presentation, and he goes out adorned like a woman; he is not out of his house before he has prepared his eyes and his visage, so that they will be quite ready when he is in public, so that he makes his appearance there entirely prepared, so that those who pass by find him already gracious and smiling at them, and so that nobody escapes him. Walking through rooms, he turns to the right, where there is a crowd, and to the left, where there is nobody; he salutes those who are there and those who are not. He embraces a man who happens to be in range, he presses his head against his chest; he then asks who that was that he embraced.]

So far, Théognis seems to be something of a buffoon, someone whose ridiculously artificial actions could hardly be expected to fool anyone. He is an automaton, whose actions are neither the result of some essential governing intelligence, nor even a response to his interlocutors, but merely the mechanical effects of the whirring of *roues* and *ressorts* within.[40] However, as the fragment continues, we discover that for all its unconscious silliness, Théognis's performance is actually quite effective:

Quelqu'un a besoin de lui dans un affaire qui est facile; il va le trouver, lui fait sa prière: Théognis l'écoute favorablement, il est ravi de lui être bon à quelque chose, il le conjure de faire naître des occasions de lui rendre service; et comme celui-ci insiste sur son affaire, il lui dit qu'il ne la fera point; il le prie de se mettre en sa place, il l'en fait juge. Le client sort, reconduit, caressé, confus, presque content d'être refusé.

[Someone needs his help in a simple affair; he goes to meet him, makes his request: Théognis listens to him favorably, he is delighted to be of help, he begs him to create occasions so that he can be of service; and as [the visitor] insists on his affair, he says to him that he will not do it; he asks him to put himself in his [Théognis's] place, he makes him the judge. The client goes out, escorted, caressed, confused, almost happy to be refused.]

The unfortunate "client," unable to penetrate behind the mask, remains baffled, to his own detriment, by the performance of Théognis; but what is truly extraordinary about this moment in the text is the way in which that bafflement is brought about. The critical instant of the performance, the move that seals the fate of the suitor-audience, comes precisely when Théognis invites his suitor to "se mettre en sa place." Théognis here pretends to abandon pretence, to drop the mask, to stop performing in order to reveal the essence of his being (which apparently prevents him from fulfilling the wishes of his suitor). The audience is invited behind the mask, to step inside the role being performed, to see literally (to pursue La Bruyère's mechanical metaphor) what makes him tick. Théognis goes still farther: he asks the audience to pass judgment: "il l'en fait juge." The suitor-audience is invited to go beyond merely exchanging roles with Théognis, and to adopt the lofty perspective of La Bruyère's merciless "on": "L'on juge…" But what happens? We might expect that the *client*, if he had been carefully reading the *Caractères*, would at this moment see through the performance, and discover the *tuf*, the *mal*, the *ridicule* of the machines behind the scenes.

We might, for example, expect a reaction along the lines of that described in *Des biens de fortune* 25. La Bruyère opens this fragment with a visit to a kitchen where a great feast is being prepared, suggesting that one's appetite for "le festin" might be adversely affected by such a visit: "…quelles saletés! quel dégoût!" ["…what filthiness! what disgust!"] He goes on to conduct a backstage tour of a theatre:

Si vous allez derrière un théâtre, et si vous nombrez les poids, les roues, les cordages, qui font les vols et les machines; si vous considérez combien de gens entrent dans l'exécution de ces mouvements, quelle force de bras, et quelle extension de nerfs ils y emploient, vous direz: "Sont-ce là les principes et les ressorts de ce spectacle si beau, si naturel, qui paraît animé et agir de soi-même?" Vous vous récrierez: "Quels efforts! quelle violence!"

[If you go backstage at the theatre, and if you count the weights, the wheels, the ropes, which produce the flights and work the machines; if you consider how many people are involved in the execution of these movements, how much labor and muscle they put into it, you will say: "So these are the principles, the springs of that spectacle, so beautiful, so natural, which seems to be alive, and to act by itself?" You will exclaim: "What efforts! what violence!"]

But the *client* of Théognis does not react this way. Indeed, the text does not inform us about the immediate response of the *client* to this invitation behind the scenes, a fact which raises multiple possibilities. First, and simplest, it may be that the invitation is itself a performance, an act of bad faith whereby Théognis pretends to drop the mask while actually revealing nothing; and it is quite clear that "nothing" is in fact what the *client* sees. Perhaps, then, the *client* simply bounces off yet another protective surface, one which, while pretending to be a window, is actually only another mirror. The non-vision of the *client* also suggests a second possibility, one reinforced by the gap or void in the text itself at the critical moment. Precisely where we might expect a description of "les principes et les ressorts de ce spectacle si beau, si naturel," we find instead nothing at all. In the text, the *client* is "fait juge" of the actions and motivations of his patron, but then the text jumps immediately to his exit: "Le client sort..." In other words, perhaps the *client* sees nothing because there is nothing to see – there is only a void at the center. Is the confused retreat of the *client* therefore the consequence of a nameless horror inspired in him by a terrifying glimpse of the abyss? Or is he simply baffled into silence by the irreducible paradox of seeing nothing where he knows he must see something? Or does his subordinate, dependent position as a *client* radically restrict his vision? There is, finally, a fourth possibility: that the question of whether or not there is an essence, or even merely a pile of *tuf*, lurking behind the dazzling surfaces is not one that can be answered at all. The *client* is unable to read behind the surface of the performance simply because it is impossible; whatever is or is not there remains permanently unobservable. In the end, we do not know which of these interpretations is correct. The text refuses to answer. We see only the result: the suitor leaves, thoroughly confounded, and yet somehow pleased that he has been so utterly stymied in his suit. Théognis's performance has succeeded.

How can this be? La Bruyère's purpose seemed to be to expose the hollowness of such elaborately contrived performances; and yet the text winds up demonstrating that despite that hollowness – or perhaps because of it – Théognis gets away with it, and even manages to please his audience into the bargain. We find ourselves as readers in a position analogous to that of the unfortunate suitor in the text: unable to explain why the performance succeeds, we are forced to admit failure, and yet despite this we exit the text somehow satisfied with that performance, impressed with La Bruyère's lapidary cleverness, almost not noticing that his text actually demonstrates the opposite of what it sets out to prove: that blatant imposture, its moral bankruptcy notwithstanding, nevertheless manages to convince its audiences – aesthetically and practically – more often than not.

This is a serious problem. How can La Bruyère account for the surprising resistance of the courtly performance to his interpretive attacks? One approach that La Bruyère tries, as has already been suggested, is to blame the audience. He recognizes the power of appearance and opinion, wishing vainly that it were otherwise:

Je vois un homme entouré et suivi; mais il est en place. J'en vois un autre que tout le monde aborde; mais il est en faveur. Celui-ci est embrassé et caressé, même des grands; mais il est riche. Celui-là est regardé de tous avec curiosité, on le montre du doigt; mais il est savant et éloquent. J'en découvre un que personne n'oublie de saluer; mais il est méchant. Je veux un homme qui soit bon, qui ne soit rien davantage, et qui soit recherché.[41]

[I see a man surrounded, with a following; but he is well-placed. I see another that everyone approaches; but he is in favor. This one is embraced and caressed, even by the great; but he is rich. That one is looked at by all with curiosity, people point him out; but he is scholarly and eloquent. I discover one that nobody forgets to salute; but he is bad. I want a man who is good, who is nothing else, and who is sought after.]

Those who are centers of attention are such, not because of their essential virtue or goodness, but because of various external trappings they have managed to attach to themselves, trappings which catch the eye of the beholder and which persuade that beholder that they are in turn the signs of some great internal worth.[42] Apparently the great mass of humanity cannot see beyond such surfaces, perhaps because they are only surfaces themselves, faceted mirrors engaged in a game of endless mutual speculation. The emblem of this game is the nameless, featureless man of *De la ville* 13: "Voilà un homme, dites-vous, que j'ai vu quelque part: de savoir où, il est difficile; mais son visage m'est familier." ["There's a man, you say, I've seen somewhere; hard to say where, but his face is familiar."] La Bruyère's imaginary interlocutor has seen this man somewhere – indeed, everywhere, as it turns out; yet he is indistinguishable from the mass, and is in fact the personification of that mass, the Audience writ large. La Bruyère's narrator asks sarcastically:

Où pourriez-vous ne l'avoir point vu? où n'est-il point? S'il y a dans la place une fameuse exécution, ou un feu de joie, il paraît à une fenêtre de l'Hôtel de ville; si l'on attend une magnifique entrée, il a sa place sur un échafaud; s'il se fait un carrousel, le voilà entré, et placé sur l'amphithéâtre; si le Roi reçoit des ambassadeurs, il voit leur marche, il assiste à leur audience, il est en haie quand ils reviennent de leur audience. Sa présence est aussi essentielle aux serments des ligues suisses que celle du chancelier et des ligues mêmes. C'est son visage que l'on voit aux almanachs représenter le peuple ou l'assistance.

[Where could you not have seen him? where is he not? If there is a big execution in the square, or a bonfire, he appears at a window of the *Hôtel de ville*; if people are waiting for a magnificent *entrée*, he has his place on a scaffold; if there's a carousel, there he is, sitting in the amphitheatre; if the King is receiving ambassadors, he sees them come in, he is present at their audience, he is standing there when they come back from their audience. His presence is as essential to the oaths of the Swiss Leagues as that of the chancellor and the Leagues themselves. It's his face that one sees in the almanacs, representing the people or the audience.]

Look in the dictionary, under "Audience": there is his portrait. In fact, he does nothing else; he is pure *regard*, a passive reflector of all that occurs, and it is precisely this vacuous purity of vision that makes him absolutely essential to the proper functioning of society.

... celui-ci voit, il a vieilli sous le harnois en voyant, il est spectateur de profession; il ne fait rien de ce qu'un homme doit faire, il ne sait rien de ce qu'il doit savoir; mais il a vu, dit-il, tout ce qu'on peut voir, et il n'aura point regret de mourir. Quelle perte alors pour toute la ville!

[... he sees, he has grown old on the job while seeing, he is a spectator by profession; he does nothing that a man ought to do, he knows nothing that he ought to know; but he has seen, he says, everything that one can see, and he will not regret dying. What a loss that will be for the whole city!]

La Bruyère goes on, in a tone laden with irony, to list the fatuous social trivia with which this man, and those like him, are eternally preoccupied; yet the very weight of that irony betrays both the immense power of those trivia to govern the lives of their audience, and the vital role played by such a man as this "spectateur de profession." He may do nothing but see, but his seeing conditions that of others, in that he informs the public what ought to be seen; he orchestrates the collective gaze. More importantly, not only does he see, he is also seen; indeed, he is seen everywhere, most often onstage as part of the spectacle. The "spectateur" is himself the object of the gaze of the audience; even the two voices heard in this fragment cannot escape this fact. His salient attribute is that he is always and everywhere visible. He may be only the audience, but in the minds of these speakers he occupies center stage. Now, if this nonentity can possess such importance, is it any wonder that a person that is merely "bon" cannot hope to attract attention?

La Bruyère hopes to combat this dangerous trend, as we have seen, through inculcating habits of good reading into his own audience. The result, he hopes, will be a reader who can see through the deceptive play of surfaces to discern the truth behind. La Bruyère's description of his own project shows how he hopes to achieve this end:

Le philosophe consume sa vie à observer les hommes, et il use ses esprits à en démêler les vices et le ridicule; s'il donne quelque tour à ses pensées, c'est moins par une vanité d'auteur, que pour mettre une vérité qu'il a trouvée dans tout le jour nécessaire pour faire l'impression qui doit servir à son dessein.[43]

[The philosopher spends his life observing men, and he consumes his intelligence in revealing their vices and ridiculousness; if he gives some style to his thoughts, it is less from authorial vanity than in order to place the truth he has found in the proper light necessary to make the impression that will serve his purpose.]

La Bruyère calls for careful observation, followed by a stripping away of pretense to reveal "les vices et le ridicule"; his results are then presented in a way calculated to attract the eye of the reader, and only after that attention has been commanded, to lead the reader to virtue. Notice, however, that the *philosophe* "consume sa vie à observer les hommes"; how, then, does he differ from the "spectateur de profession" just discussed? La Bruyère will argue that the observations of the former, rather than being a passive absorption and reflection of all that may be seen, are guided by virtuous principles, and directed towards a higher end. Not for him the empty plaudits of an uninformed public; he aims to make them better. However, as we have also seen, this is easier said than done. The audience itself, composed as it is of "de fort sottes gens, des gens fades, oisifs, désoccupés"[44] ["really stupid people, dull, lazy, idle people"], possesses considerable inertia, which will not be easily overcome. It is far more likely to be dazzled by a Théognis than persuaded by a Socrate.[45] Hence the necessity of adding "quelque tour à ses pensées," to make them more attractive to the jaded eye of the public; yet doing so is a potentially dangerous compromise with the powers of illusion. The author runs the risk of having his essential truths simply vanish behind the play of deceptive surfaces, thereby undermining his entire *dessein*.

La Bruyère therefore attempts to resist this tendency by situating his *philosophe* outside the theatre of appearances. He attempts to claim for his observer a privileged position, one that is able to discern the truth behind the theatrical illusions promulgated by the actors on the stage of the court. Hence such fragments as the famous precursor of the *Lettres persanes*, *De la cour* 74, where the court of Versailles is described from the point of view of an alien being; this is perhaps the most extreme example in the *Caractères* of La Bruyère's effort at defamiliarization. He will also insist that the *philosophe*, the *homme de bien*, is necessarily and by definition situated outside the courtly context. The court, he claims, is simply too corrupt to hold him, and therefore the only option open to him is a retreat into a kind of philosophical solitude. In *De la société et de la conversation* 12, after describing the insufferably rude courtier Théodecte, a loudmouth devoid of any sense of decorum, but one who nevertheless commands a wide audience, the speaker claims that he simply cannot remain any longer in the same universe as this unpleasant person: "Je cède enfin et je disparais, incapable de souffrir plus longtemps Théodecte, et ceux qui le souffrent." ["I give up finally and I disappear, incapable of tolerating Théodecte any longer, and those that tolerate him."] It is not just the courtier that is intolerable; it is also his enthusiastic audience, an audience apparently unable to discern the true worth of Théodecte's performance. Likewise, later in the same chapter, La Bruyère offers counsel to the reader eager to know what to do when confronted with such *mauvais plaisants*: "Ce que l'on peut faire de mieux, d'aussi loin qu'on les découvre, est de les fuir de toute sa force et sans regarder derrière soi."[46] ["The best thing to do, as soon as one spots them, is to flee them with all one's strength, and without looking back."] Why flee? First, one must run away lest one become contaminated, implicated in the corruption of the court; he says that one must "...fuir à l'orient quand le fat est à l'occident, pour éviter de partager avec lui le même tort."[47] ["...flee to the east when the fool is to the west, to avoid sharing with him the same error."] This "fat" can only be Théognis, Ménippe, Philémon; he is dangerous because, his own hollow fatuity notwithstanding, he still manages to persuade his audience.

This brings us to the second reason for flight: there is the danger that the persuasive influence of the performance of a Théodecte can turn the passive and malleable public against the sage, making *him* appear to be the one that does not belong. This is what happens in the remarkably bitter fragment *Des esprits forts* 26, where La Bruyère says that all courts are dominated either by *libertins* or by hypocrites, and then goes on to describe what happens in a court controlled by the latter (evidently much the worse of the two alternatives):

Cent fois plus épris de la fortune que les premiers, ils en sont jaloux jusqu'à l'excès; ils veulent la gouverner, la posséder seuls, la partager entre eux et en exclure tout autre; dignités, charges, postes, bénéfices, pensions, honneurs, tout leur convient et ne convient qu'à eux; le reste des hommes en est indigne; ils ne comprennent point que sans leur attache on ait l'impudence de les espérer.

[A hundred times greedier for fortune than the first, they are jealous of it to excess; they want to govern it, possess it alone, share it among themselves and exclude all others from it; dignities, offices, positions, benefices, pensions, honors, everything suits them and only them; the rest of humanity is unworthy of [such things]; they do not understand that, without their connections, one might have the impudence to hope for them.]

There is no room for anyone else, least of all the *homme de bien*. The imagery he uses to depict this moment of exclusion is most revealing:

Une troupe de masques entre dans un bal: ont-ils la main, ils dansent, ils se font danser les uns les autres, ils dansent encore, ils dansent toujours; ils ne rendent la main à personne de l'assemblée, quelque digne qu'elle soit de leur attention: on languit, on sèche de les voir danser et de ne danser point: quelques-uns murmurent; les plus sages prennent leur parti et s'en vont.

[A troop of masks enters a ball: they have first choice, they dance, they dance with each other, they still dance, they keep dancing; they ask nobody else present to dance, however worthy they might be of their attention. People get bored, annoyed to see them dancing while not dancing themselves. Some murmur; the wisest make up their minds and leave.]

This grotesque inversion of Castiglione's dance of the court is La Bruyère's nightmare: a court where the imposture of the "troupe de masques" is so successful that all those who refuse to wear a mask, to play false, are simply excluded, forced to stand on the sidelines and watch in impotent frustration as the show goes on without them. Indeed, they may even be branded as impostors themselves. "Les plus sages" may be morally superior, but it avails them naught; their only remaining option is to leave the stage.

At first glance, La Bruyère might seem here to be advocating a kind of philosophical retirement akin to that proposed by his sometime hero, Montaigne. However, as we saw in our first chapter, even for Montaigne such a quasi-Stoic retreat is both conceptually and practically impossible; and by the time La Bruyère is writing his pastiche of Montaigne[48] a century later, political conditions have changed so much that even the pseudo-retreat of a Montaigne to his country house is no longer an option. To retire to one's *terres*, in La Bruyère's time, is not just useless, it is dangerous.[49] This is not to say that the other option is any more attractive: "Un noble, s'il vit chez lui dans sa province, il vit libre, mais sans appui; s'il vit à la cour, il est protégé, mais il est esclave: cela se compense."[50] ["A noble, if he lives at his provincial home, lives free, but without support; if he lives at court, he is protected, but he is a slave. There are trade-offs."] It seems to be a question of choosing one's poison. Moreover, says La Bruyère, when trying to escape the pernicious influence of hypocritical fortune-hunters such as those described in *Des esprits forts* 26, even the country is not remote enough:

Fuyez, retirez-vous: vous n'êtes pas assez loin. – Je suis, dites-vous, sous l'autre tropique. – Passez sous le pôle et dans l'autre hémisphère, montez aux étoiles, si vous le pouvez. – M'y voilà. – Fort bien, vous êtes en sûreté.[51]

[Flee, run away; you're not far enough off. – I am, you say, beyond the other tropic. – Go beyond the pole and into the other hemisphere, climb to the stars, if you can. – Here I am. – That's fine, you're safe.]

Unfortunately, even in the absence of constraints such as the laws of physics, there are forces that prevent any complete escape from the court. We have already seen how difficult it is for La Bruyère to distinguish his careful observer, the *philosophe*, from the "spectateur de profession"; and we have also seen the corresponding, and more fundamental, difficulty he experiences in trying to demonstrate the possibility, much less the efficacy, of a gaze that will infallibly penetrate layers of illusion to discern Truth. Even such amateurs as Ménippe and Pamphile are really quite successful at foiling attempts to reveal their impostures; what can we expect, then, when more adept actors step onto the stage?

La Bruyère hints at who these actors might be in his portrait of Théognis. The victim of his baffling performance is, it will be recalled, a *client*, that is to say one who is in a position somehow subordinate to Théognis and therefore dependent upon him for favors and advancement, be it economic, political, or social. In other words, as La Bruyère himself is constrained to admit, those best placed to fool the masses are none other than the nobility themselves, a fact La Bruyère deplores: "La prévention du peuple en faveur des grands est si aveugle, et l'entêtement pour leur geste, leur visage, leur ton de voix et leurs manières si général, que, s'ils s'avisaient d'être bons, cela irait à i'idolâtrie."[52] ["The predilection of the people for the great is so blind, and the infatuation with their gestures, their visage, their tone of voice and their manners so general, that, if they [*les grands*] decided to be good, it would become idolatry."] Note that it is not the intrinsic virtue of the nobility that causes the *peuple* to worship them, but mere externalia: "... leur geste, leur visage, leur ton de voix et leurs manières..." If only they would be virtuous! And yet one cannot help suspecting that it is precisely the absence of virtue that makes them such effective performers.

La Bruyère is, as this opening fragment of the chapter *Des grands* demonstrates, perfectly capable of attacking the high nobility as a group; but he will go only so far. We suggested earlier that La Bruyère could not afford the kind of anti-courtly bitterness associated with a La Rochefoucauld; this is because his own nobility, like Montaigne's, is of rather more recent date than that of his *maxime*-writing counterpart. La Bruyère is a *robin*, not a landed warrior, and one of the consequences of this status is his dependency on some sort of pension or salary, whether royal or, as in his case, from a noble patron, the Prince de Condé, whose remarkably unpromising grandson he tutors. In other words, he is to Condé as the nameless *client* is to Théognis; his relationship to at least one particular *grand* is one of subordination and dependency. This relationship is, of course, the image of that existing between courtier and sovereign in the court of Louis XIV. The courtier may strive to dazzle, but he can throw off no light of his own; the only light source is the Sun King, around whom everyone else orbits like tiny planets, each reflecting the light given off by the central star. The courtly performance is therefore an attempt to dazzle with borrowed brilliance, to reflect the available light with a more beautifully polished surface than one's neighbor, so as to blind that neighbor while simultaneously catching the eye of the Sun at the center. Therefore, one can hardly speak of the courtly observer being able to sustain any kind of independent position from which to judge the performance of nobility. Read in this context, La Bruyère's fulsome *éloge* of his patron is open to several interpretations.

Æmile était né ce que les plus grands hommes ne deviennent qu'à force de règles, de méditation et d'exercice. Il n'a eu dans ses premières années qu'à remplir des talents qui étaient naturels, et qu'à se livrer à son génie. Il a fait, il a agi, avant que de savoir, ou plutôt il a su ce qu'il n'avait jamais appris.[53]

[Æmile was born what the greatest of men only become through rules, meditation, and practice. He had only in his first years to fulfil his natural talents, and let his genius take charge. He did, he acted, before knowing, or rather he knew what he had never learned.]

No doubt it was in La Bruyère's best practical interest to say such things, whether they were true or not; and a certain amount of this kind of pragmatic cynicism is surely present.[54] Nevertheless, it is certainly at odds with much of the rest of the *Caractères*, with their merciless attacks on all sorts of social impostors, including those at the highest levels of court society.

Indeed, what La Bruyère is most anxious to prove about Condé is that he was in no way an impostor, but instead was born with an instinctive gift for his role. It would perhaps be most accurate to say that La Bruyère is eager to show that, for Condé, there was no distance between *masque* and *visage*.[55] Æmile/Condé is the realization, the personification, of the myth of nobility: the truly noble are born that way, and, thanks to their innate virtue, they do instinctively what mere mortals can only achieve through immense effort. Æmile/Condé is in actuality what the others (Ménippe, Pamphile, *et al.*) are trying so desperately to pretend to be. It seems likely that, if he did not exist, La Bruyère would have to invent him (as he in fact seems to do in this passage), since the idea that there is a "false" version of nobility, a cheap imitation, necessarily implies that there must also exist a "real," "original" version, a model to be imitated. Moreover, La Bruyère not only posits the existence of an ideal of nobility, he also posits the existence of a time when, in contradistinction to the corrupt and debased present, this ideal nobility was the norm. In the *Discours sur Théophraste*, he talks of "cette véritable grandeur qui n'est plus" ["that true grandeur that is no more"], and then goes on to describe in some detail this golden age and its denizens:

La nature se montrait en eux dans toute sa pureté et sa dignité, et n'était point encore souillée par la vanité, par le luxe, et par la sotte ambition. Un homme n'était honoré sur la terre qu'à cause de sa force ou de sa vertu; il n'était point riche par des charges ou des pensions, mais par son champ, par ses troupeaux, par ses enfants et ses serviteurs; [...] Rien n'est plus opposé à nos moeurs que toutes ces choses...[56]

[Nature showed itself in all its purity and dignity, and was not yet corrupted by vanity, luxury, and foolish ambition. A man was honored on Earth only because of his strength or his virtue; he was not rich through offices or pensions, but through his lands, his flocks, his children and his servants; [...] Nothing is more contrary to our mores than all these things...]

This pastoral golden age was populated by Real Men, simple, strong, and virtuous; in other words, it was a world full of Æmiles. Clearly, then, this praise of Condé must not be mistaken for mere sycophancy on La Bruyère's part; he genuinely believes in the idea of nobility, as here exemplified by his employer. In particular, La Bruyère deplores the fact that the modern, post-pastoral innovation of money, in the form of "des charges [et] des pensions," has helped to erase the distinction between "true" (landed, *épée* – as represented by Æmile) and "false" (salaried, *robe*) nobility. We have already seen how La Bruyère's conservatism renders him, like the majority of his contemporaries, unable or unwilling to conceive of the possibility that the existing monarchical/aristocratic order is not divinely ordained. The portrait of Æmile not only manifests this belief; it also enacts grammatically the precise relationship that La Bruyère seems to believe ought to exist between such a paragon and his audience. The enormous final sentence of the fragment consists of a long train of descriptive phrases enumerating the superlative attributes supposedly possessed by Æmile/Condé, all dependent on a single clause at the very beginning, a clause which is the key to La Bruyère's entire project:

On l'a regardé comme un homme incapable de céder à l'ennemi, de plier sous le nombre ou sous les obstacles; comme une âme du premier ordre, pleine de ressources et de lumières, et qui voyait encore où personne ne voyait plus; comme celui qui, à la tête des légions, était pour elles un présage de la victoire, et qui valait seul plusieurs légions; qui était grand dans la prospérité, plus grand quand la fortune lui a été contraire (la levée d'un siège, une retraite, l'ont plus ennobli que ses triomphes; l'on ne met qu'après les batailles gagnées et les villes prises); qui était rempli de gloire et de modestie; on lui a entendu dire: *Je fuyais*, avec la même grâce qu'il disait: *Nous les battîmes*; un homme dévoué à l'Etat, à sa famille, au chef de sa famille; sincère pour Dieu et pour les hommes, autant admirateur du mérite que s'il lui eût été moins propre et moins familier; un homme vrai, simple, magnanime, à qui il n'a manqué que les moindres vertus.

[One looked at him as a man incapable of giving in to the enemy, of bending under the weight of numbers or obstacles; as a soul of the first order, full of resources and intelligence, and who still saw where nobody saw any longer; as he who, at the head of legions, was for them a presage of victory, and who alone was worth several legions; who was great in prosperity, greater still when fortune was contrary to him (the raising of a siege, a retreat, ennobled him more than his triumphs; one only lists afterwards the battles won and the cities taken); who was full of glory and modesty; one heard him say: *I fled*, with the same grace that he said: *We defeated them*; a man devoted to the State, to his family, to the head of his family; sincere to God and men, as much an admirer of merit as if it had been less proper to him and less familiar; a man true, simple, magnanimous, who lacked only the least of virtues.]

"On l'a regardé..." Æmile/Condé becomes the object of contemplation for the omnipresent, all-seeing "on," but this time there is no irony, no stripping away of false appearances, no revelation of the sordid truth behind the gaudy trappings; nor can there be, since for Æmile *masque* and *visage* are one and the same[57] – at least as far as "on" is able to tell. "On l'a regardé *comme*..." The sentence does not actually assert that Æmile/Condé really *was* all these things, merely that he was *seen as* possessing these attributes; but here this perception is unassailable. There is no way of checking or confirming these observations, since the seeing agency is that impersonal "on" whose vision supposedly penetrates all disguises. At least within the fragment, there is only one person whose (metaphorical?) vision is apparently superior to that of mere mortals, one who "voyait encore où personne ne voyait plus": Æmile himself.

The syntactical parade of superhuman attributes before the eyes of the reader parallels the edifying performance of nobility meant to be enacted by the truly noble before the adoring gaze of a courtly audience. There is no doubt in the author's mind that such a thing as true nobility exists;[58] nor is there any doubt that it is worthy of being thus contemplated, of being the center of attention. We observed earlier that for such a person as Ménippe to lay claim to being that center of attention was ridiculous; here, we see that, for La Bruyère, while Ménippe's claim may be preposterous, the idea of *someone* being the center of attention is far from preposterous. On the contrary, it is essential. The objection, in the case of Ménippe, is that he is trying to be something he is not; La Bruyère says of him that "[s]a vanité l'a fait honnête homme, l'a mis au-dessus de lui-même, l'a fait devenir ce qu'il n'était pas..." But even this apparently clear-cut example contains a hitch, one which radically undermines the *caractère*'s instructive value. We are told that Ménippe's vanity "l'a fait devenir" something he was not; in other words, opinion has become reality, at least as far as one beholder – Ménippe himself – is concerned.

This raises an extremely difficult problem. If opinion governs reality (and we have seen that it has the potential to do so in La Bruyère's court universe),[59] how are we to distinguish between Æmile and Théognis, between the actor playing himself and the actor playing a role, between "true" and "false" nobility? It has become clear that this is a much more formidable task than it seemed at first, since – from the outside – all courtly performances look much the same. Moreover, getting beyond the outside to the inside has proved to be virtually impossible; we find, like Théognis's unfortunate suitor, that only surfaces are observable. Even when La Bruyère tries to show the failure of a disguise, his examples resist this unmasking, sometimes betraying him, as in the case of Ménophile:

Ménophile emprunte ses moeurs d'une profession, et d'une autre son habit; il masque toute l'année, quoique à visage découvert; il paraît à la cour, à la ville, ailleurs, toujours sous un certain nom et sous le même déguisement. On le reconnaît et on sait quel il est à son visage.[60]

[Ménophile borrows his manners from one profession, and from another his clothing; he masks the whole year long, although his face is uncovered; he appears at court, in the city, elsewhere, always under a certain name and in the same disguise. One recognizes him and knows what he is by his face.]

We are told that, even though Ménophile wears attributes not his own, his "real" identity can be seen in his *visage*, openly displayed; but since he is always performing, how reliable is that *visage*, *découvert* or not, as an indicator of who he "really" is? How confident can we be in our own ability to read that *visage* correctly? Can we unerringly distinguish it from the other parts of his disguise, or is there always the risk that it is just another mask? La Bruyère has tried to convince us that an appropriately trained and situated reader/observer, one who observes carefully and methodically, can indeed penetrate these surfaces, but it seems that such genuinely infallible vision is available only to one situated wholly outside the known (that is, courtly) universe, one like the alien being examining that strange country situated "à quelque quarante-huit degrés d'élévation du pôle, et à plus d'onze cents lieues de mer des Iroquois et des Hurons."[61] ["at some forty-eight degrees North, and more than eleven hundred *lieues* of ocean from the Iroquois and the Hurons."] And we have found that his efforts to avoid implicating the observer in the corrupting stage-play of the court, through situating that observer at a vantage point outside of the world, have come to naught.[62] Even La Bruyère himself is caught in the web; and even he finds himself dazzled by certain surfaces, those of Condé and Louis XIV foremost among them. The point is not that these last are necessarily themselves impostors; the point is rather that we have no way of knowing whether they are or not. We can see only surfaces, and therefore the discernible differences between the performances we see are differences only of degree, not of kind. La Bruyère thus seems forced to accept the very mystification he spends so much time decrying.

Moreover, La Bruyère's own methods lead to a result radically different from the one at which he actually hopes his reader will arrive. La Bruyère confronts us with a text that offers a vivid representation of the glittering surfaces of court society, but without offering many hints as to what might lie behind. He eschews any overt attempt to integrate his careful observations into a synoptic view of society, preferring instead to concentrate on isolated fragments – sometimes representative, sometimes unique – of that society, leaving the effort of systematization to the reader. This synthetic effort is clearly meant to be applied not only to the *Caractères*, but also to its subject; the fragmented structure of this text, this ostensibly mimetic "portrait … d'après nature" of a society, closely mirrors the apparent structure of the world it claims to represent. We have already seen something of the sort in Bacon, where learning to interpret the text and learning to interpret the courtly performances of the world it (re)produces are parallel activities. For Bacon, reading aright is the key to survival in the dangerous ethical vacuum of the court, but there is no question of any transcendent Truth that might, by anchoring a particular interpretation, give precedence to that interpretation over any other. La Bruyère, too, recognizes the power of what Bacon calls the "naturall, though corrupt Love"[63] of the lies of theatricality, and even uses similar metaphors of ornament and decoration to describe the problem. Nevertheless, he arrives at an entirely different conclusion:

L'homme est né menteur: la vérité est simple et ingénue, et il veut du spécieux et de l'ornement. Elle n'est pas à lui, elle vient du ciel toute faite, pour ainsi dire, et dans toute sa perfection; et l'homme n'aime que son propre ouvrage, la fiction et la fable.[64]

[Man is born a liar. Truth is simple and ingenuous, and he wants speciousness and ornament. It [truth] does not belong to him, it comes from Heaven already made, so to speak, and in all its perfection; and man loves only his own work, fiction and fable.]

For La Bruyère, there is always that transcendent Truth lurking behind the veil of human pretense and illusion; and it is that Truth, the basis of moral virtue, which is meant to be the result of a careful reading of the glittering fragments of the *Caractères*. Like Bacon, La Bruyère avoids feeding the "answer" to the reader because he wants the reader to do the work; but unlike Bacon, he also feels that that "answer" is both unique and, given a sufficiently attentive reader, self-evident.[65]

However, La Bruyère's text strongly resists such a synthetic reading. Its fragmentation and surface-orientation ultimately work against the production of any "answer," acting not to eliminate but to emphasize precisely those problems about noble identity which are most urgently insoluble. Fragmentation resists synthesis, and the hard, bright surfaces of the text likewise resist any attempt to peer behind them. The text is itself a mirror of the "model" courtier it portrays. The careful, detailed readings of surfaces he collects all point inescapably towards a single conclusion: all is surface, all is theatre, all is equally false – or at least not demonstrably "true." In other words, La Bruyère's minute representation in his text of the court-world he observes has foregrounded, perhaps more than any other text here studied, the fundamental contradictions inherent in the idea and performance of late Renaissance nobility, contradictions which at once define it and undermine its very existence. Yet La Bruyère refuses to recognize this contradiction, even though it is the conclusion demanded by his own data, since it is completely at odds with his belief in the possibility of reading beyond surfaces to essences, and in the real existence of "true" nobility. Instead, he insists that, when the tough questions come up, they simply should not be asked; when pushed (by his own text), he appeals to a final, unassailable authority, one whose very unobservability places it beyond question.

La Bruyère is willing to admit that the court, which for him is a microcosm of the world, is nothing but glittering surface: "Qui a vu la cour a vu du monde ce qui est le plus beau, le plus spécieux et le plus orné; qui méprise la cour, après l'avoir vue, méprise le monde."[66] ["Whoever has seen the court has seen of the world what is most beautiful, specious, and ornate; who scorns the court, after having seen it, scorns the world."] Here, he uses the same loaded vocabulary as he does in *Des esprits forts* 22 to show that the court, *spécieux et orné*, is as far from "la vérité ... simple et ingénue" as it is possible to be; but the *mépris* here expressed is curiously double-edged. On the one hand, it is certainly an appropriately Christian conclusion at which to arrive; one should disdain the false works of man and concentrate on virtue, which "vient du ciel toute faite."[67] On the other hand, if, as his text has clearly demonstrated in spite of itself, there is nothing else but surface, or at least nothing else that is observable, perhaps to feel *mépris* for the realm of surfaces – and thereby to lay claim to a vantage point outside of it – is not only foolish but an exercise in bad faith, since the text has also demonstrated the impossibility of situating oneself outside of *le monde*.

In conclusion, then, we may say that the breakdown of the text, its inability to enact a wished-for Golden Age of ideal noble behavior, is itself only a reflection of the problem – perhaps the failure – of the idea of nobility itself. The failure of La Bruyère's text to create and sustain a distance between stage and audience may be seen as the culmination of a literary and historical evolution that began when Castiglione set forth the terms of a theatrical discourse of nobility. That evolution takes the form of an ever-increasing tension between, on the one hand, nobility's inevitable – and necessary – claim to be permanent, immutable, and self-sustaining, and, on the other, nobility's obvious historical contingency, a contingency brought increasingly to the fore in the course of the period we have studied. The literary responses to this crisis – whether real or perceived – constitute a progressive revealing of the impossibility of sustaining the discourse of nobility. Montaigne sees this problem, but for him the absolute mutability of all things human, and a consequent necessary arbitrariness, offers an escape route. His deployment of multiple selves engages and implicates the reader in a continuous *jeu* of concealment and revelation; he is less concerned with unmasking the "truth" of noble identity, whether his own or anyone else's, than with representing it as a dynamic process. For Bacon, who finds himself in a more exigent courtly context, the solution is straightforward: he comes down squarely on the side of prevarication, insisting that the unobservable is necessarily unprovable. Bacon's notion of the primacy of the public self may negate even the possibility of a private sphere – and this is a constant throughout Bacon's work – but this does not prevent Bacon from expressing a certain ironic nostalgia for the idea of a "frend," for and with whom the private might actually come into existence. Corneille's response is diametrically opposed to that of Bacon, and is even more unequivocal: he simply refuses to accept the possibility of compromise with reality, taking refuge instead in an ideal of nobility which, as we have seen, cannot be sustained in the historical theatre of the court, and hence is ultimately forced offstage into the outer darkness.

La Bruyère's intimate involvement with the greatest court in European history, together with his method of careful observation and representation "d'après nature," serves to foreground more clearly than any other text we have studied the essential contradiction at the heart of the idea of nobility; paradoxically, however, he is least able to draw the obvious conclusions, precisely because of his complete investment in the theatre of deception and mystification he so brilliantly satirizes. His apparent incapacity in turn mirrors a larger paradox, one on which the entire performance of nobility depends. The text of the *Caractères* is engaged in an effort at persuasive performance much like that of its audience. The text, in order to persuade its reader of the truth of its observations, must first persuade that reader that it (the text) sees through the masquerade of the court thanks to its vantage point outside that court; second, it must persuade the reader that he, too, can gain access to that privileged vantage point and thereby penetrate the disguises of his fellow courtiers. All readers want to see themselves as the excluded but privileged *sage*, to persuade themselves that they are not like all the other courtly impostors; and yet of course this is precisely what they are. This, then, is the purpose of the courtly performance: to persuade not only the audience but – most importantly – oneself (see the example of Ménippe) that one is not acting, that there is no difference between *masque* and *visage*, even and especially when there is in fact nothing but *masque*. Perhaps it would be more accurate to speak of a succession of *masques*, such that, even if a true *visage* were to make an appearance, as in the case of Ménophile, nobody would be able to tell the difference. The whole discourse of nobility depends on this mystification, one which the text desperately wants both to promulgate and to believe. La Bruyère wants his reader to believe in the essence of true nobility, but his discourse is inevitably dragged by its own insistence on the fascination – and the irreducible concrete reality – of the imperfect back into the realm of contingency, artifice, and deception. As is the case whenever the question of nobility arises, the Golden Age is always elsewhere.

Court society will survive in France for another century after the death of La Bruyère, but we may legitimately ask whether the collapse of La Bruyère's moralist project signals the demise of literary constructions of nobility. By emptying out the idea of nobility, by showing that the costumes, the shells, the masks are all that there is, and by depriving the performance of nobility of even the faintest glimmer of a governing consciousness, La Bruyère shows in spite of himself that the discourse of nobility is no longer sustainable. However, La Bruyère's effort to create and sustain a distance between stage and audience, despite its failure within the text itself, may have other, more constructive consequences as well. That effort depends on the text's attempted move away from a theatrical discourse and towards a narrative one; La Bruyère's "on" claims, at least, to speak as a remotely situated observer, narrating in the third person the phenomena of court society. La Bruyère's acceptance of the mystification of nobility prevents him from drawing the obvious conclusions, and thus from situating his narrator – or audience – genuinely outside the theatre of the court. However, his text's rhetorical collapse, in the face of the contradictions it reveals, simultaneously demonstrates the failure of the theatrical discourse of nobility and the necessity, or at least the possibility, of an alternative. The text of the *Caractères* gestures toward, without being able actually to articulate, a narrative, rather than a performance, of the self. The literature of the theatre of *noblesse* will be replaced, in the eighteenth century, by a narrative mode of literary self-representation, for which La Bruyère's paradoxical failure paves the way.

Notes

1   INTRODUCTION: "THE NOBLE HART"

1 Spenser seems here to prefigure, if not to confirm, Lacan's contention that the *moi* is defined only in terms of its reflection in the eyes of the other, and that it is this "la dialectique sociale qui structure comme paranoïaque la connaissance humaine." Jacques Lacan, "Le stade du miroir comme formateur de la fonction du Je telle qu'elle nous est révélée dans l'expérience psychanalytique," in *Ecrits* (Paris: Editions du Seuil, 1966): 96.

    Erving Goffman, in a particularly helpful study, offers a similarly paranoid vision of the structure of the social self, couched in terms of what he, echoing Kenneth Burke, calls a "dramaturgical approach," in his *The Presentation of Self in Everyday Life* (New York: Doubleday Anchor, 1959).

2 For a history of this notion, see Ernst Robert Curtius, *European Literature and the Latin Middle Ages*, tr. Willard R. Trask (Princeton: Princeton University Press, 1973) 138–44.

3 Our discussion will owe much to Stephen Greenblatt's Burckhardtian model of a "society which was ... deeply theatrical," and to his formulation of courtly theatricality as "both disguise and histrionic self-presentation," without however necessarily subscribing to his view of this theatricality as a kind of totalizing, self-perpetuating repression, as will be seen below. Stephen Jay Greenblatt, *Renaissance Self-Fashioning. From More to Shakespeare* (University of Chicago Press, 1980) 162. See also his *Sir Walter Ralegh. The Renaissance Man and His Roles* (New Haven, CT: Yale University Press, 1973), where many of these notions find their first expression.

4 See Norbert Elias, *The Court Society*, tr. Edmund Jephcott (New York: Pantheon, 1983), and also the two volumes of his more wide-ranging study, *The Civilizing Process: The History of Manners*, tr. E. Jephcott (New York: Pantheon, 1978), and *Power and Civility*, tr. E. Jephcott (New York: Pantheon, 1982).

    For a discussion of the "totalization of theatricality" in Jacobean England, whereby theatricality comes to pervade all of public life, see Jonathan Goldberg, *James I and the Politics of Literature: Jonson, Shakespeare, Donne, and Their Contemporaries* (Stanford University Press, 1989 (orig. pub. Baltimore, MD: Johns Hopkins University Press, 1983)). This phrase appears on p. 152.

5 See Greenblatt, *Renaissance Self-Fashioning*, 227ff., where he discusses the

211

notion of "improvisation," the ability to adapt one's identity to changing circumstances otherwise beyond one's control.

Behind Greenblatt's notion of the self is Thomas M. Greene's fundamental essay, "The Flexibility of the Self in Renaissance Literature," in *The Disciplines of Criticism. Essays in Literary Theory, Interpretation, and History*, ed. Peter Demetz, Thomas M. Greene, and Lowry Nelson Jr. (New Haven: Yale University Press, 1968): 241–64.

6 On the notion that theatrical modes of behavior helped to defuse, at least for a time, tensions and potential conflicts between members of the aristocracy and between aristocracy and Crown in Elizabethan England, see Richard McCoy, *The Rites of Knighthood: The Literature and Politics of Elizabethan Chivalry* (Berkeley: University of California Press, 1989).

For our discussion of the situation in France, we are indebted to Jean Duvignaud, *Sociologie du théâtre. Essai sur les ombres collectives* (Paris: Presses Universitaires de France, 1965); Louis Marin, *Le portrait du roi* (Paris: Les Editions de Minuit, 1981); Jean-Marie Apostolidès, *Le roi-machine* (Paris: Les Editions de Minuit (collection "Arguments"), 1981), and his *Le prince sacrifié* (Paris: Les Editions de Minuit (collection "Arguments"), 1985).

7 See, for example, Hugh Trevor-Roper's essay, "The General Crisis of the Seventeenth Century," in *Past and Present* 16 (November 1959): 31–64. Sir Hugh argues against the thesis of Maurice Dobb and E. J. Hobsbawm that the Puritan Revolution was the breakthrough of bourgeois capitalism, in part by attempting to show that that revolution was independent of specific economic forces, and that it was instead part of a larger, pan-European crisis.

8 This idea, at least as applied to England, was famously promulgated by Lawrence Stone, in his fundamental work, *The Crisis of the Aristocracy, 1558–1641* (Oxford: Clarendon, 1965). For a similar thesis applied to France, see Davis Bitton, *The French Nobility in Crisis, 1560–1640* (Stanford University Press, 1969).

9 For the English case, see Sir John E. Neale, "The Elizabethan Political Scene," (British Academy Raleigh Lecture, 1948), repr. in *Essays in Elizabethan History* (New York: St. Martin's Press, 1958): 59–84; Wallace T. MacCaffrey, "Place and Patronage in Elizabethan Politics," in *Elizabethan Government and Society*, ed. S. T. Bindoff, Joel Hurstfield, and C. H. Williams (London: Athlone Press, 1961): 95–126, and especially Mervyn James's extended essay, "English Politics and the Concept of Honor, 1485–1642," in his *Society, Politics and Culture. Studies in Early Modern England* (Cambridge University Press, 1986): 308–415, where he describes how nobility, initially the property of a "self-authenticating" (375) group in which status depended primarily on birth, gradually became the property of the State, with which it rewarded its faithful servants. See especially 375–79, and 381: "Thus the community of honour came to be that which centred on the crown, its structure that of the court and city, its service that of the state, its mark the nobility of virtue, and the dignities which this conferred. Of course, there was no explicit challenge to the hierarchical grouping of the social order, and its basis in heredity. This was taken for granted, but also, since lineage constituted the 'lowest' kind of nobility, was pushed into the background. Among the intellectuals a tendency emerges to view honour due to 'blood' as

the result of a powerful and obsessive social convention, rather than inherent in the natural order of things."

For France, the magisterial work of Roland Mousnier gives a picture at once Olympian and minutely detailed of what he envisions as a "société des ordres," governed by relations of *clientage* between its members, in which – at least at the beginning of our period – distinctions between *ordres* are made on the basis of birth and privilege. Mousnier sees this society as evolving towards a class society, in which talent and wealth become the determinants of status, thanks largely to the ongoing conflict between the hereditary *noblesse d'épée* and the *noblesse de robe*. See his *Les institutions de la France sous la monarchie absolue*, 2 vols. (Paris: Presses Universitaires de France, 1974–1980), especially I, 94ff., on definitions of *noblesse*. On the sale of offices, which gave a broader range of people access to a kind of nobility and which, in his view, helped lead to the breakdown of the society of orders, see his *La vénalité des offices sous Henri IV et Louis XIII* (Paris: Presses Universitaires de France, 1971). For a (relatively) brief and schematic summary of his views, see "Les Concepts d''ordres', d''états', de 'fidélité' et de 'monarchie absolue' en France de la fin du XVe siècle à la fin du XVIIIe," in *Revue Historique*, vol. 47 (Apr-Jun 1972): 289–312. Some aspects of Mousnier's work have met with criticism, but the vast scope and solidity of his scholarship remain unrivaled. On this, see J. H. M. Salmon's review essay, "Storm over the Noblesse," in *Journal of Modern History* 53:2 (June 1981): 242–57.

J. Russell Major, like Mousnier, sees *clientage* relationships as crucial to the French nobility of the period, but emphasizes economic interests rather than abstract values held by this or that group. See his "The Crown and the Aristocracy in Renaissance France," in *AHR*, vol. 69, no. 3 (April 1964): 631–45, where he argues that in the sixteenth century, at least, greater and lesser nobles were bound together by common interests, and were driven apart only by royal manipulation of office-holding and titles after 1604. In his "Noble Income, Inflation, and the Wars of Religion in France," in *AHR*, vol. 86, no. 1 (February 1981): 21–48, he calls into question the thesis, advanced by Mousnier and others, that the nobility generally suffered economically during this period; see also "The Revolt of 1620: A Study of Ties of Fidelity," in *French Historical Studies*, vol. 14, no. 3 (Spring 1986): 391–408.

Kristen B. Neuschel, in her *Word of Honor. Interpreting Noble Culture in Sixteenth-Century France* (Ithaca, NY: Cornell University Press, 1989), likewise emphasizes the practical aspects of *clientage*, but focuses not on institutions *per se* but rather on (16) "the manner in which the nobility actually behaved." Her study of *noblesse d'épée* situates "... the motives for nobles' political behavior within a warrior culture that was still materially and psychologically independent of the state."

10 James ("English Politics" 375–79) suggests that the pressures of the "New Men" helped to bring about a redefinition of nobility in terms of virtue, and even learning, and points out that Castiglione's *Courtier* was a major factor in advancing this Bartolist view.

Mousnier (*Les Institutions* I 96–107) gives an extremely detailed account of the various ways to gain access to nobility, and (162–68) insists that relations between *épée* and *robe* nobles were fundamentally antagonistic, while also pointing out (169) that *épée* nobles were on occasion perfectly happy to fight with one another as well. In this, he is arguing against, among others, Pierre Goubert, who, in his *L'Ancien Régime* (Paris: Armand Colin, 1969–1973), sees the nobility (I, 153) as essentially unitary – "toute la noblesse était juridique-ment la même" – and as defining itself against (I, 152) "son antonyme, la roture."

J. Russell Major's model places greater emphasis on the constructive role of social mobility, as he sees the nobility consisting essentially of *anoblis*; that is, it is constantly replenished by bourgeois buying land, noble titles, and the mental attitudes that go with them. In "The Crown and the Aristocracy in Renaissance France," he describes this movement (632) as not only common but necessary: "Indeed, if the newcomers from the town had not been accepted sooner or later by the old nobility, the ranks of the second estate would have been very thin..." Russell Major does not discount resistance from the already noble to the *anoblis*, but he suggests that this resistance was to some extent neutralized by "...the fact that the newcomer's nobility was challenged [which] made it all the more necessary for him to abandon his bourgeois ways and live nobly in every respect." Orest Ranum, in his "Richelieu and the Great Nobility: Some Aspects of Early Modern Political Motives," in *French Historical Studies*, vol. 3, no. 2 (Fall 1963): 184–204, makes a similar point (185). However, it seems more likely, as the case of Montaigne will show, that "living nobly" was to some extent redefined by those who bought into it in the course of the late Renaissance.

11 MacCaffrey ("Place and Patronage" 96–97) shows how this kind of mutual dependence was essential to the function of Elizabeth's regime, particularly because of the Crown's lack of a monopoly on violence. Sharon Kettering makes the case that ties of *clientage*, patronage, and dependency determined, to a large extent, the behavior of noble individuals during the Fronde; see her "Patronage and Politics during the Fronde," in *French Historical Studies*, vol. 14, no. 3 (Spring 1986): 409–41, esp. p. 430. See also the preceding note.

12 Perhaps the closest of these to Burckhardt's original vision is Agnes Heller, who offers (in her *Renaissance Man*, tr. Richard E. Allen (London: Routledge and Kegan Paul, 1978 (1st pub. 1967)) a kind of Marxo-Burckhardtian account of the development of the individual; for her, as for Burckhardt, this development has its roots in the economic and political situation of Renaissance Florence, spreading throughout Europe in parallel with the development of the nation-state (54–55). She also emphasizes what she calls (10) the "estrangement" of public and private, and suggests (206–09) that the separation between self and public role is a Renaissance innovation.

13 For Reiss, see his *The Discourse of Modernism* (Ithaca, NY: Cornell University Press, 1982), and especially "Montaigne and the Subject of Polity," in *Literary Theory/Renaissance Texts*, ed. Patricia Parker and David Quint (Baltimore: Johns Hopkins University Press, 1986): 115–49, discussed in our chapter on Montaigne, *infra*.

Neuschel, drawing on Elizabeth L. Eisenstein's *The Printing Press as an Agent of Change*, 2 vols. (Cambridge University Press, 1979), and on David Warren Sabean, *Power in the Blood* (Cambridge University Press, 1984), links (191) noble identity to orality and to its being publicly performed, "...in opposition to the deeply internalized and personalized conscience that both post-Tridentine Catholicism and Protestantism were seeking to recognize and develop within each individual." She argues further (192–93) that the development of this self, in the interests both of Church(es) and State, was essentially a literary one, and points out that Eisenstein's primary example of this new form of identity is Montaigne himself.

Jonathan Dewald, in his *Aristocratic Experience and the Origins of Modern Culture. France, 1570–1715* (Berkeley: University of California Press, 1993), locates the invention of modern subjectivity in the memoirs of the French nobility of the first half of the seventeenth century, and sees the development of this inner, "true" self as a response to the patriarchal oppression of the increasingly powerful State.

14 One occasionally has the sensation of being too easily persuaded; Dewald's otherwise fine book, for example, is marred by an oddly uncritical reliance, for his picture of seventeenth-century noble life in France, on the notoriously unreliable Tallemant des Réaux.

15 Sir Francis Bacon, *The Works of Francis Bacon*, 14 vols., ed. James Spedding, Robert Leslie Ellis, and Douglas Denon Heath (London: Longman *et al.*, 1858–1874; repr. Stuttgart: Frommann/Holzboog, 1963): IV, 53 (Aphorism 36). All works of Bacon other than the *Essayes* will be cited in this edition; each citation will give volume and page number for the passage cited.

16 Bacon, *Advancement of Learning*, *Works* III, 403.

17 Sir Francis Bacon, *The Essayes or Counsels, Civill and Morall*, ed. Michael Kiernan (Cambridge, MA: Harvard University Press, 1985) 8. All further references to the *Essayes* will be from this edition.

18 *Le Cid*, I, iv, 193–94. All citations of Corneille will be from Pierre Corneille, *Oeuvres complètes*, 3 vols., ed. Georges Couton (Paris: Gallimard (Pléiade), 1980–87), and will simply indicate act, scene, and line number.

19 Many critics have discussed the theatre motif in Castiglione; the most extensive treatment is Wayne A. Rebhorn's *Courtly Performances: Masking and Festivity in Castiglione's Book of the Courtier* (Detroit: Wayne State University Press, 1978). Jonas A. Barish, in his *The Antitheatrical Prejudice* (Berkeley: University of California Press, 1981), reads Castiglione from this perspective, 168ff., and goes on to discuss post-Castiglione courtesy books in similar terms, 176ff.

20 Daniel Javitch sees Castiglione's shift in emphasis, from the putatively Ciceronian ideal of the public orator to a model of artful indirection, as reflecting a contemporary set of political circumstances that demand a more oblique, less dangerous approach. While his argument may be more applicable to the Elizabethan court than to Urbino, Javitch is surely right to insist on the political and ideological dimensions of Castiglione's aestheticization of Ciceronian ideas of public performance. See his *Poetry and Courtliness in Renaissance England* (Princeton: Princeton University Press, 1978), 40ff., and 97, where he discusses the notion of "beautiful play" as a means of attracting the attention of one's prince in order to "exert positive moral influence."

21 Cicero, *De Oratore* III. lvi. 214.

22 Cicero, *De Oratore* III. lvii. 215.

23 The element of persuasion, and in particular of persuading the princely audi-

ence to follow the path of virtue, is certainly also present; the complex (and familiar) question of the degree to which this is so, and in a broader sense of the purpose(s) of the courtier's performance, continues to puzzle modern readers. Javitch, for example, responds (*Poetry and Courtliness* 40ff.) to the familiar conundrum of the relationship of book IV to the rest of the *Cortegiano* by situating book IV, and in particular Ottaviano's claim that the courtier should serve the prince for the good of the State, outside the mainstream of the book's thought. It is perhaps fairer to suggest that, by presenting Ottaviano's claim – and, in a larger sense, the work's transcendental conclusion – as an ideal, unrealizable in the fallen world of its readers, book IV explicitly reinforces the elegiac mood implicit in the first three books.

24 Baldassarre Castiglione, *Il libro del Cortegiano*, ed. Ettore Bonora and Paolo Zoccola (Milan: Mursia, 1972, 1984), book I, xvii, p. 51: "...la principale e vera professione del cortegiano debba esser quella dell'arme..."

25 Dewald (*Aristocratic Experience* 58–59) discusses this notion with regard to seventeenth-century France, saying that, like the court, war was seen as an arena of public performance, "...in which actions were carefully observed and evaluated. As at court ... the warrior had to exercise rigid self-control within a highly emotional setting."

26 Castiglione, *Cortegiano*, II, 8.

27 Rebhorn (*Courtly Performances* 30) sees the performer as constantly monitoring the audience's responses, and adjusting his own performance accordingly, leading to a kind of consensus; Frank Whigham, however, disagrees, claiming that the dependence of the performer on the audience, and of the audience on each other, leads to a kind of interpretive chaos: "no one is in charge here" (p. 39). This chaos, he goes on to argue, leads to a kind of paranoid struggle for domination on the stage of the court, at least in Elizabethan England. See Whigham, *Ambition and Privilege: The Social Tropes of Elizabethan Courtesy Theory* (Berkeley: University of California Press, 1984) 36–39, and 61–62.

Goffman offers a more general view of this kind of performance anxiety, when he speaks of the fear of audience misinterpretation that drives the social performer to attempt to control even the most trivial details of his performance. See his *The Presentation of Self in Everyday Life* 51.

28 Bacon, *Essayes* 7.

29 Goffman (*The Presentation of Self in Everyday Life* 216) refers to this as "dramaturgical discipline," pointing out that the performer must look good performing his role, "in a spontaneous, uncalculating way," and must also be "affectively dissociated from his presentation in such a way that leaves him free to cope with dramaturgical contingencies as they arise." This dissociation is exactly the point of the "abito disciolto," and of Bacon's similar sartorial advice, discussed in ch. 3.

30 Cicero, *Orator* xxiii. 78.

31 Castiglione, *Cortegiano*, I, 28, where the Count explains that *sprezzatura*, properly applied, suggests to the onlooker more than is actually there.

32 See, for example, *De Oratore* II. xxxv. 147, where, in the context of a discussion of *diligentia*, Antonius says that it is important to observe one's opponent closely, so as to discern his state of mind: "Id tamen dissimulanter facere, ne sibi

ille aliquid proficere videatur, prudentia est." ["But to do this dissemblingly, lest he think he has accomplished something, is prudence."]

33 Cicero, *De Officiis* II. ix. 34.

34 For a sensitive discussion of this point, and more generally of the nuances of certain key terms in Castiglione, see Eduardo Saccone, "*Grazia, Sprezzatura, Affettazione* in the *Courtier*," in *Castiglione. The Ideal and the Real in Renaissance Culture*, ed. Robert W. Hanning and David Rosand (New Haven: Yale University Press, 1983): 45–67.

35 Giovanni della Casa, *Galateo overo de' costumi*, ed. Emanuela Scarpa (Modena: ISR-Ferrara/Franco Cosimo Panini, 1990) 3–4.

36 Giovanni della Casa, *Galateo* 20. The Spanish connection is made explicit a little later on (25), when he speaks of the excessive "cirimonie" associated with too-fine distinctions of nobility, an import which Italy, he says, still resists.

37 I consulted the Newberry Library's copy of an edition published by Vincenzio Vangelisti in Florence in 1681. Barish offers a brief survey of much of this material in *Anti-theatrical Prejudice* 176–85.

38 See Barish's discussion of Baldi, *Anti-theatrical Prejudice* 180.

39 See, for example, his ch. 13, "Della dissimulazione che appartiene alla pietá," where he cites the examples of Noah's sons (as misappliers of dissimulation) and Joseph (as a positive example).

40 Torquato Accetto, *Della dissimulazione onesta*, in *Politici e moralisti del seicento*, ed. by Benedetto Croce and Santino Caramella (Bari: Laterza, 1930): 143–73. See Barish, *Anti-theatrical Prejudice* 182.

41 The most useful survey of this material remains Maurice Magendie's immense study, with its indispensable bibliography: *La politesse mondaine et les théories de l'honnêteté en France, au XVIIe siècle, de 1600 à 1660*, 2 vols. (Paris: Presses Universitaires de France, 1925).

42 On this, see not only Elias, *The Court Society*, but also Orest Ranum, "Courtesy, Absolutism, and the Rise of the French State, 1630–1660," in *JMH*, vol. 52, no. 3 (September 1980): 426–51, where, in an argument closely resembling that of Elias, he proposes that standards of courtly behavior were used as an instrument of coercion by the State, so as to bring about the (449) "political emasculation" of a recalcitrant nobility, making them entirely dependent on royal favor.

43 Le Sieur de Nervèze, *La Guide des Courtisans*, in *Les oeuvres morales du Sieur de Nervèze* (Paris: Du Bray, 1620 (1st pub. 1610)): 11.

44 Barish remarks (*Anti-theatrical Prejudice* 180) that this "lends a slightly schizoid air to Refuge's treatise."

45 "Mais comme la dissimulation faict part de l'Accortise, la sçavoir descouvrir en autruy, & au travers d'icelle recognoistre le fonds des pensées de ceux ausquelz nous avons à faire, est chose tresnecessaire en la Court." ["Since dissimulation is part of *Accortise*, to know how to discover it in others, and by means of it to see to the bottom of the thoughts of those with whom we have to deal, is a very necessary thing at Court."] Eustache de Refuge, *Traicté de la Court* (n. p. [Paris], 1616) 96f.

46 The edition cited here is Nicolas Faret, *L'Honeste homme. Ou, l'art de plaire à la Cour: par le sieur Faret* (Paris: Nicolas et Jean de la Coste, 1639); I have also consulted a modern critical edition: Nicolas Faret, *L'honnête homme ou l'Art de*

plaire à la cour, ed. Maurice Magendie (Paris: Presses Universitaires de France, 1925), which contains a detailed history of the reception of Faret's treatise.

2   MONTAIGNE AND THE STAGING OF THE SELF

1 Among the critics who have pointed out the importance of theatrical images and metaphors in Montaigne's discussions of human identity and society, see: Floyd Gray, *Le style de Montaigne* (Paris: Nizet, 1958) 155–58, 160; Yves Delègue, "Du paradoxe chez Montaigne," in *Cahiers de l'A. I. E. F.*, 14 (March 1962): 242, 251–52; Keith Cameron, "Montaigne and the Mask," in *L'Esprit Créateur*, VIII, 3 (Fall 1968): 198–207; R. A. Sayce, *The Essays of Montaigne. A Critical Exploration* (London: Weidenfeld and Nicolson, 1972) 296–97, 318–19; Frederick Rider, *The Dialectic of Selfhood in Montaigne* (Stanford University Press, 1973) 78–79; Richard L. Regosin, *The Matter of My Book. Montaigne's Essais as the Book of the Self* (Berkeley: University of California Press, 1977) 143–44; Jean Starobinski, *Montaigne en mouvement* (Paris: Gallimard, 1982) 260ff., 296; and François Rigolot, *Les métamorphoses de Montaigne* (Paris: Presses Universitaires de France, 1988) 162–75, 213.

2 Among those who have addressed themselves to this problem, we may cite Margaret McGowan, who insists on not only the existence but also the primacy of the private, inner, "true" self; Timothy Reiss, arguing against those who see Montaigne as a proto-Cartesian, who says that the private or inner subject in Montaigne has only the most tenuous existence, and consists solely of perpetual movement and inconstancy, while the "self" *per se* is constituted as a political subject in an external, public context; and Rigolot, who, while agreeing that the idea of the private subject is essentially foreign to the sixteenth century, does situate Montaigne at the beginning of the development of that subject, locating him at the start of a trajectory that will lead to Descartes and beyond. See Margaret M. McGowan, *Montaigne's Deceits. The Art of Persuasion in the Essais* (London: University of London Press, 1974) 148–49; Timothy J. Reiss, "Montaigne and the Subject of Polity," in *Literary Theory/Renaissance Texts*, ed. Patricia Parker and David Quint (Baltimore: Johns Hopkins University Press, 1986) 117, 137, 140, and *passim*; and Rigolot, *Les métamorphoses* 57–59.

3 Thus the title page (second state) of the first edition of the *Essais*, 1580.

4 See both his edition of the *Essais*, cited below, and his monumental two-volume *Les Sources et l'évolution des "Essais" de Montaigne* (1908; 2nd ed. Paris: Hachette, 1933).

5 Michel de Montaigne, *Essais*, ed. Pierre Villey and V.-L. Saulnier (Paris: Presses Universitaires de France, 1965) 241. All further references to the *Essais* will be to this edition, and will be indicated by parenthetical page references in the text.

6 Hugo Friedrich, *Montaigne* (Bern: A. Francke, 1949, 2nd edn 1967) 92. For his specific arguments against Villey, see *passim* and especially pp. 67–68 ("Die vielbesprochene 'stoische' Phase Montaignes gibt es nicht" ["Montaigne's much-talked-about stoic phase does not exist"]).

7 Starobinski, *Montaigne en mouvement* 85.

8 See *ibid.*, *passim*, especially pp. 28–33, 42–54, 85, 131–32, and 148–49, where he asserts that his model is not dependent on the actual chronology of Montaigne's life, but then seems to contradict himself by linking the phases of Montaigne's

thought he describes to specific *economic* moments or periods in the life of Montaigne.

9 Friedrich, *Montaigne* 309–11.

10 Wilden's reading, owing much not only to Lacan but also to René Girard, says that the Self is simply the desire for the plenitude of being represented by the (absent) Other, in this case that ideal/identical *amy*, La Boétie. Reiss (134) likewise equates the self with pure absence and desire. Terence Cave, in his brilliant and influential study, adopts in his response to Wilden an even more radical position, seemingly eliminating "audience" from the equation altogether; he sees the *Essais* as a circular process of Derridean supplementarity, forever attempting to refer to – and taking the place of – the inevitably absent double self of La Boétie/Montaigne. Starobinski and Rigolot, while perhaps less eager to eliminate entirely any notion of an extratextual audience, do agree on the ultimate necessity of an Other-as-audience to Montaigne's project of self-definition. See Anthony Wilden, "'Par divers moyens on arrive à pareille fin': A Reading of Montaigne," in *MLN*, vol. 83, no. 4 (May 1968): 577–97; Terence Christopher Cave, *The Cornucopian Text: Problems of Writing in the French Renaissance* (Oxford: Clarendon, 1979), particularly part II, ch. 4: "Montaigne," 271–321, *passim*, esp. 273, 299; Starobinski, *Montaigne en mouvement, passim*; and Rigolot, *Les métamorphoses* 175, 182–83, and 213.

11 For a discussion of this phenomenon as typical of the later sixteenth century in France, see George Huppert, *Les Bourgeois Gentilshommes: An Essay on the Definition of Elites in Renaissance France* (University of Chicago Press, 1977).

12 See, for example, "De l'institution des enfans" (I, 26, p. 175), where Montaigne is at some pains to distance himself from this aspect of nobility, telling us that if his tutor had not allowed him to read Ovid and Virgil as a child, "... j'estime que je n'eusse raporté du college que la haine des livres, comme fait quasi toute nostre noblesse." ["... I suppose that I would have brought away from school only a hatred of books, like nearly all of our nobility."]

13 See Huppert, *Les Bourgeois Gentilshommes* 89–90, where he suggests that the group of persons he defines as "gentry," bourgeois or quasi-bourgeois aspirants to noble status, often responded to this problem by adopting one of two sets of attitudes: either neo-Stoicism of the kind discussed below, or, alternatively, a kind of Ciceronian civic virtue. His paradigm for this model is Montaigne himself.

14 We are indebted here to Norbert Elias's *The Court Society*; although it focuses on the absolutist state of Louis XIV (with which our later chapters will be more directly concerned), its larger theoretical implications are relevant to the period we are here discussing.
    J. H. M. Salmon's essay, "Cicero and Tacitus in Sixteenth-Century France," helpfully surveys sixteenth-century French responses to Ciceronean and Tacitean models of civic behavior, emphasizing the links between rhetoric and public comportment. This essay constitutes the first chapter of his *Renaissance and Revolt. Essays in the Intellectual and Socal History of Early Modern France*, Cambridge Studies in Early Modern History (Cambridge: Cambridge University Press, 1987); it originally appeared in *American Historical Review*, 85 (1980): 307–31. See also his *Society in Crisis: France in the Sixteenth Century* (London:

Methuen, 1979 (1st pub. 1975)).

Kristen B. Neuschel, in her *Word of Honor*, examines the *mentalité* of the *noblesse d'épée*, insisting on the oral and therefore performative nature of noble identity in this period (23): "Noblemen made their hostilities and alliances known to others and to themselves by acting them out." See especially her ch. 4, "The Power of Words: Oral Culture and the Definition of Events."

15 On this trend in general, see Salmon, "Cicero and Tacitus in Sixteenth-Century France." Arnaldo Momigliano, in his essay "Tacitus and the Tacitist Tradition," links together Tacitus and Seneca in this context (123): "The popularity of Seneca both as a stylist and as a philosopher was mounting; Neo-Stoicism became the faith of those who had lost patience with theology, if they had not lost faith altogether. The fortunes of Seneca and Tacitus became indissolubly connected towards the end of the sixteenth century." The essay appears as ch. 5 of Momigliano's *The Classical Foundations of Modern Historiography*, Sather Classical Lectures, v. 54 (Berkeley: University of California Press, 1990) 109–31.

16 For a different view, see Gordon Braden's *Renaissance Tragedy and the Senecan Tradition: Anger's Privilege* (New Haven: Yale University Press, 1985), in which he proposes a theatrical model of the aristocratic self based on the Stoic themes and personages of Senecan tragedy. One of Braden's primary assumptions is that neo-Stoic ideology is closely identified, in the Renaissance, with aristocratic ideas of selfhood; he goes on to argue that Montaigne identifies himself more or less unambiguously with the *noblesse d'épée* (see p. 78), and therefore that – despite Montaigne's ambivalence towards Stoicism *per se* (p. 94) – he is situated on a line of development leading to an essentially Stoic kind of *arrière-boutique*, where "the self's ambitions are compromised into a new sense of distant inwardness" (p. 2). I do not feel, as will become apparent, that Montaigne is able or willing to align himself unequivocally with the ideology, neo-Stoic or otherwise, of the true *noblesse d'épée*. Gerhard Oestreich, in his *Neostoicism and the Early Modern State* (Cambridge: Cambridge University Press, 1982), articulates still another viewpoint, namely that neo-Stoic ideologies and attitudes were adopted not so much by the old nobility as by the *noblesse de robe*, court functionaries who wanted, not unlike Montaigne, to cultivate a certain posture of quasi-aristocratic independence. Sayce goes even farther, suggesting that this pose of independence is in fact a kind of proto-bourgeois individualism (pp. 239–40).

17 It should be recalled that the possibility of ending up "sans femme, sans enfans et sans biens, sans train et sans valetz" was not, for Montaigne as for anyone else in late sixteenth-century France, a mere hypothetical abstraction; the civil wars made such deprivation a very real threat. The Stoic gesture is therefore to some extent practical (as indeed it was for Seneca, echoed in this passage), and not just philosophical or ideological.

Franz Borkenau neatly sums up the political dilemma of the Stoic: "Das Lebensproblem des Stoikers ist die Haltung des Individuums in der Politik, nur sie. Die Regel ist: äußerlich in ihr stehen, innerlich sich von ihr frei halten." Franz Borkenau, *Der Übergang vom feudalen zum bürgerlichen Weltbild. Studien der Geschichte der Philosophie der Manufakturperiode* (Paris: Félix Alcan, 1934; reprint: New York: Arno (series: "European Sociology"), 1975) 190.

18 Of course Montaigne will radically contradict this thesis elsewhere, particularly in the third book; his most thorough exploration of the issue is to be found in "De l'exercitation" (II, 6). See also "Du repentir" (III, 2), and especially "De la phisionomie" (III, 12), in particular pp. 1051–52. Among the many critical discussions of this issue, see especially Starobinski, *Montaigne en mouvement* 95–99. He argues that Montaigne arrives at the anti-Stoic position represented in "De la phisionomie" after having discovered that death, which he had previously regarded as the literal Moment of Truth, may in fact be nothing more than another inauthentic performance, and one which finally reveals nothing about the inner state (if any) of the performer.

19 In some ways this almost out-Senecas Seneca, since even the Roman (*Epistulæ morales* viii, 2 and 6) indicates that his retirement from the world nevertheless benefits that world, by affording him the time to produce the letters that will so edify and improve the lot of humanity. Montaigne, as we will see in a moment, will roundly criticize just this kind of arrogance and presumption in Cicero and Pliny in "Consideration sur Ciceron" (I, 40), ironically holding up Seneca (along with Plutarch) as a counter-example.

20 Indeed, Starobinski does seem to make of Montaigne a kind of Rousseau *avant la lettre* in this respect, and many of the motifs evident in his reading of the *Essais* echo themes found in his earlier work on Rousseau (*Jean-Jacques Rousseau. La transparence et l'obstacle* (Paris: Plon, 1958)). For another discussion of this point, see Robert D. Cottrell, *Sexuality/Textuality. A Study of the Fabric of Montaigne's Essais* (Columbus, OH: Ohio State University Press, 1981) 104–09.

21 This is of course a familiar *topos* in the Renaissance; we are reminded, for instance, of the Prologue to Marguerite de Navarre's *Heptaméron*.

22 On Montaigne's attitudes, mistrustful and otherwise, with regard to rhetoric, see Friedrich, 85–87; Lawrence D. Kritzman, *Destruction/découverte. Le Fonctionnement de la rhétorique dans les "Essais" de Montaigne* (Lexington: French Forum, 1980); Edwin M. Duval, "Rhetorical Composition and 'Open Form' in Montaigne's Early *Essais*," in *BHR*, 43 (1981): 269–287; and Gérard Defaux, *Marot, Rabelais, Montaigne: l'écriture comme présence* (Paris and Geneva: Champion-Slatkine, 1987), especially ch. 4, "La présence recouvrée: Montaigne et la peinture du Moi."

23 The typically Montaignian tag at the end of the paragraph undercuts his argument at its most vehement, which should make us wonder even more just how far Montaigne is really committed to it. As we shall see, in some of the later additions to the *Essais* Montaigne goes even further, on occasion beginning to sound almost Ciceronian himself.

24 Erasmus, *Ciceronianus* LB I, 1022 B; cited by Defaux, 204. Defaux, reading Plato's *Phaedrus* via Erasmus (rather than via Nietzsche, as he says certain modern critics have done), divides language, whether written or spoken, into categories of good (reliable) and bad (unreliable), and makes the anti-Derridean argument that there can be – through an Augustinian leap of faith – a direct connection between the former category and some form of supralinguistic truth (206). I do not think that Montaigne goes as far in this direction as Defaux claims. It seems more accurate to say that, while Montaigne is willing to

distinguish between good and bad uses of language, he nevertheless maintains a clear separation between language – good, bad, or indifferent – and non-language, as expressed in the opening to "De la gloire" (II, 16, 618): [A] "Il y a le nom et la chose: le nom, c'est une voix qui remerque et signifie la chose; le nom, ce n'est pas une partie de la chose ny de la substance, c'est une piece estrangere joincte à la chose, et hors d'elle." ["There is the word and the thing; the word is a sound that marks out and signifies the thing; the word is not a part of the thing or its substance; it is an alien object attached to the thing, and outside of it."] See the following note. Defaux 202–07; see also an earlier version of the same argument: "Montaigne, Erasme, Platon, Derrida: l'écriture comme présence," in *Rivista di letterature moderne e comparate*, vol. 38, fasc. 4 (October–December 1985): 325–43.

25 This is, despite its apparent simplicity, an especially tricky passage. "Parole" here has multiple meanings; in the more general sense (and the one in connection with which this passage is most often cited, not without doing some violence to the context), it may be read to mean the word as communication, language as the (only) medium of interchange between persons. Hence it could mean, for Cave, that we are wholly dependent on language, since nothing can be shown to exist outside of it; or it could mean, for Defaux, that we must place our faith in the imperfect medium of language, while remembering that there exists a supralinguistic higher essence of which that language is only a reflection. But it must be remembered that the specific sense generated by the context of the essay remains active; at this point in "Des menteurs," "parole" means "the word/ language that is not misleading," "word (of honor)," etc. It is this latter meaning that has a more direct bearing on our argument, as will become apparent. Montaigne examines the more general sense of the word in "Du démentir" (II, 18, 666–67), where he describes *parole* as the sole means by which we can conduct our relations with one another. Even here, however, Montaigne makes no metaphysical claims for the power of *parole*; on the contrary, he strictly limits its application to the realm of the practical. While human society depends on the trustworthiness of our *parole*, it remains an "util" ["tool"], not a philosophical abstraction; whether or not it represents some transcendent truth is irrelevant.

26 He comments gleefully on the inevitable discomfiture of such persons when they become entrapped in the web of their own contradictory utterances, and then closes the essay by illustrating the point with not one but two rather Byzantine anecdotes of court life, narratives which seem to undermine Montaigne's point even as they reinforce it. To begin with, their detailed intricacy indicates a somewhat too intimate knowledge of court life, on the part of their narrator, for one who claims to be a non-courtier; moreover, they seem actually to show that it is only *ineffective* deception that does not pay. Even the "innocent" victim of the first story, the felicitously named Signor Merveille, is himself a courtier ("escuyer d'escurie chez le Roy") and professional deceiver, a spy sent to Milan as an "ambassadeur par effect, mais par apparence homme privé, qui fit la mine d'y estre pour ses affaires particulieres" ["in effect an ambassador, but in appearance a private citizen, who pretended to be there on personal business"]. Montaigne even gives details of Merveille's manufactured persona: he is dis-

patched on his mission with one set of (secret) letters and instructions for his real, covert task, and another (public) set of documents "pour le masque et la montre" ["for the mask and for show"]. The King may see through his adversary's attempts to deceive him, but in the meantime his own subterfuge has itself been discovered and foiled in a most unpleasant manner.

27 His reference to "cette nouvelle vertu de faintise et de dissimulation" also links him to a degree with the contemporary current of anti-Machiavellian thought, as exemplified in such works as the *Discours sur les moyens de bien gouverner* (popularly known as the *Anti-Machiavel*) of Gentillet (1576). However, Montaigne has too much respect for the Florentine to lend himself wholeheartedly to such polemics; later in the same essay, while discussing the unprovability of political arguments in general, he remarks (655): "Les discours de Machiavel, pour exemple, estoient assez solides pour le subject, si y a-il eu grand aisance à les combattre; et ceux qui l'ont faict, n'ont pas laissé moins de facilité à combattre les leurs." ["The discourses of Machiavelli, for example, were pretty solid, considering the subject, but they were quite easy to contest; and those who have done so, have made it no less easy to contest their own."]

28 We will ignore, for the moment, the C-text twist at the end of this paragraph. Antoine Compagnon examines Montaigne's use of this quasi-aphoristic style, showing (as we will try to do) that the reader of the *Essais* should not be fooled by Montaigne's Senecan posturing into making of him purely an author of aphorisms; Montaigne's style, he argues, is in fact a Socratic balance of the compressed and the extended, the brief and the sustained, and it is the tension between these two discursive modes, governed by the first-person authorial voice, that gives the *Essais* their organic unity. Our argument will follow a similar critical trajectory, while attempting to show that these stylistic choices, rather than existing in a vacuum, are closely linked to specific political and ideological positions. See Compagnon, "A Long Short Story: Montaigne's Brevity," in *Montaigne: Essays in Reading*, ed. Gérard Defaux (*Yale French Studies* 64 (1983)): 24–50, especially 34–37, where he discusses this passage from "De l'institution des enfans."

29 For another discussion of the connection between Montaigne's choice of linguistic style and his desire to be associated with a particular system of values, see Cottrell, *op. cit.* Cottrell highlights the sexual vocabulary and metaphors used by Montaigne to describe a "masculine" ethical stance of "vigor and valor" (p. 15), pointing out that "Montaigne ascribes to masculinity all the virtues ordinarily identified with Stoicism – virtues that imply, of course, unrelenting tension and rigidity" (p. 7). He then discusses how Montaigne moves from positive approbation of this kind of moral virtue to a more equivocal view, showing that Montaigne simultaneously "undermines the value of such behavior" (p. 15) and associates himself with its opposite, a kind of quasi-feminine laxity or *mollesse*, both linguistically and philosophically (pp. 22–23, 39ff.). However, Cottrell's psychoanalytic reading does not address, as we hope to do, the issues of class and historical context.

30 This is linked to a larger concept of the nobleman-as-dilettante, of which one of the earliest and most influential expressions is found, as we have already seen, in Castiglione's discussion of *sprezzatura*, and which is set forth in Montaigne

especially in "De l'institution des enfans." We will return to this later. For now, we may merely observe that Montaigne's claims to poor memory, inability to be polite in a courtly context, and all-round ineptitude are all part of this package – this despite Montaigne's professed distaste for Castiglione and his ideas of courtly behavior (see, for example, "De la gloire" (II, 16), 622). Many critics have commented on Montaigne's studied claims to ineptitude; see, for example, Erich Auerbach's famous essay, "L'Humaine Condition," ch. 12 of *Mimesis. The Representation of Reality in Western Literature*, trans. Willard R. Trask (Princeton: Princeton University Press, 1953): 285–311, especially 298, 306–08; Friedrich, *Montaigne* 36, 87–88; and Sayce, *Essays of Montaigne* 282–84.

31 Montaigne 784 (II, 37: "De la ressemblance des enfans aux peres"). Read in this context, this statement sounds almost like testimony before a Congressional committee ("Are you now, or have you ever been...?"); and it seems less a philosophical reappropriation of "good" language (Defaux 206) than a practical and political statement.

32 See our discussion of this point with reference to Castiglione and Bacon in the following chapter.

33 At the end of the essay, Montaigne discusses his letter-writing habits, and deplores the necessity of affixing not only the *formules de politesse*, but also "une legende de qualitez et tiltres," honorifics and titles which cannot be omitted or wrongly formulated without offending the honor of the addressee. He links this proliferation and consequent debasement of language to the inflation in the economy of nobility: "Tant d'innovations d'offices, une si difficile dispensation et ordonnance de divers noms d'honneur ... si cherement acheptez..." ["So many new offices, such a difficult dispensation and ordering of various honorific names ... so dearly bought..."]

See Rigolot's discussion of this theme, in connection with "De la gloire," in terms of the "false currency" of what he refers to as the "monde inflationniste et pervers des affaires publiques" ["inflationary and perverse world of public affairs"]: Rigolot 57.

34 Michel Eyquem de Montaigne, *Journal de Voyage*, ed. François Rigolot (Paris: Presses Universitaires de France, 1992) 214.

35 Huppert, in his discussion (p. 90) of this point, seems to take for granted the legitimacy of Montaigne's self-proclaimed connection to this class. Likewise, James J. Supple, in his *Arms and Letters. The Military and Literary Ideals in the Essais of Montaigne* (Oxford: Clarendon, 1984), argues against those who (starting in the seventeenth century, if not earlier) express skepticism regarding Montaigne's identification with the *épée* nobility (pp. 30–31, and *passim*). For reasons which will become apparent, it seems more prudent, while noting Montaigne's interest in *appearing* to belong to that class, not to take at face value the claim that he actually does belong to it. We will return to this issue farther on.

36 This is almost identical to *sprezzatura*, which likewise means scorn or disdain; but Montaigne adds to it a dimension of *rudesse*, in keeping with the quasi-martial tone he wishes to set for his French nobleman, which does not seem quite in accord with the *grazia* associated with Castiglione's courtier. On this, see Compagnon, "A Long Short Story" 39.

37 Note that the C-text addition essentially pulls the rug from under Montaigne's original argument, by suggesting that it is careful study and self-cultivation ("la philosophie") that confers upon one the capacity for free and open speech.
38 See above, ch. 1, where this contradiction in Castiglione is discussed in some detail. On the relationship between Montaigne and Castiglione, see Marcel Tetel, "The Humanistic Situation: Montaigne and Castiglione," in *Sixteenth Century Journal*, vol. X, no. 3 (Fall 1979): 69–84.
39 Braden seems to accept the identification of Montaigne with the *noblesse d'épée* when he discusses this passage, and seems to feel that Montaigne's insistent tone may be ascribed to a resistance on his part to threats to the status of the *noblesse d'épée* as a warrior class (78): "Montaigne ... does not yet assent to such a basic redefinition of his class, but its imminence clearly affects him."
    Ellery Schalk adduces this passage in support of his argument that the military profession, in the sixteenth century, is accessible to all, and that it confers the status of a *noble d'épée* upon all who practice it: " ... status, or the status of nobility at least, is *simply* a profession – the profession comes first and determines the status." *From Valor to Pedigree. Ideas of Nobility in France in the Sixteenth and Seventeenth Centuries* (Princeton: Princeton University Press, 1986) 11.
40 Ironically, the language he uses closely echoes that of Castiglione, whose Ludovico da Canossa states, as we have seen, that "la principale e vera professione del cortegiano debba esser quella dell'arme"; but Montaigne's emphasis is quite different, and (deliberately?) considerably less sophisticated. Castiglione enunciates the cliché, but immediately goes on to say that the reason for being a warrior is to make oneself look good; he is, after all, talking specifically about the courtier, and therefore does not waste time talking about racial history or national character. Montaigne, on the other hand, seems unwilling to ironize the idea as explicitly, at least at the moment he utters it; he seems to hope that if he shouts loudly enough, nobody will ask too many questions. See Castiglione, I, xvii, p. 51.
41 This is a point that Montaigne will make in considerably greater detail later on, notably in "De l'experience" (III, 13); see *infra*, pp. 56ff.
42 Friedrich 16–18.
43 See, for example, his extended discussion of the topic in "De mesnager sa volonté" (III, 10), beginning with the quote with which we opened this chapter (pp. 1011ff.).
    For a fascinating, if idiosyncratic, reading of Montaigne's *politique* persona, see Max Horkheimer's remarkable essay, "Montaigne und die Funktion der Skepsis," in *Kritische Theorie. Eine Dokumentation*, ed. by Alfred Schmidt, Band 2 (Frankfurt am Main: S. Fischer, 1968): 201–259. Horkheimer examines Montaigne's practical approach to the civil wars (215): "Er sieht die kämpfende Parteien als aufgeklärter Diplomat, Gewissensfreiheit bedeutet ihm Voraussetzung des Friedens. Nach ihm hat niemand recht, es gibt kein Recht, sondern Ordnung und Unordnung." ["He sees the warring parties from the viewpoint of an enlightened diplomat; freedom of conscience is for him a prerequisite for peace. To him, nobody is right; there is no 'right,' only order and disorder."] Horkheimer views this position of skeptic/Stoic detachment as essentially bourgeois; Montaigne is identified not with this or that ideology, but with the

interests of the bourgeoisie and the nascent absolutist State, which alone can guarantee peace and stability (209). For Horkheimer, writing in 1938, this position becomes untenable with the rise of capitalism and the attendant alienation of the individual. What works for Montaigne under the Valois is a cop-out, not to say a betrayal, for intellectuals under the totalitarian *Führerstaat* (245).

44 As will be seen in the following chapter, Montaigne is here not far from Bacon's views, set forth in the *Advancement of Learning*, on the pernicious "contract of error" that governs the exchange of ideas between persons.

45 Note that he does so in the same textual layer [A] as the discussion of the *arrière-boutique* itself.

46 See Montaigne 156ff.

47 Friedrich, in his general discussion of the *arrière-boutique*, points this out (p. 233): "Das ist keine anachoretenhafte Weltabgeschiedenheit, sondern ein stets verfügbares inneres Refugium das dem Geiste nicht verwehrt, der Welt zu geben, was sie verlangt, und von ihr zu nehmen, was ihm Freude macht." ["This is no hermit-like retirement from the world, but rather an always available inner refuge, that does not prevent the soul from giving to the world what it demands, nor from taking from it, what makes it happy."]

48 I would not, however, go so far as Thomas Greene, who, in a strenuous effort to refute Cave's argument, defines the Montaignian self as a fortress-like ensemble governed by a "unique, recognizable voice, a distinctive moral style" (129), an entity which he places at the center of the *Essais*: "It is not too much to say that the ultimate subject of the *Essais* is this transformative *stile* of their author's soul" (136). Similarly, Sayce suggests, without perhaps expending as much critical energy on the problem, that there is some constant center, a defined set of limits within which the movement of the self takes place (115–16, alluding to Montaigne's mention in "Du repentir" (III, 2) of "une forme sienne, une forme maistresse"). Both of these arguments imply an overriding consistency which seems to me to be absent, both philosophically and materially, from the *Essais*. Perhaps the most sensitive evaluation of this complex problem is that offered by Claude Blum: "...lorsqu'il se donne pour projet de peindre le moi, Montaigne ne se propose pas tant un objet à analyser que la forme d'une analyse qui restitue l'objet dans la plénitude et la complexité de son insaisissable perception" (71). See Thomas M. Greene, *The Vulnerable Text. Essays on Renaissance Literature* (New York: Columbia University Press, 1986), ch. 7: "Dangerous Parleys – Montaigne's *Essais* 1:5 and 6," pp. 116–40; Sayce, *op. et loc. cit.*; and Claude Blum, "La peinture du moi et l'écriture inachevée," in *Poétique* 53 (February 1983): 60–71. Greene's essay also appears in *Montaigne: Essays in Reading*, ed. Gérard Defaux (*YFS* 64 (1983)): 3–23. On Reiss, see *supra*, nn. 2 and 10; on Cave, see his pp. 302, 313, and *passim*, and *supra*, n.10; and see also Starobinski, p. 106, where he discusses the question of masks in Derridean terms that suggest Cave's argument.

49 As we have seen, Montaigne is very fond of claiming that he is old and decrepit, that he is soft, flabby, devoid of memory, and generally inept; here, however, this impulse takes on a special focus, as it is precisely his own *mollesse*-induced unsuitability for the Stoic form of retreat that he wishes to emphasize. (See

Cottrell's discussion of this theme, 19–41.) We will see later how Montaigne manipulates this pose of helpless incompetence. For the moment, it is sufficient to keep in mind that the veracity (dubious at best) of his claims of generalized impotence is irrelevant to his main purpose; the claims are deployed not as absolute truths but as tactics in a larger performative strategy.

Ultimately, of course, Montaigne is probably suggesting (as we will see Bacon do in the next chapter) that we are *all* "âmes communes," and therefore that Stoicism is indeed irrelevant to the conduct of daily life, except when it is utilized as a pose, a theatrical performance. Much of "De la vanité" (III, 9), is devoted to an extended consideration of the wretched and depraved nature of contemporary society; Montaigne closes one section of this discussion (955–57) by pointing out that, deplorable as that society is, it is all there is, and – despite the best efforts of Plato, Aristotle and the rest – it cannot be otherwise. To illustrate his point, he holds up that great reformer and lawgiver, Solon, as an example of pragmatic acceptance of the *status quo* (957). Even the wisest person does not live in a vacuum, and must therefore adapt to the prevailing circumstances, whatever they may be. See Starobinski's discussions of this point, pp. 113ff. and 366–67.

50 Slightly earlier in "De la phisionomie" (p. 1039), we are told that this *suffisance* is not to be had through assiduous study of edifying texts, and that it does not result from a rigorous application of stern philosophical principles in an attempt to make oneself more virtuous. Rather, it is acquired through the application of the Delphic dictum, "know thyself," in its purest sense. (This ideal of Socratic self-knowledge is, of course, one of the main themes of the *Essais*, articulated most thoroughly at the end of the entire work, in "De l'experience" (III, 13).) We should, however, be careful not to take Montaigne too literally here, lest we fall into the trap of thinking that he will henceforth base his utterances solely upon his own experiences; after all, he has hardly given up reading ancient authors himself. Perhaps a more accurate way of putting it would be to say that he is adding himself to his reading list. In other words, Montaigne (in the form of the *Essais*) has himself become a text, an (ancient) author to be read, reread, and commented upon – within the *Essais* themselves – along with Plutarch and the rest. This reflects his evident eagerness to join that exclusive club of sages "qui ne vivent qu'en la memoire des livres" to which he advises his would-be nobleman to turn for edification and self-improvement. It is interesting, in this connection, to recall Montaigne's desire (expressed in "De la vanité" (III, 9, pp. 996–97)) to become a citizen of (ancient) Rome: [B] "Me trouvant inutile à ce siècle, je me rejecte à cet autre, et en suis si embabouyné que l'estat de cette vieille Romme, libre, juste et florissante (car je n'en ayme ny la naissance ny la vieillesse) m'interesse et me passione."

51 Cottrell discusses this revalorization of weakness, with particular emphasis on the sexual metaphors used by Montaigne, and links it to what he sees as Montaigne's shift from a quasi-Stoic psychology of rigor and linearity to one more process-oriented and "circular." Cottrell 23–24 and 56–57, and *passim*.

52 Sayce (p. 148) compares this point to Diderot's *Paradoxe sur le comédien*, where Diderot discusses the same idea, albeit with the emphasis on aesthetic rather than practical concerns.

53 See Rigolot's discussion (158–59) of this passage and that on Montaigne's "cicatrice", cited below.

54 This maneuver is clearly consistent with what we have already seen of Montaigne's more or less oblique attempts to present himself as one of those virtuous ancients, or at least to align himself (as he aligns La Boétie) with them against the corruption, unwisdom, and decadence of modern times.

55 In making this comparison, Montaigne is of course alluding to the famous adage of Erasmus, *Sileni Alcibiadis* (III, iii, 1), and he may also be recalling the prologue to *Gargantua*. See Joshua Scodel's discussion of Montaigne's relationship to Socrates: "The Affirmation of Paradox: A Reading of Montaigne's 'De la Phisionomie'," in *Montaigne: Essays in Reading*, ed. Gérard Defaux (*Yale French Studies* 64 (1983)) 209–37, especially pp. 235–37, where he discusses the triangle Socrates-La Boétie-Montaigne.

56 Montaigne 640–41 ("De la præsumption" (II, 17)), where he hastens to point out that he shares these attributes with Castiglione's ideal courtier – a point to which we shall return.

57 Montaigne 1060–63. Cf. Rigolot's discussion of this portion of the essay (to which my reading is indebted) in the larger context of the semiotic complex *masque-visage-aspect-forme-figure* ... in his ch. 8, pp. 174–75.

58 Literally, "pulled the treachery from his fists."

59 Cf. his claim, in "De l'experience" (III, 13, p. 1097), that his *visage* always reveals his inner state: "[B] Mon visage me descouvre incontinent, [C] et mes yeux: [B] tous mes changemens commencent par là, et un peu plus aigres qu'ils ne sont en effect; je faits souvent pitié à mes amis avant que j'en sente la cause." ["My visage reveals me immediately, as do my eyes; all my changes start there, and [seem] more intense than they really are; I often inspire sympathy in my friends before I feel the cause myself."] But the assertion instantly deconstructs itself: his *visage* does *not* actually deliver an exact representation of his *moi*; instead, it exaggerates, seemingly of its own volition, in order to persuade more effectively. If anything, Montaigne seems rather proud of its ability to command sympathy from an audience without even any necessary correspondence between his inner state and the *visage*, much less any conscious performative effort on his part.

60 They seem not to be mere bandits, but perhaps renegade Protestant noblemen; Montaigne refers to them as "gentils-hommes masquez," and notes that they are accompanied by a troop of mounted archers.

61 Apparently their initial reason for pursuing and capturing Montaigne is political, even if their real motivations later seem to be more practical.

62 On the natural, uncultivated bravery of peasants, see, among other places in the *Essais*, "De la phisionomie" (III, 12), pp. 1040–41.

63 Cf. Supple's discussion of this passage, 169ff., where he also emphasizes Montaigne's ambivalence towards this ideal.

64 Cave and Greene, while agreeing on little else, both emphasize the martial rhetoric of this essay (referred to by Friedrich (234) as "einer Art Brevier der *honnête-homme*-Bildung" ["a kind of manual for the *honnête homme*"]). Cave (278) sees that rhetorical strategy as primarily a defensive maneuver: "The subject of the *Essais* must prove his identity (his singular coherence) by rejecting, or at least opposing himself to, alien discourse. Thus ... the discussion of the

'art of conversation' in III. viii, where conversation is defined in terms of conflict with the speech of others…" For Greene (131, and *passim*), such conflict is still threatening, but it is also essential: "The conflict of the siege then is both life-threatening and life-preserving. […] The question whether or not to parley contains the question whether or not to write. To use language is to be invaded and to invade. To parley is to assume the vulnerability of a writer, to enter the gray area of language, of interchange, of the *prinse* of oppositions."

65 As will be seen, it might be more accurate to say that the pleasure derived from this sort of *conférence* differs qualitatively from that associated with conversation by other writers on the subject.

66 This thought takes on an added dimension when Montaigne compares the violent physical excitement of conversational combat to that of sex, "és morsures et esgratigneures sanglantes."

67 In this, he differentiates his ideal conversation from the kind of domestic theatre performed, according to Neuschel, by *épée* nobles in their households, which – although separate from, and therefore maintaining a certain symbolic independence from, the court – nevertheless remained "small theatres in which dramas of honor and deference could be acted out." Neuschel 160; see 159–83, *passim*.

68 Montaigne does not miss the chance to inflate his own noble status, this time by claiming that he himself experienced such annoyingly deferential treatment in his formative years (918).

69 Besides, as we have already seen, such professional specialists are by definition excluded from the ranks of the nobility, new or old.

70 One might even argue that this process of elimination really leaves only one person, and that the *Essais* are the result: Montaigne's conversation with the only person he can stand to talk to, Montaigne …

71 On the mask as a protective mechanism, see Starobinski, *Montaigne en mouvement* pp. 317–18, where he discusses the idea in the context of a reading of "De mesnager sa volonté" (III, 10). He sees it, in somewhat Sartresque terms, as protective insofar as it serves as a barrier "qui permet la distinction entre 'se donner à autruy' et 'se donner à soy'" ["which allows the distinction between 'giving oneself to others' and 'giving oneself to oneself'"], maintaining a kind of interior space safe from the incursions of "les autres."

72 Recall that this inertia comes into play specifically when Montaigne feels it necessary to resist (through inaction?) any kind of external impulse, i.e. to maintain his freedom, and that this puts it at odds with his passivity…

73 Montaigne 993. Naturally Montaigne is also alluding to his more recent Italian counterparts.

74 Again, see Salmon, "Cicero and Tacitus in Sixteenth-Century France," and Momigliano, "Tacitus and the Tacitist Tradition."

75 This *suffisance*, for which Socrates is the prototype, is perhaps Montaigne's least ambiguous effort to identify with a philosophical paradigm from classical antiquity; David Lewis Schaefer also suggests that it makes of Montaigne "one of the key philosophic architects, and perhaps *the* original architect, of what we know as 'bourgeois' morality." Schaefer is careful to insist that Montaigne himself, far from being "bourgeois," belongs instead to the "class" of philosophers, but he nevertheless sees Montaigne as promulgating a transformative

political project in the interests of all. "Montaigne is, in short, one of the earliest philosophic advocates of the modern liberal regime." David Lewis Schaefer, *The Political Philosophy of Montaigne* (Ithaca: Cornell University Press, 1990) 340, 375.

76 Villey, in a footnote to this passage, points out that Montaigne did not actually receive the King's letter until well after his return to Bordeaux.

77 Cave 320.

78 Note that the first and last terms ("fidelité ... liberté"), apparently contradictory, are reconciled through the mediation of the one in between: "jugement." I am indebted to David Quint for pointing this out.

79 At best, the role is posited as an ideal one cannot live up to – in the meantime, though, it remains an ideal which may be cynically exploited.

80 Ironically enough, one of the demands the court *milieu* places upon the courtier is that of distinguishing himself from all the other courtiers – this in the midst of the most crushing insistence upon conformity. We have already seen Montaigne address the question of *la gloire*, but a more detailed treatment of this problem will be reserved for our final chapter.

3   MASK AND ERROR IN FRANCIS BACON

1 We also saw the dangers of taking these claims to autonomy at face value, a trap which one recent comparison of Montaigne and Bacon fails to avoid. Kenneth A. Hovey contrasts Bacon's political involvement with what he calls (79–80) "Montaigne's extremism in categorically rejecting" such involvement, but, as the preceding chapter has shown, Montaigne's various "rejections" are neither as simple nor as univocal as Hovey would seem to believe. Hovey's essay is fairer to Bacon than it is to Montaigne. Kenneth Alan Hovey, "'Mountaigny Saith Prettily': Bacon's French and the Essay," in *PMLA*, 106: 1 (January 1991): 71–82.

2 Sir Francis Bacon, *The Works of Francis Bacon*, 14 vols., ed. James Spedding, Robert Leslie Ellis, and Douglas Denon Heath (London: Longman *et al.*, 1858–1874; repr. Stuttgart: Frommann/Holzboog, 1963) III: 421. All works of Bacon other than the *Essayes* will be cited in this edition; each citation will give volume and page number for the passage cited. Except when noted, English translations of Bacon's Latin works will be taken from this edition.

3 Our reading will thus lend support to Jonathan Goldberg's more general contention that, in seventeenth-century England at least, the private is defined only as the absence of a pervasive public. See his *James I and the Politics of Literature: Jonson, Shakespeare, Donne, and Their Contemporaries* (Stanford University Press, 1989 (orig. pub. 1983)) 148–51.

4 See, for example: Geoffrey Tillotson, "Words for Princes: Bacon's *Essays*," *TLS*, 6 Feb. 1937, 81–82 (repr. *Essays in Criticism and Research* (Cambridge University Press, 1942) 31–40); Basil Willey, *The English Moralists* (London: Chatto & Windus, 1964) 141–44; and Allan H. Gilbert, *Machiavelli's Prince and Its Forerunners* (Durham, NC: Duke University Press, 1938).

5 See Napoleone Orsini, *Bacone e Machiavelli* (Geneva: Emiliano Degli Orfini, 1936); Vincent Luciani, "Bacon and Machiavelli," *Italica* 24: 1 (March 1947): 26–40; Emile Gasquet, *Le courant machiavelien dans la pensée et la littérature*

anglaises du XVIe siècle (Paris: Didier, 1974); and Brian Vickers, *Francis Bacon and Renaissance Prose* (Cambridge University Press, 1968).

6 Orsini sees this move, which he characterizes (*Bacone e Machiavelli* 78) as "il più caratteristico sviluppo del machiavellismo in Bacone," as a shift from the public to the private sphere, and, while disinclined to view it as trivializing, he nevertheless seems uneasy about it. Luciani argues that this reduction from public to private life not only devalues Machiavelli's precepts, but also shows Bacon to be "ethically inferior" to his model ("Bacon and Machiavelli" 27).

7 C[live] S[taples] Lewis, *English Literature in the Sixteenth Century Excluding Drama* (Oxford University Press, 1954) 537.

8 He remarks further that "The Prince of darkness is a Gentleman & not a Man he is a Lord Chancellor," and goes on to refer to Bacon as, among other things, a "Villain," a "Knave & Fool," a "Liar," a "Usurer," "Satan," and a "Contemptible and Abject Slave." *The Complete Poetry and Prose of William Blake*, revised edition, ed. David V. Erdman, with commentary by Harold Bloom (Garden City, NY: Anchor, 1982) 620–32.

9 William Hazlitt, "Lectures on the Age of Elizabeth": lecture no. 7, "Character of Lord Bacon's Works – Compared as to Style with Sir Thomas Brown and Jeremy Taylor," in *Collected Works of William Hazlitt*, 12 vols., ed. A. R. Walker and Arnold Glover (London: J. M. Dent, 1902) 5: 327.

10 R. S. Crane sees the *Essayes* as the fulfillment of a program, set forth in the *Advancement of Learning* and *De Augmentis*, for a systematic description of "civil knowledge." Ronald S. Crane, "The Relation of Bacon's *Essays* to His Program for the Advancement of Learning," *Schelling Anniversary Papers* (New York: Century, 1923) 89.

R. C. Cochrane elaborates upon this view, and makes of the *Essayes* a manual for the enterprising and ambitious man, one who would be the master of his own fortune. Rexmond C. Cochrane, "Francis Bacon and the Architect of Fortune," in *Studies in the Renaissance*, vol. 5, ed. M. A. Shaaber (New York: The Renaissance Society of America, 1958) 176–95.

11 Lisa A. Jardine, *Francis Bacon. Discovery and the Art of Discourse* (Cambridge University Press, 1974) 228.

12 Stanley Eugene Fish, *Self-Consuming Artifacts. The Experience of Seventeenth-Century Literature* (Berkeley: University of California Press, 1972) 94.

13 Fish, *Self-Consuming Artifacts* 151.

14 Fish, *Self-Consuming Artifacts* 153–55.

15 Fish, *Self-Consuming Artifacts* 121.

16 Sir Francis Bacon, *The Essayes or Counsels, Civill and Morall*, ed. Michael Kiernan (Cambridge, MA: Harvard University Press, 1985) 5. All further references to the *Essayes* will be from this edition.

17 Cf., as only the most famous among many such excuses to be found in Renaissance literature, the prefatory epistle to Castiglione's *Cortegiano*.

18 This is, at least, the generally accepted view; Julian Martin, however, argues otherwise, saying that Bacon in fact enjoyed considerable favor at this point in his career, but was precluded from holding certain offices because of his youth. In any event, what matters is that Bacon perceived a gap between his actual status and his deserts. See Martin, *Francis Bacon, the State, and the Reform of*

Natural Philosophy (Cambridge University Press, 1992) 98–99.

19 III: 268ff. Machiavelli makes the same point in the dedication of the *Principe*, 257.

20 There will be more to say about "rhetoric," both as a word in the Baconian lexicon and as a weapon in his intellectual arsenal. I do not wish here to engage in the rather confused critical debate on Bacon's use of the terms and concepts "rhetoric" and "dialectic"; for now, at least, I use the term "rhetoric" merely in a generic sense, as pertaining to strategies of persuasion, without intending as yet any specifically Baconian overtones.

21 As in, for example, the works of Antonio Guevara and others.

22 This translation is based on that found in Morris Croll, "Attic Prose: Lipsius, Montaigne, Bacon," *Schelling Anniversary Papers* (New York: Century, 1923) 138–39.

23 Morris Croll, "Juste Lipse et le mouvement anti-cicéronien," in *Revue du seizième siècle* II (1914): 200–42; "'Attic' Prose in the Seventeenth Century," in *Studies in Philology* 18 (1921): 79–128; "Attic Prose: Lipsius, Montaigne, Bacon," cited *supra*; "Muret and the History of 'Attic' Prose," in *PMLA* XXXIX (June 1924): 254–309; "The Baroque Style in Prose," in *Studies in English Philology*, eds. K. Malone and M. Ruud (Minneapolis: n.p., 1929): 427–56.

24 See, among others, Karl R. Wallace, *Francis Bacon on Communication and Rhetoric, Or: The Art of Applying Reason to Imagination for the Better Moving of the Will* (Chapel Hill: University of North Carolina Press, 1943); Paolo Rossi, *Francis Bacon: From Magic to Science*, tr. Sacha Rabinovitch (London: Routledge and Kegan Paul, 1968), esp. pp. 180–85; and John C. Briggs, *Francis Bacon and the Rhetoric of Nature* (Cambridge, MA: Harvard University Press, 1989) 162, and *passim*.

25 The incident in question, which occurred in 1593, is one in which Bacon seems to have incurred the long-term displeasure of Queen Elizabeth by speaking his conscience in Parliament rather too freely. See Bacon, *Works* VIII: 222–41. Levy's argument here follows that of Jonathan Marwil, who, in his *The Trials of Counsel. Francis Bacon in 1621* (Detroit: Wayne State University Press, 1976), describes this incident (74ff.) in terms of a failure of Ciceronian strategies of self-presentation. Marwil says further (88) that the first version of the *Essayes* is a direct autobiographical reflection of this experience: "In 1597 Bacon wrote as a private man bitterly disappointed in his hopes." F. J. Levy, "Francis Bacon and the Style of Politics," in *ELR*, 16: 1 (Winter 1986): 103–04, 109.

26 On this, cf. Daniel Javitch, *Poetry and Courtliness in Renaissance England* (Princeton: Princeton University Press, 1978) 65–66.

27 Levy, "Francis Bacon" 101.

28 Cf. our discussion of Montaigne's moves in this direction in the previous chapter.

29 As he calls it in the first of the *Essayes*, "Of Truth," and elsewhere. *Essayes* 8.

30 For a generally positive, but balanced, view of Bacon's endeavor, see Rossi, *From Magic to Science*, and also his article "Baconianism," in the *Dictionary of the History of Ideas*, ed. Philip P. Wiener (New York: Scribner, 1973) I: 172–79.

31 Many critics see Bacon's schemes to uncover the Secrets of Nature as of a piece with his efforts in the area of "civill Businesse"; see, for example, Timothy J.

Reiss, *The Discourse of Modernism* (Ithaca: Cornell University Press, 1982) 199; Briggs, *Francis Bacon and the Rhetoric of Nature, passim*, and likewise Martin, *Francis Bacon, the State, and the Reform of Natural Philosophy*; and also B. H. G. Wormald, in his *Francis Bacon. History, Politics, and Science, 1561–1626* (Cambridge University Press, 1993).

32 Thomas M. Greene examines this aspect of Machiavelli's writings in "The End of Discourse and Machiavelli's *Prince*," in his *The Vulnerable Text. Essays on Renaissance Literature* (New York: Columbia University Press, 1986) 61–78.

33 On the relationship between Bacon and Guicciardini, with particular reference to Bacon's historical works, see the source study of Vincent Luciani, "Bacon and Guicciardini," in *PMLA* 62: 1, 1 (March 1947): 96–113. Several recent scholars have argued that Bacon's view of history, and by extension his ideas on political action, are strongly influenced by Guicciardini's notion of history as a series of arbitrary and unique contingencies; see, for example, Ian Box, "Bacon's *Essays*: From Political Science to Political Prudence," in *History of Political Thought* III (1982): 31–49, and Markku Peltonen, "Bacon's Political Philosophy," in Markku Peltonen, ed., *The Cambridge Companion to Bacon* (Cambridge University Press, 1996): 283–310.

34 Frank Whigham (*Ambition and Privilege* 27) links the aphorism or apophthegm to courtly discourse, emphasizing the aphorism's utility and adaptability.

35 Jardine, *Francis Bacon* 227. For discussions of Bacon's categories of "magistral" and "initiative," see, for example, Wallace, *Francis Bacon on Communication* 18–21; Rossi, *From Magic to Science* 176ff.

36 Fish discusses in some detail the way in which this technique of writing and reading the *Essayes* is designed to cause the reader to reject easy assent, and to focus instead on the *process* of evaluating the data presented. See Fish, ch. 2, especially pp. 91–92.

37 Indeed, according to classical rhetorical theory, the very purpose of commonplaces is to persuade by appealing to emotion, while discouraging careful thought. See Aristotle, *Rhetoric* 1395b–1400b; the anonymous *Rhetorica ad Herennium*, II.xxx.47; Cicero, *De Inventione* I.liii.100ff., and II.xiv.47ff.; Quintilian, *Institutio Oratoria*, V.xii.6, V.xiii.56–57; etc.

38 Fish, *Self-Consuming Artifacts* 1–21, and *passim*.

39 Elsewhere in the passage, Bacon vehemently rejects Plato's condemnation of rhetoric, which would seem to undermine Fish's reliance on Plato to describe Bacon's views on and use of rhetoric.

40 Recall that this is a *critical* definition; Bacon is not here expressing approbation of the "contract of error."

41 One is of course reminded of Erasmus's *Moria*.

42 The "Father" in question is, of course, Augustine (*Contra Academicos*, I).

43 My argument is here indebted to Javitch's discussion of the linkages between that "*Vinum Daemonum*" and norms of Elizabethan courtly behavior, which, he proposes, suppress humanist models of free and open civic discourse while privileging what we might call the "contract of error" of the figurative, oblique language of poetry.

44 Bacon further refines this unappealing thought in the *De Augmentis* (I: 730), where he closes the passage by remarking that one cannot correct the wicked,

"... nisi ipse prius omnia malitiae latibula et profunda exploraverit." ["... without first exploring all the depths and recesses of their malice." (V: 17)] The image, and the kernel of the thought, are from Matthew 10:16, where Jesus is advising the apostles on how to conduct themselves among men: "Behold, I send you forth as sheep in the midst of wolves: be ye therefore wise as serpents, and harmless as doves." Cf. also Ephesians 5:15.

45 Greenblatt emphasizes this connection between Renaissance rhetoric and the social performances of the Renaissance court; indeed, he says that rhetoric is the key to the Renaissance man: "It offered men the power to shape their worlds, calculate the probabilities, and master the contingent, and it implied that human character itself could be similarly fashioned, with an eye to audience and effect. Rhetoric served to theatricalize culture, or rather it was the instrument of a society which was already deeply theatrical." *Renaissance Self-Fashioning* 162.

46 Fish 101–08.

47 In this, of course, Bacon is once again following Machiavelli; recall the former's famous remark in the *Advancement* (*Works* III, 430): "... we are much beholden to Machiavel and others, that write what men do and not what they ought to do." Later in the same work (III, 471–72), he goes into more detail: "... if a man would set down for himself that principle of Machiavel, *that a man seek not to attain virtue itself, but the appearance thereof; because the credit of virtue is a help, but the use of it is cumber*; or that other of his principles, *that he presuppose, that men are not fitly to be wrought otherwise but by fear; and therefore that he seek to have every man obnoxious, low, and in strait*, which the Italians call *seminar spine*, to sow thorns: ... and the like evil and corrupt positions, whereof, as in all things, there are more in number than of the good: certainly with these dispensations from the laws of charity and integrity, the pressing of a man's fortune may be more hasty and compendious."

48 Here again, what follows will undermine – or, perhaps more precisely, complicate – what has gone before. After making these distinctions, Bacon goes on to show what the well-prepared reader will have already guessed, namely that these discrete categories of deception tend to shade into one another, and are in fact inseparably intertwined. But the falsification inherent in easy distinctions is at least a place to start.

49 A crucial aspect of this concealment is the capacity to hide the very fact that one is able to read behind the masks of others. See, for example, this passage from essay XXII, "Of Cunning," where he talks about looking beyond and through the visages, rhetorical or physical, presented by one's interlocutor (70): "It is a point of *Cunning*; to wait upon him, with whom you speake, with your eye; As the Jesuites give it in precept: For there be many Wise Men, that have Secret Hearts, and Transparent Countenances. Yet this would be done, with a demure Abasing of your Eye sometimes, as the Jesuites also doe use." Bacon here makes some apparently simple suggestions on how to see and be seen in conversation, but the interweaving of the various acts of seeing (and not-seeing) is more complex than it first appears. This passage, like the actions it describes, has a meticulous rhetorical balance. It takes the form of an imperative ("Perform an action") followed by a qualification ("but pretend not to"); the qualification seems almost to cancel what it qualifies, but in actuality it only shifts the

original imperative from a plane of simple assertion and instruction onto a plane of rhetorical instability and moral relativity, while through its apparent simplicity concealing that such a shift has taken place. This rhetorical sleight of hand has the same structure as the behavioral procedure Bacon is here prescribing. First, one must see (through) one's interlocutor; simultaneously, of course, one must also avoid being seen through oneself. What is more, though, it is equally imperative to avoid letting oneself be perceived in the act of seeing (hence the "demure Abasing of your Eye"). The passage calls not for a straight-forward gaze of penetrating observation but for a careful balance between perception, presentation, and concealment. This kind of fan-dance is the essence not only of Baconian rhetoric but also of the comportment of the Baconian man: showing to one's audience what one thinks or hopes they want to see, based upon what one is able to discern through seeing – all the while concealing both one's own motivations and one's ability to perceive those of others.

50 "*Habit*" may here mean either "custom" or "costume"; both senses seem to be operative. Lurking behind at least the former definition seems to be Aquinas's notion of *habitus*, as laid forth in *ST* 1a2ae, 49–54. For Aquinas, *habitus* may be either natural or acquired; he defines the latter kind (q. 51, art. 2) as being produced by the action of the will upon the subject over time, through repeated practice; the result is a stable pattern of action (one which, as Aquinas notes, can be either good or bad (q. 54, art. 2)). In the same way, the Baconian Man's diligent fabrication of his (sartorial or behavioral) "*Habit*" leads to an almost automatic self-presentation, which as Bacon shows here both enables and protects.

51 This favorite among Bacon's commonplaces also serves to open essay XLIII, "Of Beauty," a piece with links both to "Of Ceremonies and Respects" and "Of Simulation *And* Dissimulation," among others. Castiglione uses the same image in his discussion (II, 39–40) of the kinds of deception permissible to his courtier; Federico defends certain modes of deceit by comparing them to the activity of a master goldsmith in setting "una gioia" to show it off to maximum advantage, insisting that such activity consists in "bon giudicio" ["good judgment"] and "arte" ["art"] rather than "inganno" ["deceit"]. Shakespeare's Prince Hal, no doubt recalling his reading of the *Cortegiano*, famously uses the same image in the same way at the end of act I, scene 2 of *I Henry IV*.

52 Cf. also the *Advancement* (*Works* III, 445–47), where he discusses this entire issue in similar terms. Especially revealing is his remark (p. 446) on the dangers of over-acting: "...if behaviour and outward carriage be intended too much, first it may pass into affection, and then *quid deformius quam scenam in vitam transferre*, to act a man's life?"

53 It is worth noting that this sentence was added to the essay in the 1625 edition. Cf. also the *Advancement*: (*Works* III, 447).

54 "The first, that *Simulation* and *Dissimulation*, commonly carry with them, a Shew of Fearfulnesse, which in any Businesse, doth spoile the Feathers, of round flying up to the Mark. The second, that it pusleth [puzzleth] and perplexeth the Conceits of many; that perhaps would otherwise co-operate with him; and makes a Man walke, almost alone, to his owne Ends." (22)

55 This emphasis on the external, public man pervades Bacon's political thought,

and may also be seen in, for example, the *Advancement* (*Works* III, 420ff.) and in the corresponding portions of the *De Augmentis*. On Bacon's preference, stated and implied, for public rather than private good, and for action in the public sphere, see e.g. Wallace, *Francis Bacon on Communication* 110–11; Wormald, *Francis Bacon* 109ff.; and Ian Box, "Bacon's Moral Philosophy," in Peltonen (ed.), *The Cambridge Companion to Bacon* 260–82.

56 Wallace T. MacCaffrey gives us a lucid description of these people, and of their prospects, in his "Place and Patronage in Elizabethan Politics," p. 101: "... the greediest and most restless were those with the least in hand and the most to wish for – the great army of younger brothers, or the jostling crowd of lesser gentry, men with little patrimony or none at all, either threatened with the loss of status or desperately anxious to attain it. For them politics was a career in a much more urgent sense than for their luckier fellows. The opportunities for making a living open to them were limited. [...] Of the two learned professions, the Church was probably somewhat in disrepute among the higher classes and in any case offered its prizes only to those of considerable learning, while the law required a formidable and special erudition and commanding talent. [...] The minority, endowed with administrative talents, would win the favour of Burghley or some other great minister and move on to the solid respectability and substantial rewards of an official career." He adds that those who were fortunate enough to possess good looks and wit could hope to become part of the Queen's circle. The "formidable and special erudition and commanding talent" are surely Bacon's own. The essay appears in *Elizabethan Government and Society*, ed. S. T. Bindoff, Joel Hurstfield, and C. H. Williams (London: Athlone Press, 1961) 95–126.

57 Insofar as it is possible, in the Baconian universe, to speak of "truth" in this connection.

58 Cf. *supra*, p. 101ff., and n.47. In essay XI, "Of Great Place," Bacon uses an image which elegantly evokes the crooked and hidden paths trodden by the seeker of power (36): "All rising to *Great Place*, is by a winding Staire ... "

59 Cf. the Horatian closing to essay II, "Of Death" (11): "*Death* hath this also; That it openeth the Gate, to good Fame, and extinguisheth Envie. *Extinctus amabitur idem.*"

60 The entire essay is illuminating in this context.

61 Note also that Honor is an attribute which exists primarily through comparison ("gained and broken upon Another"), rather than being an absolute quality. These ideas are consistent with Bacon's conception of nobility as a whole. Cf. also essay XL, "Of Fortune."

62 On this, see Whigham, *Ambition and Privilege* 32–39, and *passim*.

63 "But chiefly, the Mould of a Mans *Fortune*, is in his owne hands. *Faber quisque Fortunae suae*; saith the Poet." (122) This is of course one of Bacon's favorite themes, explored not only in essay XL, "Of Fortune" (whence this quotation is taken) but also throughout the collection, as well as in the *Advancement* and elsewhere. See Cochrane, "Francis Bacon and the Architect of Fortune."

64 Bacon discusses this topic at greatest length in "Of Envy," where the specific type of envy in question is that directed towards persons who, like himself, have risen to titled positions of power through their own efforts. "*Persons* of Noble

Bloud, are lesse *envied*, in their Rising: For it seemeth, but Right, done to their Birth." However, for those who owe their position to factors other than heredity, the situation is somewhat more dangerous, and one must take precautions accordingly, e.g. by complaining about one's workload: "Wherefore, you shall observe that the more deepe, and sober sort of Politique persons, in their Greatnesse, are ever bemoaning themselves, what a Life they lead; Chanting a *Quanta patimur*. Not that they feele it so, but onely to abate the edge of *Envy*." One should also be sure to keep one's subordinates happy, "[f]or by that meanes, there be so many Skreenes betweene him, and *Envy*" (29).

65 The radical difference between the two versions of this essay makes Marwil's comment (88) about Bacon's writing procedure seem rather strange: "Yet while successively altering his perspective, he never cuts out what has been previously said except to forestall foreign complaints or avoid verbal obscurity." This is manifestly untrue, at least in the case of this most crucial of the *Essayes*. It is, however, consistent with Marwil's book-long effort to demonstrate that Bacon is unworthy of whatever good reputation he may possess. Such animus detracts from an otherwise useful book.

66 "Speculation" here means a hypothesis, an irreal supposition of an ideal.

67 This attitude is typified by his bitter comment in essay XXXI, revealingly titled "Of Suspicion," which also made its first appearance in 1625: "What would Men have? Doe they thinke, those they employ and deale with, are Saints? Doe they not thinke, they will have their owne Ends, and be truer to Themselves, then to them?" (102)

68 Cf. 1 Cor. 13, and also the *Advancement* (*Works* III: 266).

69 This kind of mutual dependence is described at the conclusion of essay XLVIII, "Of Followers and Frends," where Bacon cynically remarks: "There is Little Frendship in the World, and Least of all between Equals, which was wont to be Magnified. That that is, is between Superiour and Inferiour, whose Fortunes may Comprehend, the One the Other." (149)

4   NOBLE ROMANS: CORNEILLE AND THE THEATRE OF ARISTOCRATIC REVOLT

1 For a discussion of Corneille's uses of Roman history, see Simone Dosmond, "La Rome de Corneille," in *L'Information littéraire*, 36: 4 (sept.–oct. 1984): 142–52. Marie-Odile Sweetser discusses the various representations of absolutist kingship *à la* Louis XIV in the theatre of Corneille in her "Images de Louis XIV chez Corneille," in *Ouverture et Dialogue. Mélanges offerts à Wolfgang Leiner à l'occasion de son soixantième anniversaire*, ed. Ulrich Döring, Antiopy Lyrouidas, and Rainer Zaiser (Tübingen: Gunter Narr, 1988): 755–768.

2 Georges Couton, *La Vieillesse de Corneille, 1658–1684* (Paris: Librairie Maloine, 1949); *Corneille et la Fronde. Théâtre et politique il y a trois siècles* (Clermont-Ferrand: Publications de la Faculté des Lettres de l'Université de Clermont (fasc. 4), 1951); *Corneille et la tragédie politique* (Paris: Presses Universitaires de France (coll. "Que sais-je?," vol. 2174) 1984).

3 André Stegmann, *L'Héroïsme cornélien. Genèse et signification*, 2 vols. (Paris: Armand Colin, 1968) II: 580, 613–14, 657–59, and *passim*.

4 Serge Doubrovsky, *Corneille et la dialectique du héros* (Paris: Gallimard, 1963) 269. See also pp. 96, 492, and *passim*.
5 Bernard Dort, *Corneille dramaturge* (Paris: L'Arche, 1957; 2nd ed., 1972).
6 Jean-Marie Apostolidès, *Le roi-machine. Spectacle et politique au temps de Louis XIV* (Paris: Editions de Minuit (coll. "Arguments"), 1981); and *Le prince sacrifié. Théâtre et politique au temps de Louis XIV* (Paris: Editions de Minuit (coll. "Arguments"), 1985), especially ch. 3, "L'univers historique."
7 See, for example, his p. 116, where he posits an identity between the political situation of the tragedies and the "ordre naturel" that produces the hero in the first place. Michel Prigent, *Le héros et l'État dans la tragédie de Pierre Corneille* (Paris: Presses Universitaires de France (coll. "Ecrivains"), 1986).
8 Marc Fumaroli, *Héros et orateurs. Rhétorique et dramaturgie cornéliennes* (Geneva: Droz, 1990) 8.
9 Fumaroli, following Octave Nadal, insists on the originary primacy of the pastoral ideal in Corneille's conception of nobility. See *Héros et orateurs*, ch. 1: "Pierre Corneille, fils de son oeuvre" 36–37, and *passim*. See also Octave Nadal, *Le Sentiment de l'amour dans l'oeuvre de P. Corneille* (Paris: Gallimard, 1948). On the relationship between the notion of pastoral retreat and the question of noble identity, see Maurice Magendie, *La politesse mondaine et les théories de l'honnêteté en France, au XVIIe siècle, de 1600 à 1660*, 2 vols. (Paris: Presses Universitaires de France, 1925), and *Du nouveau sur L'Astrée* (Paris: Honoré Champion, 1927); and Norbert Elias, *The Court Society*, tr. Edmund Jephcott (New York: Pantheon, 1983), ch. 8, "On the Sociogenesis of Aristocratic Romanticism in the Process of Courtization," especially his lengthy discussion of *L'Astrée*, 246–67.
10 Doubrovsky, *Dialectique* 125, and *passim*.
11 Paul Bénichou, *Morales du grand siècle* (Paris: Gallimard, 1948) 21–23. Opposing this view, Doubrovsky (*Dialectique* 118) proposes that the key to the *héros cornélien* is in fact a high degree of self-sacrifice; in his Hegelian terms, real "Maîtrise" depends on the sacrificial negation of the "Moi animal." It is indeed true that much of the heroism of Corneille's protagonists consists of sacrificing one set of ties or interests for another, higher set; however, this sacrifice (as Doubrovsky acknowledges) seems always to be at least as much in the service of the *moi héroïque* as in that of any purely extra-individual abstraction such as the State. This is true even in such extreme cases as those of Horace or Polyeucte.
12 Bénichou, *Morales* 22. This remark also emphasizes the intrinsic theatricality of the *héros cornélien*, a point upon which he elaborates later (as will we).
13 See, for example, *Morales* 78–79, where, after enumerating the various attributes and characteristics that go to make up the *héros cornélien*, he nevertheless insists that there exists a unitary and transcendent "moi" which subsumes these varied attributes into itself.
14 Fumaroli's version of this is characteristically erudite and sophisticated; he locates the roots of the *héros cornélien* in Aristotle (the ideal of *magnanimité*) and in Pseudo-Longinus (a rhetoric of the sublime), both Christianized by the theorists of the Counter-Reformation. *Héros et orateurs*, ch. 4: "Corneille et la rhétorique de l'humanisme chrétien," part 3: "L'héroïsme cornélien et l'éthique de la magnanimité" 324, and *passim*.

15 Couton, in the introduction to his edition of the *Oeuvres complètes*, says (p. xxxiv) that "Le théâtre cornélien, comme l'épopée contemporaine, pratique une jonction des deux langages, de la typologie et de l'allégorie morale" ["Corneille's theatre, like contemporary epic, joins two languages, that of typology and that of moral allegory"]. These two seventeenth-century discourses, says Couton, make available to both the playwright and his audience an entire vocabulary of allegorical/symbolic types, by transforming persons, through antonomasia, into *personnages* representing specific attributes or abstract qualities. Pierre Corneille, *Oeuvres complètes*, 3 vols., ed. Georges Couton (Paris: Gallimard (Pléiade), 1980–1987) I: xxix–xxxviii.

16 Dort (*Corneille dramaturge* 34) is undoubtedly right to insist on the inseparability of the character from its context. Fumaroli meanwhile likens this composite nature of the *personnage* to an orator manipulating various forms of figural speech; discussing the monologue in classical French theatre, he describes the *personnage* as "un visage à la recherche de son masque définitif" ["a visage in search of its definitive mask"]. As will be seen, however, the idea – indeed the possibility – of any "masque définitif" is ultimately open to question. ch. 4: "Corneille et la rhétorique de l'humanisme chrétien," section 2: "Rhétorique et dramaturgie: le statut du personnage dans la tragédie cornélienne" 311.

Fumaroli also offers a salutary warning against the danger of reducing the entire theatre of Corneille to the single figure of the *héros cornélien*: "... ce théâtre est moins une dramaturgie du héros, comme on s'obstine à le voir avec une constance vraiment psittaciste, qu'une *dramaturgie du couple*" ["... this theatre is less a dramaturgy of the hero, as some – with truly parrotesque constancy – insist on seeing it, than a *dramaturgy of the couple*"]. It is true, however, that the "constance ... psittaciste" of Corneille's readers in this regard is in some sense only a reflection of Corneille's own obsession with the problem. Fumaroli, *Héros et orateurs*, ch. 2: "Corneille et la Société de Jésus," section 1: "Corneille et le collège des jésuites de Rouen" 77. See also his ch. 4: "Corneille et la rhétorique de l'humanisme chrétien," part 6: "Du *Cid* à *Polyeucte*: une dramaturgie du couple" (399–413). We will have more to say later about the role(s) played by the female halves of Corneille's couples.

17 I, i, 15–16. All citations will be taken from Couton's edition of the *Oeuvres Complètes*, and will give act, scene, and line number (lines numbered continuously from beginning to end of each play).

18 Micheline Cuénin remarks that contemporaries likened Don Diègue to some of the *compagnons* of Henri de Navarre (Biron, Bassompierre), particularly one Gilles de Souvré, governor of Touraine, who in 1609, at the age of 61, was named the *gouverneur* of the future Louis XIII, then aged 8 (about the same age, presumably, as the unseen prince in *Le Cid*).

She also compares the Comte, on the other hand, to certain of the unruly *Grands* under Marie de Médicis: Rohan, Nevers, Condé, Soissons. Micheline Cuénin, "L'amour et l'ambition dans *Le Cid*," in *Pierre Corneille. Actes du colloque tenu à Rouen du 2 au 6 octobre 1984*, éd. Alain Niderst (Paris: PUF, 1985) 445–49.

19 Don Diègue's son Rodrigue says of him (II, ii, 401–02) that "... ce vieillard fut la même vertu, / La vaillance, et l'honneur de son temps..." ["... this old man was

virtue itself, / Valor, and the honor of his time…"] Don Diègue is even here equated with (reduced to?) a set of one-dimensional properties; the ultimate consequences, for Don Diègue, of this reduction are examined below.

Apostolidès points out (*Le prince sacrifié* 60) that this kind of nobility must be constantly réaffirmed and re-demonstrated in a continually renewed present, and goes on to say that Don Fernand breaks the rules of this game by insisting that the past – in this case, Don Diègue – counts as well as the present (indeed, the past counts a great deal, since it is made responsible for the future, in the person of the young Prince of Castile). While I agree that the heroic *individual*, caught permanently in the present instant, has no temporal dimension – that is, no duration – and is constantly at risk, I do not think that this is true of the heroic *role* or *function*. On the contrary, that role is a historical constant, a fact which everyone in the play except Don Gomès seems to recognize. In other words, Apostolidès's two-body argument, drawn from Kantorowicz, should apply to the nobility as well as to the king. It therefore seems to me that Don Fernand is actually playing by the rules when he tries to force the others, specifically Don Gomès, to recognize the temporal dimension of their role. For Don Gomès, he and the role are identical, and exist only in the present instant, as a kind of dimensionless point-source of heroic virtue. The task of Don Fernand is to give temporal extension to that instant by bringing it back into the continuum of history.

20 Dort (*Corneille dramaturge* 35) points out this monothematic aspect of Corneille's heroic *personnage*, and rightly emphasizes its performative nature. Oddly, however, he links these ideas to Corneille's own position as a provincial bureaucrat eager for advancement and higher social status.

21 Prigent (*Le héros* 37–38) advances a rather strange argument in an effort to demonstrate that Rodrigue is not in fact a representative of a particular social class, and furthermore that ideas of class or social stratification are not relevant to any discussion of Corneille. He asserts that Rodrigue, far from representing a given class or category of persons, or realizing the desires or needs of that class, is rather engaged in a project of transcending his origins; he insists further that the notions of heredity and origin we are here discussing have nothing to do with class, even in the rather general sense of a group of persons sharing values and political interests. "Si Rodrigue faisait preuve d'un 'courage de classe', il n'aurait aucun mérite puisque seuls les aristocrates sont présents sur la scène" ["If Rodrigue demonstrated a 'class courage,' he would have no merit, since only aristocrats are present on the stage"]. The problem is that Rodrigue incarnates not "*un* 'courage de classe'" but "*le* 'courage de classe'"; his function is to be the ultimate representative of a particular set of interests and values, interests and values both hereditary and socially defined. As such, he is in clear if implicit (potential) conflict with the king, whose interests are *not* the same. Moreover, his audience is not just other aristocrats; it is also *le peuple*, present both within the play (in IV, ii, we are told that they are one of the reasons for Rodrigue's success) and without, as a part of the "real-life" audience of *Le Cid*.

Behind Prigent's argument seems to be his concern (37) with demonstrating that the theatre of Corneille is not what Doubrovsky (*Dialectique* 96) says it is, namely a "[t]héâtre d'histoire" that is really a "théâtre de réaction contre l'histoire, théâtre *réactionnaire*" ["theatre of reaction against history, a *reactionary* theatre"]. One does not need to agree with Doubrovsky's quasi-Hegelian conclusions to see that Corneille places on stage a set of values whose very nature is to fight a continuous rear-guard action against the historical changes occurring in the France of Louis XIII and Richelieu.

22 Orest Ranum, in his "Courtesy, Absolutism, and the Rise of the French State, 1630–1660," in *JMH* 52:3 (September 1980): 426–51, sees (in a reading which seems to owe something to Elias) this kind of lack of discretion as characteristic of noble behavior in the 1630s. He describes the attempts of the Queen Mother and Mazarin to enforce a code of courtesy as a means of imposing social and political control over an unruly class, and sees *Le Cid* as exploring the dynamics of this question. See especially 444–47.

23 Or, for that matter, the *vantard* Matamore of *L'Illusion comique*. Indeed, Matamore's rhetoric is uncomfortably close to that of Rodrigue and other "serious" *héros cornéliens*; Doubrovsky (*Dialectique* 96, n. 89) attempts to differentiate between the two by pointing out that Matamore's "heroism" is "la contrefaçon de l'héroïsme, un héroïsme impur, qui se paye de *mots*" ["a counterfeit of heroism, an impure heroism, which contents itself with words"]. He goes on to try to distinguish between the comic and tragic versions of this rhetoric by assigning Matamore to the realm of the purely theatrical, while characterizing Rodrigue's performance of the heroic role as a transition from the theatrical to the "real." It is unclear, however, whether Doubrovsky's existential dialectic can rescue Rodrigue from his own theatricality. Rodrigue's role may indeed correspond to the truth of his being, his "essence," but only because his "essence" *is* that theatrical role; it is useless to speak of Rodrigue as having any "self" apart from his publicly performed function. If role and "essence" have been somehow telescoped into one, if it is no longer possible to distinguish between Rodrigue and his role, it may only be because Rodrigue is Matamore without ironic distance; that is, he has lost his sense of humor.

In the same way, Apostolidès (*Le prince sacrifié* 57–58) says (without, however, citing Doubrovsky) that, unlike the case of Rodrigue, there is a radical discontinuity between the words of Matamore and his actions, and indeed that Matamore's universe is limited to words. This distinction, however, remains insufficient; it must be recognized that even the deeds of Rodrigue have no significance until they are authenticated through the words of the king. The flesh must be made word. See *infra*, pp. 134ff.

24 Dort (*Corneille dramaturge* 59) discusses the role of the king-as-mediator, suggesting (I think correctly) that Don Fernand's function is to draw Rodrigue back into history. He does not, however, explore what it is that gives Don Fernand the ability to assume that role; nor does he explain the deferred and provisional nature of the solutions that Don Fernand is able to offer.

25 It will be noted that this descent seems to be accomplished through agamogenesis or cloning, without the intervention of any maternal agent. Is this because any genes other than those of Don Diègue, former holder of Rodrigue's unique role, might dilute and therefore endanger the inheritance of the traits essential to that role? Or is it simply a Salic means of insuring the incontrovertible legitimacy of the offspring, by eliminating even the remotest possibility of a

child resulting from conjugal infidelity? Indeed, there are plenty of children in the play, but no mothers. (Perhaps they do things differently in Spain.) Even Chimène seems to be nothing so much as a virtual clone of her father. I do not mean to suggest, as some have done, that Corneille's female characters are simply men in drag; on the contrary, as Corneille's *oeuvre* progresses, the women become increasingly complex and powerful, moving to center stage while the men recede into two-dimensionality or impotence. But of this more later.

26 That this is the key to all power in this play becomes apparent later on during Rodrigue's narration of the battle, when we find that it is the mere force of his name that causes the enemy to surrender: "Ils [les Rois] demandent le Chef, je me nomme, ils se rendent" (IV, iii, 1336) ["They [the Kings] ask for the leader, I name myself, they surrender"]. Rodrigue here launches an onomastic preemptive strike; he *names himself* (in the present tense) as the "Chef," as though nobody else were qualified to do so, thereby beating to the punch all the kings in the play, Moorish, Castillian, or otherwise. Note, too, that before anyone has a chance to draw the obvious conclusion from this event, the scene is conveniently interrupted by the arrival of Chimène.

27 Couton makes the parallel with the anti-duelling policy of Richelieu; see his notes on the play, in Corneille, *OC*, I: 1474–76.

28 This is not quite what Chimène had in mind; in a long *tirade* earlier in the same scene (1365ff.) she demands that Rodrigue be *deprived* of the opportunity to die honorably, insisting that to allow him to do so would be to defraud her of her just vengeance.

29 This scene between the Infante and Chimène is a curious one, in that the former articulates what will be the absolutist line in the plays immediately following – *Horace* and *Cinna* – namely that private honor must give way to the higher good of (public) civic virtue. Echoing her father's remarks in II, vi, cited above, she points out (1185) to Chimène that "Ce qui fut bon alors ne l'est plus aujourd'hui" ["What was then good, is no longer so."] She insists that Chimène's pursuit of her private honor is at odds with the good of the state (1192): "Tu poursuis en sa mort la ruine publique" ["You pursue, in his death, the ruin of all"]. She explicitly states that it is *more* noble, more *généreux*, to sacrifice demands of familial *honneur* to the *res publica* – precisely what Horace will do (1207–10): "C'est générosité, quand pour venger un père, / Notre devoir attaque une tête si chère: / Mais c'en est une encor d'un plus illustre rang, / Quand on donne au public les intérêts du sang." ["It is generosity when, to avenge a father, / Our duty attacks one so dear to us; / But it is an even higher level [of generosity], / When we renounce the interest of our blood in favor of the public [interest]."] The problem arises when we realize, with Chimène, that while the Infante lectures on the superiority of public to private *générosité*, she is herself behaving in a manner actually less *généreuse* than Chimène, since she is hardly disinterested. Although her request is cloaked in the discourse of nobility, she is asking Chimène to spare Rodrigue, not out of some higher sense of noble *vertu*, but so that she, the Infante, may marry him. The position she claims to espouse is therefore undermined, or at least called into question, in the larger context of the play, and indeed the play seems unwilling to commit itself wholeheartedly to

the logical consequences of the absolutist positions it advances, preferring instead to seek an uneasy – and ultimately unstable – balance between the demands of noble *honneur* and the demands of the State.

30 See Apostolidès, *Le prince sacrifié* 62.

31 As many critics have pointed out, this deferral seems stronger in the 1660 version of the play, and the likelihood of the marriage of Rodrigue and Chimène consequently seems slightly more remote. Milorad R. Margitic ("Les deux *Cid*: de la tragi-comédie baroque à la pseudo-tragédie classique," in *Papers on French Seventeenth-Century Literature*, 11:21 (1984): 411) links this to the fact that Don Fernand seems to be something more of a king in 1660. I cannot here enter into the vast critical debate on the *dénouement* of the play; see, in addition to Couton, Nadal, and Doubrovsky, Harold C. Ault, "The Tragic Genius of Corneille," in *MLR* 45 (1950): 164–76; *idem*, "The Dénouement of *Le Cid*: a Further Note," *MLR* 48 (1953): 54–56; P. J. Yarrow, "The Dénouement of *Le Cid*," in *French Studies* 14 (1960): 141–48; René Pintard, "De la tragi-comédie à la tragédie: l'exemple du *Cid*," in *Mélanges... J. A. Vier* (Paris: Klincksieck, 1973): 455–66; C. J. Gossip, "The Dénouement of *Le Cid*, yet again," in *MLR* 75 (1980): 275–81; etc.

32 This point is also made by Timothy J. Reiss, in his "La Voix royale: de la violence étatique ou, du privé à la souveraineté dans *Cinna*," in *Pierre Corneille: ambiguités*, ed. Michel Bareau (Edmonton: Alta Press, 1989) 41–54; see especially pp. 45–47. Reiss's argument parallels my own in many ways; I regret that it came to my attention only after the present chapter was completed.

33 Couton, for example, sees it as reflecting conditions under Richelieu, which he describes as a state of permanent conspiracy, this being, for lack of any other outlet, the normal and obligatory form of noble opposition. Corneille, *OC* I: 1585. On the other hand, Stegmann, as usual, refuses even such generalized historical connections, insisting, in his brief introduction to the play in his edition of the *Oeuvres complètes*, that there is no ground for seeing in *Cinna* even the slightest allusion to contemporary events. Corneille, *Oeuvres complètes*, ed. André Stegmann (Paris: Editions du Seuil (coll. "l'Intégrale"), 1963) 268.

34 This "style" of conspiracy, for Couton, is characterized by the importance of women and amorous intrigue, by confusion between private and public ends, by a lack of serious vision, etc. Corneille, *OC* I: 1585–86.

These characteristics do not mean, however, that such conspiracies are merely silly, whether we are examining the Fronde (which, Dort (*Corneille dramaturge* 157–58) reminds us, "...on aurait tort de tenir pour une guerre en dentelles ou un prétexte aux *Mémoires* de Retz..." ["...we would be wrong to consider a war in lace or a pretext for Retz's *Mémoires*..."]) or the conspiracy in *Cinna*.

35 It would also make for rather poor theatre; therefore, making credible the threat to Auguste is, as will be seen, both a political and a dramatic necessity.

36 Similarly, when Fulvie discreetly suggests that Auguste isn't so bad after all, since he has in fact displayed considerable good will towards Emilie after gaining power, Emilie dismisses his generosity as irrelevant, saying further that to be swayed by his kindness would be to betray her noble status (I, ii, 84): "Et c'est vendre son sang, que se rendre aux bienfaits." ["And it's selling one's blood

to surrender to favors."]

37 Gordon Braden points out, in his *Renaissance Tragedy and the Senecan Tradition: Anger's Privilege* (New Haven: Yale University Press, 1985), that this kind of aristocratic theatricality has its origins in Senecan Stoicism, citing (p. 26) Seneca's famous admonition, "Do whatever you do as if someone were watching" (*Ep.* 25:5). Emilie is certainly an excellent example of the uncompromising aristocratic self he describes in his ch. 5, "Towards Corneille" (151): "...individual psychology in both Seneca and Corneille mirrors political absolutism as a form of selfhood scrupulous in its rejection of emotional compromises to its integrity." However, as we will shortly see, compromises are in fact made, no matter how hard the "scrupulous" Emilie tries to avoid them.

38 It reappears, for example, in *La Mort de Pompée*, and will be the subject of *Tite et Bérénice*.

39 Although even Auguste himself is well aware of the problem, as we see at II, i, 523–25: "Cette haine des Rois que depuis cinq cents ans / Avec le premier lait sucent tous ses [Rome's] enfants, / Pour l'arracher des coeurs, est trop enracinée." ["That hatred of Kings which, for five hundred years, / Rome's children have sucked with their first milk, / Is too deeply rooted to be taken from their hearts."] The parallel between this position and that of the noble conspiracies against Louis XIII and/or Richelieu would surely not have needed spelling out to a contemporary audience. Indeed, it would almost certainly have been dangerous to state such a position too strongly or convincingly, and therefore it is not surprising that the characters who announce this position most emphatically (Emilie and, especially, Maxime) are (1) undermined in other ways, so as to render their political judgments suspect; (2) converted at the end to a royalist/absolutist position. We will have more to say about this later; see *infra*, p. 150.

40 Odette de Mourgues makes a similar point in her "Coherence and Incoherence in *Cinna*," in *Form and Meaning: Aesthetic Coherence in Seventeenth-Century French Drama. Studies Presented to Harry Barnwell*, ed. William D. Howarth, Ian McFarlane, and Margaret McGowan (Amersham: Avebury, 1982) 55. She does not, however, discuss the theatrical or performative aspects of the problem.

41 The later revelation of the speciousness of this claim will have important consequences.

42 In this respect, at least, Cinna is certainly no fool, and is clearly more astute than Emilie, who responds to his concerns by claiming that, win or lose, his "mémoire," "gloire," and "honneur" will remain intact. She also compares him, inevitably, to Brutus and Cassius (I, iii, 261ff.); but Cinna, in his speech to Auguste, will insist – with perhaps unintentional irony – that there are, in these degenerate days, no longer any potential rebels of the stature and moral authority of a Brutus (II, i, 437–38): "On entreprend assez, mais aucun n'exécute, / Il est des assassins, mais il n'est plus de Brute..."

43 II, i, 433–36, where Cinna compares Auguste's good fortune in this respect with the rather less auspicious destiny of Julius Caesar. Needless to say, Cinna does not here go into the problem of how Caesar, Auguste's legitimizing role model, managed to get himself assassinated while ostensibly under the divine protection accorded to all rulers.

44 Cinna himself points this out later on when, after his interview with Auguste, he is arguing with Emilie about the legitimacy of their chosen course of action; he offers here (III, iv, 1003–10) the standard defense of Divine Right absolutism. In his note to this passage, Couton (Corneille, *OC* I: 1613) cites in support Le Bret, Bossuet, and Louis XIV himself, and points out that the same views are to be found in *Oedipe*, V, i, 1635–39. In the present play, Livie reinforces the point at V, ii, 1609–16; see *infra*, p. 161.

That Cinna is at this point in the play able to enunciate such a view naturally indicates that he has begun to change his mind about assassinating Auguste; however, that he also brings it up in the interview with Auguste, when he is still ostensibly planning to commit precisely the kind of sacrilege to which he alludes, may seem odd. At least it strikes Maxime that way. We will see later whether or not Cinna is to be accused of hypocrisy in this regard.

45 Jean Bodin, *Six Livres de la République* (Paris: J. du Puys, 1577): II, 2, 201, cited by Couton in his notes to this *tirade*.

46 This is perhaps an opportune moment to address the question of Corneille's alleged anti-Machiavellianism. It is certainly true that Corneille participates in the theatrical tradition, widespread in both France and England throughout the late Renaissance, of making base and villainous characters repositories of so-called "Machiavellian" ideas (lying, cheating, murder, and other miscellaneous perfidy), and his participation in this tradition is customarily cited as proof of Corneille's anti-Machiavellianism. However, this has very little to do with the real Machiavelli; moreover, as is so often the case, it seems that Corneille was of the devil's party without knowing it, as the path to power, and the means of retaining it once achieved, here advocated by Cinna are precisely those put forth by Machiavelli in the first book of the *Discorsi* (I, ix–x). Machiavelli there proposes that, in order to arrive at the leadership of a state, the most efficient means available should be employed, not excluding violence; but that once the situation is stabilized, governing justly is the only prudent course of action, since it is only in this way that one's personal safety (and reputation) and that of the state may be assured. Moreover, Machiavelli insists, as will the present play, that it is only *good* ends that justify the employment of any means at all, good, bad, or indifferent; evil means in the service of evil ends are doubly unacceptable.

47 To be sure, one of the traditional criticisms leveled against Cinna is that he himself is motivated as much by his desire for Emilie as by any kind of republican fervor. However, unlike Maxime, he is able to rise above his "selfish" concerns, and comes to value the public over the private good without undergoing the same kind of radical personality switch as Maxime or Emilie. He is converted because, as we shall see, he was a believer all along.

48 Ultimately, it will be seen that one party does indeed have something of a monopoly on the powers of naming and interpretation, but this monopoly masquerades as its opposite, and comes at the cost of sacrificing any semblance of private subjectivity or *intérêt*.

49 This lays the groundwork both for Auguste's confrontation with Cinna at V, i, and for the final scene where all roles are reassigned and reconfirmed by Auguste.

50 It is also exactly what Polyeucte *will* do in the next play Corneille writes.

51 This solution is already present to a degree in *Horace*, where the hero survives only through becoming the pure instrument of the State, which imposes its own interpretation on his past, adjusting reality to suit its needs. Horace considers death – an exit from history – at the end of the play, but is told by Horace Senior that he must continue to live (V, iii, 1726): "...pour servir encor ton pays, et ton Roi" ["...to serve still your country, and your King"]. Likewise, the King himself tells him a few lines later (1763): "Vis pour servir l'Etat..." ["Live to serve the State..."] The crucial difference in *Cinna* is that the hero-transformed-into-tool-of-the-State and the incarnation of the State are one and the same *personnage*.

52 Euphorbe works systematically to remove Maxime's resistance to betraying his noble code and ideals, while simultaneously claiming that Cinna himself, rather than adhering to that code, enacts opposing values; and it is telling that his strategy is to use Maxime's own everything-is-permitted rhetoric against him (III, i, 735, 741–42): "L'amour rend tout permis, / [...] Contre un si noir dessein tout devient légitime. / On n'est point criminel, quand on punit un crime." ["Love makes everything permitted. / [...] Against such an evil plan, everything becomes legitimate. / We are not criminals, when we punish a crime."] By putting such arguments in the mouth of the irretrievably vile Euphorbe, Corneille retroactively negates whatever validity they might have possessed coming from Maxime, and thereby further undercuts Maxime's position. Paradoxically, however, this is what later saves Maxime. Euphorbe's non-noble birth renders him, like his counterparts in other plays of Corneille, the repository of all things base and ignoble, and his subsequent scapegoating and elimination serve to purge such negative forces from the court-world of the play. As a result, Maxime is absolved of any responsibility for his actions, since he can (and does) claim that he was simply the temporary dupe of his malignant servant (IV, vi, 1407–18).

53 See *supra*, p. 146.

54 I agree here with Odette de Mourgues, "Coherence and Incoherence in *Cinna*" 56–57. However, I do not think, as she does, that Cinna ends up being the tragic hero, "crucified by the dramatist" (61), of the play.

55 On this, see, in addition to the works already cited, André Georges, "L'évolution morale d'Auguste dans *Cinna*," in *L'Information littéraire*, 34:2 (March–April 1982): 86–94, where he summarizes the various critical responses to the problem, and links what he sees as a gradual process of moral evolution in Auguste with the model of spiritual development proposed in the *Imitatio Christi*, translated by Corneille.

56 Reiss situates the advice of Livie in the larger context of a contemporary debate on reason, violence, and the state. Livie, he says, represents the notion put forward by Corneille and others, in response to such antifeminist political writers as Richelieu and Le Bret, that women are not only men's equals with regard to reason, but that their reason is actually superior to that of men in a political context, because men are prisoners of their own violence. Unlike men, then, women are able to enunciate rational, non-violent solutions to political problems, as Livie does here. See Reiss, "La Voix royale..." 52, and on the

larger context see his *The Meaning of Literature* (Ithaca: Cornell University Press, 1992), ch. 4, "Violence and the Humanity of Reason," pp. 97–130, whose discussion of *Cinna* overlaps to some extent with the earlier article.

57 Fumaroli situates the theatricality of the Corneillean *personnage* in the context of seventeenth-century readings of Quintilian and Cicero, linking persuasive and performative success. Insofar as the orator can carry off his "masques" and tropes with conviction, he will succeed in swaying the audience "avec des résultats analogues à ceux du théâtre" ["with results analogous to those of the theatre"]. *Héros et orateurs*, ch. 4, "Corneille et la rhétorique de l'humanisme chrétien," section 2, "Rhétorique et dramaturgie: le statut du personnage dans la tragédie cornélienne" 292; see also pp. 321–22.

58 Cf. Dort, *Corneille dramaturge* 61, where he says that to look for the "signifcations" of Auguste's clemency is pointless; rather, he says, that clemency is itself the "source de toutes les significations," defining and constituting "la politique *et* la générosité. Elle *est* le roi. Elle est l'Etat."

59 Ellery Schalk discusses this problem in *Cinna*, but it seems to me that his reading distorts the text to fit his vision of the larger question of noble identity in early modern France. He claims that *Cinna* shows "... a change in Corneille's scheme from a view of a nobility that is free, independent, and *vertueuse* to a nobility that is essentially defined by birth, a birth or *rang* that has value only under the authority of the monarch." However, as we have seen, the contrary is true: in this play, as indeed throughout the *oeuvre* of Corneille, birth is the key to Old Nobility, as represented in *Cinna* by the discourse and *personnage* of Emilie. Schalk, *From Valor to Pedigree* 141.

60 I agree here with Doubrovsky's insistence (*Dialectique* 212) that Auguste's utterance, "Je le suis, je veux l'être," represents not an unproblematic correspondence between *vouloir* and *être* but rather a supreme effort on the part of Auguste, in the face of great resistance, to make the two correspond.

Reiss argues ("La Voix royale..." 41) that Auguste's renunciation of self is incomplete, and that he resembles a feudal or Machiavellian prince rather than an absolutist monarch. Were this the case, however, the solution Auguste represents (which Reiss (*ibid.* p. 49) sees, as I do, as a triumph of one discourse over another) would be no solution at all; his claim to *empire*, physical or linguistic, would be just as specious as that of Emilie or Cinna, and the cycle of private vengeance would continue. I have tried to show that the play insists instead on the radical and necessary completeness of Auguste's "victoire" over Octave.

61 See *supra*, p. 146.

62 She predicts (1759–60) what we have already seen enacted on the stage: a complete reversal of terms in the discourse of nobility. "Et le plus indomptés renversant leurs projets, / Mettront toute leur gloire à mourir vos Sujets" ["And the most untameable, reversing their plans, / Will find all their glory in dying as your Subjects"].

63 This is where Polyeucte will end up, for similar reasons. See Doubrovsky, *Dialectique* 217–19, where he discusses the attempt by Livie and Auguste to put the new *Etat* outside of history by making it providential. Cf. also Apostolidès, *Le prince sacrifié* 63ff.; P. J. Yarrow, "Réflexions sur le dénouement de *Cinna*," in

Papers on French Seventeenth-Century Literature, 11, no. 21 (1984): 547–58, where he points out the importance of Divine Providence at the end of the play, and André Georges, "Importance et signification du rôle de Livie dans *Cinna*, de P. Corneille," in *Romanic Review*, 79:2 (March 1988): 270–82, where he insists on the centrality of Livie as the voice of providential history. Reiss ("La Voix royale..." 53) also emphasizes the utopian fragility of Auguste's victory, and sees the plays that follow, as I do, as an attempt to grapple with the failure of that idealized vision. See also his *The Meaning of Literature* 121–23.

64 See Couton, *Corneille et la Fronde. Théâtre et politique il y a trois siècles* (Clermont-Ferrand: Publications de la Faculté des Lettres de l'Université de Clermont (Fascicule 4), 1951), ch. 4: "La saison théâtrale 1650–51 – *Nicomède*," as well as his introduction to the play in Corneille, *OC*, pp. 1458–76.

Jacques Scherer seems to want to reject the identification of Nicomède with Condé, saying that the anti-Fronde Corneille would be unlikely to make such an equation, but he does admit that, at the very least, the parallel no doubt occurred to Corneille and to his audience. Jacques Scherer, "Les intentions politiques dans *Nicomède*," in *Pierre Corneille. Actes du colloque tenu à Rouen du 2 au 6 octobre 1984*, ed. Alain Niderst (Paris: PUF, 1985) 493–99.

65 Corneille, *OC* (ed. Stegmann) 519. Although cf. his *L'Héroïsme cornélien. Genèse et signification*, tome II: *L'Europe intellectuelle et le théâtre. Signification de l'héroïsme cornélien* (Paris: Armand Colin, 1968) 613–14, where he says that there are no specific political allusions in *Nicomède*.

66 V, vi, 1693–98, where she cites the same "droit de la guerre," discussed by Bodin, that Cinna adduces to justify Auguste's seizure and retention of power in Rome.

67 This model is the Fronde, naturally, and not the events in the late Roman empire to which the play bears in any case only the faintest resemblance. As already observed, Corneille's exotic settings, Roman or otherwise, are usually thinly disguised versions of a French seventeenth-century present. Whether this present is "real" or "imagined" is one of the questions we are here attempting to answer.

68 See Couton's justification of this term, in *La Vieillesse de Corneille*, 278–83.

69 See Stegmann, *L'Héroïsme cornélien*, II: 401, where he remarks that relations between the Crown and "les généreux" must be governed by mutual confidence. "Un trop puissant sujet reste, sans cette confiance, un danger permanent pour l'État" ["A too-powerful subject remains, without this confidence, a permanent danger to the State"].

70 In his note to this passage, Couton, to reinforce what seems to be an essentially anti-Machiavellian argument, compares Arsinoé's remarks with the *Discorsi*, I, ix, ascribing to Machiavelli the commonplace belief that "the ends justify the means." However, this is an unfair oversimplification of Machiavelli's argument. What Machiavelli actually says in this famous passage is not that *any* ends justify whatever means are used, but that only *good* ends justify whatever means are used, and not by just anyone, but by "...uno prudente ordinatore d'una repubblica, e che abbia questo anima di volere giovare non a sé ma al bene comune, non alla sua propria successione ma alla comune patria..." ["...a prudent legislator of a republic, who wishes to benefit not himself but the public good, and not his own succession but his country..."] Arsinoé, unlike Auguste,

most certainly does not fall into this category; on the contrary, she is one who has only her own selfish ends in mind. Couton also cites as a parallel example the passage from *Cinna*, discussed above, where Livie justifies Auguste's seizure of power: "Tous ces crimes d'État qu'on fait pour la Couronne, / Le Ciel nous en absout, alors qu'il nous la donne." The point here, however, is that it is precisely "le Ciel" that gives one "la Couronne," and thus that the justification involved is not merely one of Might (or Villainy) Makes Right. Machiavelli, *Discorsi* I, ix, in *Tutte le opere*, ed. Martelli, 90. As Stegmann (*L'Héroïsme cornélien*, II: 369) points out, it is perhaps more useful to suggest that, if Corneille is attacking Machiavelli, he is attacking not the genuine item but rather the vulgar, demonized figure created by Gentillet and others.

71 La Bruyère will later call this remark a compliment.

72 Surely it is no accident that the female Tartuffe of Molière's *Misanthrope* will share the name of the villain of *Nicomède*.

73 The "coeurs infâmes" are naturally those of Arsinoé and her henchmen.

74 Cf. our discussion in the previous chapter of Bacon's remark on tempering "the *Truth* of civill Businesse" with an "Allay" of "Falshood."

75 This is precisely the "prudence généreuse" described by Corneille in the "Au lecteur"; speaking of "la grandeur de courage" manifested by certain characters in the play, he says: "Elle y est combattue par la politique, et n'oppose à ses artifices qu'une prudence généreuse, qui marche à visage découvert, qui prévoit le péril sans s'émouvoir, et ne veut point d'autre appui que celui de sa vertu, et de l'amour qu'elle imprime dans les coeurs de tous les peuples." ["It is attacked by politics, and opposes to its artifices only a generous prudence, which proceeds with its visage uncovered, which foresees peril without being disturbed, and wants no other support than that of its virtue, and of the love which it inspires in the hearts of all peoples."] *OC* II: 639.

76 An intervention resisted almost to the end by Prusias (V, ix, 1781–82): "Quoi, me viens-tu braver jusque dans mon Palais, / Rebelle?" ["What, you come to defy me even in my palace, / Rebel?"]

77 See *supra*, n. 75.

78 In the "Examen" of 1660, Corneille becomes even more *hardi*, daring to suggest that his bold new model of tragedy supersedes Aristotle's theory of tragedy. The "Examen" is basically the same text as the earlier "Au lecteur," with a few, mostly minor, changes and adjustments; but after the first sentence cited above, ending with the word "misères," he adds the following remark:

> "Dans l'admiration qu'on a pour sa [Nicomède's] vertu, je trouve une manière de purger les passions, dont n'a point parlé Aristote, et qui est peut-être plus sûre que celle qu'il prescrit à la tragédie par le moyen de la pitié et de la crainte. L'amour qu'elle nous donne pour cette vertu que nous admirons, nous imprime de la haine pour le vice contraire. La grandeur de courage de Nicomède nous laisse une aversion de la pusillanimité..."
>
> ["In the admiration that we have for his virtue, I find a manner of purging the passions that Aristotle did not talk about, and which is perhaps more sure than that which he prescribes for tragedy by means of pity and fear. The love which it gives us for this virtue that we admire imprints us with hatred for the contrary vice. Nicomède's grandeur of courage leaves us with an aversion for

pusillanimity…"] *OC* II: 643.
79 Corneille, *OC* III: 1676, 1677.
80 Corneille, *OC* (ed. Stegmann) 799. Here, Couton and Stegmann seem for once to be in agreement, in that they both see the play as presenting an essentially anti-Machiavellian position.
81 See Couton himself, *La Vieillesse de Corneille* 212, where he explicitly makes the comparison between *Suréna* and Racine's sealed world.
82 Indeed, the bad (ungrateful, ignoble) sovereign is here schematized through splitting him into two parts, the overtly nasty prince Pacorus and his well-meaning but morally crippled father Orode. If anything, Orode seems to be a reasonable and practical ruler, if fatally pedestrian and short-sighted. More-over, Suréna himself may not be as univocally virtuous as all that. See Dou-brovsky, *Dialectique* 454: "Car la vraie tragédie n'est pas qu'Orode soit, à l'instar de Marcelle ou de Cléopâtre, un 'monstre' qui ait tort, mais un sage qui *a raison* de redouter Suréna" ["For the real tragedy is not that Orode is, like Marcelle or Cléopâtre, a 'monster' who is wrong, but a reasonable man who is *right* to fear Suréna"]. See also Stegmann, *L'Héroïsme cornélien*, II: 407–08, where he, too, raises this possibility.
83 I, ii, 181. Palmis, Suréna's sister, is describing her brother to Eurydice.
84 Cf. *Cinna*, I, ii, 73–74.
85 Of which he speaks at IV, iv, 1349: "…hors des murs ma Suite est dispersée…" ["…outside the wall my Followers are dispersed…"] If, like Nicomède, he could rejoin his "Suite," his appreciative audience, he might be able to survive; but he cannot reach his audience, as it is sealed out of the court, the palace, the city. See also V, iv, 1669–70: Palmis: "Mais pouvez-vous, Seigneur, rejoindre votre Suite? / Etes-vous assez libre pour choisir une fuite?" ["But can you, Seigneur, rejoin your Followers? / Are you free enough to choose flight?"] The answer, of course, is no…
86 The lamenting, frustrated women are undoubtedly more lucid and complex than the men in this play, but their heightened awareness serves only to show more clearly to them the marginality of their position as helpless spectators. They seem, in fact, to represent the end-point of an evolution taking place throughout the *oeuvre* of Corneille, the inverse of that which we have observed in the male protagonists; where the men are steadily reduced to an almost two-dimensional essentiality, the women become increasingly complex, active, and visionary, ultimately perceiving far better than their male counterparts the intricacies of their collective predicament. That even this superior lucidity is ultimately of no avail dramatizes all the more strongly the failure of the discourse of nobility.

For a fuller discussion of issues of gender in Corneille, see, among others, Reiss's *The Meaning of Literature*, ch. 4, where he traces an evolution similar to the one suggested here; see *supra*, n. 56. He suggests (126, n. 53) that "Corneille seemed to give up on this issue after *Pompée*." Later female protagonists, he says, wind up isolated, despairing, suicidal, masculinized, or "resigned to suffer-ing and dominion or to joyless love," in which category he places Eurydice. While it is true that *Pompée*'s Cornélie represents a high point in the develop-ment of Corneille's women, in terms of her concrete capacity to affect political events, I am not sure that Corneille simply "gives up"; the women's articulateness seems rather to increase in proportion to the discursive resistance they encounter from the ever more debased world they inhabit.

5   LA BRUYÈRE AND THE END OF THE THEATRE OF NOBILITY

1 Jean de La Bruyère, *Les Caractères de Théophraste traduits du grec avec Les Caractères ou les Moeurs de ce siècle*, ed. Robert Garapon (Paris: Classiques Garnier, 1962) 15. All references to the *Caractères* will be to this edition, and, when referring to the text of the *Caractères* themselves, will give chapter title and fragment number. When referring to other portions of the book, such as the *Discours sur Théophraste*, the page number will be indicated.

2 Cited in Georges Mongrédien, *Recueil des textes et des documents contemporains relatifs à La Bruyère* (Paris: Editions du Centre National de la Recherche Scientifique, 1979) 87.

3 La Bruyère, *Les Caractères* xiv–xvii.

4 Contrasting him with the more vehement La Rochefoucauld, he says, "...c'est un moraliste tempéré, il ne brûle pas..." ["he is a temperate moralist, he does not burn..."] Roland Barthes, "La Bruyère," in *Essais Critiques* (Paris: Editions du Seuil (coll. "Points"), 1971) 222.

5 Louis van Delft, *La Bruyère moraliste. Quatre études sur les Caractères* (Genève: Droz, 1971) 9.

6 See van Delft, *La Bruyère moraliste* 10–13, and *passim*.

7 See the entire chapter of *Des esprits forts*, with which he chooses to close the work as a whole.

8 See *Du souverain ou de la république* 21 and 35.

9 See *Du souverain ou de la république* 35.

10 See *Du mérite personnel* 33.

11 See *Du mérite personnel* 32.

12 Barthes ("La Bruyère" 230–31) says that the question of "sincerity" in such matters is not only unanswerable but unaskable; the expression of adulation for the monarch is, for a person of the seventeenth century, merely inevitable ("fatale").

13 This is not to say that La Bruyère was incapable of thinking critically about the political institutions of his time; see, for example, the remarkable fragment *Du souverain ou de la république* 28, where he offers a kind of proto-*contrat social*.

14 La Bruyère, *Caractères*, *Préface* 61.

15 La Bruyère, *Caractères*, *Préface* 64–65.

16 *De l'homme* 156. The unicity and self-evident clarity of "la vérité" here recall Descartes.

17 Or, if they do not, the failing lies rather in the readers than in him: "Il faut chercher seulement à penser et à parler juste, sans vouloir amener les autres à notre goût et à nos sentiments: c'est une trop grande entreprise." ["We must try only to think and speak rightly, without wanting to lead others to share our taste and sentiments; that is too great an undertaking."] *Des ouvrages de l'esprit* 2. Again, the Cartesian echo is clear. On La Bruyère's alleged classificatory impulse, see Louise K. Horowitz, "La Bruyère: The Limits of Characterization," *FF* 1 (1976): 127–38, where, citing and following Foucault, she argues (129) that

La Bruyère's putative interest in distinguishing classes of objects and in establishing borders between them is typical of the *épistèmé* of the seventeenth century. The same argument is made by Normand Doiron, in his "La Bruyère naturaliste. *Pamphile, ou l'ordre des grandeurs*," in *Romanic Review* 80:1 (January 1989): 50–56, where he even cites (52) the identical passage from *Les mots et les choses* – without, however, mentioning Horowitz.

18 *Des ouvrages de l'esprit* 1.
19 Barthes, "La Bruyère" 226.
20 Abbé François-Séraphin Régnier-Desmarais, "Réponse au discours de réception de l'abbé Fleury à l'Académie française," 16 juillet 1696, in *Recueil des harangues prononcées par MM. de l'Académie française* (1714), III, 79–80; cited in Mongrédien, *Recueil* 81–82.
21 *Des ouvrages de l'esprit* 1.
22 On this subject, see Jean Lafond's excellent historical article, "Des formes brèves de la littérature morale aux XVIe et XVIIe siècles," in *Les formes brèves de la prose et le discours discontinu (XVIe–XVIIe siècles)*, ed. Jean Lafond, *De Pétrarque à Descartes*, vol. 46 (Paris: J. Vrin, 1984) 101–22.
23 *De l'homme* 147.
24 Horowitz ("Limits of Characterization" 135) argues that La Bruyère attempts to construct a stable model of the essence of the society he represents, but that the kinds of shifts apparent in this fragment doom any such attempt to failure, reducing the text to what she refers to (129) as "a mass of undifferentiated, changing matter." This seems rather too simple. La Bruyère does look for stability, order, and permanence, but the order in question is a transcendent one, and its locus is not in society but beyond it. We will have more to say on this issue later.
25 *De l'homme* 2.
26 *De l'homme* 6.
27 *De la mode* 19.
28 See *De l'homme* 157 and 158. There have been varying critical responses to the question of whether or not it is possible to say that La Bruyère has any kind of overt unifying philosophical scheme. Barthes ("La Bruyère" 233) defines the *caractère* as a "*faux récit* ... une métaphore qui prend l'allure du récit sans le réjoindre vraiment" ["*false narrative* ... a metaphor which looks like a narrative, without quite getting there"]. He goes on (234) to describe the book as "un livre de *fragments*, parce que précisément le fragment occupe une place intermédiaire entre le maxime qui est une métaphore pure, puisqu'elle *définit* ... et l'anecdote, qui n'est que récit..." ["a book of *fragments*, precisely because the fragment occupies an intermediate place between the maxim which is pure metaphor, since it *defines*... and the anecdote, which is only narrative..."] This of course fits neatly into one of Barthes's favorite schemata, that of a text whose meaning(s) can only be constituted by the reader through the act of reading – a schema which, despite its familiarity, seems particularly appropriate in the case of La Bruyère.

Horowitz ("Limits" 136) talks about what she characterizes as "the moralist's effort towards essential and summary knowledge," but says that the world is moving too fast for him to pin it down. Van Delft speaks of what he sees as La

Bruyère's effort to speak simultaneously of worldly particulars and of eternal truths, saying (*La Bruyère moraliste* 159) that for La Bruyère, "la morale" consists in reconciling these two points of view. Odette de Mourgues, in her study of La Rochefoucauld and La Bruyère, discusses (135ff.) La Bruyère's use of the concrete specifics of the material world to construct his text, citing (145) Jules Brody's remark (see *infra*, n.31) that La Bruyère is a writer "pour qui le monde extérieur existe" ["for whom the external world exists"]. Michael S. Koppisch sees La Bruyère as manifesting a unitary vision in the earlier editions of the *Caractères*, but sees this vision as breaking down in the later versions of the text. Finally, Floyd Gray insists on the fragmentary, snapshot-like nature of the text, and on the theatrical quality of many of the *personnages* La Bruyère brings before the reader, while drawing a contrast between La Bruyère's static portraits and the dynamic theatre of, say, Molière. Odette de Mourgues, *Two French Moralists. La Rochefoucauld and La Bruyère* (Cambridge University Press, 1978); Michael S. Koppisch, *The Dissolution of Character. Changing Perspectives in La Bruyère's Caractères* (Lexington, KY: French Forum, 1981); Floyd Gray, *La Bruyère amateur de caractères* (Paris: Nizet, 1986).

29 Gray (*La Bruyère amateur* 51) links these two characteristics of the text, and discusses them relative to the social nature of the text as it was read by his audience.

30 It is important to recognize the exclusive centrality of the court to the world-vision of La Bruyère. Van Delft is right to assert that La Bruyère's vision is restricted, deliberately or not, and that for him the court is a representative microcosm of the rest of the world. This does not mean, however, that La Bruyère is as encyclopedic as he pretends to be; Erica Harth rightly points out that La Bruyère does not quite know what to do with those persons (the majority of humanity) that fall outside his categories of classification. Brody and Horowitz, on the other hand, both claim that the *Caractères* at least try to represent the totality of civilization. Louis van Delft, "Les *Caractères* et l'anthropologie à l'âge classique," in *Papers on French Seventeenth-Century Literature/Biblio 17: Actes de Davis 40*, 1988: 89 (see also his *La Bruyère moraliste* 57); Erica Harth, "Classical Disproportion: La Bruyère's *Caractères*," in *L'Esprit Créateur* 15:1–2 (Spring–Summer 1975): 191; Jules Brody, *Du Style à la pensée. Trois études sur les Caractères de La Bruyère* (Lexington, KY: French Forum, 1980) 66; Horowitz, "Limits" 136.

31 Brody sees it primarily as the result of La Bruyère's apparent nostalgia for a lost world of "true" nobility (about which more later), and says ("Du style" 29) that La Bruyère therefore views his less-than-ideal present with a certain disaffection. He focuses on describing the external because, says Brody, that is all that is available in this "monde chosifié et deaspiritualisé" ["thingified and despiritualized world"]. He goes on to suggest that, if the *Caractères* are all surface, it is because his contemporaries, "surtout nobles, ne lui montraient plus autre chose..." ["especially nobles, no longer showed him anything else..."] Cf. also his pp. 59–64, where he cites the Sannions (*De la ville* 10) as an example of what he sees as La Bruyère's jaundiced view of the new *noblesse* as opposed to the old; this will be discussed further below. On the question of externality, see also Maurice Delcroix, "Dire 'je'. La Bruyère et son caractère," in *Papers on French*

Seventeenth-Century Literature/Biblio 17: Actes de Davis 40 (1988): 113–21, especially p. 117.

32 Many critics have commented upon La Bruyère's participation in the tradition of using theatrical languages and imagery to describe the court. Michel Guggenheim, in an essential article, "L'homme sous le regard d'autrui ou le monde de La Bruyère," in *PMLA* 81:7 (December 1966): 535–39, emphasizes the importance of vision and display in the text, and shows the predominance of theatrical metaphors in La Bruyère's approach to the problem of the *regard*. He takes a familiar position in describing (535) La Bruyère's own position as one of a backstage observer, comparing him in this respect to La Rochefoucauld and Saint-Simon; Brody, in his "Images de l'homme chez La Bruyère," in *L'Esprit Créateur* 15:1–2 (Spring–Summer 1975): 164–88, will do the same, 188 (this article is reprinted as ch. 2 of his book, *Du style à la pensée*, cited above). I am inclined to think, for reasons that will become apparent, that La Bruyère's claim to be observing the stage-play of the court from an offstage vantage point is something of a mystification, albeit an essential one to his project.

Doris Kirsch, in her *La Bruyère ou le style cruel* (Montréal: Les Presses de l'Université de Montréal, 1977), compares (97) the *caractères* to "marionettes." Odette de Mourgues, too, citing both Guggenheim and Brody, discusses (*Two French Moralists*, ch. 8) the theatricality of La Bruyère's world, also likening its denizens to puppets. Finally, Robert Garapon, in his thoughtful and scholarly *Les Caractères de La Bruyère. La Bruyère au travail* (Paris: SEDES, 1978), discusses not only the theatrical imagery of La Bruyère, but also what he refers to (150) as "l'allure essentiellement orale, pour ne pas dire théâtrale, du style de notre auteur" ["the essentially oral, not to say theatrical, character of our author's style"].

33 *De la cour* 40.

34 *Du mérite personnel* 27.

35 "Claim" is here the key word; what they often reveal instead, of course, is the rhetorical vacuum of the text itself, as we will attempt to show.

36 *De la cour* 83.

37 In this connection, see especially *De la mode* 12.

38 *Des biens de fortune* 4.

39 *Des grands* 48.

40 Théognis seems here very close to the mechanical *courtisan* described in *De la cour* 65: "Les roues, les ressorts, les mouvements sont cachés; rien ne paraît d'une montre que son aiguille, qui insensiblement s'avance et achève son tour: image du courtisan, d'autant plus parfaite qu'après avoir fait assez de chemin, il revient souvent au même point d'où il est parti." ["The wheels, the springs, the movements are hidden; nothing shows on a watch but its hand, which insensibly advances and finishes its round: image of the courtier, the more perfect in that having covered a lot of ground, he often comes back to the same point he started from."] La Bruyère is fond of applying mechanical metaphors to the apparently unconscious actions of his *caractères*, making frequent reference to the machines behind the scenes of the theatre of the court. Brody ("Images de l'homme" *passim*) links this mechanical imagery to what he describes as La Bruyère's Cartesian anthropology, saying that the *caractères* are, so to speak, machines

without ghosts, operating like mere automata. Harth ("Classical Disproportion" 195–96) also alludes to this Cartesian aspect of La Bruyère's vision of humanity. See also van Delft, *La Bruyère moraliste*, ch. 2.

41 *De la cour* 31.

42 In this connection, see also *De la cour* 32, where La Bruyère demonstrates at some length the degree to which opinion becomes reality at court, determining the identity of a person quite independently of whatever attributes that person may or may not actually possess. The power of opinion is likewise a major theme of *De quelques usages*; in fragment 4, for example, a *roturier* manages to persuade himself that he is of noble descent. As long as he persuades only himself, he is merely ridiculous; but as soon as he begins to persuade others, he becomes dangerous, as in fragment 6: "Il suffit de n'être point né dans une ville, mais sous une chaumière répandue dans la campagne, ou sous une ruine qui trempe dans un marécage et qu'on appelle château, pour être cru noble sur sa parole." ["It suffices not to be born in a town, but in a cottage out in the country, or in a marsh-bound ruin called a 'château,' to be believed noble on one's word."]

43 *Des ouvrages de l'esprit* 34.

44 *De la ville* 13.

45 See *Des jugements* 66.

46 *De la société et de la conversation* 27. One is naturally reminded of Molière's Alceste.

47 *De la société et de la conversation* 29.

48 *De la société et de la conversation* 30.

49 In *De l'homme* 3, La Bruyère also attacks the Stoic project on familiar philosophical grounds, comparing it unfavorably with his own corrective enterprise. Instead of making vice seem appalling or ridiculous, thereby inspiring people to change, he says, the Stoics demand an impossible perfection. La Bruyère wishes to remain firmly engaged in the world, hoping to improve it through his activity as a moralist.

50 *De la cour* 67.

51 *Des biens de fortune* 35.

52 *Des grands* 1.

53 *Du mérite personnel* 32.

54 While this fragment does not appear until the seventh edition of the *Caractères*, in 1692, long after the death of le Grand Condé in 1686, it should be remembered that, even at that late date, such flattery would have had considerable practical utility for its author, as La Bruyère remained in the employ of the family for some time after his patron's death. On the developments and changes in successive editions of the *Caractères*, see van Delft's careful examination of this question, *La Bruyère moraliste*, ch. 1. See also Koppisch, *Dissolution of Character*, whose Girardian argument owes much to van Delft's discussion.

55 *De l'homme* 140: "La différence d'un homme qui se revêt d'un caractère étranger à lui-même, quand il rentre dans le sien, est celle d'un masque à un visage." ["The difference between a man who dresses himself in an alien character, and himself, when he returns to his own, is that between a mask and a face."]

56 *Discours sur Théophraste* 12. Cf. also *Du mérite personnel* 29, where the present is compared unfavorably with the Roman past: "Chez nous le soldat est brave, et l'homme de robe est savant; nous n'allons pas plus loin. Chez les Romains l'homme de robe était brave, et le soldat était savant: un Romain était tout ensemble et le soldat et l'homme de robe." ["With us the soldier is brave, and the *homme de robe* is scholarly; we go no further. With the Romans, the scholar was brave, and the soldier was scholarly: a Roman was at once soldier and scholar."] La Bruyère's ersatz quotation from Montaigne (*De la société et de la conversation* 30) is interesting in this light; he wants to make Montaigne the representative of a golden age of nobility, but finds himself compelled to fabricate a "quote" from Montaigne in order to prove his point.

Philip R. Berk has studied the classical antecedents of the Golden Age topos in La Bruyère; see his "*De la ville xxii*: La Bruyère and the Golden Age," in *French Review* 47:6 (May 1974): 1072–80. Brody (*Du style à la pensée* 28–29) speaks of La Bruyère's nostalgia for a "true nobility," paralleling it with that expressed by the noted reactionary Joseph de Maistre a century later. On the general question of the connection between noble ideology and pastoral nostalgia, see Elias, *The Court Society*, ch. 8, "On the Sociogenesis of Aristocratic Romanticism in the Process of Courtization," especially pp. 246–67.

57 Even the slight final twist – "... à qui il n'a manqué que les moindres vertus" – acts not to undermine but to reinforce the glorious image of Æmile, since the statement merely confirms that he had all the virtues that were truly important. It is almost as though "les moindres vertus" were beneath his dignity.

58 In addition to the passages cited earlier, see, for example, *Du mérite personnel* 42, where he describes "la véritable grandeur," and compares it to the counterfeit version.

59 See *supra*, n.42.

60 *De la cour* 48.

61 *De la cour* 74.

62 As we saw earlier (*supra*, n.32), Guggenheim seems to believe that La Bruyère is indeed able to position himself "offstage," and thereby stake a claim to a privileged point of view. Likewise, Brody ("Images de l'homme," 184–85) says that La Bruyère not only situates himself outside the contingent realm of social discourse, but expects the reader to do so as well in order to share his insights. Doiron, too, says ("La Bruyère naturaliste" 51) that such a separation is in fact the only escape from the two-dimensional realm of appearances, and continues (52) by comparing the appearance of the world, thus presented at a distance, to a theatre, in which the reader suddenly becomes conscious of his role as spectator, and of his distance from the characters presented by La Bruyère. However, as we have seen, this "distance" is in fact illusory; the role of spectator is still a role played out on the stage of La Bruyère's court-world. There will be no off-stage in the theatre of La Bruyère.

63 Bacon, *Essayes* 7.

64 *Des esprits forts* 22.

65 Guggenheim points out ("L'homme sous le regard" 539) the significant loss of irony in the chapter *Des esprits forts*, where La Bruyère attacks his targets in the name of a moral and religious indignation wholly without his customary ironic

perspective. Garapon (*Les Caractères* 190ff.) sees La Bruyère as an essentially Christian moralist.

66 *De la cour* 100.

67 This is the same demand he makes in *Des esprits forts* 9, where he attacks courtiers who, "esclaves des grands" ["slaves of the great"], allow their lives to be governed not by concern for their eternal souls, but by how they appear in the eyes of their noble patrons.

Bibliography

Accetto, Torquato. *Della dissimulazione onesta.* In *Politici e Moralisti del Seicento,* edited by Benedetto Croce and Santino Caramella, 143–73. Bari: Laterza, 1930.

Apostolidès, Jean-Marie. *Le roi-machine. Spectacle et politique au temps de Louis XIV.* Paris: Editions de Minuit, "Arguments", 1981.

— *Le prince sacrifié. Théâtre et politique au temps de Louis XIV.* Paris: Editions de Minuit, "Arguments", 1985.

Auerbach, Erich. *Mimesis. The Representation of Reality in Western Literature.* Trans. Willard R. Trask. Princeton: Princeton University Press, 1953.

Bacon, Francis. *The Works of Francis Bacon.* Edited by James Spedding, Robert Leslie Ellis, and Douglas Denon Heath. 14 vols. Stuttgart: Frommann/Holzboog, 1963 [London: Longman *et al.*, 1858–1874].

— *The Essayes or Counsels, Civill and Morall.* Edited by Michael Kiernan. Cambridge, MA: Harvard University Press, 1985.

Baldi, Cammillo. *Congressi civili.* Florence: Vincenzio Vangelisti, 1681.

Barish, Jonas A. *The Antitheatrical Prejudice.* Berkeley: University of California Press, 1981.

Barthes, Roland. *Essais critiques.* Editions du Seuil (coll. "Points"), 1971.

Bénichou, Paul. *Morales du grand siècle.* Paris: Editions Gallimard, Bibliothèque des Idées, 1948.

Berk, Philip R. "*De la Ville xxii*: La Bruyère and the Golden Age." *French Review* 47 (May 1974):1072–80.

Bitton, Davis. *The French Nobility in Crisis, 1560–1640.* Stanford: Stanford University Press, 1969.

Blake, William. *The Complete Poetry and Prose of William Blake.* Revised Edition. Edited by David V. Erdman. Commentary by Harold Bloom. Garden City, NY: Anchor, 1982.

Blum, Claude. "La peinture du moi et l'écriture inachevée." *Poétique* 53 (février 1983):60–71.

Bodin, Jean. *Six Livres de la République.* Paris: J. Du Puys, 1577.

Borkenau, Franz. *Der Übergang vom feudalen zum bürgerlichen Weltbild. Studien zur Geschichte der Philosophie der Manufakturperiode.* European Sociology. New York: Arno Press, 1975 [Paris: Félix Alcan, 1934].

Box, Ian. "Bacon's *Essays*: From Political Science to Political Prudence." *History of Political Thought* 3 (1982):31–49.

Braden, Gordon. *Renaissance Tragedy and the Senecan Tradition: Anger's Privilege.*

New Haven: Yale University Press, 1985.

Briggs, John C. *Francis Bacon and the Rhetoric of Nature*. Cambridge, MA: Harvard University Press, 1989.

Brody, Jules. "Images de l'homme chez La Bruyère." *L'Esprit Créateur* 15 (Spring–Summer 1975):164–88.

Du style à la pensée. Trois études sur les Caractères de La Bruyère. French Forum Monographs, vol. 20. Lexington, KY: French Forum, 1980.

Cameron, Keith. "Montaigne and the Mask." *L'Esprit Créateur* 8 (Fall 1968):198–207.

Castiglione, Baldassarre. *Il libro del Cortegiano*. Edited by Ettore Bonora and Paolo Zoccola. Milano: Mursia, 1984 [1972].

Cave, Terence. *The Cornucopian Text: Problems of Writing in the French Renaissance*. Oxford: Oxford University Press, Clarendon, 1979.

Cochrane, Rexmond C. "Francis Bacon and the Architect of Fortune." In *Studies in the Renaissance*, edited by M. A. Shaaber, vol. 5, 176–95. New York: The Renaissance Society of America, 1958.

Compagnon, Antoine. "A Long Short Story: Montaigne's Brevity." In *Montaigne: Essays in Reading*, edited by Gérard Defaux, *Yale French Studies* 64 (1983):24–50.

Corneille, Pierre. *Oeuvres complètes*. Edited by André Stegmann. Paris: Editions du Seuil, L'Intégrale, 1963.

Oeuvres complètes. Edited by Georges Couton. 3 vols. Paris: Gallimard, Pléiade, 1980–7.

Cottrell, Robert D. *Sexuality/textuality. A Study of the Fabric of Montaigne's Essais*. Columbus, OH: Ohio State University Press, 1981.

Couton, Georges. *La Vieillesse de Corneille 1658–1684*. Paris: Librairie Maloine, 1949.

Corneille et la Fronde. Théâtre et politique il y a trois siècles. Publications de la Faculté des Lettres de l'Université de Clermont (fasc. 4). Clermont-Ferrand: Faculté des Lettres de l'Université de Clermont, 1951.

Corneille et la tragédie politique. Que sais-je?, vol. 2174. Paris: Presses Universitaires de France, 1984.

Crane, Ronald S. "The Relation of Bacon's *Essays* to His Program for the Advancement of Learning." In *Schelling Anniversary Papers*, 87–105. New York: Century, 1923.

Croll, Morris W. "Juste Lipse et le mouvement anti-cicéronien." *Revue du seizième siècle* 2 (1914):200–42.

"'Attic' Prose in the Seventeenth Century." *Studies in Philology* 18 (1921):79–128.

"Attic Prose: Lipsius, Montaigne, Bacon." In *Schelling Anniversary Papers*, 117–50. New York: Century, 1923.

"Muret and the History of 'Attic' Prose." *PMLA* 39 (1924):254–309.

"The Baroque Style in Prose." In *Studies in English Philology*, edited by K. Malone and M. Ruud, 427–56. Minneapolis: n.p. 1929.

Cuénin, Micheline. "L'amour et l'ambition dans *Le Cid*." In *Pierre Corneille. Actes du colloque tenu à Rouen du 2 au 6 octobre 1984*, edited by Alain Niderst, 445–49. Paris: Presses Universitaires de France, 1985.

Curtius, Ernst Robert. *European Literature and the Latin Middle Ages*. Translated by Willard R. Trask. Bollingen Series, vol. 36. Princeton: Princeton University Press, 1973.

Defaux, Gérard. "Montaigne, Erasme, Platon, Derrida: l'écriture comme présence." *Rivista di Letterature Moderne e Comparate* 38 (ottobre–dicembre 1985):325–43.

Marot, Rabelais, Montaigne: l'écriture comme présence. Paris and Geneva: Champion-Slatkine, 1987.

Delcroix, Maurice. "Dire 'je'. La Bruyère et son caractère." *Papers on French Seventeenth-Century Literature/Biblio 17: Actes de Davis* 40 (1988):113–21.

Delègue, Yves. "Du paradoxe chez Montaigne." *Cahiers de L'A. I. E. F.* 14 (March 1962):241–53.

della Casa, Giovanni. *Galateo overo de' costumi.* Edited by Emanuela Scarpa. Modena: Istituto di Studi Rinascimentali Ferrara/Franco Cosimo Panini, 1990.

Dewald, Jonathan. *Aristocratic Experience and the Origins of Modern Culture. France, 1570–1715.* Berkeley: University of California Press, 1993.

Doiron, Normand. "La Bruyère naturaliste. *Pamphile,* ou l'ordre des grandeurs." *Romanic Review* 80 (January 1989):50–56.

Dort, Bernard. *Corneille dramaturge.* Travaux. Paris: L'Arche, 1972 [1957].

Dosmond, Simone. "La Rome de Corneille." *L'Information littéraire* 36 (September/October 1984):142–52.

Doubrovsky, Serge. *Corneille et la dialectique du héros.* Paris: Editions Gallimard, Bibliothèque des Idées, 1963.

Duval, Edwin M. "Rhetorical Composition and 'Open Form' in Montaigne's Early *Essais.*" *Bibliothèque d'Humanisme et Renaissance* 43 (1981):269–87.

Duvignaud, Jean. *Sociologie du théâtre. Essais sur les ombres collectives.* Bibliothèque de Sociologie Contemporaine. Paris: Presses Universitaires de France, 1965.

Eisenstein, Elizabeth L. *The Printing Press as an Agent of Change.* 2 vols. Cambridge: Cambridge University Press, 1979.

Elias, Norbert. *The History of Manners.* Vol. 1 of *The Civilizing Process.* Translated by Edmund Jephcott. New York: Pantheon, 1978.

Power and Civility. Vol. 2 of *The Civilizing Process.* Translated, revised by, notes by Edmund Jephcott. New York: Pantheon, 1982.

The Court Society. Translated by Edmund Jephcott. New York: Pantheon, 1983.

Faret, Nicolas. *L'Honeste homme. Ou, l'art de plaire à la Cour.* Paris: Du Bray, 1630.

L'honnête homme ou l'Art de plaire à la cour. Edited by Maurice Magendie. Paris: Presses Universitaires de France, 1925.

Fish, Stanley Eugene. *Self-consuming Artifacts. The Experience of Seventeenth-Century Literature.* Berkeley: University of California Press, 1972.

Friedrich, Hugo. *Montaigne.* Bern: Francke, 1967 [1949].

Fumaroli, Marc. *Héros et orateurs. Rhétorique et dramaturgie cornéliennes.* Histoire des idées et critique littéraire, vol. 277. Geneva: Droz, 1990.

Garapon, Robert. *Les Caractères de La Bruyère. La Bruyère au travail.* Paris: SEDES, 1978.

Gasquet, Emile. *Le courant machiavélien dans la pensée et la littérature anglaises du XVIe siècle.* Paris: Didier, [1974].

Georges, André. "L'évolution morale d'Auguste dans *Cinna.*" *L'Information littéraire* 34:2 (March/April 1982):86–94.
"Importance et signification du rôle de Livie dans *Cinna*, de P. Corneille." *Romanic Review* 79:2 (March 1988):270–82.
Gilbert, Allan H. *Machiavelli's Prince and Its Forerunners.* Durham, NC: Duke University Press, 1938.
Gilbert, Felix. *Machiavelli and Guicciardini. Politics and History in Sixteenth-century Florence.* Princeton: Princeton University Press, 1965.
Goffman, Erving. *The Presentation of Self in Everyday Life.* New York: Doubleday, Anchor, 1959.
Goldberg, Jonathan. *James I and the Politics of Literature: Jonson, Shakespeare, Donne, and Their Contemporaries.* Stanford: Stanford University Press, 1989 [Baltimore: The Johns Hopkins University Press, 1983].
Goubert, Pierre. *L'Ancien Régime.* 2 vols. Collection U: Histoire moderne. Paris: Armand Colin, 1969–73.
Gray, Floyd. *Le Style de Montaigne.* Paris: Nizet, 1958.
La Bruyère amateur de caractères. Paris: Nizet, 1986.
Greenblatt, Stephen Jay. *Sir Walter Ralegh. The Renaissance Man and His Roles.* New Haven: Yale University Press, 1973.
Renaissance Self-Fashioning. From More to Shakespeare. Chicago: University of Chicago Press, 1980.
Greene, Thomas M. "The Flexibility of the Self in Renaissance Literature." In *The Disciplines of Criticism. Essays in Literary Theory, Interpretation, and History*, Edited by Peter Demetz, Thomas M. Greene, and Lowry Nelson, Jr., 241–64. New Haven: Yale University Press, 1968.
The Vulnerable Text. Essays on Renaissance Literature. New York: Columbia University Press, 1986.
Guggenheim, Michel. "L'homme sous le regard d'autrui ou le monde de La Bruyère." *PMLA* 81: (December 1966):535–39.
Hanning, Robert W., and David Rosand, eds. *Castiglione. The Ideal and the Real in Renaissance Culture.* New Haven: Yale University Press, 1983.
Harth, Erica. "Classical Disproportion: La Bruyère's *Caractères.*" *L'Esprit Créateur* 15 (Spring–Summer 1975):189–210.
Hazlitt, William. *The Collected Works of William Hazlitt.* Edited by A. R. Walker and Arnold Glover. 12 vols. London: J. M. Dent, 1902.
Heller, Agnes. *Renaissance Man.* Translated by Richard E. Allen. London: Routledge & Kegan Paul, 1978 [1967].
Horkheimer, Max. "Montaigne und die Funktion der Skepsis." In *Kritische Theorie*, edited by Alfred Schmidt, 201–59. Frankfurt am Main: S. Fischer, 1968 [1938].
Horowitz, Louise K. "La Bruyère: The Limits of Characterization." *French Forum* 1 (May 1976):127–38.
Hovey, Kenneth Alan. "'*Mountaigny* Saith Prettily': Bacon's French and the Essay." *PMLA* 106:1 (January 1991):71–82.
Huppert, George. *Les Bourgeois Gentilshommes: An Essay on the Definition of Elites in Renaissance France.* Chicago: University of Chicago Press, 1977.
James, Mervyn. *Society, Politics and Culture. Studies in Early Modern England.* Past

and Present Publications. Cambridge: Cambridge University Press, 1986.

Jardine, Lisa. *Francis Bacon. Discovery and the Art of Discourse.* Cambridge: Cambridge University Press, 1974.

Javitch, Daniel. "Rival Arts of Conduct in Elizabethan England: Guazzo's *Civile Conversation* and Castiglione's *Courtier.*" *Yearbook of Italian Studies* 1 (1971):178–98.

————. *Poetry and Courtliness in Renaissance England.* Princeton: Princeton University Press, 1978.

Kettering, Sharon. "Patronage and Politics During the Fronde." *French Historical Studies* 14 (1986):409–41.

Kirsch, Doris. *La Bruyère ou le style cruel.* Montreal: Les Presses de l'Université de Montréal, 1977.

Koppisch, Michael. *The Dissolution of Character. Changing Perspectives in La Bruyère's Caractères.* French Forum Monographs, vol. 24. Lexington, KY: French Forum, 1981.

Kritzman, Lawrence D. *Destruction/découverte. Le Fonctionnement de la rhétorique dans les Essais de Montaigne.* Lexington: French Forum, 1980.

La Bruyère, Jean de. *Les Caractères de Théophraste traduits du grec avec Les Caractères ou les Moeurs de ce siècle.* Edited by Robert Garapon. Paris: Garnier, Classiques Garnier, 1962.

Lacan, Jacques. *Ecrits. Le champ freudien.* Paris: Editions du Seuil, 1966.

Lafond, Jean. "Des formes brèves de la littérature morale aux XVIe et XVIIe siècles." In *Les formes brèves de la prose et le discours discontinu (XVIe–XVIIe siècles)*, edited by Jean Lafond, 101–22. De Pétrarque à Descartes, vol. 46. Paris: J. Vrin, 1984.

Levy, F. J. "Francis Bacon and the Style of Politics." *ELR* 16:1 (Winter 1986):101–22.

Lewis, C[live] S[taples]. *English Literature in the Sixteenth Century Excluding Drama.* Vol. 3 of *Oxford History of English Literature.* Oxford: Oxford University Press, 1954.

Luciani, Vincent. "Bacon and Guicciardini." *PMLA* 62 (March 1947):96–113.

————. "Bacon and Machiavelli." *Italica* 24:1 (March 1947):26–40.

MacCaffrey, Wallace T. "Place and Patronage in Elizabethan Politics." In *Elizabethan Government and Society. Essays Presented to Sir John Neale,* edited by S. T. Bindoff, J. Hurstfield, and C. H. Williams, 95–126. London: University of London, Athlone Press, 1961.

McCoy, Richard C. *The Rites of Knighthood: The Literature and Politics of Elizabethan Chivalry.* The New Historicism: Studies in Cultural Poetics, vol. 7. Berkeley: University of California Press, 1989.

McGowan, Margaret M. *Montaigne's Deceits. The Art of Persuasion in the Essais.* London: University of London Press, 1974.

Machiavelli, Niccolò. *Tutte le opere.* Edited by Mario Martelli. Florence: Sansoni, 1971.

Magendie, Maurice. *La politesse mondaine et les théories de l'honnêteté en France, au XVIIe siècle, de 1600 à 1660.* 2 vols. Paris: Presses Universitaires de France, 1925.

————. *Du nouveau sur l'Astrée.* Paris: Honoré Champion, 1927.

Major, J. Russell. "The Crown and the Aristocracy in Renaissance France." *American Historical Review* 69:3 (April 1964):631–45.

"Noble Income, Inflation, and the Wars of Religion in France." *American Historical Review* 86:1 (February 1981):21–48.

"The Revolt of 1620: A Study of Ties of Fidelity." *French Historical Studies* 14:3 (1986):391–408.

Margitic, Milorad R. "Les deux *Cid*: de la tragi-comédie baroque à la pseudo-tragédie classique." *Papers on French Seventeenth-Century Literature* 11, no. 21 (1984):409–25.

Marin, Louis. *Le portrait du roi*. Paris: Editions de Minuit, 1981.

Martin, Julian. *Francis Bacon, the State, and the Reform of Natural Philosophy*. Cambridge: Cambridge University Press, 1992.

Marwil, Jonathan. *The Trials of Counsel. Francis Bacon in 1621*. Detroit: Wayne State University Press, 1976.

Momigliano, Arnaldo. *The Classical Foundations of Modern Historiography*. With a foreword by Riccardo Di Donato. Sather Classical Lectures, vol. 54. Berkeley: University of California Press, 1990.

Mongrédien, Georges. *Recueil des textes et des documents contemporains relatifs à La Bruyère*. Paris: Editions du Centre National de la Recherche Scientifique, 1979.

Montaigne, Michel Eyquem de. *Essais. Edition conforme au texte de l'exemplaire de Bordeaux*. Edited by Pierre Villey. Revised by, preface by V[erdun]-L[ouis] Saulnier. 2 vols. Paris: Presses Universitaires de France, 1978 [1965].

Journal de voyage. Edited by François Rigolot. Paris: Presses Universitaires de France, 1992.

Mourgues, Odette de. *Two French Moralists. La Rochefoucauld and La Bruyère*. Major European Authors. Cambridge: Cambridge University Press, 1978.

"Coherence and Incoherence in *Cinna*." In *Form and Meaning: Aesthetic Coherence in Seventeenth-Century French Drama. Studies Presented to Harry Barnwell*, edited by William D. Howarth, Ian McFarlane, and Margaret McGowan, 51–62. Amersham: Avebury, 1982.

Mousnier, Roland. *La Venalité des offices sous Henri IV et Louis XIII*. 2d ed. Paris: Presses Universitaires de France, 1971.

"Les Concepts d''ordres', d''états', de 'fidélité' et de 'monarchie absolue' en France de la fin du XVe siècle à la fin du XVIIIe." *Revue historique* 47 (April–June 1972):289–312.

Les Institutions de la France sous la monarchie absolue. 2 vols. Paris: Presses Universitaires de France, 1974–80.

Nadal, Octave. *Le Sentiment de l'amour dans l'oeuvre de P. Corneille*. Paris: Gallimard, 1948.

Neale, Sir John E. "The Elizabethan Political Scene." In *Essays in Elizabethan History*, 59–84. New York: St. Martin's Press, 1958.

Nervèze. *La Guide des Courtisans*. In *Les oeuvres morales du Sieur de Nervèze*. Paris: Du Bray, 1610.

Neuschel, Kristen B. *Word of Honor. Interpreting Noble Culture in Sixteenth-century France*. Ithaca, NY: Cornell University Press, 1989.

Oestreich, Gerhard. *Neostoicism and the Early Modern State*. Cambridge Studies in

Early Modern History. Cambridge: Cambridge University Press, 1982.

Orsini, Napoleone. *Bacone e Machiavelli.* Genoa: Emiliano degli Orfini, 1936.

Palmer, Jerry. "Merit and Destiny: Ideology and Narrative in French Classicism." In *1642: Literature and Power in the Seventeenth Century. Proceedings of the Essex Conference on the Sociology of Literature, July 1980*, edited by Francis Barker, Jay Bernstein, John Coombes, Peter Hulme, Jennifer Stone, and Jon Stratton, 114–38. n.p.: University of Essex, 1981.

Peltonen, Markku, ed. *The Cambridge Companion to Bacon.* Cambridge: Cambridge University Press, 1996.

Prigent, Michel. *Le héros et l'Etat dans la tragédie de Pierre Corneille.* Paris: Presses Universitaires de France, "Ecrivains," 1986.

Ranum, Orest. "Richelieu and the Great Nobility: Some Aspects of Early Modern Political Motives." *French Historical Studies* 3:2 (Fall 1963):184–204.

"Courtesy, Absolutism, and the Rise of the French State, 1630–1660." *Journal of Modern History* 52 (September 1980):426–51.

Rebhorn, Wayne A. *Courtly Performances: Masking and Festivity in Castiglione's Book of the Courtier.* Detroit: Wayne State University Press, 1978.

Refuge, Eustache de. *Traicté de la Court.* [Paris], 1616.

Regosin, Richard L. *The Matter of My Book. Montaigne's Essais as the Book of the Self.* Berkeley: University of California Press, 1977.

Reiss, Timothy J. *Toward Dramatic Illusion: Theatrical Technique and Meaning from Hardy to Horace.* New Haven: Yale University Press, 1971.

The Discourse of Modernism. Ithaca: Cornell University Press, 1982.

"Montaigne and the Subject of Polity." In *Literary Theory/Renaissance Texts*, edited by Patricia Parker and David Quint, 115–49. Baltimore: Johns Hopkins University Press, 1986.

"La Voix royale: de la violence étatique ou, du privé à la souveraineté dans *Cinna*." In *Pierre Corneille: ambiguïtés*, edited by Michel Bareau, 41–54. Edmonton: Alta Press, 1989.

The Meaning of Literature. Ithaca: Cornell University Press, 1992.

Rider, Frederick. *The Dialectic of Selfhood in Montaigne.* Stanford: Stanford University Press, 1973.

Righter, Anne. "Francis Bacon." In *The English Mind: Studies in the English Moralists Presented to Basil Willey*, edited by Hugh Sykes Davies and George Watson, 7–29. Cambridge: Cambridge University Press, 1964.

Rigolot, François. *Les métamorphoses de Montaigne.* Paris: Presses Universitaires de France, "Ecrivains," 1988.

Rohou, Jean. "The Articulation of Social, Ideological and Literary Practices in France: The Historical Moment of 1641–1643." translated by John Coombes. In *1642: Literature and Power in the Seventeenth Century. Proceedings of the Essex Conference on the Sociology of Literature, July 1980*, edited by Francis Barker, Jay Bernstein, John Coombes, Peter Hulme, Jennifer Stone, and Jon Stratton, 139–65. n.p.: University of Essex, 1981.

Rossi, Paolo. *Francis Bacon: From Magic to Science.* London: Routledge and Kegan Paul, 1968.

"Baconianism." In *Dictionary of the History of Ideas*, edited by Philip P. Wiener, vol. 1, 172–79. New York: Scribner, 1973.

Sabean, David Warren. *Power in the Blood*. Cambridge: Cambridge University Press, 1984.

Saccone, Eduardo. "*Grazia, Sprezzatura, Affettazione* in the *Courtier*." In *Castiglione. The Ideal and the Real in Renaissance Culture*, edited by Robert W. Hanning, and David Rosand, 45–67. New Haven: Yale University Press, 1983.

Salmon, J. H. M. *Society in Crisis: France in the Sixteenth Century*. London: Methuen, 1979 [London: Ernest Benn, 1975].

"Storm Over the Noblesse." *Journal of Modern History* 53:2 (June 1981):242–57.

Renaissance and Revolt. Essays in the Intellectual and Social History of Early Modern France. Cambridge Studies in Early Modern History. Cambridge: Cambridge University Press, 1987.

Sayce, R. A. *The Essays of Montaigne. A Critical Exploration*. London: Weidenfeld and Nicolson, 1972.

Schaefer, David Lewis. *The Political Philosophy of Montaigne*. Ithaca: Cornell University Press, 1990.

Schalk, Ellery. *From Valor to Pedigree. Ideas of Nobility in France in the Sixteenth and Seventeenth Centuries*. Princeton: Princeton University Press, 1986.

Scherer, Jacques. "Les intentions politiques dans *Nicomède*." In *Pierre Corneille. Actes du colloque tenu à Rouen du 2 au 6 octobre 1984*, edited by Alain Niderst, 493–99. Paris: Presses Universitaires de France, 1985.

Scodel, Joshua. "The Affirmation of Paradox: A Reading of Montaigne's 'De la Phisionomie' (III: 12)." In *Montaigne: Essays in Reading*, edited by Gérard Defaux, *Yale French Studies*, no. 64 (1983):209–37.

Spencer, Catherine J. "*Cinna*: 'un crayon imparfait…?'" *Romanic Review* 78 (November 1987):420–31.

Starobinski, Jean. *Montaigne en mouvement*. Paris: Gallimard, 1982.

Stegmann, André. *L'Héroïsme cornélien. Genèse et signification*. 2 vols. Paris: Armand Colin, 1968.

Stone, Lawrence. *The Crisis of the Aristocracy, 1558–1641*. Oxford: Oxford University Press, Clarendon Press, 1965.

Supple, James J. *Arms Versus Letters. The Military and Literary Ideals in the Essais of Montaigne*. Oxford: Oxford University Press, Clarendon, 1984.

Sweetser, Marie-Odile. "Images de Louis XIV chez Corneille." In *Ouverture et Dialogue. Mélanges offerts à Wolfgang Leiner à l'occasion de son soixantième anniversaire*, edited by Ulrich Döring, Antiopy Lyroudias, and Rainer Zaiser, 755–68. Tübingen: Gunter Narr, 1988.

Tetel, Marcel. "The Humanistic Situation: Montaigne and Castiglione." *Sixteenth Century Journal* 10 (Fall 1979):69–84.

Thomas Aquinas, St. *Summa Theologiae*. Vol. 6 of *Opera Omnia*. Rome: S. C. De Propaganda Fide, 1882–.

Tillotson, Geoffrey. "Words for Princes: Bacon's *Essays*." In *Essays in Criticism and Research*, 31–40. Cambridge: Cambridge University Press, 1942.

Trevor-Roper, H. R. "The General Crisis of the Seventeenth Century." *Past and Present* 16 (November 1959):31–64.

van Delft, Louis. *La Bruyère moraliste. Quatre études sur les Caractères*. Genève: Droz, 1971.

"Les *Caractères* et l'anthropologie à l'âge classique." *Papers on French*

Seventeenth-Century Literature/Biblio 17: Actes de Davis 40 (1988):83–96.

Vickers, Brian. *Francis Bacon and Renaissance Prose.* Cambridge: Cambridge University Press, 1968.

Villey, Pierre. *Les sources et l'évolution des Essais de Montaigne.* Paris: Hachette, 1933 [1908].

Wallace, Karl R. *Francis Bacon on Communication and Rhetoric, Or: The Art of Applying Reason to Imagination for the Better Moving of the Will.* Chapel Hill: University of North Carolina Press, 1943.

Whigham, Frank. *Ambition and Privilege: The Social Tropes of Elizabethan Courtesy Theory.* Berkeley: University of California Press, 1984.

Whitney, Charles. *Francis Bacon and Modernity.* New Haven: Yale University Press, 1986.

Wilden, Anthony. "'Par divers moyens on arrive à pareille fin': A Reading of Montaigne." *Modern Language Notes* 83 (May 1968):577–97.

Willey, Basil. "Francis Bacon." In *The English Moralists,* 124–47. London: Chatto & Windus, 1964.

Williamson, George. *The Senecan Amble. A Study in Prose Form from Bacon to Collier.* Chicago: University of Chicago Press, 1951.

Wormald, B. H. G. *Francis Bacon. History, Politics and Science, 1561–1626.* Cambridge Studies in the History and Theory of Politics. Cambridge: Cambridge University Press, 1993.

Yarrow, P. J. "Réflexions sur le dénouement de *Cinna.*" *Papers on French Seventeenth-Century Literature* 11, no. 21 (1984):547–58.

Index

neo-Stoicism in   5, 25, 39, 45, 220 n. 16
'De l'art de conferer'   56–58, 59–60
'Consideration sur Ciceron'   27–28,
    30–34, 36–37
'Couardise mere de la cruauté'   34–35
'Du démentir'   222 n. 25
'De l'exercitation'   221 n. 18
'De l'experience'   56, 72–77, 225 n. 42,
    227 n. 51, 228 n. 60
'De la gloire'   55–56, 224 n. 30
'De l'incommodité de la grandeur'
    58–9
'De l'institution des enfans'   28–30,
    32–33, 45–47, 219 n. 12, 224 n. 30
Journal de Voyage   34
'Des livres'   41–42
'Des menteurs'   28, 29, 222 n. 25
'De mesnager sa volonté'   68–71, 225
    n. 44, 229 n. 72
'De la phisionomie'   42–43, 44, 50–55,
    221 n. 18, 228 n. 63
'De la præsumption'   29–30, 35–36,
    49–50, 63, 223 n. 27, 228 n. 57
'Que philosopher c'est apprendre à
    mourir'   25, 26
'Des récompenses d'honneur'   38–39
'Du repentir'   45, 46, 221 n. 18, 226 n. 49
'De la ressemblance des enfans aux
    peres'   224 n. 31
'De la solitude'   25–27, 43–44
'De trois commerces'   48–49, 61–62
'De l'utile et de l'honneste'   64–66
'De la vanité'   27, 66–68, 227 nn. 50,
    51
'De la vanité des paroles'   27, 60, 67
Mourgues, Odette de   188, 244 n. 40, 246 n.
    54, 253 n. 28, 254 n. 32
Mousnier, Roland   213 nn. 9, 10

Nadal, Octave   238 n. 9, 243 n. 31
Nantes, Edict of   184
Navarre, Marguerite de   221 n. 21
Neale, John E.   212 n. 9
neo-Stoicism   18, 219 n. 11, 220 nn. 15, 16.
    See also Stoicism
    in Montaigne   5, 25, 39, 45
Nervèze   16, 18, 217 n. 43
Neuschel, Kristen B.   4, 213 n. 9, 214 n. 13,
    220 n. 14, 229 n. 68
New Men   3, 6, 78, 109–16, 121, 146, 167,
    183, 213 n. 10, 236 n. 56
Nietzsche, Friedrich   126, 221 n. 24
nobility, old   3, 34, 109, 111–12, 114, 214 n.
    10, 220 n. 16
noblesse   8, 9, 19, 24, 123, 157, 159, 163,

166, 178, 220 n. 16, 213 n. 9, 214 n. 10
d'épée   3, 5, 24, 25, 29, 35–41, 57, 61, 78,
    79, 183, 203, 213 n. 9, 214 n. 10, 220 nn.
    14, 16, 224 n. 36, 225 n. 40, 229 n. 68
de robe   3, 5, 24, 25, 35, 61, 203, 220 n. 16,
    213 n. 9, 214 n. 10, 220 n. 16, 256 n. 56

Oestreich, Gerhard   220 n. 16
Orsini, Napoleone   230 n. 5, 231 n. 6
Ovidius Naso, Publius   219 n. 12

paranoia   4, 15, 211 n. 1, 216 n. 27
parole   5, 28, 33, 39, 222 n. 25, 255 n.
    42
parrhesia, in Montaigne   78
Pascal, Blaise   182, 183
passivity
    in Montaigne   53, 63–64, 70–71, 79
    of human nature, in La Bruyère   187
    of Suréna   173
persuasion   54, 98, 114, 115 *See also*
    audience, persuasion of; rhetoric
Plato   47, 57, 58, 68, 96, 221 n. 24, 233 n.
    39, 227 n. 50
pleasure
    aesthetic   11, 99, 100, 101, 102, 106
    conversational   57–60
Plinius Caecilius Secundus, Gaius (Pliny the
    Younger)   27, 30, 88, 221 n. 19
Plutarch   5, 42–45, 47, 172, 221 n. 19
Porcius Cato, Marcus (Cato the Elder,
    'Cato Censorius')   49, 50
Porcius Cato, Marcus (Cato the Younger,
    'Cato Uticensis')   25
Prigent, Michel   123, 124, 238 n. 7, 240 n.
    21
prudence   14, 18, 50, 61, 72, 134, 161, 168

Quint, David   230 n. 79
Quintilianus, Marcus Fabius   186, 233 n.
    37, 247 n. 57

Rabelais, François   51, 228 n. 56
Racine, Jean   173, 250 n. 81
Ranum, Orest   214 n. 10, 217 n. 42, 241 n.
    22
Rebhorn, Wayne   215 n. 19, 216 n. 27
Refuge, Eustache de   10, 18–20, 217 nn. 44,
    45
Régnier-Desmarais, François-Séraphin,
    Abbé   252 n. 20
Regosin, Richard   218 n. 1
Reiss, Timothy J.   4, 45, 214 n. 23, 218 n. 2,
    219 n. 20, 226 n. 49, 232 n. 31, 243 n. 32,
    246 n. 56, 247 n. 60, 248 n. 63, 250 n. 86

Cambridge Studies in Renaissance Literature and Culture

General editor
STEPHEN ORGEL
Jackson Eli Reynolds Professor of Humanities, Stanford University